COLLISION AT SEA

A guide to the legal consequences

Collision at Sea

A guide to the legal consequences

SAMIR MANKABADY

1978

NORTH-HOLLAND PUBLISHING COMPANY
AMSTERDAM · NEW YORK · OXFORD

North-Holland ISBN: 0 444 85155 0

Published by:

North-Holland Publishing Company - Amsterdam · New York · Oxford

Sole distributors for the U.S.A. and Canada:

Elsevier/North-Holland Inc.
52 Vanderbilt Avenue
New York, N.Y. 10017

Library of Congress Cataloging in Publication Data

Mankabady, Samir.
Collision at sea.

Includes index.
1. Collisions at sea. 2. Liability for marine accidents. I. Title.
JX4434.M35 341.7'566'6 78-2649
ISBN 0-444-85155-0

Printed in the Netherlands

PREFACE

In July 1970, the IMCO Sub-Committee on Safety of Navigation set up a working group to revise the Collision Regulations of 1960. After two years of discussion, the International Regulations for Preventing Collisions at Sea were approved in October 1972 and came into force at 1200 hours zone time on July 15, 1977.

In trying to teach the Law on Collision at Sea, it became apparent to me that there was a need for a textbook to deal with the new Regulations. Although these Regulations "do not contain the whole of the wisdom at sea"[1], their value "lies in the importance that must be attached to an observance of them"[2].

The first three chapters of the book deal with general legal principles of collision and the remaining chapters are devoted to the Collision Regulations. A brief, but concise description of the local rules of navigation in force in certain ports in the United Kingdom, is given in Appendix XX.

Some of the cases decided under the previous Collision Regulations are not valid under the present Rules. Therefore, reference is made only to the decisions which are not affected by the changes.

The sketches reproduced in this book are for illustrative purposes only and are reconstructions from the findings of the courts. They are intended to assist in visualizing the occurrences.

My thanks are due to Captain A.G. Bole who has read the whole work and who has made many valuable suggestions.

I should like also to express my thanks to the Consulting Editor of Lloyd's Law Reports from which I have quoted extensively.

A list of the countries which ratified the Collision Regulations, printed in Appendix II, has been reproduced by the kind permission of IMCO. I tender my thanks to the United States Coast Guard for supplying the photograph used for the cover of the book.

Liverpool
November, 1977

Samir Mankabady

---

1. *The Hardwick Grange* (1940) 67 Ll.L.Rep. 335.
2. *Orduna* (Owners) v. Shipping Controller (1921) 1 A.C. 250, at p.263.

CONTENTS

PREFACE v

LIST OF THE SKETCHES xiii

LIST OF CASES CITED xv

INTRODUCTION: Growing hazards at sea 1
Safety measures 1
Co-operation between States 5
The Collision Regulations: historical background .. 6
The plan of the book 8

Chapter 1

CIVIL LIABILITY FOR COLLISION

(I) THE CONCEPT OF "FAULT" 9
Duty to use proper skill and care 9
Breach of statutory duty 11
Faults-mixed 12
Faults-successive: Faults-separated; Faults-interlocked .. 12
Faults causing damage without a collision 14
Inevitable accident 14
Agony of the moment 17
Removal of wreck 18
Faults in towage operations 19
Duties of the tug 19
Duties of the tow 20
Liability for collision 21
Faults in pilotage operations 21
Meaning and need for pilotage 21
Relationship between master and pilot 22
Liability for negligence of pilots 22
Faults in salvage operations 23

(II) DAMAGES 24
Division of damages 25
Difficulties in apportionment 27
Revision of apportionment by the Court of Appeal .. 30
Damage to the cargo 31
Damages in foreign currency 32
Right of recovery against two negligent ships .. 34
Remoteness of damages 34

(III) CAUSATION 36
Negligence must be a contributory cause of the collision 36

(IV) LIMITATION OF LIABILITY 38
The meaning of "ship" 39
Persons entitled to limit liability 39
"Fault or privity" 40
The amount of limitation 43
Limitation by a tug and tow 45
Limitation by a pilotage authority 47
Period within which action must be taken 48

Chapter 2

CRIMINAL LIABILITY FOR COLLISION

(I) THE JURISDICTIONAL ZONES 51
Territorial waters 51
High seas 51

(II) OBSERVANCE OF COLLISION REGULATIONS 53
Duty to assist after collision 54
Distress signals 55
Other offences 55

(III) INQUIRIES AND INVESTIGATIONS 56
Formal investigation 58
Published reports 60

Chapter 3

JURISDICTION, RULES OF EVIDENCE AND INTERPRETATION

(I) JURISDICTION 61
(i) Actions *in rem* and *in personam* 61
The exercise of jurisdiction 61
Service out of the jurisdiction 65
(ii) Practice and procedure 66
Nautical assessors 66
Consolidation 68
Staying actions 68
Costs 69
(iii) Lien and arrest of ship 71
Maritime liens 71
Arrest of ship 72
Lashes 74

(II) RULES OF EVIDENCE 75
Direct evidence or inference 75
Notices to Mariners 77

(III) INTERPRETATION OF THE COLLISION REGULATIONS 77

Chapter 4

GENERAL RULES STATED BY THE COLLISION REGULATIONS

Rule 1 - Application 81
Rule 2 - Responsibility 89
Rule 3 - General definitions 96

Chapter 5

STEERING AND SAILING RULES

(I) CONDUCT OF VESSELS IN ANY CONDITION OF VISIBILITY .. 105

Rule 4 - Application 105
Rule 5 - Look-out 105
Meaning of look-out 105
The duties of the person on look-out 106
Cases where bad look-out contributed to collision 108
Rule 6 - Safe speed 112
Meaning of "safe speed" 113
Factors to be taken into account 115
Consequences of excessive speed 118
Rule 7 - Risk of collision 118
The use of radar for collision avoidance 121
Plotting 122
Cases on failure to use the radar properly 122
Rule 8 - Action to avoid collision 131
Rule 9 - Narrow channels 142
Meaning of "narrow channel" and "fairway" 144
Cases on collision in narrow channels 146
Rule 10 - Traffic separation schemes 155
Aim of the traffic separation schemes 156
The methods used for a separation scheme 157
The traffic schemes and the rules 158
Location of the traffic separation schemes 159

(II) CONDUCT OF VESSELS IN SIGHT OF ONE ANOTHER 161

Rule 11 - Application 161
Rule 12 - Sailing vessels 162

Rule 13 - Overtaking 163
Duty of overtaking vessel 164
Cases on overtaking 165
Interaction 170
Rule 14 - Head-on situation 170
Rule 15 - Crossing situation 171
Crossing rules - when to apply 174
Crossing rules - when to cease 177
Failure to observe the crossing rules 178
Crossing situations in approaching a pilot station and in narrow channel 183
Distinction between overtaking and crossing situations 186
Rule 16 - Action by give-way vessel 190
Rule 17 - Action by stand-on vessel 197
Course and speed 193
Take action 197
Sub-paragraphs (c) and (d) 201
Rule 18 - Responsibilities between vessels .. 201
Paragraph (d) 204

(III) CONDUCT OF VESSELS IN RESTRICTED VISIBILITY .. 205

Rule 19 - Conduct of vessels in restricted visibility 205
Cases which have a bearing upon Rule 19 208

Chapter 6

LIGHTS, SHAPES; SOUND, LIGHT SIGNALS; AND EXEMPTIONS

(I) LIGHTS AND SHAPES 215

Rule 20 - Application 215
Rule 21 - Definitions 216
Rule 22 - Visibility of lights 217
Rule 23 - Power-driven vessels underway 218
Rule 24 - Towing and pushing 219
Rule 25 - Sailing vessels underway and vessels under Oars 220
Rule 26 - Fishing vessels 221
Rule 27 - Vessels not under command or restricted in their ability to manoeuvre 222
Rule 28 - Vessels constrained by their draught .. 224
Rule 29 - Pilot vessels 224
Rule 30 - Anchored vessels and vessels aground .. 225
Rule 31 - Seaplanes 226

(II) SOUND AND LIGHT SIGNALS 227

Rule 32 - Definitions 227
Rule 33 - Equipment for sound signals 227
Rule 34 - Manoeuvring and warning signals 228
Rule 35 - Sound signals in restricted visibility 231
Rule 36 - Signals to attract attention 233
Rule 37 - Distress signals 234

(III) EXEMPTIONS 234

Rule 38 - Exemptions 234

APPENDICES

Appendix I - The Annexes to the International Regulations for Preventing Collisions at Sea, 1972 237
Appendix II - List of the States which ratified the Collision Regulations, 1972 248
Appendix III - The Collision Regulations and Distress Signals Order, 1977, and its amendment.. 251
Appendix IV - IMCO recommendation on basic principles and operational guidance relating to navigational watch-keeping 255
Appendix V - Notice No. M. 685 on Keeping a Safe Navigational Watch, as amended by M. 708 264
Appendix VI - Notice No. M. 517 on the Use of Radar 265
Appendix VII - Notice No. M. 626 on the Use of Radar for Collision Avoidance 268
Appendix VIII - Notice No. M. 535 on Radar in Merchant Ships: Siting Precautions 269
Appendix IX - Notice No. M. 767 on Standard Marine Navigational Vocabulary 278
Appendix X - Maritime buoyage - harmonization of systems in North-West Europe 283
Appendix XI - Recommendations applicable to nuclear ships 285
Appendix XII - The International Convention for the Unification of Certain Rules of Law with Respect to Collision between Vessels, 1910 290

Appendix XIII	-	The International Convention on Certain Rules Concerning Civil Jurisdiction in Matters of Collision, 1952	294
Appendix XIV	-	The International Convention for the Unification of Certain Rules Relating to Penal Jurisdiction in Matters of Collision or Other Incidents of Navigation, 1952	297
Appendix XV	-	The International Convention for the Unification of Certain Rules Relating to the Arrest of Sea-going Ships, 1952	299
Appendix XVI	-	The Convention Relating to the Unification of Certain Rules Concerning Collisions in Inland Navigation, 1960	305
Appendix XVII	-	IMCO Convention on Limitation of Liability for Maritime Claims, 1976 ..	311
Appendix XVIII	-	Lloyd's Standard Form of Arbitration Agreement in Cases of Collision ..	321
Appendix XIX	-	Lloyd's Standard Form of Salvage Agreement	327
Appendix XX	-	A summary of the local rules of navigation applied in some ports in the United Kingdom	333

INDEX 339

LIST OF THE SKETCHES

The Adolf Leonhardt (1973) 152
The Alletta and The England (1965) 16
The Almizar (1969) 209
The Anneliese (1969) 139
The Aracelio Iglesias (1968) 173

The Ballylesson (1968) 154
The Boleslaw Chrobry (1974) 112
The Bonifaz (1967) 132
The Bovenkerk (1973) 125
The Bowbelle (1967) 92
The British Aviator (1964) 136
The British Patrol (1967) 147

The Cadans (1967) 165
The Carebeka 1 (1973) 203

The Djerada (1976) 100

The Ek (1966) 197
The Elazig (1972) 210
The Esso Brussels (1972) 117
The Esso Wandsworth (1970) 150

The Fogo (1967) 167
The Forest Lake (1967) 180
The Francesco Nullo (1973) 86
The Frosta (1973) 169

The Gannet (1967) 123

The Hagen (1973) 126
The Homer (1972) 196

The Jan Laurenz (1972) 85
The Judith M (1968) 38

The Linde (1969) 130
The Lucile Bloomfield (1966) 230

The Marimar (1968) 213
The Martin Fierro (1974) 134

The Nipigon Bay (1975) 29

The Oldekerk (1974) 90
The Orduna (1920) 177
The Osprey (1967) 212

The Royalgate (1967) 183

The Sabine (1974) 149
The Salaverry (1968) 128
The Santander (1966) 185
The Savina (1974) 176
The Schwarzburg (1976) 94
The Sestriere (1976) 175
The Statue of Liberty (1970) 182

The Tojo Maru (1968) 110
The Toni (1973) 179
The Troll River (1974) 143

TABLE OF CASES

A

Abadesa, The (1968) 44
Adam v. The British and Foreign Steamship Co., Ltd. (1898) 83
Adolf Leonhardt, The (1973) 108, 115, 151, 152
Albion v. The Admiralty, The (1952) 76, 99
Alletta and The England, The (1965) .. 15, 108, 197, 198, 230
Alletta and The England, The (1973) 41, 42, 71, 74
Almizar, The (1969) 106, 108, 208, 209
American and The Syria, The (1874) 220
American Jurist, The (1958) 144
Andrea Ursula, The (1971) 73
Anglo-Newfoundland Development Co. v. Pacific Steam Nav. Co. (1924) 12
Anna M. Fahy (1907) 18
Anneliese, The (1969) 28, 108, 138, 139, 140, 191
Annie Hay, Coldwell-Horsfall v. West Country Yacht Charters, The (1968) 42
Anonity, The (1961) 42
Aracelio Iglesias (1968) 172, 173, 194
Atlantic Star, The (1973) 68
Auriga, The (1977) 164, 188, 189
Australia (Owners) v. Owners of Cargo of S.S. Nautilus, The (1927) 66, 67

B

Ballylesson, The (1968) 108, 153, 154, 171
Banshee (1887) 186, 190
Batavier III (1925) 27
Bellanoch (1907) 131, 170
Berny, The (1977) 74
Beryl, The (1884) 78, 79, 170
Betty Moran, The (1974) 20
Billings & Sons v. Riden (1958) 10
Billings Victory, The (1949).. .. .. 190, 197
Boanergers and the Anglo-Indian (1865) 93
Boleslaw Chrobry (1974) 10, 111, 112
Bonifaz, The (1967) 131, 132, 133
Bourhill v. Young (1943) 10
Bovenkerk, The (1973) 36, 109, 118, 124, 125, 147
Bowbelle, The (1967) 91, 92, 93
Boy Andrew v. St. Rognvald (Owners) (1947) 75
Bramley Moore, The (1964) 45
Bristol City, The (1956) 70
British Aviator, The (1965) 9, 76, 135, 136, 137

British Confidence, The (1951) 106, 109
British Patrol, The (1967) 70, 147, 148
British Tenacity, The (1963) 28, 144
Burns, Philip & Co. v. Nelson & Robertson (1958) 27
Bywell Castle, The (1879) 17

C

Cadans, The (1967) 165, 166
Cairnbahn, The (1958) 27
Cairnbahn, The (1914) 34
Calliope, The (1970) 35
Carebeka 1, The (1973) 202, 203, 204
Carl Julius, The (1963) 12
Carlotta, The (1899) 99
Cederic, The (1924) 193
Centurity, The (1963) 14, 76
Chartered Mercantile Bank of India v. Netherlands India Steam Navigation Co. (1883) 83
Chattahoochee, The (1899) 31
Chugaway II, The (1969) 43
Chyebassa, The (1919) 23
Claiborne McCarty Service Contracting Ing. (1971) 98
Clarence L. Blakeslee, The (1917) 78
Conoco Britannia and Other Vessels (1972) 61, 62
Convallaria, The West and Others v. Ritchie and Others, The (1969) 108, 225, 226
Corocraft Ltd. and Another v. Pan American Airways (1939) 78
Crackshot (1949) 144
Craiova, First Thames Land Holding Ltd. and Another v. Craiova (Owners), The (1976) 65

D

Dalhanna and Staxton Wyke (1960) 233
Davidson v. Hill (1901) 83
Dayspring, The (1968) 41, 70, 108
Deacon v. Evans (1911) 53
Delius, The (1954) 76
Despina R, The (1977) 33
Devonshire (Owners) v. Barge Leslie (Owners)(1912) .. 21, 34
Dimitrios N. Rallias (1922) 15
Djerada, Ziemia Szczecinska (Owners) v. Djerada (Owners), The (1976) 100, 101, 102
Donoghue v. Stevenson (1932) 9

E

Eland and the Monte Urquiola, The (1969) 115
Elazig, The (1972) 12, 108, 122, 210, 211
Ellen M. (Owners) v. Great Yarmouth Port and
Haven Commissioners, The (1967) 13, 77
Elk, The (1966) 70, 198, 199
Empire Jamaica, The (1957) 42, 43
Ercole, The (1977) 122, 140, 141
Eschersheim, The (1974) 62, 73
Esk and The Gitana, The (1869) 225
Esso Brussels, The (1972) 108, 116, 117, 118
Esso Malaysia, The (1974) 83
Esso Wandsworth (1970) 121, 122, 150, 151
Estrella, The (1977) 11, 159, 200, 201
Eurymedon, The (1938) 36

F

Ferranti, The (1942) 144
Festivity (1974) 59
Fina Canada, The (1962) 67
Firston, The (1963) 227
Fogo, The (1967) 35, 119, 166, 167
Folias, The (1977) 33
Forest Lake, The (1967) 108, 179, 180
Fowles v. Eastern, etc. S.S. Co., Ltd. (1916) 23
Francesco Nullo, The (1973) 11, 86, 87, 108, 115
Franconia, The (1878) 45, 164
Fritz Thyssen, The (1967) 35, 36, 37, 66
Frosta, The (1973) 168, 169
Funabashi, The (1972) 44

G

Gannet, The (1967) 115, 122, 123, 124, 232, 233
Genimar, The (1977) .. 11, 156,158, 159, 160, 161, 191, 192
George H. Jones, The (1928) 114
Giacinto Molta, The (1977) 44
Gilbert v. Corporation of Trinity House (1886) 19
Gilda, The (1961) 114
Glanfala v. Texas Company (1960) 98
Glasgow Corporation v. Muir (1948) 10
Golden Trader, The (1974) 72

H

Hagen, The (1973) 12, 24, 76, 126, 127
Halcyon, The (1976) 63, 70, 72
Heranger, The (1939) 75
Hermes, The (1969) 147

Hildina (1957) 42, 43
Homer, The (1973) 106, 108, 195, 196
Hook v. Consolidated Fisheries Ltd. (1953) 42
Hughes v. Lord Advocate (1963) 35
Humbergate, The (1952) 12
Huntingdon, Federal Steam Navigation Co., Ltd.
v. Department of Trade and Industry, The 78

J

Jaladhir, The (1961) 93
Jan Laurenz, The (1972) 26, 66, 84
Jaroslaw Dabrowski (1952) 144
Jean Kraut AG v. Albany Fabrics Ltd. (1976) 33
Judith M, The (1968) 37, 38, 66, 108

K

Kathy K, The (1976) 20, 42, 234
Kennedy v. The Sarmation (1880) 77
Kingston Diamond, The (1964) 45
Koningin Juliana, The (1974) 28, 30, 78, 145, 146
Kozara, Yugoslavenska Oceanska Plovidba
v. Castle Investment Co., Inc., The (1973) 32
Kurt Arlt, The (1962) 12

L

Lady Gwendolen, The (1965) 40, 43, 54, 206
Lake Atlin, The (1972) 74
Lastrigoni, Shell Oil Company v. The ship
Lastrigoni (1975) 72
Lennard's Carrying Co. v. Asiatic Petroleum Co. (1915) .. 40
Libra, The (1881) 78
Linde, The (1969) 129, 130
Llanover, The (1945) 9
Lotus, The (1927) 52
Lucile Bloomfield, The (1967) 26, 108, 161, 229, 230

M

MacGregor, The (1943) 27, 30
Maid of Kent, The (1973) 14
Main, The (1886) 186
Manchester Regiment, The (1938) 186, 190
Manners v. Pearson & Sons (1898) 32
Mansoor, The (1968) 69
Margaret, The (1881) 10, 36
Marimar, The (1968).. .. ..10, 147, 213, 214

Marine Drilling Co. v. Autin (1966) 90
Marine Sulphur Queen, The (1970) 15
Martin Fierro, The (1974) 133, 134, 147
Mauroux v. Sociedade Commercial Abel
Pereira da Fonseca (1972) 65
Mary A. Bickel-Pocomoke (1931) 18
Mary Moxham, The (1876) 83
Mecca, The (1968) 44
Mendip Range, The (1921) 99
Merchant Prince, The (1892) 16
Merkur, Corporation of Trinity House v. Maritime
Salvors Ltd., The (1923) 19
Mersey No. 30, The (1952) 143, 144
Milan, The (1861) 31
Miliangos v. George Frank (Textiles) Ltd. (1976) 32
Miraflores (Owners) v. The George Livanos
(Owners), The (1967) 9, 13, 27, 28
Mount Athos, The (1962) 114

N

Nassau, The (1964) 137
Netuo, The (1974) 83
Newby v. General Lighterage (1955) 75
Nipigon Bay, Liquilassie Shipping Ltd. v. M.V.
Nipigon Bay, The (1975) 29, 30
Nora, The (1956) 120
Norman, The (1960) 42, 43
Norwhale, Owners of Barge Norwhale v. The
Ministry of Defence, The (1975) 26
Nowy Sacz, The (1976) 186, 187, 188

O

O'Boyle, Lim-Procs (1974) 18
Octavian, Geelong Harbour Trust Commissioners
v. Gibbs Bright & Co., The (1974) 17
Offshore Co. v. Robinson (1959) 98
Oldekerk, The (1974) 11, 17, 18, 89, 90, 120
Orduna (Owners) v. Shipping Controller (1920) 177
Oregon, The (1895) 22
Orlik, The (1964) 70
Oropensa, The (1942) 34
Osprey, The (1967) 70, 211, 212, 213
Oteri v. The Queen (1977) 52
Otranto, The (1931) 194, 197, 198

P

Paris v. Stepney, B.C. (1951) 11
Pink v. Fleming (1890) 35
Putbus, The (1969) 39
Producers Drilling Co. v. Gray (1966) 98

Q

Queen Mary, The (1949) 90, 170

R

Rankin v. De Coster (1975) 82
Rattray Head/Tillerman (1970) 138, 207
Reanoke, The (1908) 193
Re United Railways of Havana and Regla
Warehouses Ltd. (1961) 32
Robin Hood Mills, Ltd. (1937) 40
Rosstrum (1974) 59
Royal Eagle, The (1950) 14
Royalgate, The (1967) 108, 183, 184
Royal Sovereign, The (1962) 14
R. v. Wreck Commissioners, Ex parte Knight (1976) 59

S

Sabine, The (1974) 12, 108, 148, 149, 233
Sagacity and The Icemaid, The (1948) 115
Salaverry, The (1968).. 70, 108, 109, 121, 127, 128, 129, 147
Salman v. Commissioners of Customs and Excise (1966) .. 78
Salt Union v. Wood, The (1893) 82
Santander, The (1966) 105, 108, 184, 185
Savina, The (1976) .. 28, 30, 31, 67, 108, 174, 176, 191, 200
Schorsch Meier G.m.b.H. v. Hennin (1975) 32
Schwarzburg, Sagittarius (Owners) v. Schwarzburg
(Owners), The (1976) 94, 95
Sea Star, Horta Barbosa (Owners) v. Sea
Star, The (1976) 29, 106
Sedgepool, The (1956) 120
Sestriere, Alonso De Ojeda (Owners) v. Sestriere
(Owners), The (1976) 13, 91, 174, 175, 184
Shell Spirit 2, The (1962) 14
Sir John Snell, The (1958) 45
Sir Joseph Rawlinson (1972) 46
Sitala, The (1963) 114
Smith v. Marriott (1954) 75
Smith v. Voss (1857) 144
Sobieski, The (1949) 27
Sparto, The (1956) 198

Spontaneity, The (1962) .. .. [illegible]

Standard Oil Co. of New York v. Clan Line Steamers Ltd. ([illegible]) 43

Statue of Liberty, The (1971) 36, 70, 108, 181, 182

St. Blane, The (1974) 24

St. Merriel, The (1963) 73

Synova, The Admiralty Marshal v. Calder, The (1967) 72

T

Taunton, The (1928) 194

Test, The (1847) 93

Texaco Caribbean, The (1976) 65

Thames, The (1940) 42

Theems, The (1938) 44

Tillie Lykes, The (1977) 68

Toju Maru, The (1969) .. 23, 42, 82, 110, 111, 163, 200, 215

Tolten, The (1946) 82

Toni, The (1974) 70, 108, 178, 179, 191, 194

Troll River, The (1974) 143, 144

Truculent, Admiralty v. Owners of Divina, The (1952) 40, 42

Turquoise, The (1908) 225

U

United States of America v. Chesapeake & Delaware Shipyard Inc. (1974) 19

United States of America v. Raven (1975) 18

U.S. v. Atlantic Mutual Ins. Co. (1952) 31

Utopia, The (1893) 18

V

Vasilia, The (1972) 72

Vechtstroom (1964) 120

Verena, The (1961) 12, 121, 138

Volturno, The (1921) 32

Volute, The (1922) 12, 13, 24

W

Wagon Mound, Overseas Tanship (U.K.) v. Mort's Dock and Engineering Co., The (1961) 35

Walter Raleigh (1953) 15

Waziristan, The (1953) 23

Whitley Abbey, The (1962) 12

Woomera, Quinn and Others v. Associated Steamships Proprietary, Ltd., The (1968) 108

INTRODUCTION

GROWING HAZARDS AT SEA

Safety at sea is of paramount importance to all nations; coastal and land locked States. To ensure safety, a number of legal measures, on both international and national levels, have been adopted with regard to the ship, the crew and the environment. Technological developments and scientific progress in the shipping industry have brought new hazards. The current exploration for oil, gas and other resources on the continental shelf, together with the large increase in the size of ships, has resulted in significantly greater risks to safety at sea. Added to this, the introduction of vessels with "special characteristics", such as giant oil tankers, gas carriers, chemical carriers and nuclear vessels, gives genuine cause for concern. Perhaps the greatest potential danger from chemicals and gas carriers arises from the uncertainty of how these materials will be dispersed in the event of an accident. The Dover Strait and the approaches to the North Sea give a clear and striking picture of the growing hazards, since they are among the busiest areas of the seas.

Safety measures

Safety measures may be classified from different points of view, e.g. objectives, character, etc., and these classifications would necessarily overlap. Those set out under any one heading can be used as sub-divisions under any of the others. Classification, by reference to the objectives of the safety measures, may be grouped under four categories.

(1) *Measures to prevent accidents to ships*

Illustrations of such measures are numerous, the most important one being the Regulations for Preventing Collisions at Sea, 1972. Similarly, the traffic separation schemes approved by IMCO are valuable and practicable measures. The different languages used at sea could present an obstacle to interchange of information between the vessels. Therefore, IMCO introduced an Internationally Acceptable English Marine Vocabulary[1]. More recently, a

---

1. See Appendix IX.

new system[1] of maritime buoyage in North-West Europe was adopted and started to apply in the English channel in April, 1977[2]. This new system brought two major changes in the navigational rules for buoyage. The traditional black painted buoys used for starboard marks (indicating the limit of a safe water on the right-hand side of a channel) are now coloured green. The existing red can buoys, sometimes red and white, marking the port side (left) remain the same.

The second change was in the marking of wrecks. They have always been indicated in waters around the British Isles by a single green buoy, usually anchored over the wreck itself if submerged. Under the new system the position of a wreck is shown by a single "cardinal" buoy, a pillar buoy with a mark on top. A cardinal buoy marks safe water around the wreck by indicating the appropriate quarter of the compass in which it lies[3].

The Navigation Information Service[4] which was established experimentally in 1972 in Dover Strait is continuing on a permanent basis. Other measures which may be adopted in the future are the setting up of a navigation warnings system similar to the

---

1. The new system came as a result of accidents in 1971 in the Dover Strait when *The Brandenburg* struck a wrecked ship, *The Texaco Caribbean*, and sank. A few weeks later, in spite of the two wrecks being marked by two light vessels and 14 green buoys, another vessel, *The Niki*, ploughed into the wreckage and sank. Altogether 51 lives were lost and there was controversy over the effectiveness of the navigational marks.
2. See Appendix X.
3. The IALA system "A" is an attempt to combine the best features of the lateral system commonly used in British waters with the more widely used continental cardinal system. In addition to the change in colour and the introduction of cardinal pillar or spar buoys, the colours of lights and their flashing sequences are altered as well. The light sequences for the cardinal buoys are quite ingenious, and should bring instant recognition to the navigator as the number of flashes is based on the clock face -
   north - uninterrupted;
   east - three flashes in a group;
   south - six flashes (equivalent to six o'clock); and
   west - nine flashes (nine o'clock).
   The cardinal buoys also have distinctive "top marks" to aid their visual recognition - double cones apex up for north, double inverted cones for south, and so on.
4. Notice No. 772 of August, 1976.

one established in 1976 for the Baltic and the requirements calling for all ships to carry radar[1], echo sounders and gyro compasses.

Limitation of speed in certain busy and congested areas, the introduction of a system to control the movement of vessels within a traffic separation scheme, and compulsory pilotage for certain classes of vessels, would make a valuable contribution to safety at sea. Automation, which is already being used on a limited scale, could well be used for collision avoidance systems.

(2) *Measures to minimise the risks after accidents*

The starting point here is that if accidents at sea could not be avoided or eliminated, at least certain measures should be adopted to minimise the risks. The rules on survival capability of ships after the accident, the Search and Rescue (SAR), and the Maritime Distress System, are obvious examples of measures of this kind. More recently, a Convention on the "international Maritime Stalellite Organisation" (INMARSAT) was agreed "to adopt criteria and procedures for the approval of earth stations on ships for access to the space segment"[2]. The aim of the INMARSAT[3] is to establish new means of communication by satellite for ships at sea. When the INMARSAT agreements come into force[4], the use of satellite would remedy the deficiencies and the dangerous situations which exist at present for

---

1. From April 1, 1976, all British merchant vessels over 1,600 tons gross are required to carry an approved radar installation. See S.I. No.302, 1976.
2. In September 1976, IMCO approved the INMARSAT Convention which still needs to be ratified by member governments of IMCO. However, a preparatory committee has been set up to handle the interim stage before the deposit of the ratification.
3. It is interesting to note that INMARSAT is a combination of an inter-governmental organisation enjoying privileges and immunities, and a commercial enterprise formed by public and private "shareholders". This means that the Organisation enjoys both the political authority and commercial flexibility.
4. There are two instruments, the convention which sets out the structure of the Organisation and the operating agreement which spells out how the Organisation can raise its financial resources. The idea of having separate operating agreements is to avoid the domination of the Organisation by the major investors.

radio telephone communication at sea. There are, at present, long delays, poor quality in transmission and areas of black-out. The maritime satellite system will,

(1) relieve the pressure on the MF and HF bands;
(2) improve the quality in transmission;
(3) improve the geographical coverage; and
(4) improve distress communications.

It is estimated that this system would ultimately operate for all maritime regions between latitudes 70° north and 70° south by three geostationary satellites over the Atlantic, Indian and Pacific Oceans.

(3) *Measures to raise the standard of safety*

Illustrations on measures to raise the standard of safety are not lacking. IMCO agreed on a Resolution on Standards of Training and Watchkeeping (STW) of seafarers[1]. This Resolution deals with:

(a) basic principles to be observed in keeping a navigational watch[2]; and
(b) operational guidance for the officers in charge of a navigational watch.

The requirements of the Convention for the Safety of Life at Sea (SOLAS), 1974; the IMCO Code for the Construction and Equipment of Ships carrying dangerous chemicals in bulk[3]; and the IMCO Code for the Construction and Equipment of Ships carrying liquefied gases in bulk[4], all aim at ensuring the physical fitness of the vessel[5]. As for the operational side in shipping, the various rules on safe working practices aim at having a high standard in performing the work.

Similarly, the International Convention for Safe Carriage of

---

1. Resolution A.285 (VIII) approved at the Eighth IMCO Assembly in 1974.
2. Notice No.756 of April 1976. There is concern among the Maritime States of the dangers posed by ships which do not meet agreed standards laid down by the International Labour Organisation in its October 1976 Convention on the manning of ships.
3. Resolution A.212 (VII).
4. Resolution 328 approved on Nov.12, 1975.
5. The idea of ensuring the physical fitness of the vessel came as a result of well known casualties such as *The Titanic*, *The Morro Castle*, *The Andrea Doria*/Stockholm, *The Yarmouth Castle* and *The Torrey Canyon*.

Containers 1974[1] provides for regulations for the testing, inspection, approval and maintenance of containers.

(4) *Measures to establish liability and/or to ensure that adequate compensation is available to persons who suffer damage*

Even with the most precautionary measures, accidents do happen. Therefore, there is a need to establish[2] liability and to ensure that adequate compensation is available. In the field of oil pollution[3] there are the two conventions on Intervention on the High Seas in Cases of Oil Pollution Casualties and on Civil Liability for Oil Pollution Damage, 1969[4]. Also, there is the Convention on the Establishment of an International Fund for Compensation for Oil Pollution Damage, 1971[5]. More recently, the Convention for the Prevention of Pollution from Ships, 1973 was approved.

CO-OPERATION BETWEEN STATES

The effectiveness of the safety measures depends on the co-operation between States, and unilateral measures to deal with particular problems would not be the ideal solution. The standards and requirements in different countries vary considerably. The present international system, based on the interdependency of sovereign states, is the material from which solutions must come[6]. This system has both considerable capacity and serious

---

1. IMCO publication, sales no. 74.10.E.
2. The measures may only provide for the apportionment of liability, e.g. the Convention for the Unification of Certain Rules of Law with Respect to Collision between vessels, 1910 as incorporated into the Maritime Conventions Act, 1911, provides for the apportionment of liability according to the degree of fault.
3. In the nuclear field, the Brussels Convention Relating to Civil Liability in the Field of Maritime Carriage of Nuclear Material, 1971 sets up a system for liability arising out of the maritime carriage of nuclear materials.
4. These are incorporated into the Prevention of Oil Pollution Act 1971, and the Merchant Shipping (Oil Pollution) Act, 1971 respectively.
5. This Convention is incorporated into the Merchant Shipping Act, 1974.
6. The present system leaves to every State the freedom to enforce international conventions by means of its own municipal legislation. In the United Kingdom international conventions are implemented and given the force of law by legislation passed by, or under the authority of, Parliament.

limitations for dealing with safety at sea. Even if international conventions are concluded, the crucial matter is the coming into force of these conventions. Many conventions concerned with the sea are not yet ratified internationally.

THE COLLISION REGULATIONS : HISTORICAL BACKGROUND

This book is devoted to one of the means which promote safety at sea, namely the Collision Regulations.

At the beginning of the nineteenth century, collisions between wooden vessels under sail were very rare. With the advent of steel construction and steam propulsion in the latter half of the nineteenth century, many serious collisions started to occur, especially in ports and their approaches. Therefore, Trinity House felt the need to organise navigation and, to this end, it issued certain rules in 1840[1]. Although they had no statutory authority, nevertheless they were enforced by the Admiralty Court as they were considered to represent the practice of good seamanship. Over the years other regulations were approved, and by the Merchant Shipping Act, 1862 these regulations were repealed and substituted by one code in 1863.

The Merchant Shipping Act, 1894, s.419 (1) provided that all owners and masters shall obey the Collision Regulations, and shall not carry or exhibit any other fog signals than those required by the Regulations.

Further amendments were carried out and the most important was the introduction of the Maritime Conventions Act, 1911 which abolished the presumption of fault of vessels infringing the Collision Regulations, and which provided for apportionment of liability according to the degree of fault. The Collision Regulations were made by Order in Council of October 13, 1910[2]. In 1954, a Statutory Instrument[3] revoked the 1910 Regulations and introduced new Regulations which came as a result of the Conference of Safety of Life at Sea, 1948. The great virtue of these Regulations was to set up a uniform system on an international level to prevent collision at sea. They sought to develop "common rules which apply irrespective of frontiers to matters which are of wider than national concern...a law which is broader in scope than municipal law"[4].

1. Before 1840, there were rules established by custom to enable approaching vessels to keep clear from each other.
2. S.R. & O. 1910, No.1113.
3. S.I.1557 of 1953 made October 28, 1953 and came into operation on January 1, 1954.
4. C.W. Jenks, The Common Law of Mankind (1958), p.81.

The Convention on Safety of Life at Sea was revised in 1960, and Annex B to the final Act of the Conference contained the Collision Regulations which came into force in the United Kingdom on September 1, 1965.

Nearly twelve years have passed since these Regulations were adopted. During that time, the practice and the technological developments in shipping have revealed that the Regulations have become seriously out of date. The time has now come to amend them and remedy these deficiencies. IMCO took on this task and the revised Regulations were adopted in 1972[1]. Article IV (1) (a) provides:

> "The present Convention shall enter into force twelve months after the date on which at least 15 States, the aggregate of whose merchant fleets constitutes not less than 65 per cent by number or by tonnage of the world fleet of vessels of 100 gross tons and over have become Parties to it, whichever is achieved first."

The conditions laid down in this article were fulfilled[2] on July 14, 1976 and therefore the Collision Regulations came into force at 1200 local time on July 15, 1977.

NON-PARTY STATES TO THE COLLISION REGULATIONS

Some States are not yet party to the Collision Regulations, 1972, but they may be party to the 1960 Rules. This would present a real difficulty. The crucial point seems to be whether it is reasonable for those on board a vessel to assume that the other vessel is party to the new Regulations, or whether they should have anticipated the possibility that the other vessel is not party to the new Regulations and bound by the old ones.

To put the problem in another way, the fact that the Collision Regulations, 1960 would be allowed to remain effective after July 15, 1977, would increase the hazards in sea traffic for those ships which are about to enter the indefinable borderline between the high seas and the territorial waters of a non-party State. Added to this, ships may be forced to equip themselves with the special lights and signals that would meet the requirements of both the 1960 and 1972 Collision Regulations.

---

1. English and French are the two authoritative texts of the Collision Regulations.
2. See the list of the States which have ratified the Collision Regulations, Appendix II.

THE LAYOUT OF THE COLLISION REGULATIONS

The Rules are presented in a logical order. They are divided into five parts, A to E, followed by four annexes. Part A deals with the application of the Rules, responsibility to obey them and definitions which apply to all the Rules. Part B contains the steering and sailing rules. The technical details on lights and shapes are dealt with in Part C, while Part D is devoted to sound and light signals. Part E deals with exemptions.

Annex I on "Positioning and technical details of lights and shapes" contains details on the placing of lights. It also contains technical details on the navigational lights to ensure uniform colour intensities. Annex II on "Additional signals for fishing vessels fishing in close proximity" aims at the standardisation of the signals. Annex III is entitled "Technical details of sound signal appliances", while Annex IV is on "Distress signals".

THE PLAN OF THE BOOK

The first three chapters of the book deal with general legal principles of collision and preliminary considerations. Thus, chapter 1 is on civil liability, chapter 2 on criminal liability and chapter 3 on jurisdiction, rules of evidence and interpretation of the Collision Regulations. The remaining chapters are devoted to the Collision Regulations annotated. Chapter 4 is on general rules stated by the Collision Regulations, chapter 5 on the steering and sailing rules and chapter 6 on lights, shapes, sounds, light signals and exemptions.

Chapter 1

CIVIL LIABILITY FOR COLLISION

Civil liability is based on the existence of "fault" which causes or contributes to the collision. So, in order to establish liability an inquiry as to the fault, damages and causation is needed. Such liability may, under certain conditions, be limited. Thus, the following points call for consideration:

(I) the concept of "fault" in collision;

(II) damages;

(III) causation; and

(IV) limitation of liability.

(I) THE CONCEPT OF "FAULT"

"Fault" involves both causative potency and blameworthiness of any navigational shortcoming[1]. The Collision Regulations did not attempt to define "fault"[2] which might be described as conduct involving a risk of causing damage. Fault implies negligence, or in the words of Viscount Maughm[3]: "a failure to exercise that degree of the skill and care which are ordinarily to be found in a competent seaman ... It is negligence not to take all reasonable steps to avoid danger in navigation, and the nature of those steps must of course depend on the surrounding circumstances, and they may call for the utmost possible precautions."

Duty to use proper skill and care

It is the duty of the master to act with proper skill and care[4] towards other users of the sea in order to avoid exposing them to

---

1. Per Willmer, L.J. in *The British Aviator* (1965) 1 Lloyd's Rep. 271, at p.277; per Lord Pearce in *The Miraflores* (1967) 1 A.C. 826, at p.845.
2. This is inevitable because no-one would expect Member States to amend their concept on this issue as it is basic to the law of tort and therefore of a wide-reaching significance.
3. *The Llanover* (1945) 78 Ll.L.Rep. 461.
4. Lord Atkin in *Donoghue* v. *Stevenson* (1932) A.C. 562, at p.580.

any risk[1]. The test is: could the collision have been prevented by the exercise of ordinary care, caution and maritime skill?

The scope of this duty is simply expressed in terms of an act which is reasonably foreseeable, but the master "is presumed to be free both from over-apprehension and over-confidence"[2]. "A reasonable man does not mean a paragon of circumspection"[3]. According to Brandon J.[4]: "the standard of skill and care to be applied by the Court is that of the ordinary mariner and not of the extraordinary one, and seamen under criticism should be judged by reference to the situation as it reasonably appeared to them at the time, and not by hindsight."

However, an error of judgment may amount to fault. In *The "Marimar"* the Court observed[5]: "...the Marimar was a less well equipped vessel than The Scotland, having no radar, her bridge being subject to more engine noise and there being possible difficulty of communication because of difference of language between the pilot and officers. Her pilot may have misjudged the extent of visibility, but if he was travelling too fast when approaching the North West Goodwin it does not appear that this was the cause of his subsequent procedure. My advisers take the view that while he was reasonably reluctant to anchor to the east of the channel, the risk he would have incurred in doing so was less than the risk of crossing the channel when the visibility was so low. In my view, there was a misjudgment on his part in deciding to cross and it was a misjudgment sufficiently serious to amount to a fault."

The standard of care is the same for all vessels irrespective of size, type of cargo or nature of their employment. The law does not recognise different standards of care or degrees of fault. But the master is entitled to proceed more or less on the assumption that others will do what it is their duty to do, namely to observe the Collision Regulations. Obviously, the amount of

---

1. "The duty is owed to those to whom injury may reasonably and probably be anticipated if the duty is not observed.". Per Lord Macmillan, in *Bourhill* v. *Young* (1943) A.C. 92, at p.104.
2. Per Lord Macmillan in *Glasgow Corporation* v. *Muir* (1948) A.C. 448, at p.457.
3. Per Lord Reid in *Billings & Sons* v. *Riden* (1958) A.C. 240, at p.255.
4. *The Boleslaw Chrobry* (1974) 2 Lloyd's Rep. 308, at p.316.
5. (1968) 2 Lloyd's Rep. 165, at p.171. But the mere fact that a ship is involved in a collision creates no liability, see *The Margaret* (1881) 6 P.D. 76.

care required will differ and depend on the circumstances. In *The "Oldekerk"*[1], the Court found that the manoeuvre which the *Oldekerk* announced her intention of performing was an ordinary and normal one for such a ship in the port of Rotterdam.

Another important point was made by Brandon, J. in *The "Francesco Nullo"*[2], when he said: "it seems to me, of what is perhaps a more important fault, which is that instead of erring on the side of safety, she erred on the side of danger. There was no difficulty for her in holding back, she was navigating against the tide; there was no need for her to come out of the Boudewijn Lock like a bullet out of a gun, and proceed down almost regardless. There is no evidence that there was any reason for her gaining a minute here or there. It seems to me that her navigation was so faulty as to be rash. Against that it seems to me that, while the *Francesco Nullo* was at fault in allowing herself to get so far to the north, it was a less serious fault in that turning is a difficult operation and it is not always possible to turn exactly as a ship would wish, or to control a ship completely in the course of a turn."

In fact, the master must know the manoeuvring capacity of his vessel and he would be guilty of negligence if his vessel, due to her deficiencies in power, collided with another. The precautions which the master ought to take should be to make due allowance for the state of his vessel. Further, the more serious the damage, the more thorough are the precautions which the master must take[3]. Fault of one vessel does not excuse fault of the other.

Breach of statutory duty

Where a statutory duty is imposed and that duty is broken, criminal liability to the penalty under the statute incurs[4] without the need for an inquiry into fault. As for civil liability, a breach of a statutory duty may not necessarily be the cause of collision. For instance, a vessel navigating in the wrong lane in a traffic separation scheme may not be held liable for the collision[5]. However, fault may be inferred from the failure to observe navigation rules without statutory authority or recommendations in notices to mariners if they are regarded as part of

---

1. (1974) 1 Lloyd's Rep. 95, at p.103.
2. (1973) 1 Lloyd's Rep. 72, at p.78.
3. *Paris* v. *Stepney, B.C.* (1951) A.C. 367; 1 All E. R. 42, H.L., per Lord Morton, 51.
4. The Maritime Conventions Act, 1911 abolished the statutory presumption of fault of a vessel infringing the Collision Regulations because it is quite possible that the infringement of the Regulations did not cause the collision.
5. *The "Estrella"* (1977) 1 Lloyd's Rep. 525; *The "Genimar"* (1977) 2 Lloyd's Rep. 17.

good seamanship[1].

Faults-Mixed

Sometimes there is a considerable overlap between the faults of the two vessels involved in a collision. In *The "Elazig"*[2], the Court found that the failure in keeping a proper look-out was not so much a separate fault as faults in keeping a speed of nine knots until far too late and in not going full astern at once were all closely interlocked.

Similarly, in *The "Hagen"*[3], the Court held that the fault in going hard to starboard at the last moment was a consequence of bad radar look-out and appreciation rather than a separate fault. Further, the failure to take the way off when fog thickened was an aggravation of the excessive initial speed in fog.

Again in *The "Sabine"*[4], the Sabine was at fault in three respects, namely, bad look-out, failure to sound a warning signal and failing to use her engines in sufficient time in order to take her further to the northward. Brandon J.[5], on examining these faults, held that the first led to the second and the third. Therefore, they cannot be regarded as a separate fault. Furthermore, the third fault was clearly causative.

Faults-Successive

Faults-separated. A clear line may be drawn between the initial fault of one vessel and the subsequent fault of the other. This comes within the classic judgment of Lord Birkenhead in *The Volute*[6]. However, if one vessel is negligent for a considerable time apparent to the other, which could have avoided the collision by adopting proper measures, the latter may well be the only one to blame. In *Anglo-Newfoundland Development Co.* v. *Pacific Steam Nav. Co.*[7], Lord Shaw observed: "... And I take the principle to be that, although there might be ... fault in being in a position which makes an accident possible yet, if the position

---

1. See *The Humbergate* (1952) 1 Lloyd's Rep. 168, followed in *The Whitley Abbey* (1962) 1 Lloyd's Rep. 110. See also *The Verena* (1961) 2 Lloyd's Rep. 127, at pp. 132, 133; *The Kurt Arlt* (1962) 1 Lloyd's Rep. 31; *The Carl Julius* (1963) 1 Lloyd's Rep. 104.
2. (1972) 1 Lloyd's Rep. 355.
3. (1973) 1 Lloyd's Rep. 257, at p.265.
4. (1974) 1 Lloyd's Rep. 465.
5. Ibid., at p.473.
6. (1922) 1 A.C. 129, at p.144.
7. (1924) App. Cas. 406, 16 App. 385; (1924) 18 Ll.L.Rep. 140.

is recognized by the other prior to operations which result in an accident occurring, then the author of that accident is the party who, recognizing the position of the other, fails negligently to avoid an accident which, with reasonable conduct on his part, could have been avoided. Unless that principle be applied it would be always open to a person, negligently and recklessly approaching, and failing to avoid a known danger, to plead that the reckless encountering of danger was contributed to by the fact that there was a danger to be encountered. There is a period of time during which the causal function of the act of approach operates and it is not legitimate to extend that cause backwards to an anterior situation."[1]

Faults-interlocked. In certain situations the respective negligence of two vessels becomes so close that "the second act of negligence is so much mixed up with the state of things brought about by the first act, that party secondly negligent ... might ... invoke the prior negligence as being part of the cause of collision so as to make it a case of contribution".[2]

In *"Alonso De Ojeda"* (Owners) v. *"Sestriere"* (Owners), (*The "Sestriere"*)[3], Brandon J. said: "It was argued for the plaintiffs that the greater blame should attach to the Sestriere on the ground that it was her initial fault which created the risk of collision, and that the fault of the Alonso lay only in her negligent reaction to the situation of risk so created. It was argued for the defendants, on the other hand, that the fault of the Alonso was a grave one, in that to go full ahead in the face of danger was so plainly wrong as to amount to rashness, and that the fault of the Sestriere was more excusable in that those on board her could not reasonably have foreseen that the Alonso would take such action.

I think that there is force in both these arguments. It was certainly the initial fault of the Sestriere which brought about the situation of danger. But on the other hand the action taken by the Alonso to deal with the situation was plainly wrong and made inevitable the collision which it was intended to avoid.

---

1. Lord Pearce in *The Miraflores* (Owners) v. *The George Livanos* (Owners) and Others (1967) A.C. 826, at p.847; (1967) 1 Lloyd's Rep. 191, at p.200, made the following observation: "It is axiomatic that a person who embarks on a deliberate act of negligence should in general bear a greater degree of fault than one who fails to cope adequately with the resulting crisis which is thus thrust upon him...".
2. *The Volute* (1922) 1 A.C. 129, at p.144.
3. (1976) 1 Lloyd's Rep. 125, at p.131.

In the result, it seems to me that both ships were guilty of serious errors of appreciation due, I think, to an inadequate look-out which could, and should, have been avoided.

Having weighed both the culpability and the causative potency of the faults on either side, I have come to the conclusion that both ships were equally to blame."

Again, in "*The Ellen M.*" (Owners) v. *Great Yarmouth Port and Haven Commissioners*[1], Brandon J. found that the initial negligence of the bridgemaster forced the master of the Ellen M. to undertake a difficult emergency manoeuvre. While performing that manoeuvre the master of the Ellen M. made a grave mistake; he was induced to do so, in part at least, by further confused operation of the bridge by the bridgemaster.

Fault causing damage without a collision

Fault could cause damage without a collision. A vessel, for instance, may sink as a result of the swell raised by the excessive speed of another[2]. In *The Maid of Kent*[3], a Trinity House pilot was killed while boarding the Dunedin Star from the pilot launch outside Dover harbour. The accident was caused by the defendant's ferry, Maid of Kent, which crossed the bow of the Dunedin Star, making a wash which caused the pilot launch to roll violently resulting in the death of the pilot. The Court of Appeal held that the Maid of Kent should have realized, from the time of her clearing the breakwater in Dover harbour, that if she passed Dunedin Star at a distance of about half a mile, and at a speed of nearly 20 knots, the wash might create a danger for the pilot launch.

Inevitable accident

Inevitable accident[4] describes a collision which was not intended and which could not have been foreseen and avoided by the exercise of reasonable care and skill. However, in order to succeed in the plea of "inevitable accident", it must be proved that there was no fault in getting into a situation where collision became inevitable. In other words, it is not sufficient

---

1. (1967) 2 Lloyd's Rep. 247.
2. See *The Royal Eagle* (1950) 84 Ll.L.Rep. 543; *The Royal Sovereign* (1950) 84 Ll.L.Rep. 549; *The Shell Spirit 2* (1962) 2 Lloyd's Rep. 252; *The Centurity* (1963) 1 Lloyd's Rep. 99.
3. (1973) 1 Lloyd's Rep. 49; on appeal (1974) 1 Lloyd's Rep.434.
4. Inevitable mistake is quite different. It means that, although the act and its consequences were intended, the defendant acted under an erroneous belief.

to show that the accident was unavoidable at the moment of, or for some moments before, its occurrence, but to show that all precautions have been taken and there was no fault in getting into such a position.

Among the examples of well known situations of inevitable accidents is the case where collision was caused by the force of wind in parting the lines of a moored or anchored vessel. However, three conditions must be fulfilled:

(1) the force of wind could not have been anticipated;

(2) the vessel had been moored or anchored properly; and

(3) there was no negligence on the part of those in charge of her.

The failure of machinery, and in particular the breakdown of steering gear, is another situation where the plea of "inevitable accident" is usually raised. The defendant here must prove that the defect is latent[1] and could not be discovered by reasonable diligence or inspection. Also, he must establish that the collision was the result of the defect or the breakdown and could not be avoided by proper navigation after the trouble developed.

In *The "Alletta"* and *The "England"*[2] the plea of inevitable accident failed. In this case, a collision occurred between the *England* (2271 tons gross) and the *Alletta* (500 tons gross) at night, in Halfway Reach, River Thames. The *Alletta* had been moored alongside Ford's Jetty at Dagenham with her head downstream. She left the jetty loaded with spare parts of motor cars and proceeded right across the main channel in the river intending to anchor on the south side at a position slightly up river of Ford's Jetty. In so doing she crossed the course being taken by the *England*, which was proceeding downstream; the stem of the *England* struck the starboard side of the *Alletta*. The master of the latter vessel did what he could in the emergency to save her by ordering full speed ahead and hard-a-starboard in order to ground her. In spite of this she sank, but before doing so she collided with a number of moored dumb barges, damaging them and their cargo, and also with another moored vessel,

---

1. Latent defects are those defects which could not be discovered by any visual inspection which could reasonably be required according to the standards current at the time. See *Dimitrios N. Rallias* (1922) 13 Ll.L.Rep. 363, at p.366. See also *The Walter Raleigh* (1952) A.M.C.618 at p.637; *The "Marine Sulphur Queen"* (1970) 2 Lloyd's Rep. 285.
2. (1965) 2 Lloyd's Rep. 479.

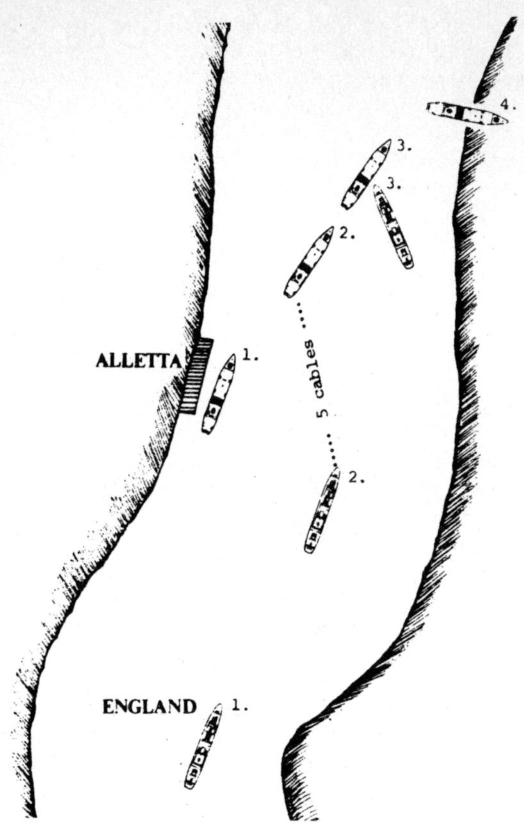

the *Mare Liberum*. Actions were brought by barges against *England* and *Alletta* and by *England* against *Alletta*.

On the issue of whether the collision with the barges was an inevitable consequence of the first collision, Hewton, J. held that *Alletta's* manoeuvres after the first collision were proper and seamanlike. Further, no new cause intervened between the first and the second collision. Therefore, the second collision was wholly foreseeable as a reasonable consequence of the first collision.

Cause of collision could not be determined

Where the cause of a collision could not be determined, the plea of "inevitable accident" could not be sustained. In *The Merchant Prince*[1], a vessel entering the Mersey collided with an anchored

---

1. (1892) Prob. Div. 179.

vessel because of the failure of her steering gear. The cause of the failure could not be determined. The Court of Appeal held that, so long as the cause of the accident was unknown, it would not be said that that cause was unavoidable. Lord Esher, M.R. said: "In this case it is beyond dispute that the defendants are unable to tell what the cause of the accident was, or how or why it happened. It occurs to me that that being so, it cannot be said that they have discharged the burden fastened upon them by showing that what heppened was inevitable. Can they say that they could not avoid a thing when they did not know what the thing to be avoided was? I think not"[1].

Agony of the moment

Where a vessel, without any fault, is placed in a position of sudden danger, she is not liable if the action which she takes in the stress of the emergency proves to be wrong. In *The Bywell Castle*[2] James, C.J. observed: "A ship has no right, by its own misconduct, to put another ship into a situation of extreme peril, and then charge that other ship with misconduct. My opinion is that if, in that moment of extreme peril and difficulty, such other ship happens to do something wrong, so as to be contributory to the mischief, that would not render her liable for the damage, inasmuch as perfect presence of mind, accurate judgment, and promptitude under all circumstances are not to be expected. You have no right to expect men to be something more than ordinary men."

Again, when the master is placed, through no fault of his own, in a real dilemma and has to take one of two courses, each of which involves risks, he is not guilty of negligence if he takes the course involving the least risk. In *The "Oldekerk"*[3], the Court found that the action of the *Anvers* was not unreasonable as it was taken in the agony of the moment. Brandon, J. said[4]: "It seems to me that, once the *Oldekerk* announced that she was coming

---

1. See also *Geelong Harbour Trust Commissioners* v. *Gibbs Bright & Co;* (*The Octavian*) (1974)1 LMCLQ, pp. 90, 91. In this case the m.v. *Octavian*,which was properly moored, was driven from her moorings by a sudden strong squall and collided with a beacon owned by the Harbour Commissioners. The latter claimed damages but the plaintiffs denied liability on the ground that the damage was caused by Act of God or by inevitable accident without negligence on their part. The High Court of Australia accepted this defence and the House of Lords refused to interfere with the Australian decision.
2. (1879) 4 Prob. Div. 219.
3. (1974) 1 Lloyd's Rep. 95.
4. Ibid., at p.105.

out, it ceased to be safe and practicable for the *Anvers* to keep more than marginally on her own starboard side of mid-river, and that, on my findings, she did until she went hard to port... In my view, therefore, there was no departure (from the Regulations) at this stage. When the *Anvers* went hard to port at the last it was, in my view no longer safe or practicable for her to remain on the south side at all, in that, if she had done so, she would have collided with the *Oldekerk* further aft and at a still broader angle... Even if going hard to port was not the best possible action, it was not unreasonable action to take in the agony of the moment."

Removal of wreck

It is the owner's duty to mark his sunken ship[1] properly[2]. By failing to do so, the owner may be guilty of negligence and consequently liable for damages to other vessels which collide with it. Marking the wreck must be carried out within a reasonable time after having full knowledge of it, and without any delay. The reasonable time is a matter of fact[3]. Furthermore, it is the duty of the owner to remove the wreck in navigable waters[4].

Since the owner's liability is based on his possession and control of the wreck, his liability ceases when he sells the wreck or abandons it to the insurer[5]. Therefore, the owner's duty will not come to an end by marking the wreck, he must maintain such marks until the sunken ship is removed or abandoned. One of the earliest cases on this issue is *The Utopia*[6] where it was held that: "so long as and as far as possession, management and

---

1. Under s. 510 of the Merchant Shipping Act, 1894, the expression "wreck, includes jetsam, flotsam, lagan and derelict found in or on the shores of the sea, or any tidal water".
2. In *Mary A. Bickel-Pocomoke* (1931) A.M.C. 1127, the buoy marking a sunken ship was not over the ship but 180 feet away. The shipowner was held negligent for not properly marking the wreck.
3. In *O'Boyle, Lim-Procs* (1947) A.M.C. 1127, a two-hour delay on the part of a barge owner in marking a wreck occurring at night in New York Harbour was held not unreasonable under the circumstances. In the *Anna M. Fahy* (1907) 153 Fed. 866, a delay of six hours in marking the wreck after notice, was held to be too long, where the circumstances would have permitted it to be done within an hour.
4. *United States of America* v. *Raven* (1975) A.M.C. 603.
5. See Protection of Wreck (Designation) Regulations 1975 (Amendment) Order, 1975 S.I. No. 262 which came into force March 25, 1975.
6. (1893) A.C. 502.

control of the wreck be not abandoned or properly transferred, there remains on the owners an obligation in regard to the protection of other vessels from receiving injury from her"[1].

Some port authorities have statutory powers to remove the wreck[2] in the port area or its approaches[3] and to recover the expenses from the owners[4].

FAULTS IN TOWAGE OPERATIONS

Frequently, a tug collides with her tow, or the tug and tow foul a third vessel. Accidents in this respect may be explained by the fact that two or more vessels are navigating and one of them is leading the flotilla.

Duties of the tug

It may be useful, in this respect, to recall the duties of the tug.

(1) The tug-owner owes a duty to tow-owners to provide a seaworthy tug, properly manned and equipped. The tug must have sufficient capacity to perform the service undertaken unless the capacity of the tug is known to the tow-owner.

(2) The tug has a duty to use reasonable care and skill in performing the towage service. Thus, it is the duty of the tug to properly supervise its towlines and make sure of the

---

1. In *United States of America* v. *Chesapeake & Delaware Shipyard Inc.* (1974) A.M.C. 511, the Court held that even though a barge had been sunk by its owner for almost a year, it was still a vessel capable of being pumped out and used again after minor repairs.
2. See also s. 530 of the Merchant Shipping Act, 1894 on removal of wreck by harbour or conservancy authority and s. 531 on power of lighthouse authority to remove the wreck.
3. As to the powers of Trinity House to deal with wrecks, including their marking and lighting, see *Corporation of Trinity House* v. *Maritime Salvors Ltd. (The Merkur)* (1923) 14 Ll.L.Rep. 91. Cf. *Gilbert* v. *Corporation of Trinity House* (1886) 17 Q.B.D. 795.
4. The owners, in turn, may recover from their Protection and Indemnity (P. & I.) clubs the costs and expenses or incidental charges of raising, removal, destruction, lighting or marking of the wreck of the ship, when such raising, removal, destruction, lighting or marking is compulsory by law or the costs thereof are legally recoverable from them. The value of the wreck saved will be deducted from such costs, charges or expenses, and only the balance, if any, is recoverable from the clubs.

appropriate length of the ropes as this factor has a considerable bearing on the safety of the towing manoeuvre[1]. It is also the duty of the tug to navigate the flotilla prudently in order to avoid any damage to the tow from swells of passing vessels or other causes. The tug must maintain a safe speed so as to keep the tow under control. Further, the tug must keep its tow in line to prevent it from sheering.

(3) The tug must obey the orders of the ship in tow. If no orders are given, the tug must perform her service with prudence. Where the orders are manifestly wrong, it is the duty of tug-master to warn the tow-master of the consequences of such orders.

(4) It is the duty of the tug to display proper lights or shapes in conformity with Rule 27(c)[2] which states: "A vessel engaged in a towing operation such as renders her unable to deviate from her course shall, in addition to the lights or shapes prescribed in sub-paragraphs (b) (i) and (ii) of this Rule, exhibit the lights or shapes prescribed in Rule 24(a)."

(5) If no time for completion of the towage operation is specified, the law implies that it will be completed within a reasonable time.

Duties of the tow

(1) It is the duty of the ship in tow to give orders regarding the movement of the two ships. Consequently, the crew on board the tow must be competent and sufficient. However, in case the tow is unmanned, the tug will be the "dominant mind".

(2) Cargo must be stowed in a manner which ensures the stability and safety of the tow. The tow must also be properly equipped with anchors and lights.

---

1. *Stein and others* v. *The "Kathy K"* (also known as *"Stormpoint"*) and *"S.N. No.1", Egmont Towing & Sorting Ltd. Shields Navigation Ltd., Helsing and Iverson* (1976) 1 Lloyd's Rep. 153. See also *The Betty Moran* (1974) A.M.C. 545, where the Court of Appeal held that (1) there was no international rule limiting the length of a tow-line, even in a "restricted area" where anchoring, trawling, fishing and dragging are prohibited; and (2) The Trial Court had erred in holding that the tug was at fault because her towing hawser was 1100 ft. longer than the 450 ft. maximum prescribed by the Inland Rules.
2. See infra chapter 6.

(3) The tow must exhibit the lights prescribed in Rule 24. In restricted visibility, the tow if manned, shall, at intervals of not more than two minutes, sound four blasts in succession (Rule 35, d).

It must be noted that these duties may be modified by express terms in the towage contract such as the terms to be found in the United Kingdom Standard Towage Conditions.

Liability for collision

The old rule used to be that the tug "is the servant or in the service of the tow" and regarded the tug and the tow as one unit. This rule is no longer correct[1] and at present it is a question of fact, in each case, whether the tug and tow are to be considered as one unit or not. Various situations in towage may exist. For example:

1. The tug may be in charge of an unmanned tow; or the tow is a disabled ship.
2. The tow has competent crew and all necessary equipment.
3. The tow is rigidly connected in a composite unit with the tug.
4. The tug is simply an ice breaker.

If either the tug or tow is solely to blame, and they are considered to be two units, the liability will rest with the one at fault. When a collision occurs between the tug and a third vessel through the fault of the tow, the tow-owner will be liable. However, the innocent ship may sue either or both vessels. A similar rule applies when the collision between the tow and a third vessel happens through the fault of the tug. Finally, when both the tug and the tow are to blame, they shall jointly and severally be liable for the damage with right of contribution or indemnity between them according to the degree of blame.

FAULTS IN POLOTAGE OPERATIONS

Meaning and need for pilotage

The term "pilot" is used in two contexts: (1) an officer serving on board the ship and having charge of the helm and the route of the ship; and (2) an independent person taken on board at a particular place for conducting the vessel through a stretch of

---

1. *S.S. Devonshire* (Owners) v. *Barge Leslie* (Owners) (1912) A.C. 634.

water[1].

Pilotage may be voluntary or compulsory. Where it is compulsory, s. 11 of the 1913 Act provides that certain classes of vessels shall be exempted. The exemptions cover H.M. ships, yachts, fishing vessels, harbour ferries and ships of less than 50 tons gross. Further exemptions could be made by bye-laws.

Relationship between master and pilot

When the ship is being piloted, it is the duty of the pilot to give directions as to speed, course, and any necessary manoeuvre. However, the master does not relinquish command of his ship and must be close at hand to assist the pilot. In fact, the relationship between the pilot and the master is difficult, if not impossible to define. It was expressed in the following terms[2]: "While the pilot doubtless supersedes the master for the time being in the command and navigation of the ship, and his orders must be obeyed in all matters connected with her navigation, the master is not wholly absolved from his duties while the pilot is on board, and may advise him, and even displace him in case he is intoxicated or manifestly incompetent. He (the master) is still in command of the vessel, except so far as her navigation is concerned, and bound to see that there is a sufficient watch on deck, and that the men are attentive to their duties".

Liability for negligence of pilots

If the ship is involved in a collision as a result of a wrong order from the pilot, the owner is liable whether pilotage is voluntary or compulsory. S.15 (1) of the Pilotage Act, 1913[3] provides: "Notwithstanding anything in any public or local Act, the owner or master of a vessel navigating under circumstances in which pilotage is compulsory, shall be answerable for any loss or damage caused by the vessel or by any fault of the navigation of the vessel in the same manner as he would if pilotage

---

1. In the past, the employment of a pilot was necessary because of his knowledge of local conditions. Nowadays, the route is marked on the chart and there is no need to have someone to show the way. But, there is still a need for someone to act as an agent for the enforcement of the local *modus operandi* and to assist the master in appreciating the local pattern of the traffic.
2. *The Oregon* (1895) 158 U.S. 186, 194.
3. See "Marine Pilotage in the United Kingdom", a Report to the Secretary of State for Trade by the Steering Committee on Pilotage. At present (1977), a bill is before Parliament for the revision of the 1913 Act.

were not compulsory"[1].

The pilot may be personally liable for his own negligence. However, the pilot's liability was held not to extend to the pilots' association to which he may belong[2].

FAULTS IN SALVAGE OPERATIONS

Following a collision which occurred between *The "Tojo Maru"* and *The "Fina Italia"*, an agreement on a Lloyd's Standard Form of Salvage was signed to render salvage services to *Tojo Maru*. A diver employed by the salvors negligently fired a bolt through plating into the tank of the vessel which had not been gas freed. As a result, an explosion occurred causing severe damage to *Tojo Maru*. The House of Lords[3] found that there was no principle of English maritime law which, by reason of "more good than harm", protected a salvor against a counterclaim in damages where the salved vessel suffered damage caused by the negligence of the salvor. Lord Reid said[4]: "The maritime law of England has a long history. It differed in many respects from the common law; statutory amendment of the common law has removed some of these differences but by no means all. So if examination of the authorities led me to the conclusion that any such rule or principle as that for which the salvors contend has been established, I would have no hesitation in giving effect to it. But after hearing full argument I have come to the conclusion that no such

---

1. See *The "Chyebassa"* (1919) P. 201. However, the Court took into account the defence of compulsory pilotage in foreign waters, see *The "Waziristan"* (1953) 2 Lloyd's Rep. 361 (collision in Iraq).
2. *Fowles* v. *Eastern, etc. S.S. Co., Ltd.* (1916) 2 A.C. 556. It must be noted that attempts to make the pilot association liable were based either on the theory of agency or partnership. However, as the pilot is not the agent or servant of the association, it has no right to direct him on his duties of pilotage.
3. *The "Tojo Maru"* (1969) 1 Lloyd's Rep. 133; on appeal (1969) 2 Lloyd's Rep. 193; H.L. (1971) 1 Lloyd's Rep. 341. Lower Court held that the owners were entitled to counterclaim for damages and not merely to reduce the salvage award. The Court of Appeal held that the owners were not entitled to counterclaim for damages caused by the salvors' negligence but the House of Lords reversed the decision of the Court of Appeal and confirmed the decision of the lower Court.
4. (1971) 1 Lloyd's Rep. 341 at p.346.

rule exists"[1].

As to the assessment of the award, the House of Lords held that the award was to be based on what would have been the salved value of the vessel had there been no negligence on the part of the salvors. This sum was then to be off-set against the damages awarded to the owners of the salved vessel.

(II) DAMAGES

As mentioned earlier, an inquiry into fault will be followed by an inquiry as to the damage[2] and causation.

At common law, if the plaintiff's injuries have been caused partly by the negligence of the defendant and partly by his own negligence, he cannot claim anything. This rule of "contributory negligence" caused hardship where one of the two negligent parties suffered the greater loss, although his negligence was not the major cause of the accident.

The Maritime Conventions Act,1911 adopted the concept of apportionment of damages in collision cases. The House of Lords in *Admiralty Commissioners* v. *S.S. Volute*[3] held that even where the defendant's negligence is subsequent to that of the plaintiff,

---

1. In *The "St. Blane"* (1974) 1 Lloyd's Rep. 557, Brandon, J. said (at p.560): "It is well established that the Court takes a lenient view of the conduct of salvors and would-be salvors, and is slow to find that those who try their best, in good faith, to save life or property in peril at sea, and make mistakes, or errors of judgment in doing so, have been guilty of negligence. Nevertheless, it is not in doubt that the Court may, in a proper case, after making all allowances, find negligence against salvors and, having done so, award damages against them in respect of it... In deciding such matters the Court looks at all the circumstances of the case, including the status of the salvors - whether amateur or professional - and the question whether they have acted at request or on their own initiative."
2. The damage may give some indication on the speed of the vessel. This is the observation made by Brandon, J. in *The "Hagen"* (1973) 1 Lloyd's Rep. 257, at p.262, where he said: "It is my belief, based on considerable experience of collision cases, that, without full and accurate information about the damage to both ships involved in a collision, it is extremely difficult for surveyors, however skilled, to reach reliable conclusions about their angle of blow or speeds, especially speeds."
3. (1922) 1 A.C. 129, at pp. 144, 145.

nevertheless the plaintiff's negligence is still contributory to the collision if there is not "a sufficient separation of time, place, or circumstance" between the plaintiff's negligence and the defendant's negligence to make the defendant's the sole cause of the collision[1].

Division of damages

At common law, the rule is that where two vessels were negligent, damages would be equally divided regardless of the degree of fault. This rule found justification on the idea that it induces care and vigilance on both sides in the negitation. However, this rule was abolished in cases where the Maritime Conventions Act, 1911[2] applies[3]. S.1 of this Act provides:

" (1) Where, by the fault of two or more vessels, damage or loss is caused to one or more of those vessels, to their cargoes or freight, or to any property on board, the liability to make good the damage or loss shall be in proportion to the degree in which each vessel was in fault:

Provided that:

(a) if, having regard to all the circumstances of the case, it is not possible to establish different degrees of fault, the liability shall be apportioned equally; and

(b) nothing in this section shall operate so as to render any vessel liable for any loss or damage to which her fault has not contributed; and

(c) nothing in this section shall affect the liability of any person under a contract of carriage or any contract,

---

1. The Law Reform (Contributory Negligence) Act, 1945 applies the principles on which the Maritime Conventions Act, 1911 was based to contributory negligence on land. Consequently, the courts are to take account of both culpability and causative potency.
2. In 1910, the International Convention for the Unification of Certain Rules of Law with Respect to Collision between Vessels was signed. In the same year, the Convention for the Unification of Certain Rules of Law Relating to Assistance and Salvage at Sea was also signed. The provisions of these two Conventions were incorporated into the Maritime Conventions Act, 1911. It must be noted that in 1967 a Protocol was signed to amend the Assistance and Salvage Convention, see Conventions on Maritime Law, p.15.
3. Liability arising from contact between a vessel and a pier or any floating object which is not covered by the definition "vessel" is still governed by the common law rule; that is damages will be divided equally.

or shall be construed as imposing any liability upon any person from which he is exempted by any contract or by any provision of law, or as affecting the right of any person to limit his liability in the manner provided by law.

(2) For the purposes of this Act, the expression 'freight' includes passage money and hire, and reference to damage or loss caused by the fault of a vessel shall be construed as including references to any salvage or other expenses, consequent upon that fault, recoverable by law by way of damages."

Thus, the Court must apportion the liability in proportion to the degree to which each vessel was at fault[1] unless it is impossible to do so. Winn, L.J. in *The "Lucile Bloomfield"* said[2]: "...the primary task of the Court is to apportion liability according to fault. This is followed by the proviso that if the Court finds it not possible to apportion different degrees of fault, the Court is to declare an equal distribution of fault. It is, therefore, as a matter of construction, a condition precedent to a declaration that liability be apportioned equally that the Court has found it impossible to establish different degrees of fault. To my own mind that is not the same thing as saying that where different degrees of fault cannot be established, then the liability should be equal. When Lord Atkinson in *The Peter Benoit* in 1915 spoke of the need to justify differentiation between the blameworthiness of two vessels, and of the need that there should be 'a clear preponderance of culpability', those words may not mean more than this, that one is not to seek to distinguish a mere 5 per cent., 7½ per cent. and 10 per cent., by way of distinction, and that it is only where there is a marked distinction of material amount that it is right to depart from 50 per cent."

The words by "fault of two or more vessels" in s.1 (1) of the 1911 Act cover all cases of damage or loss caused by one vessel to another by reason of negligence, whether there was a collision or not and whether the fault concerned was in respect of navigation or of management apart from navigation. In *Owners of Barge Norwhale* v. *The Ministry of Defence (The Norwhale)*[3] an attempt to

1. Brandon, J. in *The "Jan Laurenz"* (1972) 1 Lloyd's Rep. 404, at p.410 said that it would be wrong to differentiate between the faults of "two bull-headed navigators, each determined not to give way to the other, and as a result, taking or persisting in action which was almost certain to end up in a collision." Both vessels were held to be equally to blame.
2. (1967) 1 Lloyd's Rep. 341 at p.351.
3. (1975) 1 Lloyd's Rep. 610.

limit the scope of s. 1 (1) of the Act to (a) cases of damage by collision or (b) cases of damage caused without actual collision by navigational fault, failed[1].

Usually, the courts apportion the liability for the damage or loss by deciding separately, in reference to each vessel, what was the degree in which the fault of each one caused the damage or loss. This process involves comparison and it requires an assessment of the interrelationship of the respective faults of each vessel.

Difficulties in apportionment

It is commonplace that the courts attribute the greater blame to the ship which creates the position of difficulty. However, many courts find it not easy to assess the causative potency in terms of percentages. In the words of Lord Wright[2]: "(Apportionment) is a question of the degree of fault, depending on a trained and expert judgment considering all the circumstances, and it is different in essence from a mere finding of fact in the ordinary sense. It is a question, not of principle or of positive findings of fact or law, but of proportion, balance and relative emphasis, and of weighting different considerations. It involves an individual choice of discretion, as to which there may well be differences of opinion by different minds."

In *The "Miraflores"* and *The "Abadesa"*[3], plaintiff's tanker *George Livanos* (18,790 tons) grounded while manoeuvring to avoid first defendant's tanker *Miraflores* (20,776 tons) and second defendant's tanker *Abadesa* (13,570 tons) which collided in River Scheldt. All vessels were laden and tide was flooding at 1 to 2 knots. In consolidated actions, it was held, by Hewson, J. that:

(1) *Abadesa* was two-thirds and *Miraflores* was one-third to blame; and

(2) *George Livanos* was 50 per cent to blame and was entitled to recover remaining 50 per cent from *Abadesa* and *Miraflores* in proportions of two-thirds and one-third respectively.

---

1. As to the principles of construction where a court had to interpret an obscure or ambiguous statute provision, the preamble of the Act could be looked at. See *The Cairbahn* (1914) P. 25; *Burns, Philip & Co.* v. *Nelson & Robertson* (1958) 1 Lloyd's Rep. 342; *The Batavier III* (1925) 23 Ll.L.Rep 21; *The Sobieski* (1949) P. 313.
2. *The MacGregor* (1943) A.C. 197; (1942) 74 Ll.L.Rep. 82 at pp. 199 and 85 respectively.
3. (1967) 1 Lloyd's Rep. 191.

On appeal by *George Livanos*, it was held that the distribution of fault and liability should be: *Abadesa* 45 per cent; *Miraflores* 30 per cent; and *George Livanos* 25 per cent.

On appeal by *Miraflores*, it was held by the House of Lords that the apportionment of blame should be: *Abadesa*, two-fifths (40%); *Miraflores*, one-fifth (20%); *George Livanos* two-fifths (40%). In this case, Lord Pearce expressed the following rule[1]: "To get a fair apportionment it is necessary to weigh the fault of each negligent party against that of each of the others. It is or may be quite misleading to substitute for a measurement of the individual fault of each contributor to the accident a measurement of the fault of one against the joint fault of the rest"[2].

Brandon, J. in *The "Anneliese"*[3], after giving careful consideration to the faults on each vessel, came to the conclusion that: "with such serious faults on both sides, it is impossible to say that there is any clear preponderance of blame on the *Arietta*. That being so, s. 1 of the Maritime Conventions Act, 1911, requires me to say that both vessels were equally to blame."

Lord Simon of Glaisdale in *The "Savina"*[4] pointed out that: "A positive fault (deliberate breach of a rule) is not necessarily more blameworthy than negligent navigation. But that it may be so is apparent from taking extreme cases - grossly negligent navigation causing a collision compared with the deliberate running-down of one vessel by another... It is, in my view, open to an Admiralty Court ... to attach more blame to any deliberate breach of a rule than to a fault or omission. Whether the Court should do so depends on all the circumstances - in particular, the nature of the rule and the mode of its breach, on the one hand, and the degree of negligence in navigation on the other."

Lord Denning, M.R. in *The "Koningin Juliana"*[5] formulated the following rule: "The degree of fault is not to be measured by counting up the number of faults on each side. It is to be measured by assessing both their blameworthiness and their causative effect."

In certain cases, the serious fault of one ship would be so obvious that there would be no difficulty in apportionment. In

---

1. Ibid., at p.199.
2. See also *The British Tenacity* (1963) 2 Lloyd's Rep. 1.
3. (1969) 2 Lloyd's Rep. 78 at pp. 92, 93.
4. (1976) 2 Lloyd's Rep. 123 at p.134.
5. (1974) 2 Lloyd's Rep. 353, at p.356.

"Horta Barbosa" (Owners) v. *"Sea Star"* (Owners), (*The "Sea Star"*)[1], Brandon, J. held that:

"(1) the *Sea Star* was very seriously to blame for the collision for altering course to starboard at an improper time and it was to be inferred that this improper manoeuvre was caused by previous defective look-out, or defective appreciation of the situation, or both.

(2) *Horta Barbosa* was also to blame for not taking proper avoiding action in time...

(3) as to apportionment, there was no doubt that the situation of danger was created by the fault of *Sea Star*, and that the fault of *Horta Barbosa* lay only in her failure to react properly to the situation so created."

A similar Canadian case, the *Liqilassie Shipping Ltd.* v. *M.V. "Nipigon Bay"*, Her Owners and Charterers (*The "Nipigon Bay")*[2] where the Federal Court held that:

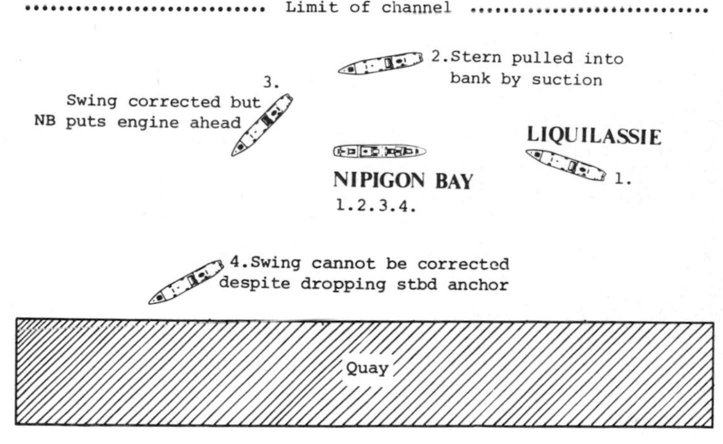

(1) *Nipigon Bay* was, if not actually on the wrong side of the channel, at least in the dead centre;

(2) the bank suction which forced the initial sheer to port of Liquilassie resulted not so much from any errors of judgment

1. (1976) 1 Lloyd's Rep. 115.
2. (1975) 2 Lloyd's Rep. 279.

on her master's part in going too close to the bank or too fast as from the fault of *Nipigon Bay* in not allowing *Liquilassie* the full half of the navigable space to which she was entitled;

(3) the damage was caused not by the initial sheer but by the kick delivered to *Nipigon Bay's* engines when *Liquilassie* was so close to *Nipigon Bay's* stern;

(4) the damage was primarily the fault of *Nipigon Bay* but some fault was attributable to *Liquilassie* for not giving a danger signal to *Nipigon Bay* and coming to a dead stop while waiting for her to move over, or for not passing at such a slow speed as to eliminate any risk of bank suction.

Apportionment of blame: *Nipigon Bay* 80 per cent., *Liquilassie* 20 per cent.

Revision of apportionment by the Court of Appeal

The apportionment of liability will often depend on the determination of difficult questions of fact and seldom of questions of law. As the trial judge is in a better position than judges on appeal, it is only in quite exceptional circumstances that the Court of Appeal should revise his apportionment[1]. In *The "Koningin Juliana"*, Lord Wilberforce said[2]: "...any other rule would encourage a proliferation of appeals, in the hope of finding an appellate tribunal which might attach different weights to the various considerations. It is an undoubted advantage of our own system of judicature that so few of the cases which come to trial are taken to appeal. This brings me to a fourth reason for the rule, though it is one which I feel some diffidence in expressing. No judge, instance or appellate, is properly equipped without both intuition and a capacity for logical analysis. But the latter quality is the more called-for in an appellate tribunal; while intuition, as Roscoe Pound was wont to emphasize, is the prime and essential quality required in a trial judge. The balancing of a number of conflicting considerations of fact (such as is called for in matters like apportionment of fault or quantifying damages or exercising discretion as to the custody of a child) is generally more a matter of intuition than of logical analysis. Finally, the trial judge deals with such matters day in, day out, and his judgment is thereby reinforced by constant experience."

Lord Diplock, in *The "Savina"*[3] explained the policy of non-interference by the Court of Appeal in the apportionment save in

---

1. See Lord Wright in *The "MacGregor"* (1943) A.C. 197 at p.199.
2. (1975) 2 Lloyd's Rep. 111 at pp. 115, 116.
3. (1976) 2 Lloyd's Rep. 123, at p.125.

exceptional circumstances in the following words: "... The costs of both sides in settling or litigating claims arising out of collisions are borne by the hull and P. & I. insurers of the vessels involved. They have to be recovered in the market rates of premiums charged to shipowners who in turn must make provision for their costs of insurance in the freight rates charged to shippers...under the English judicial system collision cases are now tried by a specialist Judge whose experience in cases about faults of navigation is much greater than that of most of those who compose the membership of Appellate Courts. This should give to the Admiralty Judge's apportionments a greater predictability than those of Appellate Courts if their members treated themselves as uninhibited in substituting their own view of the respective degrees of blame for those of the trial Judge."

Damage to the cargo

As mentioned earlier, the kinds of damage covered by Section 1 of the Maritime Conventions Act, 1911 are the ships in fault, their cargoes and freights. Each ship would be severally liable in proportion to the degree of her fault. The Admiralty rule[1] that cargo is to be identified so far as fault is concerned with its carrying ship, is still valid under the 1911 Act.

The United States did not adopt the Brussels Collision Convention 1910, and, therefore, when both vessels involved in a collision are to blame, the damage is apportioned equally, whatever the degree of blame. Also, the rule[2] is that cargo-owners may recover in full from the non-carrying vessel if it is at fault. The non-carrying vessel may then claim from the carrying vessel one half of the amount paid.

The result is that cargo-owners prefer to sue in American courts, or at least to have the American rules applied. Shipowners sought to circumvent this result by including in their documents a "both to blame collision" clause to divide the damages on a proportionate and not on an equal basis. The validity of the clause was tested in *U.S.* v. *Atlantic Mutual Ins. Co.*[3] where the Supreme Court held that the "both to blame collision" clause was null and void.

---

1. *The "Milan"* (1861) Lush 388.
2. *The "Chattahoochee"* (1899) 173 U.S. 540.
3. (1952) A.M.C. 659.

Damages in foreign currency

In *The "Volturno"*[1], the House of Lords decided that:

(1) judgment could only be given in sterling and the Court had no power to give judgment in a foreign currency; and

(2) in assessing damages in a currency other than sterling, it was to be converted into sterling. The date for conversion was in debt cases, at the time when the debt fell due, in breach of contract cases, at the time of breach, and in tort cases, at the date when the loss or expenditure concerned was incurred[2].

The reasons for these rules were that sterling was a stable currency and it was considered contrary to public policy to give judgments in foreign currency. However, when the pound was floated with different rates of exchange, the old rules seemed to be unfair[3] as they could have a substantial effect on the amount of damages received by a successful litigant.

Recently, the issue came before the House of Lords in *Miliangos* v. *George Frank (Textiles) Ltd.*[4] where it reversed its previous decision. It recognised that English Courts were entitled to give judgment for a sum of money in a foreign currency[5] where:

(a) the obligation to pay that sum arose under a contract whose proper law was that of a foreign country; and

(b) the money of account and payment was in that country's currency. The date of conversion to sterling was held to be the

---

1. (1921) 8 Ll.L.Rep. 449. See also *Manners* v. *Pearson & Sons* (1898) 1 Ch. 581. There was, however, an exception to these rules, in that it was possible for parties in an arbitration to ask the arbitrator to make his award in a foreign currency.
2. Re *United Railways of Havana and Regla Warehouses Ltd.*, (1961) A.C. 1007.
3. *Yugoslavenska Oceanska Plovidba* v. *Castle Investment Co., Inc. (The "Kozara")* (1973) 2 Lloyd's Rep. 1.
4. (1976) 1 Lloyd's Rep. 201.
5. A few days before the *Miliangos* case, the Court of Appeal held in *Schorsch Meier G.m.b.H.* v. *Hennin*(1975) 1 Lloyd's Rep. 1 that the Courts had power to give judgment in foreign currency when it was the currency of the contract.

date of the enforcement of the judgment[1].

However, as the *Miliangos* rules are only binding in contract, Brandon, J. in *The "Despina R"*[2] had to consider whether these rules would also be applicable for damages in tort. In that case, a collision occurred between two Greek ships, *The "Eleftherotria"* and *The "Despina R"*. The parties agreed that the owners of the Despina R were 85% to blame and the Eleftherotria were 15%, but the issue was whether the agreed damages would be payable in sterling or other currency. Brandon, J. awarded the owners the damages in the currency of the loss or expenditure, which was in four currencies.

On appeal[3], Lord Justice Stephenson agreed with Mr. Justice Brandon that the Court was not bound by the *Volturno* to accept the sterling solution but was free to give damages for negligence in a foreign currency. His Lordship added that as long as sterling remained in a weak position in relation to other currencies, the *Miliangos* rule applied the principle more justly than the *Volturno* rule. The Court, however, must be satisfied that the plaintiffs' own currency was the currency in which the loss was effectively felt or borne, and with which the loss was most closely connected. Accordingly, the Court held that the plaintiffs were entitled to be awarded as damages the amounts of reasonable expenditure and loss expressed in U.S. dollars or the sterling equivalents as at the date of payment. The Court also declared that where the expenditure and loss of the plaintiffs was directly and immediately incurred in any currency other than U.S. dollars, the sum representing such expenditure and loss should be converted into U.S. dollars as at the date when it was incurred.

---

1. In *Jean Kraut AG* v. *Albany Fabrics Ltd.* (1976) 2 Lloyd's Rep. 350, Mr. Justice Eveleigh awarded damages in Swiss francs to a Swiss plaintiff for non-acceptance of cloth deliveries by English defendants. The Swiss currency in that case was the agreed currency of compensation under the contract.
   In *The Folias* (1977) 1 Lloyd's Rep. 39, the clim was for damage caused to the cargo and the dispute was over which foreign currency the award should be. Robert Goff, J. made the award of damages in Brazilian cruzerios on the basis that that was the currency in which the loss was directly and immediately incurred.
2. (1977) 1 Lloyd's Rep. 618.
3. Lloyd's List July 9, 1977 - Leave to appeal to the House of Lords was granted.

Right of recovery against two negligent vessels

It has long been settled that when an innocent vessel suffers damage through the combined negligence of two other vessels, the whole damage may be recoverable from either wrongdoer. *The S.S. Devonshire* (Owners) v. *Barge Leslie* (Owners)[1] was an action against the owners of the *Devonshire*, one of the two negligent ships. They were condemned in the full amount of the damage sustained. In the course of his reasons for judgment, Viscount Haldane, L.C. said[2]: "I have come to the conclusion that the appellants (the *Devonshire* owners) have failed to show that there was a rule in force in the Court of Admiralty that the owners of an innocent ship could not recover the whole of the damage she had sustained against one of two ships both to blame for a collision with her..."

Lord Atkinson referred to[3]: "...the general rule or principle of law, common to Courts both of common law and admiralty, that there is not to be contribution between two tortfeasors, and that each is liable for the entire damages inflicted on an innocent person by their joint wrong."

Where one vessel has been held to pay the entire damage resulting from a collision for which another vessel was similarly to blame, the former may recover a contribution from the latter. *The Cairnbahn*[4] is a good illustration. In that case, the *Cairnbahn* collided with a barge being towed by a second vessel. The barge-owners sued both vessels which were held equally to blame. The towing vessel was not contractually exempted from liability and judgment was given for the barge-owners jointly and severally against both vessels. However, the barge-owners proceeded successfully to enforce the judgment solely against the owners of the *Cairnbahn* which itself claimed to recover over from its codefendant half the amount of the judgment. It was held, and affirmed on appeal, that they were entitled to do so, because the damages paid by the *Cairnbahn* were part of the damage or loss caused to it by the combined faults of both vessels within s. 1 of the Maritime Conventions Act, 1911.

Remoteness of damages

Damage which is too remote cannot be recovered. In *The Oropesa"*[5], a vessel was badly damaged in a collision, for which she was four-fifths to blame. Fifty of her crew left in two lifeboats and reached the other ship safely. About an hour-and-a-half after the collision the master launched another boat, in

---

1. (1912) A.C. 634.
2. Ibid., at p.647.
3. Ibid., at p.651.
4. (1914) P. 25.
5. (1942) P. 140. See also *The "Spontaneity"* (1962) 1 Lloyd's Rep. 460.

which he, the sixth engineer and other members of the crew under his orders embarked, in order that the master might confer with the master of the other vessel on salvage measures. The boat capsized in an unexpected cross-sea, drowning the engineer. It was held that his representatives could recover against the other ship, the death being directly caused by the collision. The test seems to be: "was the damage in question, resulting from a chain of events following the collision, brought about by something unreasonable, extraneous or extrinsic? If so, then it could not be held to be caused by the collision; if not, it could".

Willmer, L.J. in *The "Miraflores"* and *The "Abadesa"*[1] said: "Where as in the present case, the damage sued for is consequential damage said to result from the prior negligence of another or other vessels, it seems obvious that the more remote that prior negligence, is, whether in time or space, the more its causative potency must diminish until eventually it disappears altogether."

In another case, *The "Fogo"*[2], the *Trentbank* was found wholly to blame for a collision with the *Fogo*. Subsequent to the collision, the *Trentbank* sank and the Court found that the sinking was due to her failure to employ a tug for assistance. This failure was considered as a *novus actus interveniens* which broke the chain of causation. In contrast, in *The "Calliope"*[3], the Court found that the subsequent negligence of the plaintiffs did not break the chain of causation as this would amount to a resurrection of the "last opportunity" rule[4].

---

1. (1966) 1 Lloyd's Rep. 97, at p.110.
2. (1967) 2 Lloyd's Rep. 208.
3. (1970) 1 Lloyd's Rep. 84.
4. In *Overseas Tankship (U.K.)* v. *Mort's Dock and Engineering Co. (The Wagon Mound)* (1961) A.C. 388, The Privy Council held that a plaintiff can recover as damages for the negligence of the defendant, only if that damage could have been foreseen by a reasonable man. It is not enough for him to show that the damage was a direct physical consequence of negligent act. See also *Hughes* v. *Lord Advocate* (1963) A.C. 837. In *Pink* v. *Fleming* (1890) 25 Q.B.D. 396, two ships collided and one of them had to put in to port for repairs. In order to effect the repairs, it was necessary for her cargo of fruit to be discharged from the ship. The fruit was damaged because of removal from the ship and the delay. It was held that the loss of the fruit did not arise from the collision. See also *The Fritz Thyssen* (1967) 1 Lloyd's Rep. 104, where it was held that the loss of a ship following a collision could not be held to be caused by the collision because the loss was the result of the master's action and indecision in failing to accept offers of assistance.

(III) CAUSATION

Negligence must be a contributory cause of the collision

Negligence must cause or contribute to the collision which in its turn brought about the damage, in order to be actionable[1]. Lord Reid, in *The "Statue of Liberty"*[2] found that *The "Andulo's"* fault in not taking more accurate observations at the earlier stage, had no causative effect and it should be left out of account in the final assessment of the degree in which *Andulo* was to blame for the collision.

In *The "Bovenkerk"*[3], Brandon, J. held that the presence of the dredger while creating the occasion of the collision was not, in law, a contributory cause of it because its presence was well-known to the pilots of both vessels.

Similarly, in *The "Fritz Thyssen"*[4], the Court found that the sinking of the vessel was not caused by collision but because of her failure to take the necessary action. In this case, the plaintiff's vessel *"Mitera Marigo"* laden with iron ore, sustained damage below water line in collision at 02 10 hours on May 29, 1959, with defendant's vessel *Fritz Thyssen*, off Ushant. *Mitera Marigo* refused assistance from *Fritz Thyssen* and the salvage tug *Englishman*, and continued her voyage to Rotterdam. At 05 20 hours, she altered her course for Falmouth because water was increasing in No.1 hold. Her speed was 7½ knots. At 11 00 hours she engaged *Englishman* as escort and those vessels sighted each other at 17 00 hours, 11 miles from Falmouth, but *Mitera Marigo* refused a tow by *Englishman*. *Mitera Marigo* was taking water into No.1 hold at 70 to 80 tons per hour when she was towed into Falmouth Harbour by three harbour tugs. At that time, *Mitera Marigo's* owners gave her master authority to engage *Englishman* for any services required. At 20 00 hours she was moored stern

---

1. In *The Margaret* (1881) 6 P.D. 76, although both vessels were guilty of negligence, only one of them caused the collision. In this case, the *Clan Sinclair* was required by the Thames Rules to wait below a point in the river until The Margaret passed, and was in that respect guilty of negligence. Yet, it was held that this negligence was not a cause of the collision. The Margaret was held to be alone to blame because, knowing where the other vessel was she had not waited as far up as she ought, and with ordinary care she could have avoided the collision. See also *The Eurymedon* (1938) P. 41; (1937) 59 Ll.L.Rep. 214.
2. (1971) 2 Lloyd's Rep. 277 at p.280.
3. (1973) 1 Lloyd's Rep. 63.
4. (1967) 2 Lloyd's Rep. 199 (the Court of Appeal affirmed).

first to buoys with *Englishman* standing by. At 22 00 hours, an alarming noise was heard on *Mitera Marigo*, and *Englishman* was asked to pump. Pumps with capacity of 400 tons per hour were started, but 45 minutes later, when *Mitera Marigo* cast off from the buoy, preparatory to beaching, she sank.

Karminski, J. said that if *Englishman's* pumps had been used at 20 00 hours, *Mitera Marigo* probably would not have sunk. His Lordship held that *Mitera Marigo* omitted to take vital precautions which good seamanship required, and, if those precautions had been taken over two hours earlier, loss would probably have been averted.

Where the collision and the damage are due to a combination of causes, the main cause is that which is proximate in efficacy. In *The "Judith M"*[1], both vessels were to blame, but one was more substantially than the other. The collision in this case occurred in the English Channel, in fog, between plaintiff's vessel *"Glaciar Azul"* and defendant's steamship *Judith M*. *Glaciar Azul* was proceeding on course of 056 deg. (true) at stand-by full speed (13½ knots), not sounding fog signals. According to her second officer, an echo of *Judith M* was seen on radar distant 8 miles, 5 deg. on port bow. When echo was six miles distant it had broadened on the port bow and *Glaciar Azul* altered 15 deg. to starboard. When four miles distant, the echo broadened further and *Glaciar Azul* altered further 10 deg. to starboard. One minute before collision, *Judith M's* green was sighted visually distant about three cables, 5 deg. on port bow. *Glaciar Azul's* wheel was put hard-a-starboard and engines slow ahead (without sounding one-short-blast). Shortly before the collision, the engines of *Glaciar Azul* were ordered full astern and three-short-blasts were sounded. *Judith M* was proceeding on course of 228 to 230 deg. (true) at stand-by reduced full speed (8½ knots) sounding fog signals. The second officer saw the echoes of four ships approaching in line on the starboard bow but did not plot them. *Glaciar Azul's* green was sighted at a distance of two cables bearing about 25 deg. on starboard bow, followed by her green and red. *Judith M's* wheel was put hard-a-port (without sounding two-short-blasts) and her engines full ahead. Shortly before collision her wheel was put amidships, then hard-a-starboard. The collision occurred between stem of *Glaciar Azul* and starboard quarter of *Judith M* at angle of about 75 deg. leading forward on *Judith M*.

Both parties admitted blame for excessive speed, failing to reduce speed and bad radar look-out. *Glaciar Azul* contended, inter alia, that *Judith M* ported before sighting; was keeping bad

---

1. (1968) 2 Lloyd's Rep. 474.

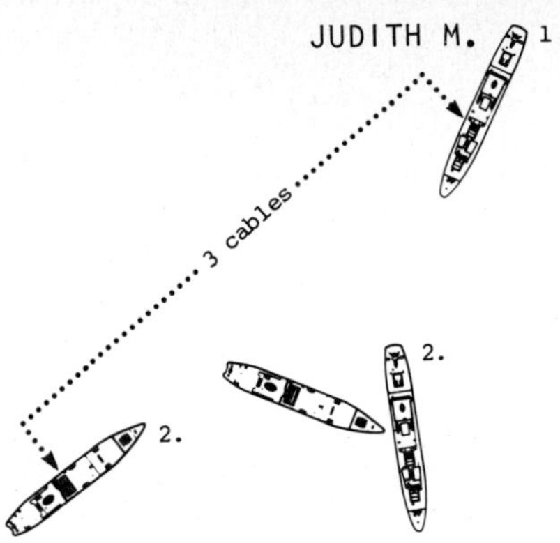

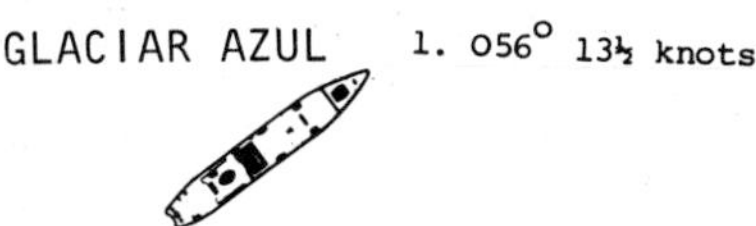

visual look-out; took wrong action after sighting and failed to sound two short blasts when she altered to port after sighting. *Judith M* contended that *Glaciar Azul* was to blame for altering to starboard before sighting, not hearing *Judith M's* fog signals and taking wrong action on sighting.

It was held that *Judith M* did not alter course to port before sighting, but was steering a more southerly course than those on board her intended. *Glaciar Azul* altered about 45 deg. to starboard and *Judith M* about 30 deg. to port between sighting and the collision. Although *Judith M* was negligent in not seeing *Glaciar Azul* earlier, it was not proved that that fault caused or contributed to the collision. To consider whether such failure was causative (on the ground that if avoiding action had been taken earlier, collision might have been avoided) was too speculative. The two small alterations of *Glaciar Azul* before sighting were unseamanlike and contributed to the collision. *Glaciar Azul* was further to blame for her starboard wheel action after sighting. Apportionment of blame: *Judith M*, 40 per cent; *Glaciar Azul*, 60 per cent.

(IV) LIMITATION OF LIABILITY

Maritime law has for a long time recognised the right of the shipowner to limit his liability in case of collision to the value of the ship and freight. The limitation of the shipowner's liability which is a kind of statutory insolvency was introduced in English law by the Merchant Shipping Act, 1894. S. 503 provides for the limitation of liability of shipowners and others to an amount calculated by reference to the tonnage of the ship.

As a result of the International Convention relating to the Limitation of the Liability of Owners of Sea-going Ships, signed at Brussels in 1957[1], the Merchant Shipping (Liability of Shipowners and Others) Act, 1958 was passed. The scope of limitation in respect of claims for loss of life or personal injury has been extended by the 1958 Act to claims for damage to property including harbour works, basins and waterways, and claims for wreck-raising charges[2].

The meaning of "ship"

By s. 742 of the Merchant Shipping Act, the word "ship" is defined, and includes every description of vessel used in navigation not propelled by oars. It is provided by the Merchant Shipping (Liability of Shipowners and Others) Act, 1958, s. 4(1) that Part VIII (the limitation provisions) of the 1894 Act shall apply to any structure, whether completed or in the course of completion, launched and intended for use in navigation as a ship or part of a ship[3].

Persons entitled to limit liability

Those entitled to limit liability are:

1. Owners of the ship, registered or not, whether British or foreign.
2. "Any charterers and any person interested in, or in possession of the ship and, in particular, any manager or operator of the ship".
3. Master and members of the crew notwithstanding actual fault or privity if the claim arises from an act or omission in the course of their employment.

---

1. Cmnd. 353. IMCO approved on November 19, 1976, a Convention on Limitation of Liability for Maritime Claims, to replace the present one. See Appendix XVII.
2. Subsection (2) of section 2 of the 1958 Act only applies to liability for wreck raising expenses incurred through the exercise of statutory powers. Thus, it gives rise to a claim for a debt and not for damages. See *The Putbus* (1969) 1 Lloyd's Rep. 253.
3. Owners of oil and gas rigs, if they are not considered as a "ship" according to the definition would not be entitled to limit liability.

4. Hirers of lighters, barges or like vessels, who, by the Act of 1921, are to be included within the meaning of "owners".
5. Owners of docks and canals as defined by the Merchant Shipping (Liability of Shipowners and Others) Act, 1900, s. 2 (4) and (5), and harbour and conservancy authorities.
6. The crown and persons entitled to limit their liability under the Crown Proceedings Act, 1947, ss. 5 and 7.

Fault or privity

The person entitled to limit liability must not be guilty of "fault or privity". In order to prove such "privity" it is necessary to prove knowledge on the part of that person. Knowledge means not only positive knowledge but the sort of knowledge expressed in "turning a blind eye" which is far more blameworthy than mere negligence.

The meaning of the words "fault or privity" have been authoritatively declared by the House of Lords in *Lennard's Carrying Co.* v. *Asiatic Petroleum Co.*[1] Lord Haldane was of opinion that the fault or privity of somebody who is not merely a servant or agent for whom the company is liable upon the basis *respondeat superior*, but somebody for whom the company is liable because his action is the very action of the company itself.

Lennard's case was followed in *Paterson Steamships Ltd.* v. *Robin Hood Mills, Ltd.*[2]. In that case, Lord Roche said: "But another and very important principle is to be derived from a consideration of the section, namely, that the fault or privity of the owners must be fault or privity in respect of that which causes the loss or damage in question, a proposition which was acted upon and illustrated in Lennard's case."

In *Admiralty* v. *Owners of Divina, The Truculent*[3], the Crown attempted to limit its liability in respect of claims which arose out of a collision between H.M.S. *Truculent* and the *Divina*. The Court held that there was a fault in relation to the lights exhibited by H.M.S. *Truculent* and that as that fault was one of which the Third Sea Lord, a responsible member of the Board of Admiralty, was or must be deemed to have been aware, the claim of the Crown to limit liability failed.

Again, in *The "Lady Gwendolen"*[4], the directors of Guinness's

---

1. (1915) A.C. 705.
2. (1937) 58 Ll.L.Rep. 33.
3. (1952) P. 1.
4. (1965) 1 Lloyd's Rep. 335, C.A.

brewery sent stout from Dublin to Liverpool in a ship whose master relied entirely on the radar when going up the Mersey at full speed. The Court found that the collision was caused by an inadequate use of radar and excessive speed. It was held that the directors were guilty of actual fault, in failing to supervise the master and consequently were not entitled to the limitation. Willmer, L.J. said[1]: "It seems to me that any company which embarks on the business of shipping must accept the obligation to ensure efficient management of its ships if it is to enjoy the very considerable benefits conferred by the statutory right to limitation."

In *The "Dayspring"*[2], the owners were unable to limit their liability because they failed to keep a proper log-book and this happened with their knowledge and consent. Similarly, in *The "England"*[3], the owners of the *England* contended: "...that the collision was caused or contributed to by the actual fault or privity of the *Alletta's* managing owners in failing to ensure that the *Alletta's* master did not navigate in the River Thames without a pilot, and ensure that the master had sufficient knowledge himself to navigate in the River Thames (in particular, failed to ensure that there were copies of the relevant by-laws on board). There was evidence that the day-to-day running of the vessel was left to the discretion of the master, and that, as a matter of practice, questions of pilotage were left to the master's discretion, no compulsory pilotage being applicable to this ship of only 500 tons".

It was held in the Admiralty Court that the practice in this case was reasonable, and that the managing owners were not at fault in leaving the decision whether or not to take a pilot to the master's discretion. It was also found that the *Alletta's* master had been competent and conscientious, and that, therefore, the managing owners were entitled to foresee that the master would not navigate in the River Thames without a pilot unless he felt competent to do so, and that before doing so the master would have familiarised himself with the port of London river by-laws.

The Court of Appeal said that it would be highly unwise for any master of a vessel such as the *Alletta*, whether or not she was at all times subject to compulsory pilotage, to allow his vessel to trade regularly to the port of London without having in his possession a copy of the by-laws, and without having familiarised himself with at least a substantial part of the contents of the

---

1. Ibid., at p.346.
2. (1968) 2 Lloyd's Rep. 204.
3. (1973) 1 Lloyd's Rep. 373.

by-laws. The case of the *Alletta* was that the managing owners were entitled to assume that the master would, without specific orders or instructions to that effect, do what was necessary to familiarise himself with such matters set out in the by-laws as it was requisite for him to know, and in particular that he would not navigate the vessel at any time in the port of London without a pilot unless he had so sufficiently familiarised himself, whether from the book of by-laws or from some other source.

The Court held that the managing owners were under a duty at least to give instructions to the master that, in trading to the port of London, he must have available a copy of the by-laws. The right to limit liability was refused.

The fact that the loss or damage is caused by the fault of one or several part-owners would not deprive the co-owners of the right to have their liability limited. As mentioned earlier, a master or member of the crew may, notwithstanding his actual fault or privity, limit his liability[1] in relation to a claim arising from an act or omission in his capacity as master or member of the crew. An owner who is also the master of the vessel at the time of the loss or damage is entitled to limit his liability even though the loss or damage has been caused by his negligence[2]. The fault or privity could result from the non-observance of a legal duty[3].

---

1. See s. 3 of the Merchant Shipping (Liability of Shipowners and Others) Act, 1958. In *The Tojo Maru* (1969) 2 Lloyd's Rep. 193, the salvors failed to limit their liability because the act which caused the damage came from under the water and was not an act or omission of a person "on board the ship".
2. See s. 2 of the 1958 Act. See also *Coldwell-Horsfall* v. *West Country Yacht Charters, The Annie Hay* (1968) P. 341.
3. See *Admiralty* v. *Owners of Divina, The Truculent*(1952) P. 1 (defective lights); *Hook* v. *Consolidated Fisheries Ltd.* (1953) 2 Lloyd's Rep. 467 (unsafe system of work); *The Thames* (1940) P. 143 (failure by hirer of barge to inquire when it was last surveyed or to take steps to ascertain conditions); *The Hildina* (1957) 2 Lloyd's Rep. 247 (failure to fit a cut-out to a trawling winch); *The Empire Jamaica* (1957) A.C. 386 (H.L.) (appointment of an uncertificated officer); *The Norman* (1960) 1 Lloyd's Rep. 1 (H.L.) (failure to communicate the latest navigational information to a ship at sea); *The Anonity* (1961) 2 Lloyd's Rep. 117 (C.A.) (inadequate steps to prohibit use of galley stove at oil jetty); *The Kathy K* (1976) 1 Lloyd's Rep. 153, Canada Sup. Ct. (the tugmaster failed to keep his tow close hauled, travelling at an excessive speed and failing to get out of the way of the sailboat).

The onus of proving the absence of actual fault or privity lies upon the party who claims it[1]. This is a heavy one and is not discharged by showing that his acts were not "the sole or next chief cause" of the mishap. As Viscount Haldane stated in *Standard Oil Co. of New York* v. *Clan Line Steamers Ltd.*[2]: "They must show that they are themselves in no way in fault or privity to what occurred."

The fault or privity of the servants, e.g. master or member of the crew, would not affect the right of the shipowner to limit his liability. Where the owners are a company, the fault or privity must be of the person who is the very *ego* and the directing mind of the company, in order to deprive the owners of the benefits of limitation[3].

The amount of limitation

Where there is loss of or damage to goods, merchandise, or other things on board the vessel, the maximum liability will be 1,000 gold francs. The maximum amount for loss of life or personal injury is 3,100 gold francs. Where there are claims both for loss of life and personal injury as well as for loss of, or damage to, goods, the former claims fall under the 2,100 gold francs per ton. If the fund is insufficient they rank *paru passu* with the latter claims against 1,000 gold francs per ton in respect of the balance left out of the 2,100 gold francs per ton[4].

---

1. *Standard Oil Co.* v. *Clan Line* (1924) A.C. 100; *The Empire Jamaica* (1956) 2 Lloyd's Rep. 119 (H.L.); *The Hildina* (1957) 2 Lloyd's Rep. 247; *The Norman* (1960) 1 Lloyd's Rep. 1. In *The Chugaway II* (1969) 2 Lloyd's Rep. 526 (Canada Exc. Ct.) the Court held: (1) that onus was on plaintiff to prove (a) the defendant whose action is the action of the company; (b) that such person has not been guilty of fault or privity; and (c) that if there was fault it did not contribute to the accident... that instructions not to tow under Fraser Street Bridge at high water would require the master to determine the existence of the high water and since the practice of counting the planks was the best method, such instructions would not have avoided the mistake. No fault of plaintiff contributed to the collision since the failure of the master to count the planks correctly or to remember to count correctly was not foreseeable. Therefore, the plaintiff was entitled to limit liability. On appeal, see (1973) 2 Lloyd's Rep. 159.
2. (1924) A.C. 100 at p.113.
3. *The Lady Gwendolen* (1965) 1 Lloyd's Rep. 335, C.A.
4. It must be noted that a writ in a limitation action may be served out of the jurisdiction in the circumstances set out in R.S.C., Ord. 75, r. 4 (R.S.C., Revision, 1969).

The Merchant Shipping (Limitation of Liability) (Sterling Equivalents) Order 1976 provides for the sums of £132.81 and £42.84 as the amounts which shall be taken as equivalent to 3,100 and 1,000 gold francs respectively[1]. The shipowner is liable beyond this statutory limit for interest and costs[2]. Interest is not awarded on the total gross figure of each claim unless the limitation fund proves sufficient to meet all claims, interest[3] and costs in full.

In *The "Giacinto Motta"*[4], Brandon, J. said that it was well-established right of a shipowner, who had already paid a claim arising out of a collision or other casualty caused by the fault of his ship, when limiting his liability under the Merchant Shipping Acts 1894 to 1974, to have taken into account in the distribution of the fund the sum previously paid by him in respect of such claim.

His Lordship added that this right further existed whether the payment was made by way of settlement of the claim out of court in the United Kingdom or abroad, or in satisfaction of the judgment of a foreign court. However, this right could not be described as a legal right of the shipowner to claim against his own limitation fund because it was not possible to bring a claim against himself. It was rather an equitable right to be given credit in the distribution of the fund... clearly the amount of the notional claim put against the fund in respect of the payment made outside could not be more than the actual claim which the claimant concerned would have been entitled to bring against

---

1. S.I. 1031 of 1976. It also provides that for the purposes of s. 4 of the Merchant Shipping (Oil Pollution) Act, 1971, £85.69 and £8,997,093 are specified as the amounts which shall be taken as equivalent to 2,000 gold francs and 210 million gold francs respectively. The Statutory Instrument is procedural and is retrospective in its effect. See *The Abadesa Furness-Houlder Argentine Lines, Ltd.* v. *Owners of Steam Tankers Miraflores* (1968) 2 All E.R. 726; *The Mecca* (1968) 2 All E.R. 731; (1968) P. 665.
2. *The Theems* (1938) P. 197.
3. In *The Funabashi* (1972) 1 W.L.R. 666; (1972) 2 All E.R. 181; (1972) 1 Lloyd's Rep. 371, the rate of interest on the limitation fund ordered by the Registrar, in limitation proceedings, was fixed at 5½% following the decision in *The Mecca* (1968) P. 665. However, the Court reviewed this percentage and fixed it on the average of the rates of interest obtainable on short term investment from the date of casualty to the date of payment into Court by the plaintiffs. Consequently, the Court fixed the rate of interest at 6½%.
4. Lloyd's List, April 16, 1977.

the fund if he had not accepted the payment.

The tonnage is that appearing on the ship's register in force at the time of the collision[1]. When the actual tonnage of the ship is less than 300 tons, the registered tonnage, for the purpose of limiting liability for claims in respect of loss of life or personal injury, shall be taken as 300 tons. Added to the tonnage of a steamship will be any engine-room space deducted to ascertain that tonnage. For example, if the net registered ton is 750 tons and the engine-room allowance is 250 tons, the limitation will be based on 1,000 tons[2]. For dock and canal owners and harbour conservancy authorities the limitation will be based on the largest registered British ship which, at the time of such loss or damage occurring is, or was within a period of five years previous thereto, within the area over which they perform any duty or exercise any power.

Limitation by a tug and tow

In *The Bramley Moore*[3], a limitation action was brought by the owners of the tug which had in tow barges, and which did not belong to the same owner. This flotilla came into collision with a third vessel. The issue on the limitation action was whether there was any basis for aggregating the tonnage of the tug and the tows by treating them as a flotilla or as a single unit, as both were under the same ownership. The Court of Appeal held that the plaintiffs were entitled to limit their liability on the basis of the tonnage of the tug alone. Lord Denning, M.R. giving the judgment of the Court, said: "If those on board the tug are

---

1. However, the register is not a conclusive evidence. See *The Franconia* (1878) 3 P.D. 164. See also S.I. 1967 Nos. 172 and 1093.
2. The procedures to be followed in limitation actions are prescribed in Order 75. Rule 1(2) defines the limitation action and contains provisions with regard to the parties to the action.
   Where there are claims for loss of life following a collision, an admission by the shipowner who is seeking a decree of limitation that he is liable for those claims only, is not accepted. In *The Sir John Snell* (1958) Fo. 77, a partial admission of blame, in the affidavit in support of the summons for decree, which does not specify to what extent liability is admitted, e.g. solely to blame or three-quarters to blame, is not acceptable unless these particulars can be ascertained from some document which has been lodged or filed. If a defence is withdrawn, the plaintiff should issue a new summons for a decree, *The Kingston Diamond* (1964) 1 Lloyd's Rep. 384.
3. (1964) 1 All. E.R. 105.

negligent and those on board the tow are not, and the tow comes into collision with another vessel, then clearly the damage is caused through an 'act or omission of any person on board the tug'."[1]

The *"Sir Joseph Rawlinson"*[2] was a collision between a tug and its tow and a third vessel. The plaintiffs were owners of both tug and tow and the collision was caused by the negligence of the master of the tug and the master of the other vessel. The tow, a dumb hopper barge, which carried a crew of five and had a helmsman at the wheel at the time of the collision, was not negligent in any way. In limitation proceedings, the owners of the other vessel contested the right of the tug owner to limit his liability to the tonnage of the tug alone and claimed that he had to limit his liability to the combined tonnage of the tug and tow. Kerr, J. held that: "Where a tug and its tow are under common ownership, those owners may limit their liability for collision damage to an amount calculated by reference to the tonnage of the tug alone where there is negligence for which they are liable on the part of the person in charge of the tug but no negligence on the part of anyone on the tow"[3].

However, in *The "Kathy K"*[4], a collision occurred between a yacht and an unmanned barge which was being towed by the *Kathy K*, in

---

1. Ibid., at p.109.
2. (1972) 2 Lloyd's Rep. 437.
3. He added: "It seems to me that...the only causative negligence, which is the negligence to which one must look, must in cases such as this be regarded as negligence in the navigation of the tug, and not negligence in the navigation of the tow or negligence in the navigation of both tug and tow. Accordingly, whilst it is apparently still correct to say that a person who negligently navigates a tug towing something may be negligent in the navigation of the tug and the tow, in particular where the damage is caused wholly or as in the present case partly by the tow, it seems to me that the effect of the decision of the Court of Appeal is that the causative negligence is in such cases to be treated as negligence in the navigation of the tug alone." Ibid., at p.445.
4. (1976) 1 Lloyd's Rep. 153.

the English Bay, Vancouver. The Exchequer Court of Canada held that both vessels were at fault and apportioned the blame as follows: *Kathy K*, 75 per cent and the yacht 25 per cent[1].

In an action for damages by the deceased's widow against the owners and the master of the *Kathy K*, the Court held that the owners were not entitled to limit their liability because they were actually privy to the fault. However, the master was entitled to limit his liability which was calculated on the aggregate tonnage of the wrong-doing mass, i.e. the tug and tow[2].

Limitation by a pilotage authority

The Pilotage Act, 1913, s. 35 (1), provides:

"A licensed pilot, who has given a bond in conformity with bye-laws made for the purpose under this Act, shall not be liable for neglect or want of skill beyond the penalty in the bond, and the amount payable to him on account of pilotage in respect of the voyage in which he was engaged when he became so liable."

It is provided in section 17 (1) (i) that the bond shall not exceed £100.

Where a pilotage authority incurs liability, as where it is the actual employer of pilots, the Pilotage Authorities (Limitation of Liability) Act, 1936 applies in the absence of actual fault or privity, to a sum arrived by multiplying the amount of £100 by

---

1. (1972) 2 Lloyd's Rep. 36.
2. (1976) 1 Lloyd's Rep. 153, at p.162.

the number of pilots holding licences for the district[1].

Period within which action must be taken

Under Section 8 of the Maritime Conventions Act, 1911, proceedings in a collision suit against the *other* ship[2] must be taken within two years of the date when the damage, loss or injury was caused. Time ceases when the writ is issued. The writ may be issued whether the defendant ship is within the jurisdiction or not, and the Court may extend the time limit and must do so where there has been no reasonable opportunity of arresting the vessel within the two years.

The limitation Act 1963 and the R.S.C. Ord. 110, provide for extension of the limitation period in personal injury cases in

---

1. As for the limitation of liability against the harbour authorities in exercising their statutory powers to remove the wreck, see *The "Berwyn"* (1977) 1 Lloyd's Rep. 17; on appeal (1977) 2 Lloyd's Rep. 99. In this case, a ship sank in the Liverpool Bay and the harbour authorities exercised their statutory powers and removed the wreck. They sold certain articles from her for £225 which they retained to reimburse themselves in part for the costs of removal. The harbour authorities then brought an action against the owners to recover: (1) damages for negligence and (2) £25,263.28 being the balance of the costs of removal. The owners agreed that they were entitled to limit their liability to a sum of £19,163.47. This argument was not accepted and the Court held that the harbour authorities have the right to recover the full amount of its loss without limitation.
2. Claims against the carrying vessel are not affected by this period of limitation.

special circumstances[1].

Section 9 provides that the Act shall also apply to persons, other than the owners, responsible for the fault of the vessel. It states: "This Act shall apply to any persons other than the owners responsible for the fault of the vessel as though the expression 'owners' included such person, and in any case where by virtue of any charter or demise, or for any other reason, the owners are not responsible for the navigation and management of the vessel, this Act shall be read as though for references to the owners there were substituted references to the charterers or other persons for the time being responsible."

---

1. As for limitation of liability and conflict of laws, see *The "Steelton"* (1977) 1 Lloyd's Rep. 310. In this case the vessel collided with a bridge in the St. Lawrence Seaway causing extensive damage both to herself and the bridge. Claims were brought against the owners in the United States. The owners argued that as the collision occurred within a Canadian waterway the Canada Shipping Act in its entirety governed the action and in particular the Canadian provisions for limitation of liability had to apply as a part of the substantive law of Canada. It was held by the District Court that:
(1) since the collision occurred within a Canadian waterway the rights and liabilities of the parties arising as a result of that collision, were governed by the law of Canada.
(2) on consideration of the material before the Court, the limitation of liability provisions of the Canada Shipping Act were found to be procedural, and the law of the forum would determine the maximum limitation of the fund created.

Chapter 2

CRIMINAL LIABILITY FOR COLLISION

(I) THE JURISDICTIONAL ZONES

In the United Kingdom, the policy adopted for many years is to abstain from interfering with foreign vessels, except in cases specified by the law or where the peace of the port or the good order of the territorial waters are affected, such as for offences resulting from collision. However, it is necessary to distinguish between offences committed on the territorial waters and those on the high seas.

Territorial waters

All offences, including those resulting from collision, committed in any part of the territorial waters, may be prosecuted in English courts. Proceedings for most offences can be instituted only with the consent of the Attorney-General, a Secretary of State or the Director of Public Prosecutions[1]. For this reason, agreements with certain countries[2] have been signed to ensure that personnel on their ships are immune from prosecution except for offences such as those involving the peace of the port. Section 5 of the Consular Relations Act, 1968, provides that no criminal proceedings may be instituted without the consent of the consul of the country concerned in connection with an incident alleged to have occurred on board a ship belonging to such a country, unless the offence:

(1) has been committed by or against a United Kingdom citizen; or

(2) is one "involving the tranquility or safety of a port, or the law relating to safety of life at sea, public health, oil pollution, wireless telegraphy, immigration or customs"; or

(3) is an arrestable offence.

High seas

The criminal law of England extends to British ships upon the

---

1. See for example the Territorial Waters Jurisdiction Act, 1878, s. 3, in relation to indictable offences.
2. Agreements are made with Austria, Belgium, Denmark, the Federal Republic of Germany, Hungary, Italy, Japan, Spain, the U.S.S.R. and Yugoslavia.

high seas. In *Oteri* v. *The Queen*[1], the Judicial Committee of the Privy Council said that: "It is trite and ancient law that the criminal law of England extends to British ships upon the high seas - an expression which in the context of Admiralty jurisdiction includes in addition to the open sea all waters below low-water mark where great ships can go... the explanation sometimes given of this extension of the applicability of English law that 'an English ship may be considered as a floating island' ... should, however, be understood metaphorically rather than literally. A British ship is not accurately described in law as part of the United Kingdom. A more acceptable rationalization juristically is that at common law a British ship fell under the protection of the sovereign; those on board her were within the King's peace and subject to the criminal law by which the King's peace was preserved. However this may be, the applicability of English law to"treasons, felonyes, robberies, murders and confederacies ... committed upon the sea" was recognized by a statute of 1536, An Acte for the Punysshement of Pyrotes and Robbers of the See. The Offences at Sea Act 1799 was but expository of the common law in providing: 'that all and every Offence and Offences, which, after the passing of this Act, shall be committed upon the High Seas, out of the Body of any county of this Realm, shall be, and they are hereby declared to be Offences ... liable to the same punishments respectively as if they had been committed upon the shore'. This is the only part of the Act of 1799 which was left unrepealed by the Criminal Law Act, 1967."

In 1952, the Brussels Convention (Penal Jurisdiction) was signed. Article 1 states: "In the event of a collision or any other incident of navigation concerning a sea-going ship and involving the penal or disciplinary responsibility of the master or of any other person in the service of the ship, criminal or disciplinary proceedings may be instituted only before the judicial or administrative authorities of the State of which the ship was flying the flag at the time of the collision or other incident of navigation."

This Convention reverses the rule laid down by the Permanent Court of International Justice in *The Lotus*[2]. It provides that the flag State can only institute criminal or disciplinary proceedings against the master or any other person in the ship's service.

The provisions of this Convention were not given the force of law in the United Kingdom. At the time of ratification, the

---

1. (1977) 1 Lloyd's Rep. 105.
2. PCIJ, Ser. A, No. 10 (1927).

British Government made the following reservation: ".... the right not to observe the provisions of Article 1 of the said Convention in the case of any ship of the State whose flag the ship was flying has as respect that ship or any class of ship to which that ship belongs consented to the institution of criminal or disciplinary proceedings before the judicial or administrative authorities of the United Kingdom"[1]. As a result of this reservation, there is no restriction on prosecutions resulting from collisions on the high seas.

(II) OBSERVANCE OF COLLISION REGULATIONS

In addition to the civil liability for damages, the master, or any member of the crew, may be criminally prosecuted for any act or omission which causes or is likely to cause loss of life, serious injury or serious damage to the ship. Section 27 of the Merchant Shipping Act, 1970 provides: "If the master or any member of the crew of a ship registered in the United Kingdom

(a) does any act which causes or is likely to cause the loss or destruction of or serious damage to the ship or the death of or serious injury to a person on board the ship; or

(b) omits to do anything required to preserve the ship from loss, destruction or serious damage or to preserve any person on board the ship from death or serious injury;

and the act or omission is deliberate, or amounts to a breach or neglect of duty, or he is under the influence of drink or a drug at the time of the act or omission, he shall be liable, on conviction on indictment, to imprisonment for a term not exceeding two years or to a fine, and, on summary conviction, to a fine not exceeding £200."

The lack of proper care in performing a duty would not amount to a "breach or neglect of duty". Thus, the failure of the person in charge of look-out to keep a proper watch would not be considered a criminal offence under s. 27[2].

S. 73 of the same Act states that in case of collision, the incident shall be reported to the Department of Trade.

"(1) Where any such casualty as is mentioned in section 55 (1) of this Act has occurred in the case of a ship or ship's boat and, at the time it occurred, the ship was registered in the United Kingdom, the owner or master of the ship shall, as

1. See Conventions on Maritime Law, 1968, p.61.
2. *Deacon* v.*Evans* (1911) 1 K.B. 571.

soon as practicable, and in any case not later than twenty-four hours after the ship's arrival at the next port, report the casualty to the Board of Trade, giving a brief description of it and stating the time and place where it occurred, the name and official number of the ship, its position at the time of the report and the next port of call.

(2) If the owner or master of a ship fails without reasonable cause to comply with the preceding provisions of this section he shall be liable on summary conviction to a fine not exceeding £100."

Inquiries and formal investigation, as we will see, may be carried out in collision cases under sections 55 and 56[1] of the Merchant Shipping Act, 1970. The Court of Inquiry may cancel or suspend any certificate issued to the officer or censure him.

The Merchant Shipping Act, 1894, requires owners and masters to observe the Collision Regulations. S.419 provides:

"(1) All owners and masters of ships shall obey the Collision Regulations[2], and shall not carry or exhibit any other lights, or use any other fog signals, than such as are required by those Regulations.

(2) If an infringement of the Collision Regulations is caused by the wilful default of the master or owner of the ship, that master or owner shall, in respect of each offence, be guilty of a misdemeanour.

(3) If any damage to person or property arises from the non-observance by any ship of any of the Collision Regulations, the damage shall be deemed to have been occasioned by the wilful default of the person in charge of the deck of the ship at the time, unless it is shown to the satisfaction of the court that the circumstances of the case made a departure from the Regulations necessary."

Duty to assist after collision : Section 422 of the Merchant Shipping Act, 1894 provides: "In every case of collision between two vessels, it shall be the duty of the master or person in charge of each vessel, if and so far as he can do so without danger to his own vessel, crew, and passengers (if any) -

---

1. S. 55 & s. 56 are not yet in force and inquiries and investigations as to shipping casualties are governed by the Merchant Shipping Act, 1894, sections 464-466.
2. The extent of the owner's obligations to observe the Collision Regulations was considered in *The Lady Gwendolen* (1964) 2 Lloyd's Rep. 99.

(a) to render to the other vessel, her master, crew, and passengers (if any) such assistance as may be practicable, and may be necessary to save them from any danger caused by the collision, and to stay by the other vessel until he has ascertained that she has no need of further assistance, and also

(b) to give to the master or person in charge of the other vessel the name of his own vessel and of the port to which she belongs, and also the names of the ports from which she comes and to which she is bound.

If the master or person in charge fails without reasonable cause to comply with this section, he shall be guilty of a misdemeanour, and, if he is a certificated officer, an inquiry into his conduct may be held, and his certificate cancelled or suspended."

Distress signals

S. 21 of the Merchant Shipping (Safety Convention) Act, 1949 provides for penalties[1] for the use of signals of distress except in the prescribed circumstances. S. 22 deals with answering distress calls. Under it, the master of a British ship, on receiving a signal of distress from any other ship, is required to go to its assistance, unless he is unable or considers such action to be unnecessary or unreasonable. If he does not answer the distress call, he shall record this fact and the reasons for not going to its assistance in the Log Book. As for the ship in distress, she may, after consultation with other ships answering the signals, call upon one or more of them to render assistance thereby relieving all other vessels from liability.

Other offences

The most frequent, prosecuted offences are those committed in breach of the Collision Regulations (Traffic Separation Schemes) Order, 1972. This Order makes it obligatory for ships navigating in a traffic lane to proceed in the recommended direction. If they are crossing a lane then they must do so "at right-angles or as near thereto as is reasonably practicable."

As regards drunkenness on duty, section 28 of the Merchant Shipping Act, 1970 states:

---

1. See the Collision Regulations and Distress Signals Order, 1977 (S.I. No. 982 of 1977) which came into operation on July 15, 1977 as amended by S.I. No. 1301 of 1977. The Schedule of this Order contains a list of foreign countries to whose vessels the Collision Regulations and Distress Signals Rules apply while beyond the limits of British Jurisdiction.

"If a seaman employed in a ship registered in the United Kingdom is, while on duty, under the influence of drink or a drug to such extent that his capacity to carry out his duties is impaired he shall be liable on summary conviction to a fine not exceeding £50."

Discharge of oil at sea is another offence under the Prevention of Oil Pollution Act, 1971. However, when a collision occurs and oil escapes, it is a defence for the master if he proved that he took all reasonable steps to prevent or stop the escape of oil. Section 5 (2) (a) provides:

"Where a person is charged as mentioned in subsection (1) of this section, it shall also be a defence to prove

(a) that the oil or mixture escaped in consequence of damage to the vessel, and that as soon as practicable after the damage occurred all reasonable steps were taken for preventing, or (if it could not be prevented) for stopping or reducing, the escape of the oil or mixture."

(III) INQUIRIES AND INVESTIGATIONS

In the nineteenth century, many accidents occurred as a result of the introduction of steam vessels and parliamentary inquiries were held to find out the causes of these accidents. This led to the enactment of the Shipping Casualties Investigations Act, 1879 and to the establishment of the post of Registrar General of Shipping and Seamen. The main function of the Registrar was to collect facts and figures that would assist in commerce and defence. Later, the Registrar started to collect details of deaths, accidents and casualties[1] and a duty was placed upon the Board of Trade, now the Department of Trade, to inquire into marine casualties and deaths[2].

---

1. For the year ending June 30, 1894, the Return of Shipping Casualties and Deaths contained details showing the position of wrecks around the coast of the United Kingdom.
2. At present, it is estimated that the Department of Trade processes about 2,000 reports of casualties every year.

An inquiry may be carried out into casualties[1] of sufficient public interest as, for example, where there has been loss of life or where an extensive oil pollution results from the accident. Such inquiries mainly deal with British or foreign ships in the United Kingdom territorial waters[2] and are generally concerned with ascertaining individual responsibility and failure to comply with statutory regulations[3]. S. 55 of the Merchant Shipping Act, 1970 provides:

"(1) Where any of the following casualties has occurred, that is to say

(a) the loss or presumed loss, stranding, grounding, abandonment of or damage to a ship; or

(b) a loss of life caused by fire on board or by an accident to a ship or ship's boat, or by any accident occurring on board a ship or ship's boat; or

(c) any damage caused by a ship;

and, at the time it occurred, the ship was registered in the United Kingdom or the ship or boat was in the United Kingdom or the territorial water thereof, the Board of Trade

(i) may cause a preliminary inquiry into the casualty to be held by a person appointed for the purpose by the Board; and

---

1. Regulation 21 of Chapter I of the Convention for the Safety of Life at Sea, 1974, states:
"(a) Each Administration undertakes to conduct an investigation of any casualty occurring to any of its ships subject to the provisions of the present Convention when it judges that such an investigation may assist in determining what changes in the present Regulations might be desirable.
(b) Each Contracting Government undertakes to supply the Organization (IMCO) with pertinent information concerning the findings of such investigations. No reports or recommendations of the Organization based upon such information shall disclose the identity or nationality of the ships concerned or in any manner fix or imply responsibility upon any ship or person."
See also Regulation 12 of Chapter VIII for accidents of a nuclear ship.
2. If, however, the accident occurs on the high seas or involves foreign ships considerable difficulty may arise in obtaining information from such vessels who may refuse to be represented.
3. Such inquiries may also deal with the certificates of the master or the officers involved and the Department of Trade may issue M Notice drawing attention to any special aspects.

(ii) may (whether or not a preliminary inquiry into the casualty has been held) cause a formal investigation into the casualty to be held, if in England, Wales or Northern Ireland, by a wreck commissioner and, if in Scotland, by the sheriff.

(2) A person appointed under this section to hold a preliminary inquiry shall for the purpose of the inquiry have the powers conferred on an inspector by section 729 of the Merchant Shipping Act, 1894."

Formal investigation

S. 56 of the 1970 Act, provides:

(1) A wreck commissioner or sheriff holding a formal investigation into a casualty under section 55 of this Act shall conduct it in accordance with rules under section 58 (1) of this Act, and those rules shall require the assistance of one or more assessors and, if any question as to the cancellation or suspension of an officer's certificate is likely to arise, the assistance of not less than two assessors.

(2) Subsections (1), (3) and (4) of section 77 of the Magistrates' Courts Act 1952 (which provide for the attendance of witnesses and the production of evidence) shall apply in relation to a formal investigation held by a wreck commissioner as if the wreck commissioner were a magistrates' court and the investigation a complaint; and the wreck commissioner shall have power to administer oaths for the purposes of the investigation.

(3) Where a formal investigation is held in Scotland the sheriff shall, subject to any rules made under section 58 (1) of this Act, dispose of it as a summary application, and, subject to section 57 of this Act, his decision on the investigation shall be final.

(4) If as a result of the investigation the wreck commissioner or sheriff is satisfied, with respect to any officer, of any of the matters mentioned in paragraphs (a) to (c) of section 52 (1) of this Act and, if it is a matter mentioned in paragraph (a) or (b) of that section, is further satisfied that it caused or contributed to the casualty, he may cancel or suspend any certificate issued to the officer under section 43 of this Act or censure him; and if he cancels or suspends the certificate the officer shall deliver it forthwith to him or to the Board of Trade.

(5) The wreck commissioner or sheriff may make such order with regard to the costs of the investigation as he thinks just and shall make a report on the case to the Board of Trade.

(6) Any costs which a person is ordered to pay under the preceding subsection may be recovered from him by the Board of Trade.

In practice, the Department of Trade send a letter to the master, or an officer, informing him of the decision to hold a formal investigation and advise that charges and criticisms, which the Department's letter details, will be made against him at the hearing. In determining the circumstances in which the collision has occurred, the seamanship of the master or the officer will be under critical review by the wreck commissioner[1].

Another type of judicial inquiry is the one mentioned in chapter 3, that is the jurisdiction of the Admiralty Court over British and foreign vessels, subject to the provisions of the Administration of Justice Act, 1956, whether the collision occurs in foreign waters or on the high seas. The Court decides questions of negligence in order to apportion the blame and to determine the liability of each vessel. The Court cannot take action against the master or a member of the crew, but it may, in certain circumstances, draw the attention of the appropriate authority to the facts of the case.

A number of collision incidents are settled by agreement which may take into account non-legal factors such as when one vessel is hired by the owners of the other vessel. Lloyd's have prepared a form called "Lloyd's Standard Form of Arbitration Agreement in Cases of Collision"[2]. In cases of collision involving

---

1. See *R.* v. *Wreck Commissioner, Ex parte Knight*, Lloyd's List June 12, 1976. The Commissioner absolved the master of one vessel involved in a collision from blame and awarded him £1,500 for costs, although the master claimed that his actual costs came to £3,600. In a motion for *certiorari mandamus,* the Court made an order of *certiorari* quashing the commissioner's award and an order of *mandamus* requiring him to reconsider the application for costs. The Court said: "if in the exercise of his discretion the learned commissioner decides to award a lesser amount than the £3,600 expended, a clear statement of his reasons for so doing" would be necessary. See also Formal Investigation - *Motorship "Festivity"* (1974) 3 LMCLQ p.337. This was a formal investigation into the circumstances attending the abandonment of the ship in the North Sea on Nov. 21, 1971. The Court found that the casualty was caused by the severity of the weather conditions and as a result of the breakdown of the steering gear and the rudder indicator. The Court, however, found that the ship was undermanned through not having a third hand who was capable of assisting in watch keeping duties. In another Investigation - Stranding of *"Rosstrum"* (1974) 3 LMCLQ, pp.338, 339, the Court found that Notices M. 566 and M. 621 were completely ignored although they were relevant to the casualty.
2. See Appendix XVIII.

salvage claims, they are usually settled by arbitrators appointed by Lloyd's[1].

Perhaps the most important type of inquiry is the one carried out privately by the owners and in the light of their inquiry, they may amend their instructions to the master and officers. However, owners are reluctant to take any action against the master or a member of the crew which could be interpreted in a court of law as admission of fault.

Published reports

Information on collision is published by various bodies and there are also statistics on marine casualties[2]. The "Lloyd's Weekly Casualty Reports" contain the casualty reports which have been published in Lloyd's List. Reference to these "Weekly Casualty Reports" is simplified by the publication of an index each quarter. The General Council of British Shipping published a "Marine Casualty Report Scheme" which contains a thorough examination of certain incidents of collisions and groundings.

The Return of Shipping Casualties and Deaths published by the Department of Trade includes 17 statistical tables. Casualties to ships are divided into three categories, these are: total losses; serious casualties; and minor casualties. The year's total losses and serious casualties are classified in three tables by type of casualty against: (a) the number, type and gross tonnage of ships involved; (b) tonnage group and age; and (c) main causes[3].

---

1. See Appendix XIX.
2. The Liverpool Underwriters Association publishes data on marine casualties.
3. A very valuable source of statistics is the information on the movement of ships given by the radar surveillance information service of the Dover Strait.

Chapter 3

JURISDICTION, RULES OF EVIDENCE AND INTERPRETATION

(I) JURISDICTION

(i) *Actions in rem and personam*

Admiralty actions are either *in rem*[1] or *in personam*. The term "*in rem*" means against a *res* or a thing and the term "*in personam*" means against a person. Actions *in rem*[2] may be against the ship, her cargo and the freight for its arrest and subsequently its sale to satisfy the claim. The hardship of this practice is mitigated by the fact that bail or other security may be given to prevent or to secure the release of the *res* from arrest.

Collision and limitation of liability actions are matters within the jurisdiction of the Admiralty Division[3]. The majority of the actions *in personam* which are dealt with in the Admiralty Division could also be tried in the Queen's Bench Division.

The exercise of jurisdiction

The jurisdiction of a court[4] is based on the actual presence of

---

1. No action *in rem* can be brought against the Crown.
2. In *The Conoco Britannia and Other Vessels* (1972) 1 Lloyd's Rep. 342 at p.347, it was alleged that an order for specific performance as an equitable remedy lies only in an action *in personam* but the Court refused this contention. The question of what steps the Court should take if the defendant did not appear in an action *in rem* was left open.
3. The jury is unknown in practice in Admiralty Division.
4. The general rule is that the procedure in collision cases is governed by the law of the tribunal (*lex fori*) whilst the liability is governed by the law of the place of collision (*lex loci*).
   It may be useful to mention some of the latin terms which are frequently used in this respect.
   Lex loci solutionis: means the law of the place of performance.
   Lex fori: means the law of the court in which the case is tried.
   Lex loci delicti: means the law of the place where the offence is committed.
   Lex situs: means the law of the place where the property lies.

the defendant within its jurisdiction at the date of the issue of the writ, or upon the submission by the parties to the jurisdiction[1]. It must be noted that a writ *in rem* cannot be served abroad and can only be effected within the jurisdiction of a court in the United Kingdom.

In the Convention on Certain Rules Concerning Civil Jurisdiction in Matters of Collision, 1952[2], it was agreed to indicate where disputes could be settled[3]. The provisions of this Convention were incorporated in the Administration of Justice Act, 1956. S.1 of this Act defines the jurisdiction of the Court whether *in personam* or *in rem*[4]. The Act lists some eighteen "questions or claims" of a maritime nature which may be brought by way of

---

1. An arbitration agreement cannot oust the jurisdiction of the Court and therefore it is possible to issue a writ *in rem*.
2. See Appendix XIII. Another International Convention on the Unification of Certain Rules Relating to Penal Jurisdiction in Matters of Collision or Other Incidents of Navigation, was approved in 1952, see Appendix XIV. No legislation has been enacted to implement this Convention. At the same time, a third Convention for the Unification of Certain Rules Relating to the Arrest of Seagoing Ships, was concluded. Important changes were made by subsection (4) of section 3 of the Administration of Justice Act, 1956 which was enacted to implement this Convention.
3. One must distinguish between choice of jurisdiction and choice of law. An English court can, and often does, decide questions of foreign law on the basis of expert evidence from foreign lawyers. The fact that the forum possessed jurisdiction would not mean that it would be compelled to exercise it. The doctrine of *forum non conveniens* could be used to decline jurisdiction in appropriate cases. The forum would thus be able to exercise a measure of discretion.
4. In *Conoco Britannia and Other Vessels* (1972) 1 Lloyd's Rep. 342, an action *in rem* by tug-owners for payment of indemnity under a towage contract as a result of collision between the tug and tow, was allowed under s. 3 (4) of the Act. See also *The "Eschersheim"* (1974) 2 Lloyd's Rep. 188, (H.L.), (1976) 2 Lloyd's Rep. 1, where the Court stated that all the paragraphs of s. 1 (1) of the Administration of Justice Act, 1956 should be construed in the usual way, giving their words their ordinary and natural meaning in the context of which they appear.

actions *in rem*[1]. It also extends the jurisdiction of the Court to "all ships ... whether British or not and whether registered or not and wherever the residence or domicile of their owners may be." Section 4 of the Act provides:

"(1) No court in England and Wales shall entertain an action *in personam* to enforce a claim to which this section applies unless -

(a) the defendant has his habitual residence or a place of business within England and Wales; or

(b) the cause of action arose within inland waters of England and Wales or within the limits of a port of England and Wales; or

(c) an action arising out of the same incident or series of incidents is proceeding in the court or has been heard and determined in the court.

In this subsection -

'inland waters' includes any part of the sea adjacent to the coast of the United Kingdom certified by the Secretary of State to be waters falling by international law to be treated as within the territorial sovereignty of Her Majesty apart from the operation of that law in relation to territorial waters;

'port' means any port, harbour, river, estuary, haven, dock, canal or other place so long as a person or body of persons is empowered by or under an Act to make charges in respect of ships entering it or using the facilities therein, and 'limits of a port' means the limits thereof as fixed by or under the Act in question or, as the case may be, by the relevant charter or custom;

'charges' means any charges with the exception of light dues, local light dues and any other charges in respect of lighthouses, buoys or beacons and of charges in respect of pilotage.

---

1. In *The "Halcyon"* (1976) 1 Lloyd's Rep. 461, the plaintiff, a deck officer claimed that the defendant failed to pay the employer's contributions in respect of him to the fund. Brandon, J. held that the claim, whether it was in debt or damages, was a claim for wages within s. 1 (1) (O) of the 1956 Act, so the plaintiff could invoke the Admiralty jurisdiction of the Court. The plaintiff also had a maritime lien for the claim so that:
(a) he could proceed *in rem* against the proceeds of sale of the ship under s. 3 (3) of the 1956 Act; and
(b) he was entitled to priority over the competing claim of the second defendants as second mortgagees against the same fund.

(2) No court in England and Wales shall entertain an action *in personam* to enforce a claim to which this section applies until any proceedings, previously brought by the plaintiff in any court outside England and Wales, against the same defendant in respect of the same incident, or series of incidents, have been discontinued or otherwise come to an end.

(3) The preceding provisions of this section shall apply to counterclaims (not being counterclaims in proceedings arising out of the same incident or series of incidents) as they apply to actions *in personam*, but as if the references to the plaintiff and the defendant were respectively references to the plaintiff on the counterclaim and the defendant to the counterclaim.

(4) The preceding provisions of this section shall not apply to any action or counterclaim if the defendant thereto submits or has agreed to submit, to the jurisdiction of the court.

(5) Subject to the provisions of subsection (2) of this section, the High Court shall have jurisdiction to entertain an action *in personam* to enforce a claim to which this section applies whenever any of the conditions specified in paragraphs (a) to (c) of subsection (1) of this section are satisfied, and the rules of court relating to the service of process outside the jurisdiction shall make such provision as may appear to the rule-making authority to be appropriate, having regard to the provisions of this subsection.

(6) Nothing in this section shall prevent an action or counterclaim which is brought in accordance with the provisions of this section in the High Court or the Liverpool Court of Passage being transferred, in accordance with the enactments in that behalf, to some other court.

(7) The claims to which this section applies are claims for damage, loss of life or personal injury arising out of a collision between ships or out of the carrying out of or omission to carry out a manoeuvre in the case of one or more of two ships or out of non-compliance, on the part of one or more of two or more ships, with the collision regulations.

(8) For the avoidance of doubt it is hereby declared that this section applies in relation to the jurisdiction of any court not being Admiralty jurisdiction, as well as in relation to its Admiralty jurisdiction, if any."

Thus, in collision cases, the court has jurisdiction over foreign vessels and subject to the provisions of the Administration of Justice Act, 1956 whether the collision occurs in foreign waters or on the high seas.[1]

Service out of the jurisdiction

An action *in personam* for damages in respect of collision cannot be brought unless the conditions set out in section 4 of the Administration Act, 1956 are fulfilled. There are, however, other occasions when the courts are empowered to assume jurisdiction in actions *in personam* although the defendant is resident abroad. The rules allowing service out of the jurisdiction in collisions and other maritime casualties are to be found in the Rules of the Supreme Court (R.S.C.) which are modified and revised from time to time[2]. In this respect, the courts laid down two principles. The first is that the court should always be cautious in granting leave to a plaintiff to sue a foreign defendant unless certain criteria for the protection of the defendant are satisfied. The criteria as stated in *The Hagen*[3] are:

(1) that a foreign defendant ought not to be unreasonably put to the expense and inconvenience of defending proceedings in England;

(2) any ambiguity in the construction of R.S.C. Order 11 is to be resolved in favour of the foreign defendant; and

(3) because proceedings in which leave is sought to serve the foreign defendant are usually *ex parte*, the plaintiff has a special duty to bring all the facts (including those favourable to the defendant) to the attention of the court.

The second principle[4] is that the burden of establishing, not only that a case comes within R.S.C. Ord. 11, r. 1(1), but also that it is a proper case for service out of the jurisdiction under R.S.C. Ord. 11, r. 4 (2), lies with the party seeking leave to effect such service[5].

---

1. There is, however, nothing in the 1956 Act, or in English Law to prevent parties from agreeing to submit the disputed maritime claim to foreign jurisdiction or to arbitration.
2. It must be noted that the plaintiff is not entitled to service out of the jurisdiction as a right. It is a discretionary remedy and the question which is the *forum conveniens* for the trial is a matter to be considered by the court. See *Hapag-Lloyd A.G., Stork Amsterdam N.V. and Fitzgerald* v. *Texaco Inc. and Texaco Panama Inc. (The "Texaco Caribbean")* (1976) 1 Lloyd's Rep. 565.
3. (1908) P. 189.
4. *Mauroux* v. *Sociedade Commercial Abel Periera da Fouseca S.A.R.L.* (1972) 1 W.L.R. 962.
5. *First Thames Land Holding Ltd. and Another* v. *Craiova (Owners) and Another (The "Craiova")* (1976) 1 Lloyd's Rep. 536.

(ii) *Practice and Procedure*

Nautical Assessors

In collision cases, the assessors advise the court on nautical matters and in particular issues of seamanship. The opinion of the assessors is not binding although the court gives it great attention. "... the Elder Brethren of Trinity House are in a unique position to advise the Judge in the Admiralty Court in the light of their experience; indeed, it is for this very purpose that they are summoned to assist the Judge at the trial of an Admiralty suit. Their advice is, of course, in no sense conclusive; it becomes in effect part of the evidence in the case, which has to be weighed in conjunction with all the other evidence. It always remains for the Judge himself to decide whether he accepts the advice that is tendered to him"[1].

Brandon, J. in *The "Judith M"*[2] made the following observation: "It seems to me that the question which arises is very much one of good seamanship, the question being, what is the seamanlike action to take in a situation of extraordinary difficulty created by numerous earlier faults on both sides?

While I have had my own doubts about the matter, I feel that the Court should, on a question of that kind, be guided largely by the advice of the Elder Brethren and should not readily or quickly disagree with it."

Assessors differ in their view

When the assessors differ in their view, Lord Sumner thought that the Court must regard the point as not proven[3]. His Lordship added: "After all, experience at sea is not everything. Assessors are not chosen for their personal conversance with collisions, and an experienced judge or counsel may boast that he has, in a sense, been in hundreds of collisions while the assessors have hardly seen tens."

In *The "Jan Laurenz"*, Lord Roskill observed[4]: "There being this marked differences of view between two experienced Elder Brethren, this Court is not only free to make up its own mind but is in duty bound to make up its own mind in the light of its own

1. Per Willmer, L.J. in *The "Fritz Thyssen"* (1967) 2 Lloyd's Rep. 199 at p.203.
2. (1968) 2 Lloyd's Rep. 474, at p.486.
3. *The Australia (Owners)* v. *Owners of Cargo of S.S. Nautilus* (1927) A.C. 145; (1926) 25 Ll.L.Rep. 141, at pp.153 and 144 respectively.
4. (1973) 1 Lloyd's Rep. 329, at pp.336, 337.

assessment of the evidence and of the conflicting advice and, of course, paying due regard to the findings of the learned trial Judge as well as to the challenge made to those finding in this Court."

Sometimes, the view of the assessors in the Admiralty Court differs from those in the Court of Appeal. Viscount Dunedin, in *The Australia*[1] said:"There is no hierarchy of assessors. They occupy much the same position as do skilled witnesses, with this difference, that they are not brought forward as the partisans of the one side or the other."

In *The Fina Canada*[2] Willmer, L.J. said: "We are just as free to consult our Assessors as the judge was to consult the Elder Brethren. We are not bound to accept their advice, any more than we or the learned judge would be bound to accept the advice tendered by the Elder Brethren. If there is a divergence of view between the Assessors advising this Court and the Elder Brethren who advised the Admiralty Court, those advising us are not to be regarded as speaking with any greater authority because they happen to be advising the Court of Appeal. This, I understand, is what is meant by the phrase that there is no appeal from Assessors to Assessors. If there is such a divergence of view, the position is that this Court must make up its own mind as to which advice be accepted."

Lord Simon of Glaisdale in *The "Savina"*[3] accepted the above-mentioned statement of Lord Justice Willmer and he added the following riders: "First, where there is no challenge to the advice accepted by the learned Judge, the Court of Appeal, by asking the Nautical Assessors the same questions that were asked by the trial judge of the Elder Brethren, is at least inviting embarrassment and complication.

Secondly, any Court consulting assessors must bear in mind the danger that Counsel may not have the opportunity by addressing the Court on all the evidence - since assessors occupy much the same position as do skilled witnesses, with this difference, that they are not brought forward as the partisans of the one side or the other...

Thirdly, an Appellate Court must also bear in mind that its assessors may not have heard the whole of the evidence, and will in any event not have enjoyed the advantage of having heard it given orally.

---

1. (1927) A.C. 145, at p.149.
2. (1962) 2 Lloyd's Rep. 445, at p.454.
3. (1976) 2 Lloyd's Rep. 123, at p.131.

Fourthly, therefore, the observations of Lord Dunedin in *The Australia* at p.150 are salutory: ... speaking for myself, except for the purposes of explanation, I shall always ask an assessor as little as possible. Certainly to find ... different assessors are at variance is much more of a hindrance than an assistance.

I, therefore, venture to suggest that it should be exceptional that the same questions should be put by an Appellate Court to its Nautical Assessors as the Court of first instance puts to the Elder Brethren - unless, of course, the advice given by the latter is challenged in the notice of appeal."

Consolidation

When actions are brought by different plaintiffs in respect of the same collision, they may be consolidated in Admiralty. If an action is brought by the owners of the ship and another by the cargo-owners, the usual practice is to order a stay of the cargo action until after the decision in the ship action.

Staying actions

Where an action *in rem* or *in personam* is pending in a foreign court in respect of the same collision, the court has a discretion to stay the proceedings in England, or to ask the plaintiff to elect one of the actions or to grant the injunction restraining the plaintiff from prosecuting the proceedings abroad. In *The Atlantic Star*[1], a collision occurred on Jan. 27, 1970, in Belgian waters, in the River Scheldt, between *Atlantic Star* (owned by the appellants, the Dutch Holland-America Company) and two barges (the Belgian *Bona Spes* owned by the respondent and the Dutch *Hugo van der Goes*). The respondent applied to the Antwerp Commercial Court to appoint a Surveyor to investigate the collision. The Court Surveyor's report tended to exonerate *Atlantic Star* from any fault. Therefore, the respondent began an action *in rem* in England against *Atlantic Star* and obtained security. Although the respondent subsequently began another action before the Antwerp Commercial Court, it was conceded that this action was brought solely to preserve the time limit in Belgium. Meanwhile, the number of actions brought in the Anwerp Court by various interests involved in the collision had risen to four. The appellants applied to stay the action on the ground that it was oppressive, vexatious and an abuse of the process of the Court. In the first instance the Court found that the Antwerp Commercial Court was the more appropriate forum, but the English

---

1. (1973) 2 All E. R. 1975 (H.L.); (1972) 1 Lloyd's Rep. 534 (first instance); (1972) 3 W.L.R. 746, C.A. See also *The "Tillie Lykes"* (1977) 1 Lloyd's Rep. 124.

authorities did not justify staying the action. As the Court of Appeal affirmed the decision, the appellants appealed to the House of Lords. The majority (Lord Reid, Wilberforce and Kilbrandon, Lord Morris and Simon dissenting) held that:

(1) the mere existence of a multiplicity of proceedings was not to be taken into account as a disadvantage to the defendant and there had to be something more than that;

(2) a clear case of oppression or vexation had to be made to justify a stay. The words "vexatious and oppressive" ought not to be too narrowly interpreted and that, on a wide interpretation of those words, the respondent's action was vexatious and oppressive and ought to be stayed.

In *The "Mansoor"*[1], a collision occurred between the m.v. *Mansoor* and the m.v. *Paranagua* in the River Scheldt. As a result, the *Mansoor* was arrested in Antwerp and released on provision of security. *Mansoor* commenced proceedings in the Antwerp Court in respect of her damage. The plaintiffs, the owners of *Paranagua*, commenced an action *in rem* in the Admiralty Court against the owners of *Mansoor* but they did not arrest her.

The defendants moved to set aside the writ and to stay all further proceedings in action on the grounds that proceedings were pending in Antwerp where *Mansoor* was arrested and released. Further, the action in the Admiralty Court was a breach of faith.

It was held, by Cairns, J. that the plaintiffs were entitled to bring an action in Court of another country notwithstanding their acceptance of the defendants' undertaking. The action did not amount to a breach of faith. Further, it could not be said that remedy in a Belgian Court was an equally effective remedy to that obtainable in the Admiralty Court.

The court usually exercises its discretion to stay an action only if either:

(1) there is *lis alibs pendens* and the plaintiff can gain no substantial advantage from prosecuting both suits;

or (2) the action is not brought *bona fide*;

or (3) the action is not well-founded and has no chance of success.

Costs

The question of costs is within the discretion of the Court which

---

1. (1968) 2 Lloyd's Rep. 218.

must be exercised judicially[1]. In general, if only one vessel is to blame the successful party will not have to bear any costs. Under certain circumstances, this may not be the rule. For instance, a successful plaintiff may recover half of his costs or no costs at all because of his conduct of the litigation[2].

Where both vessels are to blame costs may be ordered in the same proportion of blame[3]. Again, the question is at the discretion of the Court[4] and the costs may not necessarily be in the same proportions as the damages.

In *The "Osprey"*[5], Brandon, J. held one vessel two-fifths to blame and the other three-fifths. He added that under R.S.C., Ord. 62, r. 3 (2), costs were to follow the event and that where one party had done better than the other,this fact ought to be reflected in the order for costs unless there were circumstances in which some other order ought to be made as to the whole or any part of the costs. The learned judge explained the various forms which the order for costs might take[6]:

"The first method is to make cost orders in the same proportions as the proportions of blame...

Another method is to order the less successful party to pay a proportion of the taxed costs of the more successful party...

The third method ... is to make an order that the less successful party should pay a certain sum by way of contribution to the costs of the more successful party."

Costs in case an offer to settle the dispute

Megaw, J.[7] said that the Court in exercising her discretion is entitled to disregard an offer made to settle the dispute and which was refused: "It is no doubt convenient in Admiralty actions that a party should be able to encourage the other party to

---

1. See R.S.C., Ord. 62.
2. *R. & J. Rea Ltd.* v. *A.J. King & Sons (The Bristol City)* (1956) 1 Lloyd's Rep. 35.
3. *The "Dayspring"* (1965) 1 Lloyd's Rep. 103; *The Orlik* (1964) 2 Lloyd's Rep. 177.
4. *The British Patrol* (1967) 2 Lloyd's Rep. 16; *The Salaverry* (1968) 1 Lloyd's Rep. 53; *The Ek* (1966) 1 Lloyd's Rep. 440 (where the plaintiffs were given full costs although partly to blame for the collision); *The Halcyon the Great No.3* (1975) 1 Lloyd's Rep. 527.
5. (1967) 1 Lloyd's Rep. 76.
6. Ibid., at p.95.
7. *The "Toni"* (1974) 1 Lloyd's Rep. 489, at p.496.

settle by making an open offer. It is no doubt right that, normally, where such an offer has been made and maintained, but not accepted by the other party, and the party who has made the offer obtains a result in the litigation no less favourable to him than the terms of the offer, the Judge should have a discretion to make a special order as to costs in his favour. The normal exercise of the discretion would be to give the offeror his costs from the date of the offer. But it seems to me that, normally at least, the discretion would not properly be exercised in favour of the offeror unless he had maintained the offer up to the commencement of the trial of the action. I do not see why it should be thought that the offeror should acquire some kind of moral or discretionary right to the whole of the costs thereafter incurred merely because he has for a period of time ending before the start of the hearing held out an offer which has not been accepted during that period."

(iii) *Lien and arrest of ship*

Maritime liens

The word lien denotes the right to retain possession of the goods or the ship as security. Maritime lien arises in the following cases: collision; salvage; seamen's wages; master's wages and disbursements; bottomary and respondentia; fees and expenses of the receiver of wreck[1]; and damage sustained by the owner or occupier of lands by means of which assistance is rendered to a wreck[2].

Accordingly, where a vessel is involved in a collision, a lien exists in favour of the injured party on the ship. This lien can only be exercised by an action *in rem* even if the vessel has been sold to a *bona fide* purchaser[3]. It attaches to the hull of the

---

1. The Merchant Shipping Act, 1894, s. 567, para.2.
2. The Merchant Shipping Act, 1894, s. 513, para.2.
3. In *The "Alletta"* (1974) 1 Lloyd's Rep. 40, Mocatta, J. said (at p.50): "If a ship may be arrested after judgment has been obtained against her and she is at the date of her arrest the property of a third party who bought her without knowledge of the maritime lien, grave injustice may be done. The third party may have no right of indemnity or, which is a less likely supposition, his indemnity may be worthless. His vendor may, through lack of adequate funds, incompetent legal advice or other reason, not properly and fully have contested the issue of liability. Despite (Counsel's) efforts to answer these supposed circumstances by saying that the Court would find some method of re-opening the issue of liability so as to enable the third party to contest it properly and anew. I cannot see how such an end could be achieved."

ship and other equipment on board, but it does not extend to the cargo. However, the cargo may be detained in order to receive any freight due to the owner.

Arrest of ship

Arrest of the ship is an incident in proceedings *in rem*. It[1] derives either under a maritime lien or under a statutory right of lien under the Administration of Justice Act, 1956. The ship may be arrested for other reasons such as salvage award, towage, necessaries[2] and damage to the cargo. The ship may be released after arrest[3] when bail or other security is given to satisfy the plaintiff's claim[4].

The provisions of the International Convention Relating to the Arrest of Seagoing Ships, 1952 were incorporated into the Administration of Justice Act, 1956. Section 3 (3) and (4) provides:

---

1. In *The Admiralty Marshal* v. *Calder (The Synova)* (1967) 1 Lloyd's Rep. 40, the Court imposed a fine of £100 on the master because he removed twice the arrest documents affixed by the Admiralty Marshal.
2. See *Shell Oil Company* v. *The ship ("Lastrigoni")* (1975) 3 LMCLQ, p.311. The High Court of Australia held that a supplier of bunkers under a contract with a charterer to which the owner is not party cannot sustain a claim *in rem* in Admiralty.
3. In *The "Golden Trader"* (1974) 1 Lloyd's Rep. 378, the defendants asked the Court to make an order setting aside the warrant of arrest. Brandon, J. (at p.380) criticised this way, and felt that the right way was to make an order for the release of the ship under Order 75, r. 13 (4).
4. In *The Vasilia* (1972) 1 Lloyd's Rep. 51, the mortgagees arrested the vessel in a foreign port and they obtained an order for appraisment and sale. Negotiations started for the wages of the crew and expenses for repatriation and the mortgagees asked leave to make payment of $4,500 through the Admiralty Marshal. Although the master and the crew claimed $17,000, the Court granted leave to make the payment offered by the mortgagees.
   See also *The Halcyon The Great (No.1)* (1975) 1 Lloyd's Rep. 518, where the Court ordered the Admiralty Marshal to invite offers to sell the ship in foreign currency to obtain the best price. But the Court should not go further and make an order that, in the event of a dollar sale, the proceeds should be paid into Court without prior conversion into sterling, and, after such payment, to be placed to a dollar account, without good reasons for doing so. In that case, the risk of depreciation of sterling was considered to be a good reason.

"3. (3) In any case in which there is a maritime lien or other charge on any ship, aircraft or other property for the amount claimed, the Admiralty jurisdiction of the High Court, (and) the Liverpool Court of Passage may be invoked by an action *in rem* against the ship, aircraft or property.

(4) In the case of any such claim as is mentioned in paragraphs (d) to (r) (which include claims arising from collisions) of subsection (1) of section 1 of this Act, being a claim arising in connection with a ship, where the person who would be liable on the claim in an action *in personam* was, when the cause of action arose, the owner or charterer of, or in possession or in control of, the ship, the Admiralty jurisdiction of the High Court and (where there is such jurisdiction) the Admiralty jurisdiction of the Liverpool Court of Passage may (whether the claim gives rise to a maritime lien on the ship or not) be invoked by an action *in rem* against -

(a) that ship, if, at the time when the action is brought it is beneficially owned as respects all the shares therein by that person; or

(b) any other ship which, at the time when the action is brought, is beneficially owned as aforesaid."

Accordingly, to arrest a ship, two conditions must be fulfilled -

(a) the ship at the time when the writ in the action is issued must be "beneficially owned as respects all the shares therein" by the same person, owner or charterer, who was liable to an action *in personam* at the time when the cause of action arose in respect of the incident complained of. In other words, the ship must be the property of the defendant[1] to the action; and

(b) the ship must be identifiable as the ship "in connection with" which the claim made in the action arose (or a sister ship of that ship). So one had to look at the description of each of the maritime claims in the s. 1 (1) list in order to identify the particular ship in respect of which a claim of that description could arise[2].

---

1. In *The "Andrea Ursula"* (1971) 1 Lloyd's Rep. 145, the Court found that a demise charterer was a "beneficial owner". Cf. *The "St. Merriel"* (1963) 1 Lloyd's Rep. 63.
2. Salvage agreements were held to be agreements to the use of the ship and for the purpose of saving her and her cargo and bringing them to a place of safety. Therefore, they are claims in connection with the ship and enforceable under s. 3 (4) by an action *in rem* against the ship or any of her sister ships. See *The "Eschersheim"* (1976) 1 Lloyd's Rep. 81.

The Administration of Justice Act, 1956 extends the right of arrest to the sister ship. By the issue of a writ, the plaintiff creates a situation in which as soon as a sister ship whose value is sufficient to provide adequate security for his claim arrived within the jurisdiction, the writ could be amended. In *The Berny*[1] Brandon, J. said: "To renew writs where it had not been possible to effect service on a ship, a plaintiff, in order to show good and sufficient cause for renewal must establish that:

(1) none of the ships proceeded against in respect of the same claim had been or would be within the jurisdiction within the currency of the writ; or

(2) if any of the ships had been or would be within the jurisdiction the length of the visit would not afford reasonable opportunity to effect service on her; or

(3) if any of the ships had been or would be present within the jurisdiction, the value of such a ship was not great enough to provide adequate security for the claim."

Laches

Maritime liens may be lost by "laches" which means delay in the judicial enforcement of the lien. Under proper circumstances, laches constitute a valid defence. In *The Lake Atlin*[2], the Court was asked to strike out an action for want of prosecution. The initial cause of action arose through a collision on Dec. 5, 1964 where both vessels were to blame. Procedures started on Oct. 15, 1966 but there was delay by the defendants for about three years, three months. It was accepted that in order to succeed, the plaintiffs must show (1) that the delay by the defendants in prosecuting their counterclaim was inordinate; (2) that the delay was inexcusable; and (3) that the plaintiffs were likely to be seriously prejudiced if the counterclaim were not dismissed. The Court found that the delay was serious but not inordinate. On the question of inexcusable delay, the plaintiffs to a limited degree had shared in some of the delays. On the third point, the Court said: "An order dismissing the counterclaim would be a Draconian order and should not be made lightly"[3]. Consequently, the Court refused to strike out the action.

---

1. The Times, July 15, 1977.
2. (1972) 2 Lloyd's Rep. 489.
3. Ibid., at p.495. In *"The Alletta"* (1974) 1 Lloyd's Rep. 40, the objections to the plaintiffs' right to arrest the ship based on laches, failed.

(II) RULES OF EVIDENCE

Direct evidence or inference

Proof may be by direct evidence or inference. Fault may be inferred from certain circumstances thus easing the burden of proof[1]. An example of such inferences is a collision in daylight between a ship under way and another lying at anchor in a proper place.

Evidence usually consists of oral evidence or signed declaration of such persons as the master, the pilot, chief officer, second officer, cadet, helmsman, chief engineer and second engineer. Various ship"s documents such as the working chart, bridge and engine movement books, deck log, radar work book, and master's report and sketches could be used. Other documentary evidence

---

1. A distinction must be made between the rules on the burden of proof and the rules of evidence. According to *S.S. Heranger (Owners) v. S.S. Diamond (Owners), The Heranger* (1939) A.C.94, the plaintiff, in a claim or by counterclaim, must prove:
   (1) the fault of the defendant or of some person for whose acts he is responsible; and
   (2) the casual connection between the fault and the damage.
   Difficulties arise when the fault on both vessels contributes to the collision. In *Boy Andrew* v. *St. Rognvald* (Owners) (1948) A.C. 140; (1947) 2 All E.R. 350, H.L., the *St.Rognvald* was at fault in overtaking too close, and the *Boy Andrew* was at fault in altering course while being overtaken. It was held that both acts caused the collision. Lord Simon (at p.149) observed: "The suggested test of last opportunity seems to me inaptly phrased and likely in some cases to lead to error, as the Law Reform Committee said in this respect: 'In truth, there is no such rule - the question, in all cases of liability for a tortious act, is, not who had the last opportunity of avoiding the mischief, but whose act caused the wrong'."
   Once the plaintiff proved fault and causation, the burden of proof shifts to the defendant to show that his negligence in no way contributed to the loss. In *Newby* v. *General Lighterage* (1955) 1 Lloyd's Rep. 273, C.A., an unattended barge went adrift. The defendants failed to discharge the burden of proof and the Court found that they were liable because there was the possibility that some malicious third party would interfere. The Court concluded that the defendants had not proved that they had taken reasonable precautions against such interference. See also *Smith* v. *Marriott* (1954) 2 Lloyd's Rep. 358.

includes the British and Foreign Admiralty Charts, tidal information, local regulations governing navigation translated into English.

In *The "Statue of Liberty"*[1], the plaintiffs contended that mechanically recorded film strip of radar echoes of vessels was admissible in evidence. The defendants contended that evidence was produced without human intervention and was not therefore admissible under the hearsay rule. It was held by Sir Jocelyn Simon, P. that the evidence in question was admissible. He added: "If tape recordings are admissible, it seems equally a photograph of radar reception is admissible - as, indeed, any other type of photograph. It would be an absurd distinction that a photograph should be admissible if the camera were operated manually by a photographer, but not if it were operated by a trip or clock mechanism. Similarly, if evidence of weather conditions were relevant, the law would affront common sense if it were to say that those could be proved by a person who looked at a barometer from time to time, but not by producing a barograph record, so too with other types of real recordings... The law is bound these days to take cognisance of the fact that mechanical means replace human effort."

Records made by gyro-compasses, weather equipment and photographs[2] may be used in evidence. In *The Centurity*[3] a photograph taken of the two vessels by a holiday-maker on a nearby pier was admitted in evidence. And in *The British Aviator*[4], a photograph of the engine-room blackboard of one of the ships involved in the collision was put before the court[5]. Conflict in evidence is resolved in the usual way as in ordinary cases.

Usually collision cases are heard after a certain period of time, and some statements or estimates may not be accurate. In this respect, Lord Sterndale, M.R.[6] made the following observation:

---

1. (1968) 1 Lloyd's Rep. 429, at p.430.
2. Photographs of the coastguard's radar screen in the Dover Strait are taken every minute throughout each watch.
3. (1963) 1 Lloyd's Rep. 99.
4. (1964) 2 Lloyd's Rep. 403.
5. In *Thomas Stone (Shipping) Ltd.* v. *The Admiralty and Others (The Albion)* (1952) 1 Lloyd's Rep. 38, the Court considered photographs taken of the collision on the following day. See also *The Delius* (1954) 1 Lloyd's Rep. 307. See the remark made by Brandon, J. in *The Hagen* (1973) 1 Lloyd's Rep. 257, at p.262, that the damage may give some indication on the speed of the vessel.
6. *Shipping Controller (The Plumleaf)* v. *The Australia* (1921) 7 Ll.L.Rep. 207, at p.209.

"It was argued that on these findings the collision could not have come about at all, whereas in fact it did happen, and the usual propositions were put before us that, if you take the bearings given and the distance given and work out from that what happened, you will find the vessels will not come together. The answer so often given to such arguments and the answer which I suppose will continue to be given, is that you cannot take these estimates and statements as to bearings, distance and time with the accuracy which enables you to work out a sort of Chinese puzzle in that way by taking them as data. They are only estimates, and the headings are only estimates, and it is impossible to place such specific reliance on such matters as to enable you with certainty to say they are the factors which are necessary to consider in coming to a conclusion as to the collision"[1].

Similar remarks were made by Brandon, J. in *The "Ellen M"*[2] about the reliability and credibility of the witnesses: "I thought all three of the plaintiffs' witnesses were trying to tell the truth as they remembered it and were reasonably reliable, but I was far from satisfied that all their estimates of headings and positions were correct."

Notices to Mariners

Although Notices to Mariners have no statutory authority, they are of considerable importance in a court of law. These notices contain information primarily for the correction of Admiralty Charts, Sailing Directions, and List of Lights of Radio Signals[3].

(III) INTERPRETATION OF THE COLLISION REGULATIONS

Interpretation, in general, is not an exact science and cannot be regarded as the mechanical drawing of meanings from the words in a text. In most instances interpretation involves giving to a particular text a meaning which, in the circumstances of the particular case, appears to be logical, reasonable and most likely to agree with the purpose of the law.

---

1. "Mere estimates, by witnesses in collision cases, as to time and distance can rarely be relied on with confidence. It is always safer in determining such questions to be governed by the attending facts and circumstances."
   See *Kennedy* v. *The Sarmation* (1880) 2 Fed. 911, 914.
2. (1967) 2 Lloyd's Rep. 247, at p.258.
3. Notices are published daily and are numbered consecutively commencing at the beginning of each year. They are also issued in the form of two separate weekly editions and one quarterly edition.

Interpreting the Collision Regulations is obviously of great importance and regard shall be made to its international character[1] and to the need to promote uniformity[2]. Four fundamental rules of interpretation were laid down by the courts.

(1) The Rules have to be read and interpreted by seamen and, therefore they should be interpreted from the point of view of mariners. Lord Denning, M.R. said[3] the Collision Regulations: "...should be interpreted by the Courts in the same way as seamen should interpret them"[4].

An American court took the same view[5]: "Navigators are not to be charged with negligence, unless they make a decision which nautical experience and good seamanship would condemn as unjustifiable at the time and under the circumstances shown."

(2) "The (Rules) are issued for the guidance of masters of vessels; and, therefore, the proper mode of construing them is to read them literally..."[6].

(3) "The basis of the regulations for preventing collisions at sea is, that they are instructions to those in charge of ships as to their conduct; and the legislature has not thought it enough to say, 'We will give you rules which shall prevent a collision'; they have gone further and said that 'for the safety of navigation we will give you rules which shall prevent risk of collision' "[7]. Lord Buckmaster in his speech in *S.S. Kitano Maru* v.

---

1. The international character of the Collision Regulations, due to constitutional differences, is not always preserved in the different legal systems. In some countries, the Collision Regulations, as international rules, are taken *in toto* and are allowed to take effect as they stand. In other countries, they are incorporated in municipal acts and thus are transformed into municipal rules and severed from their origin. They, therefore, cease to be an expression of the will of an international conference but become the expression of the will of a national parliament. For the position of a municipal act giving the force of law to a convention, see Lord Diplock in *Salman* v. *Commissioners of Customs and Excise* (1966) 2 Lloyd's Rep. 460.
2. *Corocraft Ltd. and Another* v. *Pan American Airways* (1939) 1 Q.B. 616, at pp.654, 655.
3. The "*Koningen Juliana*" (1974) 2 Lloyd's Rep. 353, at p.354.
4. See per Lord Reid in *Federal Steam Navigation Co. Ltd.* v. *Department of Trade and Industry, the "Huntingdon"* (1974) 1 Lloyd's Rep. 520 at p.521.
5. *The Clarence L. Blakeslee* (1917) 223 Fed. 365.
6. Jessel, M.R. in construing the Thames Rules in *The Libra* (1881) 6 P.D. 139, at p.142.
7. Per Brett, M.R. in *The Beryl* (1884) 9 P.D. 137, at p.138.

S.S. Otranto[1] said: "In obeying and construing these Rules due regard shall be had to all dangers of navigation and collision, and to any special circumstances, including the limitations of the craft involved, which may render a departure in order to avoid immediate danger."

(4) "The (Rules) are all applicable at a time when the risk of collision can be avoided - not that they are applicable when the risk of collision is already fixed and determined"[2].

1. (1931) A.C. 194 at p.201; (1930) 38 Ll.L.Rep. 204, at p.208.
2. Per Brett, M.R. in *The Beryl* (1884) 9 P.D. 137, at p.140.

Chapter 4

GENERAL RULES STATED BY THE COLLISION REGULATIONS

Rule 1 - *Application*

(a) These Rules shall apply to all vessels upon the high seas in all waters connected therewith navigable by seagoing vessels.

In this paragraph two points call for examination:

(1) the meaning of a vessel; and
(2) the meaning of the high seas and all waters connected therewith navigable by seagoing vessels.

A vessel

The Rules apply to all vessels, i.e. merchant vessels, warships[1], state-owned vessels used for non-commercial or commercial services and vessels flying the flag of an international organisation. The word "vessel" is defined in Rule 3 (a) and includes "every description of water craft, including non-displacement craft and seaplanes, used or capable of being used as a means of transportation on water."

On the high seas and in all waters connected therewith navigable by seagoing vessels

Article 1 of the Geneva Convention, 1958 defines "high seas" as "all parts of the sea that are not included in the territorial sea or in the internal waters of a State."

However, the Rules apply to all vessels, on the high seas as well as to vessels in all waters - whether they are territorial or internal, e.g. river, strait, canal, lake, gulf, bay... etc. connected with the high seas - provided that these waters are

---

1. Warships are bound by the Queen's Regulations and Admiralty Instructions which contain exactly the same provisions as the Collision Regulations and by the Admiralty Notice to Mariners.

navigable[1] by seagoing[2] vessels.

Under English law, if the collision occurs in British waters, it would be governed by English law as the sovereignty of the State extends to her internal and territorial zone[3]. As Lord Diplock observed in *The "Tojo Maru"*[4], English law does not recognise a "Maritime Law of the World". This expression refers only to English municipal law as applied by English courts and in particular the Admiralty Court.

Although the continental shelf is part of the high seas[5], the Continental Shelf (Jurisdiction) Order 1965[6] provides that "questions arising out of acts or omissions taking place in the designated areas, or in any part of such an area in connection with the exploration of the sea-bed or subsoil or the exploitation of their natural resources" are determined in accordance with the law in force in such part of the United Kingdom as is specified in the Order in Council. Accordingly, if a collision occurs, for

---

1. The Hovercraft (Application of Enactments) Order 1971 (S.I. 971, 1972) art. 2 (1) provides that: " 'Navigable water' means any water which is in fact navigable by ships or vessels whether or not the tide ebbs or flows there, and whether or not there is a public right of navigation in that water."
   In *Rankin* v. *De Coster* (1975) 2 Lloyd's Rep. 84, Ashworth, J. considered the meaning of the provision "all other waters ... which are ... navigable by seagoing ship" in s. 2 (2) of the Prevention of Oil Pollution Act, 1971, by saying: "The provision has a geographical basis ... which refers to the whole of the sea within the seaward limits of the territorial waters of the United Kingdom ... It would I suppose have been possible to include in a schedule a list identifying all the other waters which the paragraph was intended to cover, but the draftsman preferred to use what I consider are general words of description, namely, waters which are navigable by seagoing ships. In my view, waters in the drydock fall within this general description and can properly be called waters navigable by seagoing ships."
2. For the meaning of a "seagoing ship", see *The Salt Union* v. *Wood* (1893) 1 Q.B. 370.
3. The sovereignty of the coastal state would not, however, extend to the proposed Exclusive Economic Zone (EEZ) which is suggested to be limited to 200 miles.
4. (1972) A.C. 242 at p.291. See also *The Tolten* (1946), P. 135.
5. The Continental Shelf Act, 1964 was passed to give effect to certain provisions of the Geneva Convention on the High Seas, 1958.
6. Continental Shelf (Jurisdiction) Order 1975 (S.I. 1881 of 1965).

example, between a ship and an oil rig in a designated area and is connected with the exploration or the exploitation of the continental shelf, the designated areas, for the purposes of conflict of laws, will be treated as territorial waters. If it is not connected with the exploration or exploitation, the Order would not apply, and consequently the designated area, for the purposes of collision, would be considered as part of the high seas.

Where two vessels are involved in a collision on the high seas, the courts apply the "general maritime law" which consists of English law and other international shipping legislation[1]. It is immaterial whether either or both of the ships are flying a foreign or a British flag[2]. However, the wrongful act[3] must constitute a tort both by the general maritime law and by English law of tort, before it will be actionable in the English courts.

Where a collision occurs in internal or territorial waters of a foreign country, the act must be actionable as a tort in England and not justifiable under the law of that country. In *The Mary Moxham*[4], action was brought in the English courts by the owners of a pier in Spanish territorial waters against British owners whose ship had collided with the pier. The Court of Appeal accepted the defence that the shipowners were not liable under Spanish law for the negligence of their servants who were navigating the ship[5].

---

1. In *Chartered Mercantile Bank of India* v. *Netherlands India Steam Navigation Co.* (1883) 10 Q.B.D. 521 (C.A.) the plaintiff brought an action for the damage to his cargo caused by one of the two Dutch ships which had collided on the high seas. The Court held that negligence was "to be tried, not indeed by the common law of England, but by the maritime law, which is part of the common law of England as administered in this country."
2. The law of the flag in maritime wrongs lost its significance as a result of the flag of convenience system.
3. The Fatal Accidents Act 1846 to 1959 gives a right of action against a foreign defendant in a suit of dependents of deceased foreigners when the deaths occurred outside British territorial waters. See *Adam* v. *The British and Foreign Steamship Co., Ltd.* (1898) 2 Q.B. 430; *Davidsson* v. *Hill* (1901) 2 K.B. 606; *The Esso Malaysia* (1974) 2 All E.R. 705.
4. (1876) L.R. 1 P.D. 107.
5. See also *The Netuo* (1974) A.M.C. 147, where the U.S. District Court held that although the United States is not party to the Brussels Convention on Civil Jurisdiction in Collision Cases, 1952, the Court would apply the provisions of this Convention in actions involving vessels whose flag countries have ratified it.

(b) Nothing in these Rules shall interfere with the operation of special rules made by an appropriate authority for roadsteads, harbours, rivers, lakes or inland waterways connected with the high seas and navigable by seagoing vessels. Such special rules shall conform as closely as possible to these Rules.

In some countries, there are local regulations enforced in ports[1] and their approaches or in rivers, canals, straits ... etc. These local regulations relate to various matters such as ships' lights, speed, anchorage areas, docking, etc. As mentioned earlier, under para.(a), the Rules might well apply to vessels in these areas. However, in order to avoid any interference with the right of each state to pass acts and/or regulations relating to its internal or territorial waters, para.(b) states that the local regulations shall conform, as closely as possible, to the Rules[2]. The application of the latter could be considered as supplementary to the local regulations. In case there is any conflict, it seems that the application of the local regulations will prevail over the Rules. The International Collision Rules or notions of good seamanship could apply only to fill in gaps in the local regulations and not to contradict them.

The State, where its local regulations contradict the Rules, could - if she is party to the Rules - be under a moral obligation to other party-States to bring her local regulations into conformity with the Rules.

Local rules applied by the Courts

International law empowers the coastal state to prescribe within its territorial sea the conditions under which navigation should be carried out.

Local rules in the United Kingdom

The "Jan Laurenz"[3] concerns a collision which occurred in the Manchester Ship Canal on Mar. 22, 1968. *Saint William* was lying moored at a berth when she observed *Jan Laurenz* proceeding down the canal at a distance of ½ mile. *Saint William* commenced to move as soon as a large vessel, the *Dimitris X*, which was proceeding up the canal, had passed. *Saint William* proceeded to the centre of the canal. *Jan Laurenz* passed *Dimitris X* safely and increased her speed. *Saint William* continued down at reduced speed

---

1. See Appendix XX on the local rules of navigation in some of the important ports in the United Kingdom.
2. As there is no visible line of separation between the high seas and the territorial waters, confusion may occur if the local rules are in conflict with the Collision Rules.
3. (1972) 1 Lloyd's Rep. 404.

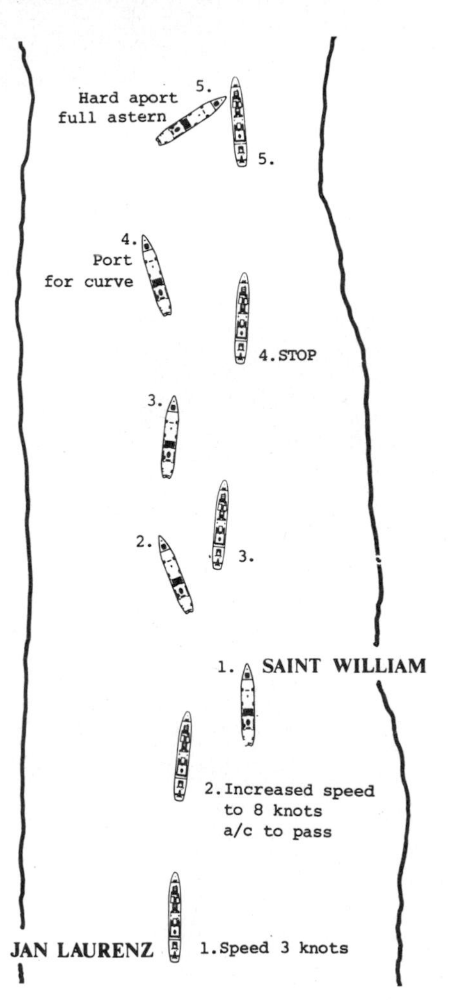

prior to passing *Pass of Glencunie* which was moored in the vicinity. *The Jan Laurenz*, making about 8 knots, commenced overtaking *Saint William*, and in the narrows approaching the Cadishead Viaduct *Saint William* ported slightly and then steadied to keep clear of the canal bank. *Jan Laurenz* continued overtaking on *Saint William's* starboard side and heading to port. *The Saint William* paid off to starboard due to the close proximity of *Jan Laurenz*. Her wheel was put hard-a-port, but her bows continued to starboard. *Saint William* put her engines full astern but *Jan Laurenz* came on and with her port side struck the starboard bow of *Saint William*.

It was held by Brandon, J. that:

(1) *Saint William* was to blame for (l) leaving her berth at an improper time, and being in breach of the General By-laws for the Harbour and Port of Manchester, 1963, by-laws 7 and 42; and (ii) persisting in going down the canal and not holding back;

(2) *Jan Laurenz* was to blame for (l) increasing her speed and making to pass *Saint William* in the way she did; and (ii) being in breach of by-laws 7, 8, 11, 18, and 27;

(3) that there was no clear preponderance of blame, and therefore

blame should be apportioned equally[1].

Local rules in foreign waters

When a collision occurs in foreign waters, the courts apply the rules of navigation applicable in these waters. In *The "Francesco Nullo"*[2] the Court found that *The Stuttgart* was in breach of the local rules. In this case a collision occurred in the River Scheldt between *The Stuttgart* and *The Francesco Nullo*. The tide was flood, of a force of two to three knots.

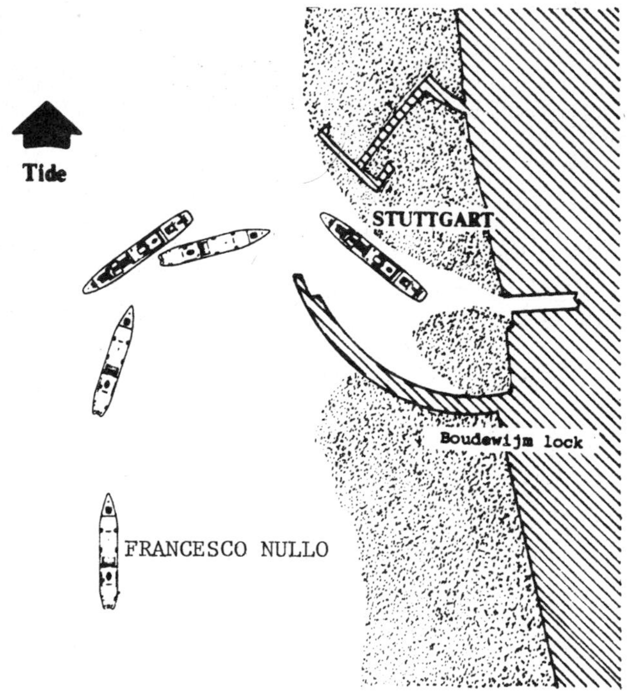

1. Appeal by *Saint William* was dismissed (1973) 1 Lloyd's Rep. 329. Lord Denning, M.R. (dissenting) held that: (1) *Saint William* was not at fault in casting off her mooring when she did; (2) *Jan Laurenz* was clearly at fault in not holding back and, on the evidence, *Saint William* was not at fault in not holding back; that *Saint William* was entitled to proceed on the assumption that *Jan Laurenz* would observe the rules by proceeding at dead slow and not overtaking; and that; therefore, *Jan Laurenz* had made the collision inevitable and was solely to blame.
2. (1973) 1 Lloyd's Rep. 72.

Francesco Nullo had come up river and intended to turn round and anchor until she was free to enter Boudewijn Lock. Seventeen minutes before the collision (c minus 17) she made fast a tug on starboard bow and put her engines dead slow ahead. C minus 15: stopped engines. C minus 10: as she was passing an anchored vessel, she sounded twice a signal of one long and one short blast (a local signal indicating her intention to turn to starboard). C minus 9: engines were put dead slow ahead and her wheel hard-a-starboard, the tug towing her head to starboard. C minus 8: engines were put half and then full astern. C minus 6: engines half astern. C minus 5: engines full astern and then slow astern. C minus 2: engines half astern and then stopped (she was then athwart the fairway). She sounded a 7-short-blast signal as a warning to *Stuttgart* which was approaching from up river and shaping to pass astern. C minus 1: *Francesco Nullo* put her engines full ahead, but there was a collision between the stern of *Francesco Nullo* and the port side of *Stuttgart* about amidships.

Five minutes before the collision, *Stuttgart* had left the Boudewijn Lock and let go her tugs. At C minus 4 she put her engines slow and then half ahead and proceeded down river. C minus 3: she put her engines full ahead. C minus 1: put her rudder at 20 deg. in order to pass under the stern of *Francesco Nullo* and gave one sustained blast as a warning.

It was held by Brandon, J.:

(1) that according to the local rules, where a vessel was turning so as to become a hindrance to passing, or when she was turning in circumstances where it could reasonably be foreseen she would become a hindrance to passing, only then were obligations imposed upon up-going or down-going vessels to stop or reduce speed as the case might be.

(2) that at C minus 3 when *Stuttgart* put her engines full ahead it was or should have been apparent that *Francesco Nullo* was turning in such a way that she either would or might become a hindrance to passage astern; and that, therefore, *Stuttgart* was to blame for going full ahead and not stopping engines.

(3) that those on board *Francesco Nullo* should have kept a look-out for down-going and up-going vessels and should if necessary have adjusted their method of turn so as not to become an obstruction to such vessels if it was not reasonably necessary so to do; she was further to blame in that her master should have recognized earlier that with *Stuttgart* persisting in coming down at a high speed it was necessary to take some avoiding action.

(4) that, since *Stuttgart* was guilty of a clear breach of the local rules and was also guilty of a more important fault in that she erred on the side of danger, she was more to blame.

Apportionment of blame: *Stuttgart*: two-thirds; *Francesco Nullo*: one-third.

(c) *Nothing in these Rules shall interfere with the operation of any special rules made by the Government of any State with respect to additional station or signal lights or whistle signals for ships of war and vessels proceeding under convoy, or with respect to additional station or signal lights for fishing vessels engaged in fishing as a fleet. These additional station or signal lights or whistle signals shall, so far as possible*[1]*, be such that they cannot be mistaken for any light or signal authorized elsewhere under these Rules.*

In case there are special rules made by a State relating to additional station or signal lights or whistle signals for warships, vessels in convoy or fishing vessels engaged in fishing as a fleet, measures must be taken to avoid any confusion with the lights and signals required by the Rules.

(d) *Traffic separation schemes may be adopted by the Organization for the purpose of these Rules.*

This paragraph provides that the application of the Rules extends to areas where IMCO adopted traffic separation schemes. Rule 10 deals with traffic separation schemes in detail[2].

(e) *Whenever the Government concerned shall have determined that a vessel of special construction or purpose cannot comply fully with the provisions of any of these Rules with respect to the number, position, range or arc of visibility of lights or shapes, as well as to the disposition and characteristics of sound-signalling appliances, without interfering with the special function of the vessel, such vessel shall comply with such other provisions in regard to the number, position, range of arc of visibility of lights or shapes, as well as to the disposition and characteristics of sound-signalling appliances, as her Government shall have determined to be the closest possible compliance with these Rules in respect of that vessel.*

In view of the special characteristics of certain vessels, they could be exempted from certain parts of the Rules, mainly those

---

1. The Civil Aviation Organisation criticised the words "so far as possible" because they would "leave room for widely different interpretations" and could be used as an "escape clause". CR/CONF/3, p.19.
2. See infra Rule 10 in Chapter 5.

relating to the number, position, range or arc of visibility of lights or shapes as well as to sound signalling equipment. Para. (e) applies to all vessels of special construction and not only to naval or military vessels. The special requirements of lights on some warships are reported in the Admiralty Notice to Mariners. For example, aircraft carriers have their masthead lights placed permanently off the centre line of the ship with a considerably reduced horizontal separation. Their sidelights may be on either side of the hull or on either side of the island structure. When at anchor, aircraft carriers may show four white lights, one at each bow and one at each quarter, each visible over an arc of at least 180°.

Rule 2 - *Responsibility*

(a) Nothing in these Rules shall exonerate any vessel or the owner, master, or crew thereof from the consequences of any neglect to comply with these Rules or of the neglect of any precaution which may be required by the ordinary practice of seamen, or by the special circumstances of the case.

"The consequences[1] of any neglect to comply with these Rules" can be illustrated by *The "Oldekerk"*[2]. In this case, a multiple collision took place in the Nieuwe Mass at Rotterdam, on Oct.17, 1969, between the *Anvers* and the *Oldekerk*, which in turn both collided with the *Perija*. All the vessels had pilots on board. *Anvers* was proceeding up river on the south side of the river whilst *Perija* was going down river on the north side. *Oldekerk* was being towed as a dead ship by four tugs from a berth on the south side to another berth downstream on the north side. She indicated her intention of leaving the berth to a shore radar station, which transmitted the information to the other two vessels, and said that she would hold back. Shortly afterwards she signalled the station that she was coming out of the berth and that she was going to port. *Anvers* proceeded up the river at half speed and ported a little. The tow ropes parted and *Oldekerk* went across the river at considerable speed. *Anvers*

1. The Netherlands proposed that: "The meaning of this Rule is not clear since the present draft does not contain any further provision whatsoever as regards the consequences of non-compliance with the Rules. Therefore, no reference should be made here to such consequences, which could be numerous and which are dealt with in other international instruments or in national legislation. There is only a need for a provision establishing the general obligation to take precautions as required by the ordinary practice of seamen." CR/CONF/3, p.20.
2. (1974) 1 Lloyd's Rep. 95.

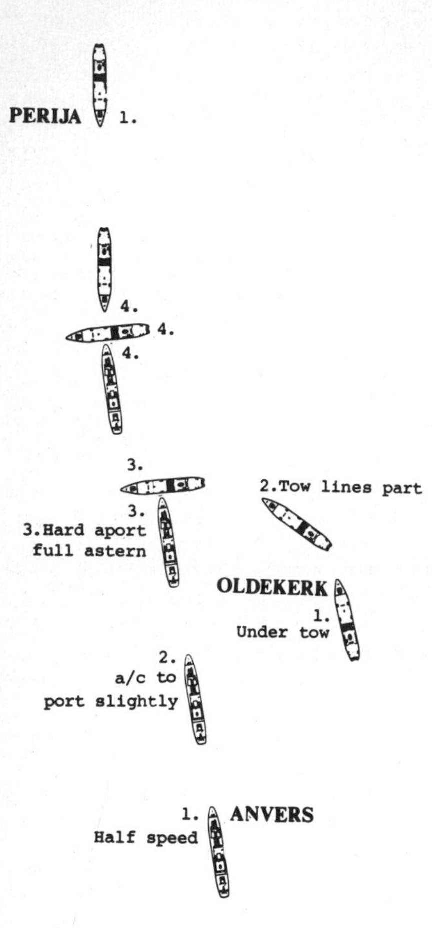

struck her, and then both *Oldekerk* and *Anvers* collided with *Perija*. *Oldekerk* admitted liability, but her owners obtained a decree of limitation of liability to £200,000 on the ground that the collision had occurred without their actual fault or privity. However, *Perija* alleged that *Anvers* was partly to blame.

It was held by Brandon, J. that:

(1) *Anvers* was not guilty of negligence in failing to stop her engines, for the pilot was negligent in assuming that *Oldekerk*, when she announced her intention of carrying out the manoeuvre would be capable of carrying it out.

(2) *Anvers* was not in breach of the local regulations or the Collision Rules, 1960 because once the *Oldekerk* announced that she was coming out, it ceased to be safe and practicable for the *Anvers* to keep more than marginally on her own starboard side of mid-river. When the *Anvers* went hard to port at the last it was no longer safe or practicable for her to remain on the south side at all. Consequently, the *Oldekerk* was alone to blame for the collision.

It is clear that para.(a) of Rule 2 is merely stating a general principle of law and giving a strong warning to seamen to observe and comply with the Rules. In *The Queen Mary*[1], Lord MacDermott said: "In my opinion, it (art.29)[2] is not aimed at authorising

1. (1949) 82 Ll.L.Rep. 303, at p.341 (H.L.).
2. Art. 29 of the old Rules is similar to para.(a) of Rule 2.

departure from the regulations, and I doubt if it is more than a solemn warning that compliance therewith does not terminate the ever present duty of using reasonable skill and care."

Ordinary practice of seamen

There is no rigid test for what is meant by "ordinary practice of seamen". This is a question of fact to be decided in the light of all the relevant circumstances. The case of *The Bowbelle*[1] is a good illustration. In this case, the *Catford* collided with the *Bowbelle* in the River Thames in daylight on the flood tide. *Catford* had come up river and intended to turn on to a down-river heading. Five minutes before collision *Catford* put her wheel hard-a-starboard with engines stopped. On beginning her turn she sounded a turning signal of four short blasts followed by one short blast. *Bowbelle* was half a mile distant coming down river at six knots in mid-channel with engines at half-speed ahead. *Bowbelle* heard *Catford's* turning signal and increased speed to full ahead to pass to south of *Catford* before *Catford* was athwart river. One and a half minutes later *Catford* put her engines full astern to assist her turn. *Catford* sighted *Bowbelle* coming down river and sounded a second turning signal. Half a minute later, *Bowbelle* put her engines to half ahead. Half a minute later *Catford* dropped her starboard anchor when vessels were quarter of a mile apart. One and a half minutes later *Catford* put her engines to slow ahead and sounded a third turning signal. At same time *Bowbelle* went slow ahead. Half a minute later *Catford* put her engines half and then full ahead and put her wheel hard-a-port. At same time *Bowbelle* stopped her engines and quarter of a minute later put them full astern. Quarter of a minute later collision occurred between stern of *Bowbelle* and port side aft of *Catford* at about a right angle. After collision *Catford* moved forward and, shortly after putting her engines astern, collided with a barge.

It was held by Brandon, J.:

(1) that *Catford* did not begin her turn at the improper time;

(2) that *Catford* was in breach of the By-laws, in that the first signal was not sounded when about to turn but when beginning to turn; but that breach did not in any way cause collision;

(3) that the master of *Catford* was not negligent in keeping his engines at full astern for 2½ minutes in executing turning manoeuvre;

---

1. (1967) 2 Lloyd's Rep. 138. See also *"Alonso De Ojeda" (Owners)* v. *Sestriere (Owners), (The "Sestriere")*, (1976) 1 Lloyd's Rep. 125.

(4) that the master of *Bowbelle* misjudged the possibility of getting past *Catford* without appropriate alteration of course on his part.

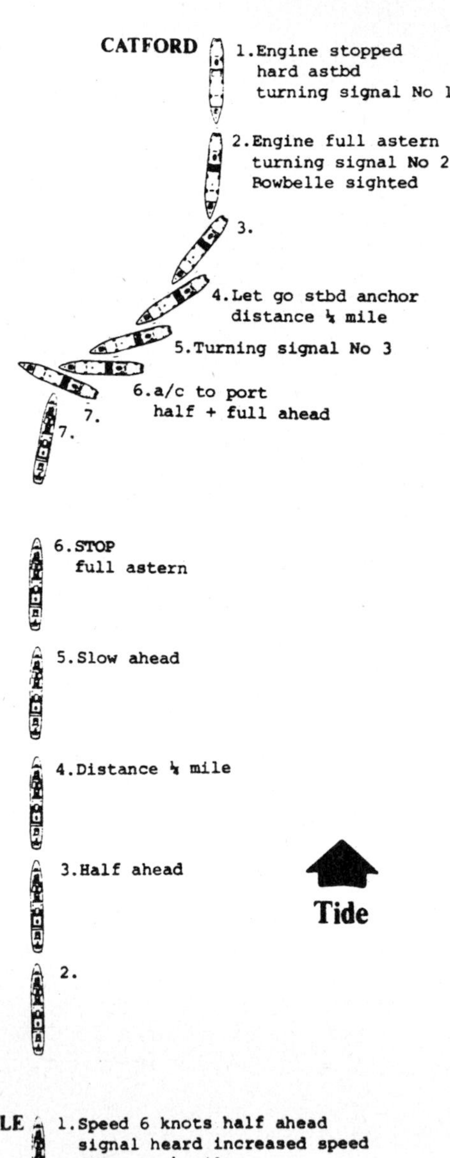

(5) that *Bowbelle* was negligent in not either altering to starboard to pass under stern of *Catford* or in taking off her way and stemming tide until *Catford* had swung round further;

(6) that although it would have been better for the master of *Catford* to have taken action earlier, he was not negligent in not doing so;

(7) that the master of *Catford* was not negligent in colliding with barge. *Bowbelle* found alone to blame.

The ordinary practice of seamen is required of all vessels regardless of their size. Hewson, J. in *The Jaladhir*[1] pointed out: "Trawlers, like all other vessels which use the high seas, do encounter, and have to manoeuvre for, all types of vessels, and they must be handled with competence and skill."

(b) *In construing and complying with these Rules due regard shall be had to all dangers of navigation and collision and to any special circumstances, including the limitations of the vessels involved, which may make a departure from these Rules necessary to avoid immediate danger.*

Departure from the Rules

The Rules are not merely of a prudential character and therefore they must be rigorously obeyed. The obligation to obey the Rules is imperative and the courts have always emphasised that departure from the Rules is recognised only to avoid immediate danger.

"You may depart, and you must depart, from a rule if you see with perfect clearness, almost amounting to a certainty, that adhering to the rule will bring about a collision, and violating a rule will avoid it"[2].

"The principle of law that you are not to adhere to strict rules of navigation but avoid an accident, if possible, is a doctrine to be very carefully watched"[3].

A vessel may assume that other vessels will observe the Rules and navigate prudently and therefore may determine her own course accordingly. Thus, a vessel is not justified in departing from the Rules merely because she fears that the other ship will not comply with them. A disabled vessel is required to take all precautions in time, and do all she can to comply with the Rules,

---

1. (1961) 2 Lloyd's Rep. 13.
2. Per Dr. Lushington in *The Boanergers and the Anglo-Indian* (1865) 2 Mar.L.Cas. (O.S.) 239.
3. Per Dr. Lushington in *The Test* (1847) 5 Not. of Cas. 276.

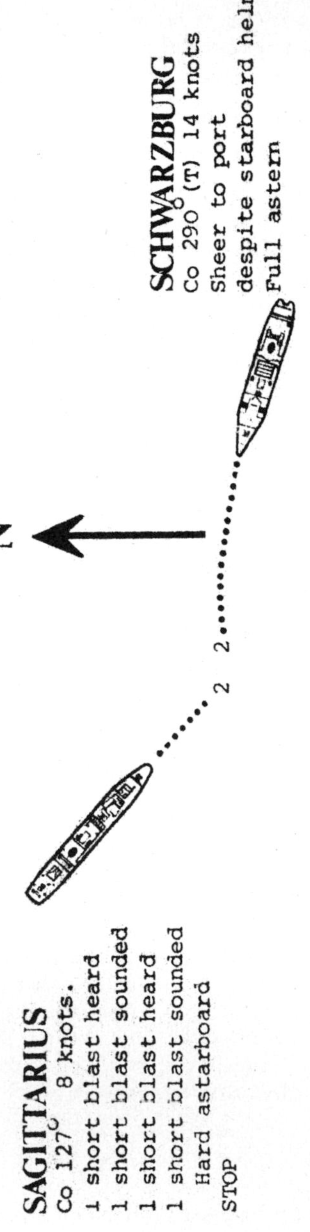
SCHWARZBURG
Co 290° (T) 14 knots
Sheer to port
despite starboard helm
Full astern
N
2
2
SAGITTARIUS
Co 127° 8 knots.
1 short blast heard
1 short blast sounded
1 short blast heard
1 short blast sounded
Hard astarboard
STOP

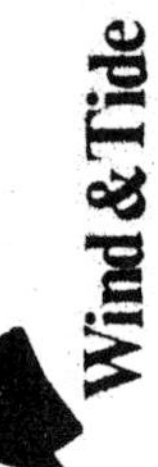
Wind & Tide

although it is the duty of the other vessels to keep clear of her. A potential difficulty in relation to other ships does not justify the departure from the Rules. In *Sagittarius (Owners)* v. *Schwarzburg (Owners) (The "Schwarzburg")*[1], the *Sagittarius* was going at her full speed of eight knots down the Canal Punta Indio (Argentina). When she passed buoys 25 at 21 45, she saw two vessels coming in the opposite direction and the first was *Schwarzburg*. When they were about ½ to one mile apart, both *Sagittarius* and *Schwarzburg* sounded two signals each of one short blast and then one of three short blasts.

Schwarzburg did not hear *Sagittarius'* signals, but the latter did those of *Schwarzburg* and put her wheel hard to starboard and stopped her engines. About this time *Schwarzburg* appeared to swing rapidly to port - later it transpired that this was due to an involuntary sheer, and expert evidence stated that this was due to hydrodynamic causes which had the effect of sucking the stern of the ship towards the bank and making her yaw to port. Her engines were put full astern and some two or three minutes later, about 22 21, the collision occurred inside the channel.

It was held, by Q.B. (Adm.Ct.) (Brandon, J.) that the *Schwarzburg* would not have got into the difficulty, and would accordingly not have sheered uncontrollably to port across the channel, if she had not been going so fast; the dangers of interaction between a ship and the bottom and sides of a channel such as the Punta Indio at anything but carefully controlled speeds should have been well known to the pilot of *Schwarzburg*, and that, having regard to those dangers, the speed of *Schwarzburg* was excessive while approaching a passing with *Sagittarius*.

The Court added that, although *Sagittarius* would have had difficulty in complying with the local rules of navigation in relation to ships following *Schwarzburg*, it was possible for her to comply largely with those rules in relation to the *Schwarzburg*, and her failure to do so could not be justified or excused on the ground that she might not have been able to comply with it in relation to those other ships. The International Collision Regulations authorized departures from other rules only when those were necessary in order to avoid immediate danger within the meaning of those rules, and in the instant case the immediate danger was that of passing *Schwarzburg* at a prohibited place and there was no good reason why the *Sagittarius*, from the point of good seamanship, should not have done her best to comply with the local rules.

As to division of blame, the fault of the *Sagittarius* was a less

---

1. (1976) 1 Lloyd's Rep. 26.

direct and immediate cause than the fault of the *Schwarzburg*. *Schwarzburg* was two-thirds to blame and the *Sagittarius* was one-third.

Burden of proof

In cases of departure from the Rules, the burden of proof is a heavy one. It must be shown that:

(1) the circumstances were exceptional or the departure was necessary in order to avoid an immediate danger; and

(2) the course adopted was reasonable in the prevailing circumstances.

Rule 3 - *General Definitions*

For the purpose of these Rules, except where the context otherwise requires:

(a) The word "vessel" includes every description of water craft, including non-displacement craft and seaplanes, used or capable of being used as a means of transportation on water.

Vessel

The definition of "vessel" includes non-displacement craft and seaplanes. Thus, hovercraft[1], hydrofoils and seaplanes are considered "vessels" subject to the Rules. Section 4 (1) of the Hovercraft Act, 1968[2] defines the hovercraft as: "a vehicle which is designed to be supported when in motion wholly or partly by air expelled from the vehicle to form a cushion of which the boundaries include the ground, water or the surface beneath the vehicle". The Collision Regulations (Ships and Seaplanes on the Water) and Signals of Distress (Ships) Order, 1965 states in article 3 that:

"The Collision Regulations shall apply to all United Kingdom registered hovercraft, and to all other hovercraft within the United Kingdom territorial waters."

Article 4 (2) provides:

"The provision of the said section 21 (of the Merchant Shipping (Safety Convention) Act 1949) - signals to be used by ships as

---

1. The word hovercraft is not precise and the correct term is air cushion vehicle. It came from the name of a manufacturer called Hovercraft Development Ltd. However, the word hovercraft is widely used in practice.
2. The Act was passed on July 26, 1968. It is an enabling act and indicated the kind of legal regime which would be created for hovercraft by further Orders in Council.

signals of distress) shall apply to all United Kingdom hovercraft, and to all other hovercraft within the United Kingdom territorial waters."

Although the application of these provisions seems to be limited to British hovercraft or all other hovercraft in British waters, para. (a) of Rule 3 of the Collision Regulations makes it clear that the Rules apply to all hovercraft[1].

The legal status of a rig[2] is not clear. The (Registration) Regulations, 1972, passed under the Mineral Workings (Offshore Installations) Act, 1971[3] mention two types of installations[4] namely the mobile and fixed installations (art. 2, 1). However, this distinction is adopted only with regard to the particulars required for the registration[5]. Thus, certain types of rigs, e.g. drill ships, are considered covered by the definition of "vessel" and will be subject to the Merchant Shipping Act, 1894[6]

---

1. Article 6 of the Hovercraft (Civil Liability) Order, 1971 provides that Part VIII of the Merchant Shipping Act, 1894, and the Merchant Shipping (Liability of Shipowners and Others) Act, 1958, shall apply subject to certain modificiations.
2. There are three different types of rigs: the jack-up, the semi-submersible and the drill ship rig. In addition, the submersible barges and fixed platforms can be used in shallow waters.
3. This Act applies to all offshore installations without any distinction (art. 1).
4. The (Construction and Survey) Regulations, 1974, also adopted this distinction with regard to the requirements for moving the offshore installations (art. 3, 1).
5. Both types, and also any part of an offshore installation capable of being manned by one or more persons, are subject to the (Registration) Regulations (art. 2, 3). The only installations which are exempted from registration are dredging installations which are registered as vessels (whether in the United Kingdom or elsewhere). Thus, all rigs whether they are considered "vessels" or not and also all foreign rigs operating in British waters must be registered under the Mineral Workings (Offshore Installations) Act, 1971.
6. Section 742 of the Merchant Shipping Act, 1894 states that "ship includes every description of vessel used in navigation not propelled by oars." Navigation in this respect means the safe conduct of a craft. Therefore, any rig which is covered by the definition of s. 742 such as a mobile rig in transit or a drill ship must conform with the provisions of the Merchant Shipping Act.

while others will not fall within this definition[1].

(b) *The term "power-driven vessel" means any vessel propelled by machinery.*

Power-driven vessel

The definition is identical to Rule 1 (c) (ii) of the 1960 Rules.

(c) *The term "sailing vessel" means any vessel under sail provided that propelling machinery, if fitted, is not being used.*

Sailing vessel

If a sailing vessel is partly under sail and also using machinery as an additional means of propulsion, she is not considered a "sailing vessel".

(d) *The term "vessel engaged in fishing" means any vessel fishing with nets, lines, trawls or other fishing apparatus which restrict manoeuvrability, but does not include a vessel fishing; with trolling lines or other fishing apparatus which do not restrict manoeuvrability*[2].

Vessel engaged in fishing: the definition is clear.

---

1. In many American cases, rigs were considered as ships for the application of the Jones Act. See *Claiborne McCarty Service Contracting Inc.* (Dist. Ct.) (1971) A.M.C. 90, where the court said: "An invaluable aid in offshore oil exploration, a submersible drilling barge is a unique craft whose specialized purpose is the location and commercial production of oil reserves found beneath the surface of the water. By the very nature of their job these specialised craft must be capable of at least some degree of mobility on navigable waters and there is now simply no question but that such craft are "vessels" within the import of both the Jones Act and General Maritime Law."
   See also *Glanfala v. Texas Company,* 350 U.S. 879 (1960) A.M.C. 1955; *Marine Drilling Co. v. Autin* (1966) A.M.C. 2013; *Producers Drilling Co. v. Gray* (1966) *A.M.C. 1260;* Offshore Co. *v.* Robinson *(1959) A.M.C. 2049.*
2. The U.S.S.R. suggested the following text: "The term 'vessel engaged in fishing' means any vessel fishing with nets, lines, or other non-towed trolling lines, trawls or other fishing apparatus which restricts manoeuvrability, but does not include a vessel fishing with towed trolling lines or other fishing apparatus which does not restrict manoeuvrability." CR/CONF/3, p.21.

(e) *The word "seaplane" includes any aircraft designed to manoeuvre on the water.*

Seaplane

The definition of seaplane is similar to Rule 1 (c) (ii) of the 1960 Rules.

(f) *The term "vessel not under command"*[1] *means a vessel which through some exceptional circumstance is unable to manoeuvre as required by these Rules and is therefore unable to keep out of the way of another vessel.*

Vessel not under command

A vessel is considered "not under command" if she is unable to manoeuvre sufficiently to get out of the way[2], for example, caused by an engine or steering breakdown or an accident[3]. In *The Mendip Range*[4], Lord Atkinson said: "I confess I have difficulty in seeing on what principle, if the captain of a ship injured by accident comes, after due and reasonable examination and inquiry to the conclusion that the facts then by him ascertained constitute reasonable grounds for the belief and opinion that his ship is not under command, he would not be held justified in having hoisted the appointed signals, at all events if the Court before which the question comes for decision concurs with him in thinking that the facts at the time so discovered do afford reasonable grounds for the opinion he has formed, even though facts should subsequently be discovered which would show that the supposed facts upon which he formed his opinion were erroneous"[5].

---

1. Bulgaria proposed that: "the term 'vessel not under command' means a vessel which through internal or external circumstances is unable to get out of the way of another vessel." Ibid, p.21.
2. *The Albion* (1952) 1 Lloyd's Rep. 38; (1953) 1 Lloyd's Rep. 239.
3. This rule has been held to refer to a ship afloat and moving, not to a ship hard and fast aground, see *The Carlotta* (1899) P. 223.
4. (1921) 6 Ll.L.Rep. 375; (1921) 1 A.C. 556 at p.581.
5. Viscount Haldane said (ibid at pp.376, 562 respectively): "A vessel cannot give herself a licence to escape from her duty to give way by claiming a special protection to which she is not entitled."

In "*Ziemia Szczecinska*" *(Owners)* v. "*Djerada*" *(Owners)*, *(The "Djerada")*[1], the *Djerada* had been in some difficulties because of the heavy weather, but she was not disabled and she had full use of her engines and steering. Consequently, the defence of a vessel not under command failed. In this case a collision occurred between the plaintiffs' motor vessel *Ziemia Szczecinska* and the defendants' motor ship *Djerada* in the Dover Strait some 5½ miles from the Dyck Light Vessel at about 02 59 on Nov. 10, 1969. The weather at the time was fine and clear, the visibilty good, the wind force eight, and the tide flood about one knot. Before the collision the speed of *Ziemia* had been about 15 knots, that of the *Djerada* about 6½ knots, and at collision the angle of blow was about 65 to 70 deg., *Djerada* striking the *Ziemia* in way of

DJERADA 1. About 117° (T)

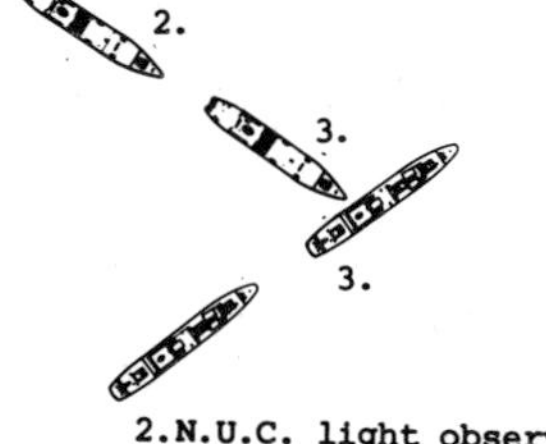

ZIEMIA 1. 041° (T) 15 knots
white + red observed
on port bow

---

1. (1976) 1 Lloyd's Rep. 50.

no. 6 hold. Both vessels had their second officers in command and both were fully laden.

Djerada had been subject to four days heavy weather and was carrying "not under command" lights, although she had full use of her engines and steering. Her master had left the bridge some two hours before the collision, leaving the second officer in charge. In addition to the "not in command" lights, the *Djerada* was carrying a white masthead light, two red lights and a green side light. She was steering a course 095 deg. (T) until very shortly before the collision when she was steering between 115 deg. (T) and 120 deg. (T). Her second officer probably did not see *Ziemia's* lights nor make any alteration to port. Meanwhile, the second officer of *Ziemia* saw the lights of *Djerada* for the first time when the latter was only a short distance away, recognizing the two red lights as not under command lights and the green light as navigation side light and appreciated that *Djerada* was on a collision course.

He ordered the wheel of the *Ziemia* hard to starboard about one minute before the collision, steering 041 deg. (T) at the time. The angle of the two courses being steered by the two ships was 70 to 75 deg.

It was held by Q.B. (Adm.Ct.) (Brandon, J.) that

(A) as to *Djerada*:

(1) the lookout on the *Djerada* was extremely bad, as a result of which the lights of the *Ziemia* were not properly observed, nor her course and speed properly appreciated during the 45 minutes leading up to the collision;

(2) as to lights, *Djerada* was not justified in carrying not under command lights and should in any case not have carried a white masthead light as well as such lights[1].

(B) as to *Ziemia*:

(1) her second officer did not appreciate what lights *Djerada*

---

1. The learned Judge made the following observation (ibid at p.58): "It is important that ships which are genuinely disabled from manoeuvring adequately should have both the right and the duty to advertise that fact by exhibiting appropriate signals and to make it clear to other ships that they must take steps to keep clear of them. It is equally important that ships which are not genuinely disabled, although they may be under certain difficulties, should not claim this special right and privilege...without proper justification."

was carrying, or what course she was on, until about one minute before the collision - that could only have been due to his extremely bad lookout;

(2) as to failure to keep clear: if the second officer had recognized the lights of *Djerada* earlier, he would, despite the element of confusion introduced by the masthead light, have taken action to keep clear, which would have been his duty to do as a matter of good seamanship under the Collision Regulations and might have been successful in avoiding a collision.

As for the apportionment of blame, *Djerada* was 60 per cent and *Ziemia* 40 per cent[1].

(g) *The term "vessel restricted in her ability to manoeuvre" means a vessel which from the nature of her work is restricted in her ability to manoeuvre as required by these Rules and is therefore unable to keep out of the way of another vessel.*

The following vessels shall be regarded as vessels restricted in their ability to manoeuvre:

(i) a vessel engaged in laying, servicing or picking up a navigation mark, submarine cable or pipeline;

(ii) a vessel engaged in dredging, surveying or underwater operations;

(iii) a vessel engaged in replenishment or transferring persons, provisions or cargo while underway;

(iv) a vessel engaged in the launching or recovery of aircraft;

(v) a vessel engaged in minesweeping operations;

(vi) a vessel engaged in a towing operation such as severely restricts the towing vessel and her tow in their ability to deviate from their course[2].

---

1. The appeal by the *Djerada* was dismissed (1976) 2 Lloyd's Rep. 40. The Court of Appeal made it clear that the *Djerada* was not entitled to carry the lights prescribed for vessels not under command.
2. This paragraph was proposed by the Netherlands who made the following comments: "A vessel engaged in a difficult towing operation, which is severely restricted to deviate from the course she is following and also is restricted to apply astern power, should be given some privilege. It should be stressed that a vessel engaged in a difficult towing operation should be regarded as a hampered vessel. CR/CONF/3, p.35.

Vessel restricted in her ability to manoeuvre

This is a new definition and differs from para. (f) in that it applies to those vessels which, due to the nature of their work, are restricted in their ability to manoeuvre. The list of the types of vessel in this category is not exhaustive. With the development in shipbuilding technology, new types of vessels could be added to this category.

(h) *The term "vessel constrained by her draught" means a power-driven vessel which, because of her draught in relation to the available depth of water, is severely restricted in her ability to deviate from the course she is following.*

Vessel constrained by her draught

This is also a new definition concerning vessels which may be restricted in their ability to deviate from their courses because of their draught in relation to the depth of water. Accordingly, two conditions are required: (1) a power-driven vessel; and (2) her draught in relation to the depth of water results in a severe restriction in her ability to deviate from the course she is following. Definition (h) is not limited to large deep draught vessels[1] nor to certain geographic areas of the water. However, it is clear that a vessel on the high seas cannot claim that she is constrained by her draught. Also, if a channel offers sufficient manoeuvring room for a vessel to deviate safely from her course, she could not be regarded as constrained by her draught[2].

(i) *The word "underway" means that a vessel is not at anchor, or made fast to the shore, or aground.*

Underway

A vessel is considered to be "underway" as soon as she ceases to be held by and under the control of her anchor. Thus, if a vessel is drifting in the sea, she is "underway". However, if the vessel is fast to another that is moored or brought up, or to a buoy, or any fixed object, she is not underway within definition (i).

---

1. The Netherlands proposed to use the term "deep draught vessels" and not a vessel "constrained by her draught" as the draftsmen of the Rules were mainly concerned with vessels in excess of 100,000 dwt or those whose draught is in excess of 40 feet. However, definition (h) applies to small boats, say, with a 4-foot draught in a 5-foot channel. See Conference Document 3 at p.23.
2. For further discussion on vessels constrained by their draught see infra Rule 18 (d) (ii).

(j) *The words "length" and "breadth" of a vessel mean her length overall and greatest breadth.*

Length and breadth

The length and breadth of a vessel are given a definite meaning.

(k) *Vessels shall be deemed to be in sight of one another only when one can be observed visually from the other.*

The word "visually" clarifies the meaning of the words "in sight of one another".

(l) *The term "restricted visibility" means any condition in which visibility is restricted by fog, mist, falling snow, heavy rainstorms, sandstorms or any other similar causes*[1].

Restricted visibility

The definition of the words "restricted visibility" is useful so as to avoid any repetition of the varying visibility conditions in other parts of the Rules. Sandstorms are included among the conditions which might restrict the visibility.

---

1. In a note presented from the United Kingdom to the drafting Committee, it was suggested that the rules should also include definitions on: "risk of collision"; "end on or nearly end on vessel"; "overtaking vessel"; and "a giving way vessel" (on file with author).

Chapter 5

STEERING AND SAILING RULES

(1) CONDUCT OF VESSELS IN ANY CONDITION OF VISIBILITY

Rule 4 - *Application*

Rules in this Section apply in any condition of visibility.

Thus the rules of this Section[1], namely Rule 5 to Rule 10, apply in both clear and restricted visibility.

Rule 5 - *Look-out*

Every vessel shall at all times maintain a proper look-out by sight and hearing as well as by all available means appropriate in the prevailing circumstances and conditions so as to make a full appraisal of the situation and of the risk of collision.

The obligation to keep a proper look-out derives from the ordinary practice of seamen as well as from the rules of prudence. It is clear that in order to avoid any danger, one must be aware of its existence. Therefore, Rule 5 requires from all vessels and at all times to maintain a vigilant and sufficient look-out by all available means appropriate in the prevailing circumstances.

Meaning of look-out

Look-out means "an appreciation of what is taking place"[2]. A good look-out involves not only a visual look-out, and not only the use of ears, but it also involves the intelligent interpretation of the data received by way of these various scientific

1. Rule 4 is a mere repetition of the title.
2. Per Willmer, L.J. in *The "Santander"* (1966) 2 Lloyd's Rep. 77.

instruments[1].

The person on look-out

The person on look-out must be a competent seaman of adequate age and with a reasonable amount of experience. Most important, he must be properly instructed in his duties.

Ordinarily, one person on look-out is sufficient. However, in special circumstances, two or more persons should be on duty for look-out. The question of the number of persons on look-out depends on various factors such as the size of the vessel, the amount of traffic and the degree of visibility.

The place of look-out

There is no specific place on the vessel for the look-out. However, the person on look-out must be properly stationed in order to have an unobstructed view. The usual place of look-out is on the bridge or in some other proper place[2]. At night, in fog, or in congested waters, the person on the look-out should not be stationed in or near the pilothouse.

The duties of the person on look-out

Apart from keeping a vigilant look-out, the person entrusted with look-out must keep the officer in charge fully informed. He must report not only lights and whistles but any movement of vessels which may affect his own course. He reports occurrences and leaves the decision to the master.

The person on look-out should not leave his post even for a short time and in principle he must have no other duties to perform. In *"Horta Barbosa" (Owners)* v. *"Sea Star" (Owners), (The "Sea Star")*[3], the Court found that the second officer was negligent in going to the chartroom and remaining there for about six or

---

1. Willmer, J. in *The Anna Salen* (1952) 1 Lloyd's Rep. 475, at p.488. Karminski, J. in *The "Almizar"* (1969) 1 Lloyd's Rep. 1 requires in certain circumstances "extra look-outs" as a special precaution, while Brandon, J. in *The "Homer"* (1973) 1 Lloyd's Rep. 501 refers to bad aural and visual look-out. The obligation to keep a look-out may include a look-out astern. A vessel starting her propeller prior to going astern, must look to see whether there are vessels near her stern which may be endangered.
2. In *The British Confidence* (1951) 2 Lloyd's Rep. 615, the Court said (at p.621) that if the person on look-out was away from the bridge and preferably at the fore end of the ship, his attention would not be diverted.
3. (1976) 1 Lloyd's Rep. 115 at p.124.

seven minutes before the collision. He should have stayed in the wheelhouse or on the starboard wing of the bridge to watch the approach of the other vessels.

Notice on Look-out

M Notice 685 explains Rule 5 and specifies the requirement for maintaining a proper look-out.

"Every ship shall at all times maintain a proper look-out by sight and hearing as well as by all available means appropriate in the prevailing circumstances and conditions so as to make a full appraisal of the situation and of the risk of collision, stranding and other hazards to navigation. Additionally, the duties of the look-out shall include the detection of ships or aircraft in distress, shipwrecked persons, wrecks and debris. In applying these principles the following shall be observed:

(1) whoever is keeping a look-out must be able to give full attention to that task and no duties shall be assigned or undertaken which would interfere with the keeping of a proper look-out;

(2) the duties of the person on look-out and helmsman are separate and the helmsman should not be considered the person on look-out while steering; except in small vessels where an unobstructed all round view is provided at the steering position and there is no impairment of night vision or other impediment to the keeping of a proper look-out;

(3) there may be circumstances in which the officer of the watch can safely be the sole look-out in daylight. However, this practice shall only be followed after the situation has been carefully assessed on each occasion and it has been established without doubt that it is safe to do so. Full account shall be taken of all relevant factors including but not limited to the state of weather, conditions of visibility, traffic density, proximity of navigational hazards and if navigating in or near a traffic separation scheme.

Assistance must be summoned to the bridge when any change in the situation necessitates this and such assistance must be immediately available"[1].

---

1. Added by M. Notice 708.

Cases where bad look-out contributed to collision

There are many cases[1] where bad look-out contributed with other causes to collision. As Brandon, J. said in *The "Anneliese"*[2]: "It is right to observe, however, that in some cases the faults of bad look-out were not separate from the other faults but are bound up with them."

In *The "Statue of Liberty"*[3], the collision occurred on a fine, moonlit night, with excellent visibility. The Court said: "The Elder Brethren have advised me, first, that in the visibility prevailing the lights of the *Andulo* could have been seen at about seven miles and should have been watched from five miles onwards; and second, that the bearing of those lights should have been checked by compass as she approached. They advise me, third, that the radar should have been used to check the distance of the *Andulo* as she approached. There were two radar sets available for this purpose. I accept this advice. I find that the look-out on the *Statue of Liberty* was totally inadequate in all these respects."

In *The "Salaverry"*[4], the Court held that the speed of *Jamunda* was 7 knots at sighting and 6 knots at collision, and that of *Salverry* was 10 knots at sighting and collision. Both vessels were sounding fog signals, but neither heard those from the other vessel.

---

1. *The "Royalgate"* (1967) 1 Lloyd's Rep. 352; *The "Forest Lake"* (1967) 1 Lloyd's Rep. 171; *The "Lucille Bloomfield"* (1966) 2 Lloyd's Rep. 289, on appeal (1967) 1 Lloyd's Rep. 341; *The "Santander"* (1966) 2 Lloyd's Rep. 77; *The "Alletta"* and *The "England"* (1966) 1 Lloyd's Rep. 573; *Quinn and Others* v. *Associated Steamships Proprietary Ltd., (The "Woomera")* (1968) 2 Lloyd's Rep. 271 (N.S.W. Australia); *The "Dayspring"* (1968) 2 Lloyd's Rep. 204; *The "Ballylesson"* (1968) 1 Lloyd's Rep. 69; *The "Judith M"* (1968) 2 Lloyd's Rep. 474; *The West and Others* v. *Ritchie and Others (The "Convallaria")* (1969) 1 Lloyd's Rep. 328; *The "Almizar"* (1969) 1 Lloyd's Rep. 1; *The "Homer"* (1972) 1 Lloyd's Rep. 429, C.A., (1973) 1 Lloyd's Rep. 501; *The "Esso Brussels"* (1972) 1 Lloyd's Rep. 286, C.A., (1973) 2 Lloyd's Rep. 73; *The "Elazig"* (1972) 1 Lloyd's Rep. 355; *The "Adolf Leonhardt"* (1973) 2 Lloyd's Rep. 318; *The "Francesco Nullo"* (1973) 1 Lloyd's Rep. 72; *The "Toni"* (1973) 1 Lloyd's Rep. 79, (1974) 1 Lloyd's Rep. 489, C.A.; *The "Sabine"* (1974) 1 Lloyd's Rep. 465; *The "Savina"* (1974) 2 Lloyd's Rep. 317.
2. (1969) 2 Lloyd's Rep. 78 at p.92.
3. (1970) 2 Lloyd's Rep. 151, at pp.152, 159.
4. (1968) 1 Lloyd's Rep. 53.

Jamunda was to blame:

(a) for bad look-out:

(i) in not watching echo of *Salaverry*; and

(ii) in not hearing *Salaverry's* fog signals.

Salaverry was to blame:

(a) for bad look-out:

(i) she should have seen *Jamunda* on her radar and kept careful watch on her; and

(ii) she should have heard fog signals of *Jamunda* before sighting; and that as a result she was not aware of *Jamunda* until sighting.

In *The "Bovenkerk"*[1], the *Bovenkerk* was at fault because:

(a) her radar look-out was defective in that:

(i) $1\frac{1}{2}$ mile range should have been tried or the vessel should have been navigated with the limitation of $\frac{3}{4}$ mile range fully in mind;

(ii) a continuous watch should have been kept by one man;

(iii) the echo of *Antonio Carlos* should have been seen and identified earlier.

The *Antonio Carlos* was at fault:

(a) in her wrong appreciation of the V.H.F. information relating to *Bovenkerk*; and

(b) in failing to keep a radar look-out.

The conversation on the bridge could divert the attention of the man entrusted with the look-out and this was considered by Willmer, J. in *The British Confidence*[2]. The learned Judge said: "Too often, I am advised, a look-out who is posted on the bridge has his attention diverted, by hearing such conversations going on around him, from the things for which he ought to be looking. Any conversation he hears may very likely be with reference to lights which are observed, and, perhaps unconsciously,his attention may be diverted to the light, or lights, that he hears being talked about. If, on the other hand, he is away from the bridge - and preferably at the fore end of the ship - his attention is not so diverted, and there is nothing to prevent him

1. (1973) 1 Lloyd's Rep. 63.
2. (1951) 2 Lloyd's Rep. 615, at p.621.

keeping the sharp look-out which is expected of the man on duty, in a forward direction, in order he be able to see not only lights but also any other object which may be of interest to those in charge of the ship."

In *The "Tojo Maru"*[1] a collision occurred between the *Fina Italia* and the *Tojo Maru* at Mena al Ahmadi, Persian Gulf, at night.

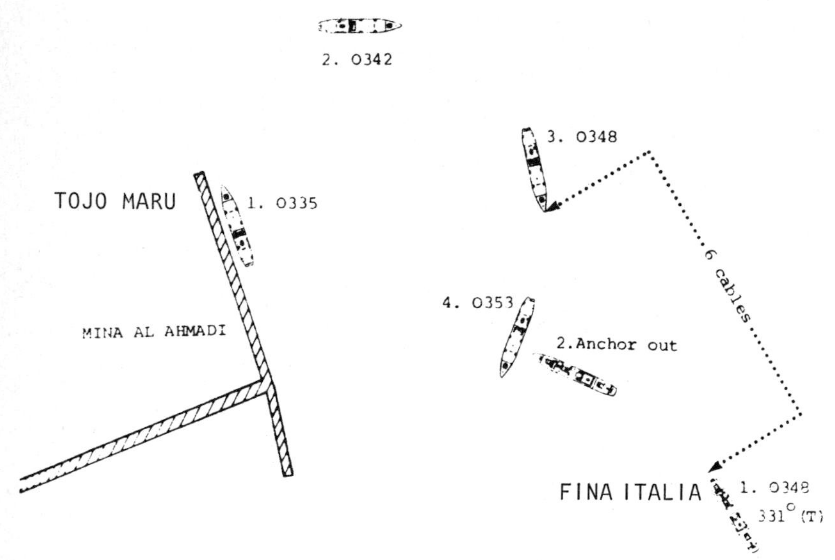

Fina Italia, with deck lights switched off, was proceeding on course of 331 deg., working up to full speed (12 knots), heading off North Pier where she was to berth. *Tojo Maru* was sighted leaving North Pier and drawing away to eastward opening her masthead lights and green light. At 03 42 hours *Fina Italia* reported her position to North Pier and reduced engines to half speed; shortly afterwards she altered course to port on heading for south end of pier. At 03 45 hours her engines were reduced to slow, at 03 47 hours to dead slow and at 03 48 hours to stop, *Tojo Maru* having drawn on to starboard bow showing her green and

1. (1968) 1 Lloyd's Rep. 365.

masthead lights open. Shortly afterwards *Fina Italia* sounded signal of two short blasts and put her wheel hard-a-port. *Tojo Maru* (then distant about six cables bearing about 35 deg. on starboard bow) replied with two short blasts but was seen to alter to starboard. *Fina Italia* put engines full astern and then emergency full astern and let go her starboard anchor. *Tojo Maru* came on across head of *Fina Italia* and collision occurred at 03 53 hours when *Fina Italia* was stopped in water.

It was held, by Willmer, L.J., (i) that, the principal cause of collision was bad look-out on part of both vessels; (ii) that *Fina Italia* failed to obey the crossing rules; (iii) that both vessels were at fault in respect of courses they were steering; (iv) that *Fina Italia* maintained her speed to the northward too long; (v) that *Tojo Maru* should have taken action to avert collision by putting engines full astern. As it was not possible to establish different degrees of fault, the Court held that both vessels were equally to blame.

In *The "Boleslaw Chrobry"*[1], the *Melide* was proceeding down the River Tagus in Lisbon harbour towards the sea. The *Boleslaw Chrobry* assisted by a tug shifted from a berth at the lower end of the Gara Maritima quay of Alcantara on the north side and turned in the river in order to go to an anchorage on the south side. The weather was overcast with rain showers from time to time. A collision occurred between the two vessels at 18 43, the stern of *Boleslaw Chrobry* coming into contact with the starboard side of *Melide* a little forward of midships. The angle of blow was between 90 deg. and 80 deg. leading forward on *Melide*. Serious damage was done to both vessels.

It was held, by Q.B. (Adm. Ct.) (Brandon, J.) that:

(1) *Boleslaw Chrobry* was not at fault in failing to see *Melide* when she herself left the jetty, for she had left when *Melide* was about 1½ miles away, and visibility was reduced by rain, and there were a number of other vessels anchored in the vicinity of *Melide* or up river of her; but she was at fault in not seeing *Melide* after she herself had embarked on the turning manoeuvre; for it was her duty to keep a good look-out for any vessel going down or coming up river;

(2) *Melide* was not at fault in altering course to port, for it was not unreasonable to expect that *Boleslaw Chrobry* would be aware of *Melide's* approach early enough to avoid collision by her own action alone, and *Melide* had reduced her speed which gave

---

1. (1974) 2 Lloyd's Rep. 308.

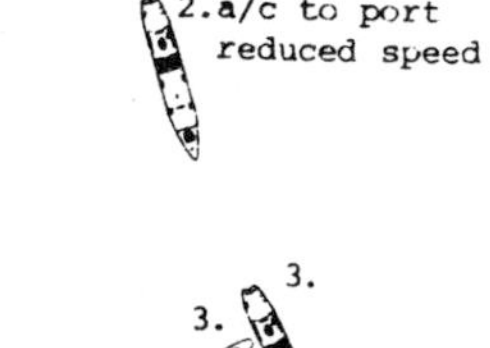

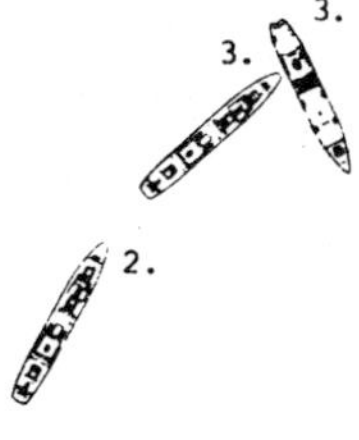

Boleslaw Chrobry more time in which to act; nor had she altered course to starboard at an improper time.

(3) *Boleslaw Chrobry* was solely to blame for the collision.

Rule 6 - *Safe Speed*

Every vessel shall at all times proceed at a safe speed so that she can take proper and effective action to avoid collision and be stopped within a distance appropriate to the prevailing circumstances and conditions.

In determining a safe speed the following factors shall be amongst those taken into account:

(a) By all vessels:

(i) the state of visibility;

(ii) the traffic density including concentrations of fishing vessels or any other vessels;

(iii) the manoeuvrability of the vessel with special reference to stopping distance and turning ability in the prevailing conditions;

(iv) at night the presence of background light such as from shore lights or from back scatter of her own lights;

(v) the state of wind, sea and current, and the proximity of navigation hazards;

(vi) the draught in relation to the available depth of water.

(b) Additionally, by vessels with operational radar:

(i) the characteristics, efficiency and limitations of the radar equipment;

(ii) any constraints imposed by the radar range scale in use;

(iii) the effect on radar detection of the sea state, weather and other sources of interference;

(iv) the possibility that small vessels, ice and other floating objects may not be detected by radar at an adequate range;

(v) the number, location and movement of vessels detected by radar;

(vi) the more exact assessment of the visibility that may be possible when radar is used to determine the range of vessels or other objects in the vicinity.

Meaning of "safe speed"

The term "safe speed" replaces the term "moderate speed". It is difficult to define "safe speed", but it refers to a speed which would not result in any risk to the vessel or to other vessels[1].

Safe speed cannot be measured in a number of knots. However, Rule 17 (a) (i) states "where by any of these Rules one of two

---

1. In a note dated February, 1970, presented from the Government of the United Kingdom to IMCO, safe speed is defined as "a speed such that at any distance a vessel can remove all her way through the water before reaching the collision point" (on file with the Author).

vessels is to keep out of the way the other shall *keep* her course and speed". As for speed in restricted visibility, Rule 19 (b) provides that "Every vessel shall proceed at a safe speed adapted to the prevailing circumstances and conditions of restricted visibility".

Thus, a speed in the open sea may well be unlawful in a crowded channel under similar circumstances. "Speed is clearly relative to the situation of the ship; what is proper at sea is ordinarily improper in a harbour and one harbour speed should differ from another. *The Jones* was moving into crowded waters; besides the *Sunco* and the tow, there were several small tugs thereabouts, and she was to pass within four or five hundred feet of a ferry slip from which at any time a ferry might emerge, and into which another was bound. At such a place and at such a time she was bound to hold herself in reserve against possible miscarriage on the part of any of these vessels"[1].

In *The Gilda*[2], a collision occurred in Suez Bay. As the *Naess Commander* was too late for the north-bound convoy, she proceeded at slow ahead (6 knots) through congested area to anchor. The *Gilda* was the first vessel in the north-bound convoy and was manoeuvring to get on her course. However, the *Naess Commander* was unable to pull up or alter course and consequently collision occurred. The Court found that the *Gilda* was guilty of excessive speed and bad look-out and the *Naess Commander* failed to take earlier astern action. Apportionment of blame: *Gilda* two-thirds and *Naess Commander* one-third.

In *The Mount Athos*[3], the collision occurred in the Dover Strait. The *St.Ronan* was the eastward bound vessel and was going on slow speed while the *Mount Athos* was westward bound and doing five knots. *St.Ronan* reduced her speed on hearing the fog signal of *Mount Athos* and her engines were put full astern when a further signal was heard. The vessels were sighted by each other at a distance of half a cable. The Court found that *Mount Athos* was alone to blame for excessive speed, bad look-out and failure to hear fog signals sounded by *St.Ronan*. *St.Ronan* was justified in not stopping her engine on hearing the fog signal as, being in a busy shipping lane, it would have been dangerous to lose steerage way[4].

Safe speed must be maintained at all times and in all conditions

---

1. *The George H. Jones* (1928) A.M.C. 1504.
2. (1961) 2 Lloyd's Rep. 286.
3. (1962) 1 Lloyd's Rep. 205.
4. *The Sitala* (1963) 1 Lloyd's Rep. 205.

of visibility[1]. It is no excuse for excessive speed that the vessel could not be kept under control by going at any less speed. Willmer, J.[2] said in such a case: "the vessel ought not to be under way at all."

Factors to be taken into account

Rule 6 states some of the important factors - which are not classified in any special order - which are to be taken into account:

(1) "the state of visibility";

(2) "the traffic density including concentrations of fishing vessels or any other vessels";

(3) "the manoeuvrability of the vessel with special reference to stopping distance and turning ability in the prevailing conditions". The manoeuvrability of the vessel depends on several considerations such as its size and the astern power. The words "prevailing conditions" cover the state of wind, wave directions and current and tidal conditions;

(4) "At night the presence of background light such as from shore lights or from back scatter of her own lights";

(5) "the state of wind, sea and current, and the proximity of navigational hazards";

(6) "the draught in relation to the available depth of water".

Vessels which have radars in working order[3] need in addition to the previous factors, to take into account:

(1) "The characteristics, efficiency and limitations of the radar equipment". This refers to the condition of the radar equipment, the types of display, plotting devices ... etc.

(2) "Any constraints imposed by the radar range scale in use". A constraint may be imposed on a particular range scale for a variety of reasons such as a strong radar, or electrical interference.

---

1. *The "Gannet"* (1967) 1 Lloyd's Rep. 97; *The "Eland"* and *The "Monte Urquiola"* (1969) 2 Lloyd's Rep. 328; *The "Francesco Nullo"* (1973) 1 Lloyd's Rep. 72; *The "Adolf Leonhardt"* (1973) 2 Lloyd's Rep. 318.
2. *The Sagacity* and *The Icemaid* (1948) 81 Ll.L.Rep. 237, at p.241.
3. The French text uses the words "en etat de marche", instead of the word "operational" in the English text. Thus, if a vessel has a radar "in proper working order" and fails to use it in the circumstances mentioned above, she will be in breach of this Rule. It should be emphasized that this Rule applies in clear weather as well as in restricted visibility.

(3) "The effect on radar detection of the sea state, weather and other sources of interference". This factor covers a situation where excessive noise, sea clutter, bad weather conditions or electrical interference may affect receiving the necessary information or may require additional time to obtain this information.

(4) "The possibility that small vessels, ice and other floating objects may not be detected by radar at an adequate range". This possibility could happen as a result of atmospheric conditions or of poor response from the object until a late stage in the encounter, leaving little time to avoid it.

(5) "The number, location and movement of vessels detected by radar". Time would be required to determine the actions of the various targets. Radar would also provide a more exact assessment of the situation than is possible in (2) above.

(6) "The more exact assessment of the visibility that may be possible when radar is used to determine the range of vessels or other objects in the vicinity". This is possible by observing the ranges at which the various ships or their lights become visible. Use in this way can also be of assistance in determining when "in *or near*" an area of restricted visibility especially at night.

In *The "Esso Brussels"*[1], a collision occurred between the *Aldebaran* and the *Esso Brussels* in the Antwerp Docks, in fog. Both vessels were engaged in moving from a Lock to discharging berths. It was necessary for them to proceed out of the lock, turn to starboard down a canal and proceed along the canal through the Lillo Bridge.

At 02 40 *Aldebaran* began leaving the lock (in good visibility), with two tugs fast ahead. One of those tugs was then secured aft, and *Aldebaran* put engine slow and dead slow ahead. By 03 20 fog had become dense; at 03 23, *Aldebaran* sounded three short blasts, put her engine full astern and let go both anchors. At 03 30 *Aldebaran* sounded a 10-second blast (attention signal under local rules).

Esso Brussels cleared the lock at 03 10 in good visibility with one tug forward and one tug in attendance. At 03 11 her engines were put half ahead; 03 12 engines full ahead; 03 17 half ahead; 03 18, second tug made fast aft. At 03 21 fog was seen, engines were put slow ahead and fog signal sounded. At 03 23½ her engines were put dead slow ahead; at 03 26 fog became dense and the engines were stopped, the after tug being ordered to pull astern. At 03 30 her engines were put full astern and port anchor let go. At 03 31½ lights of *Aldebaran* and her stern tug

---

1. (1972) 1 Lloyd's Rep. 286; on appeal (1973) 2 Lloyd's Rep. 73.

ALDEBARAN
Aldebaran
Anchored at 0323
one tug ahead and
one tug astern
attention signal at 0330

4. 0333
COLLISION

3. 0331½
Aldebaran and
tug sighted

2. 0330
Full astern
let go port anchor
ESSO BRUSSELS
1. 0326
Engines stopped
dense fog

were seen. At 03 33, port bow of *Esso Brussels* collided with starboard quarter of *Aldebaran* at an angle of four points leading forward on *Aldebaran*.

It was held by Brandon, J.:

(1) that *Esso Brussels* was not at fault in failing to prepare her anchor for letting go before encountering fog but she was at fault in (i) failing to appreciate that *Aldebaran* might have anchored before reaching Lillo Bridge; and (ii) failing to take off way, and anchor more quickly and earlier;

(2) that *Aldebaran* was not at fault in anchoring partially athwart the canal; but she was at fault for waiting until 03 30 before sounding attention signals, and such fault contributed to the collision.

Apportionment of blame: *Esso Brussels* 75 per cent.; *Aldebaran* 25 per cent.

On appeal by *Aldebaran* and cross-appeal by *Esso Brussels*, it was held that *Aldebaran's* failure to sound the signal would not have been causative because if *Esso Brussels* had heard such a signal she would have been more likely to gain the impression that *Aldebaran* was under way rather than stopped and anchored. Accordingly, the appeal was allowed and the cross-appeal dismissed. *Esso Brussels* held solely to blame.

Consequences of excessive speed

Brandon, J. in *The "Bovenkerk"*[1] summarised the consequences of excessive speed as follows: "... firstly, in creating or increasing the risk of collision, and secondly, in making damage worse if a collision occurs.

The excessive speed of the *Bovenkerk* means that the time available to both ships for hearing fog signals, making radar observations, obtaining V.H.F. information, and taking avoiding action, was reduced. It also means that, when a collision did take place, very serious damage was inflicted on the *Antonio Carlos*, as the photographs show."

Rule 7 - *Risk of Collision*

(a) Every vessel shall usc all available means appropriate to the prevailing circumstances and conditions to determine if risk of collision exists. If there is any doubt such risk shall be deemed to exist.

---

1. (1973) 1 Lloyd's Rep. 63, at p.72.

(b) Proper use shall be made of radar equipment if fitted and operational, including long-range scanning to obtain early warning of risk of collision and radar plotting or equivalent systematic observation of detected objects.

(c) Assumptions shall not be made on the basis of scanty information, especially scanty radar information.

(d) In determining if risk of collision exists the following considerations shall be among those taken into account:

(i) such risk shall be deemed to exist if the compass bearing of an approaching vessel does not appreciably change;

(ii) such risk may sometimes exist even when an appreciable bearing change is evident, particularly when approaching a very large vessel or a tow or when approaching a vessel at close range.

The Rule in paragraph (a) is mandatory requiring all vessels to be continuously aware of the risk of collision.

Paragraph (b) does not require vessels to carry radar, otherwise all vessels without radar might be condemned as unseaworthy. For many old vessels, the installation of radar may not be an economic viable proposition[1]. However, if a vessel is equipped with radar in working order, proper use, including early warning of collision risk on the longer range scales, shall be made of it.

---

1. When radar started to be used in merchant vessels, many shipowners were reluctant to install it on board their ships because they were not sure that the officers could use it properly. Also the argument that the presence of radar might give a "false sense of security" and undue reliance upon it was frequently raised in the past. In *The "Fogo"* (1967) 2 Lloyd's Rep. 208, Cairns, J. said (at p.221): "It is on men that safety at sea depends and they cannot make a greater mistake than to suppose that machines can do all their work for them."

In *The Sedgepool*[1] it was stated: "An instrument such as radar is supplied to be used, and I think its very possession does impose some additional duty on the vessel fortunate enough to be equipped with it."

In fact, the shipowner who voluntarily equipped his vessel with radar will assume greater liability in the event of collision than the one who did not provide the equipment. This is so because through the radar information the master of the vessel would have better appreciation of the situation at sea, and proceed more safely at a certain speed. Further, a vessel with an inoperative radar might be considered in law as one with no radar at all, unless the fault in the radar could be repaired by the crew during the voyage.

It must be noted that from April 1, 1976, all merchant vessels[2] registered in the United Kingdom over 1,600 ton gross, are required to carry an approved radar installation.

Scanty, in paragraph (c), covers an omission of a plot, an incomplete plot or a plot based on an insufficient number of observations. Errors in plotting can be due to a number of reasons such as; errors in bearings, errors in ranges; wrong estimation of the course or errors in the time of the plotting interval.

Paragraph (d) indicates that an appreciable change in bearing does not always indicate a safe passing.

---

1. (1956) 2 Lloyd's Rep. 668, at p.679; see also *The Nora* (1956) 1 Lloyd's Rep. 617. As for the shore radar station, Brandon,J. in *The Oldekerk* (1974) 1 Lloyd's Rep. 95 said (at p.97) that their function is "to receive and pass on information about... movements, positions and intentions" of the ships. As for the advice given by these stations, Hewson, J. in *The Vechtstroom* (1964) 1 Lloyd's Rep. 118 said: "... these facilities of radar advice are made and supplied and established for the greater safety of shipping in general and for greater accuracy in navigation... We can only presume that it was put there for a good purpose and to be used in such conditions as prevailed on that morning. A vessel which deliberately disregards such an aid when available is exposing not only herself, but other shipping to undue risks, that is, risks which with seamanlike prudence could and should be eliminated. As I see it, there is a duty upon shipping to use such aids when readily available - and when I say 'readily available' I am not saying instantly available - and if they elect to disregard such aids they do so at their own risk."
2. S.I. No. 302, 1976.

The use of radar for collision avoidance

M.626 states:

"(i) *Performance of the Radar:* The ability of the radar to display echoes at their maximum detection range is dependent on the overall quality of performance of the radar equipment. Users of radar are reminded that frequent checks of the radar performance should be made to ensure it has not deteriorated.

(ii) *Choice of Range Scales:* Although the choice of range scales for observation and plotting is dependent on several factors such as traffic density, speed of the observing ship and the frequency of observation, it is not generally advisable to commence plotting on short range scales. In any case advance warning of the approach of other vessels, or changes in traffic density, should be obtained by occasional use of the longer scales. This advice applies particularly when approaching areas of expected high traffic density when information obtained from the use of the longer range scales may be an important factor in deciding on a safe speed."

There is no obligation that the radar shall be used continually under all conditions, e.g. during daylight in clear weather. Karminski, J. said[1]: "there was no need to keep the radar switched on in the open sea in clear weather unless fog was anticipated." The use of radar is left to the discretion of the navigator and this seems to be an application of the rule of good seamanship. In fact, it would be better to approach this issue in a different way by saying that the radar shall be switched on all the time and the person on the look-out will have a glance at it from time to time. In certain circumstances, which are left to the discretion of the master, and which may be called the "circumstances test", there shall be a person on the radar watch.

Radar watch does not replace look-out but augments it: The use of radar does not replace look-out. In *The "Esso Wandsworth"*[2], the Court found that both the radar watch and the visual look-out were defective. Brandon, J. said[3]: "... it seems to me

---

1. *The Verena* (1960) 2 Lloyd's Rep. 286; (C.A.) (1961) 2 Lloyd's Rep. 127. In *The "Salaverry"* (1968) 1 Lloyd's Rep. 53, Brandon, J. said (at p.62): "The Elder Brethren advise me that, in their view, despite the difficulties of manning, a continuous radar watch ought to have been maintained. They point out that the passage down the Mersey Channel is not a very long one, and say that, while different considerations might apply at sea, in this channel, which is a busy one, a continuous watch ought to have been maintained."
2. (1970) 2 Lloyd's Rep. 303.
3. Ibid., at p.312.

clear that, if a good radar watch had been kept and the pilot kept informed of its result, the pilot would have been aware much earlier than he was that there was s ship coming up...towards him. In fact, as a result of erroneous observations by the third officer and the master, or through lack of communication between them and the pilot, or both, the pilot was not made aware of this fact until a little over a minute before the collision. In these circumstances it seems to me inescapable that the radar, as well as the visual look-out and appreciation of the Moerdyk, were defective."

Plotting: By plotting, the navigator could ascertain the course, speed and the closest point of approach of the other vessel[1]. M.517 states:

"To estimate the degree of risk of collision with another vessel it is necessary to forecast her nearest approach distance. Choice of appropriate avoiding action is facilitated by knowledge of the other vessel's course and speed, and one of the simplest methods of estimating these factors is by plotting. This involves knowledge of own ship's course and distance run during the plotting interval."

A mere glance at the radar screen will give limited information, mainly the direction (bearing) and distance (range) of the other vessels. Plotting must be carried out in good time in order to take an action to avoid the risk of collision. However, in certain circumstances, e.g. in a narrow channel crowded with vessels and when the bearings are continually changing, plotting may not be practical.

Cases on failure to use the radar properly

There are many reported cases[2] where the failure to use the radar properly or to interpret the information intelligently was among the reasons for the collision. In *The "Gannet"*[3], a collision occurred between the *Katharina Kolkmann* and the *Gannet* in the Dover Strait. Both vessels were on opposite courses and were proceeding at full speed. They were using radar, but *Gannet* was not plotting and *Katharina Kolkmann* ceased to plot at six miles range. *Katharina Kolkmann* was proceeding at 10 knots in rapidly

---

1. In *The "Ercole"* (1977) 1 Lloyd's Rep. 516, Brandon, J. said (at p.523): "... if piloting is necessary in order to enable a navigator to ascertain correctly the course of an approaching ship, then either he should make a plot, or he should not draw conclusions about the course of that ship which are unwarranted without one."
2. See *The Elazig* (1972) 1 Lloyd's Rep. 355.
3. (1967) 1 Lloyd's Rep. 97.

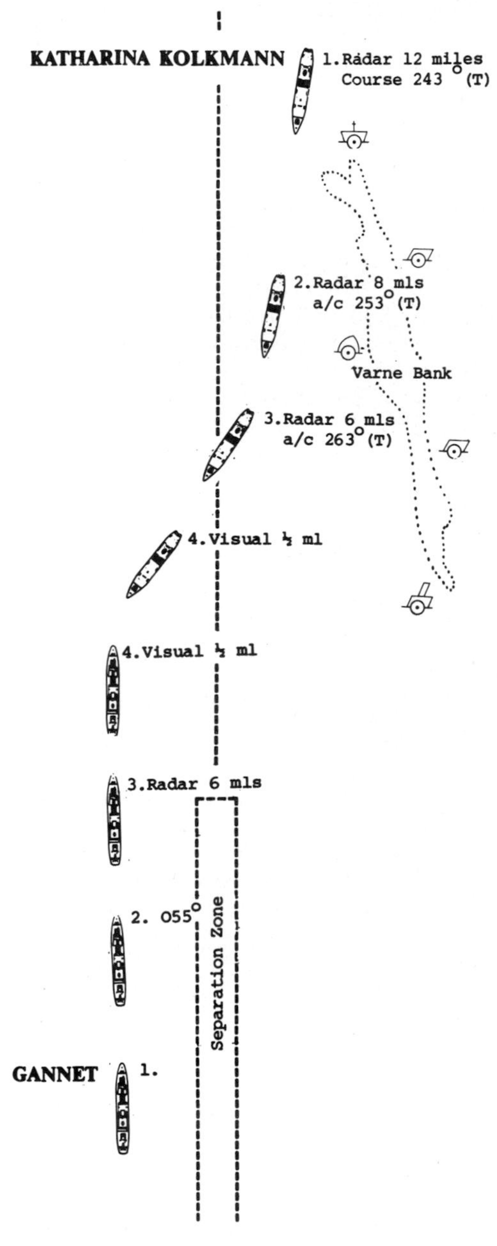
KATHARINA KOLKMANN
1.Radar 12 miles
Course 243° (T)
2.Radar 8 mls
a/c 253° (T)
Varne Bank
3.Radar 6 mls
a/c 263° (T)
4.Visual ½ ml
4.Visual ½ ml
3.Radar 6 mls
2. 055°
Separation Zone
GANNET
1.

deteriorating visibility. She observed echo of *Gannet* on her radar at 12 miles on her port bow. When *Gannet's* echo was at eight-mile range, *Katharina Kolkmann* went 10 deg. to starboard and about six minutes later, when *Gannet* closed to six miles, *Katharina Kolkmann* altered course further 10 deg. to starboard. *Gannet*, on automatic steering, was proceeding, in dense fog, at 11½ knots. *Katharina Kolkmann* was observed on *Gannet's* radar about 7½ deg. on starboard bow, at distance of six miles (after *Katharina Kolkmann's* alterations to course). The vessels sighted each other at under half a mile. *Gannet* collided with *Katharina Kolkmann* at about a right angle, and *Katharina Kolkmann* sank.

It was held, by Karminski, J., that both vessels were equally to blame. They failed to use their radars properly, in that they did not plot at less than six miles. The court added[1]: "The main difficulty in this case arises from the use, or the misuse, of the radar. Neither side plotted their radar after six miles.. plotting radar is the safest way of observing the bearing of an approaching vessel, in a sense watching the compass to check the bearing; and that duty is in no way abrogated by the use of radar, which is an extra eye when watching by eye is ineffective or only partly effective."

In *The "Bovenkerk"*[2], a collision occurred in fog, between the *Antonio Carlos* and the *Bovenkerk* in the River Elbe. The tide was ebb of a force of 1½-2 knots.

Antonio Carlos, with engines at dead slow ahead, was on an up-river course of 101 deg. (true) with her radar on the three-mile range. The pilot of *Antonio Carlos* had heard on V.H.F. that *Bovenkerk* was coming down river. The *Bovenkerk* was proceeding on a course of 270 deg. (true) at about 8½-9 knots. Her V.H.F. was ineffective and her radar was on ¾ mile range. She was approaching a dredger which was moored slightly to the north of mid-channel and which was indicating signals that the fairway to the north was closed and that ships passing either way should do so to the south. *Antonio Carlos* altered to 105 deg. (true) and reduced to "slow ahead". She then heard, on her V.H.F., that *Bovenkerk* was about to pass the dredger and ordered her engines "stop". The masthead lights and green of *Bovenkerk* were seen bearing about 15-20 deg. on the port bow distant about one cable. *Antonio Carlos* ordered engines "full astern", but a collision occurred.

---

1. Ibid., at p.102. Both vessels were also at fault for excessive speed. They relied upon their radar and took very little notice of the fog.
2. (1973) 1 Lloyd's Rep. 63.

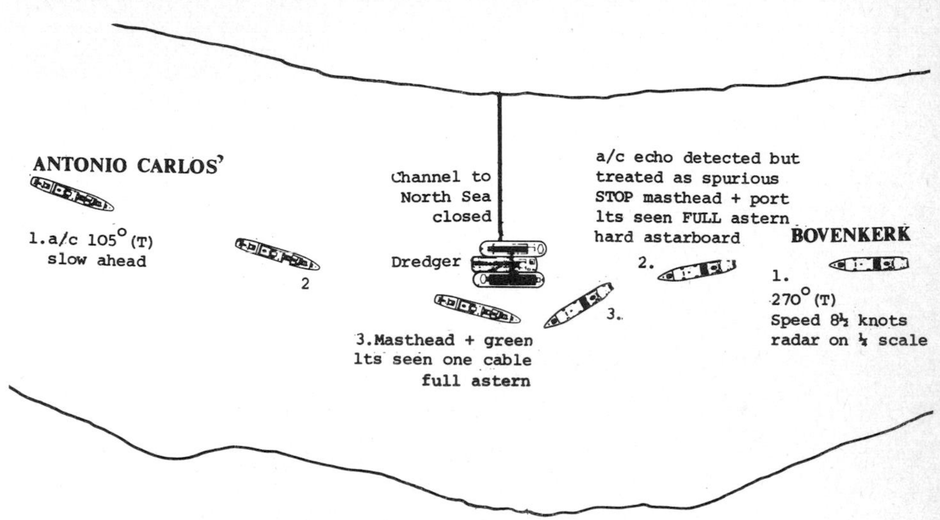

It was held by Brandon, J.

(A) that *Bovenkerk* was at fault because

(1) her radar look-out was defective in that (a) 1½ mile range should have been tried or the vessel should have been navigated with the limitation of ¾ mile range fully in mind; (b) a continuous watch should have been kept by one man; (c) the echo of *Antonio Carlos* should have been seen and identified earlier;

(2) she was proceeding at excessive speed;

(3) she should have passed the dredger on a direct down-river course.

(B) *Antonio Carlos* was at fault

(1) in her wrong appreciation of the V.H.F. information relating to the *Bovenkerk*;

(2) in failing to keep a radar look-out;

(3) in proceeding up river at the narrow angle which she did.

Apportionment of blame: *Bovenkerk* 60 per cent.; *Antonio Carlos* 40 per cent.

The collision in *The "Hagen"*[1] resulted in a loss of life of seventeen of the crew of the *Boulgaria*. Both the *Hagen* and the *Boulgaria* were proceeding at an average speed of 11½ knots even when the fog thickened.

The *Boulgaria* was proceeding on a course of 244 deg. (true) and sounding fog signals, while the *Hagen* was on a course of 071 deg. (true) and with engines at full ahead. She was making about 12 knots through the water and sounding fog signals.

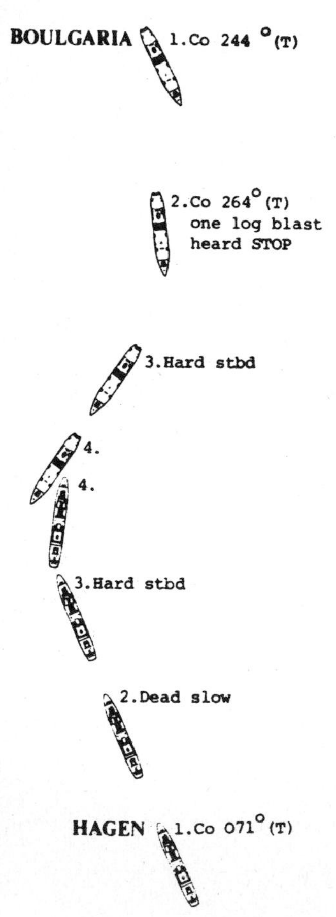

The radar echo of the *Hagen* was observed on the port bow of the *Boulgaria* and was watched. The course of *Boulgaria* was altered to 264 deg. (true) by two successive alterations of 10 deg. When a single prolonged blast was heard on *Boulgaria's* port bow, her engines were immediately stopped. Two more single prolonged blasts were heard and *Hagen* was first sighted distant one to two cables. *Boulgaria's* helm was put hard-a-starboard. *Hagen* came on at speed and with her stem and port bow struck *Boulgaria's* port side aft at an angle of 75 deg. leading aft on *Boulgaria*.

The *Hagen's* case was that *Boulgaria* was seen distant about two cables and bearing about three points on the starboard bow with *Boulgaria* on a north-west heading swinging to starboard to cross ahead of *Hagen*. *Hagen's* wheel was immediately put to starboard and her engines were ordered dead

1. (1973) 1 Lloyd's Rep. 257.

slow astern and then full astern. *Boulgaria* continued across *Hagen's* head and *Boulgaria's* port side in way of her engine-room struck *Hagen's* stem at between 50 deg. and 90 deg. leading aft on *Boulgaria*.

It was held, by Brandon, J. that:

the *Hagen* was to blame for excessive initial speed in fog; and this fault was one of the main causes of the collision;

the *Boulgaria* was at fault for she was guilty of bad radar look-out and appreciation; excessive speed and failure to take off way when the fog thickened and *Hagen* approached; and going hard to starboard before sighting.

Apportionment of blame: *Boulgaria* 60 per cent.; *Hagen* 40 per cent.

In *The "Salaverry"*[1], a collision occurred in fog in the Mersey Channel, between *Jamunda* and *Salaverry*. Both vessels were in the charge of pilots. *Jamunda* was proceeding at half speed, in visibility of about half a mile and sounding fog signals. Her radar was at three-mile range, but no continuous watch was being kept. Echo of *Salaverry* was observed at two miles range. At 22 06 hours, *Jamunda* reduced speed to dead slow ahead and echo of *Salaverry* was seen at one mile. *Jamunda* was then under 10 deg. starboard wheel to round bend in channel. *Jamunda's* wheel was put hard-a-starboard. At 22 08 hours, two masthead lights and green light of *Salaverry* were sighted fine on port bow, at distance of half a mile. Pilot of *Jamunda* maintained course and speed, expecting *Salaverry* to alter course to starboard. At 22 09 hours, pilot of *Jamunda* put engines emergency full astern and sounded series of three-short-blasts signals. Two-short-blasts signal was heard from *Salaverry*. Collision occurred about 45 seconds later.

The *Salaverry's* case was that at 22 01 hours she was proceeding down river at half ahead, sounding fog signals, and with her radar switched to one-mile range in order to pick up buoys. *Salaverry* was rounding bend in channel to port. At 22 08 hours, two masthead lights and red light of *Jamunda* were sighted by *Salaverry*, one point on starboard bow, at distance of four cables. Pilot of *Salaverry* put engines to dead slow ahead and one long blast was sounded. At 22 09 hours engines were put full ahead, and wheel hard-a-port and two short blasts were sounded. Collision occurred between stem of *Jamunda* and starboard side of *Salaverry* at about a right angle in southern half of channel (*Salaverry's wrong water*). Both vessels contended that the other

---

1. (1968) 1 Lloyd's Rep. 53.

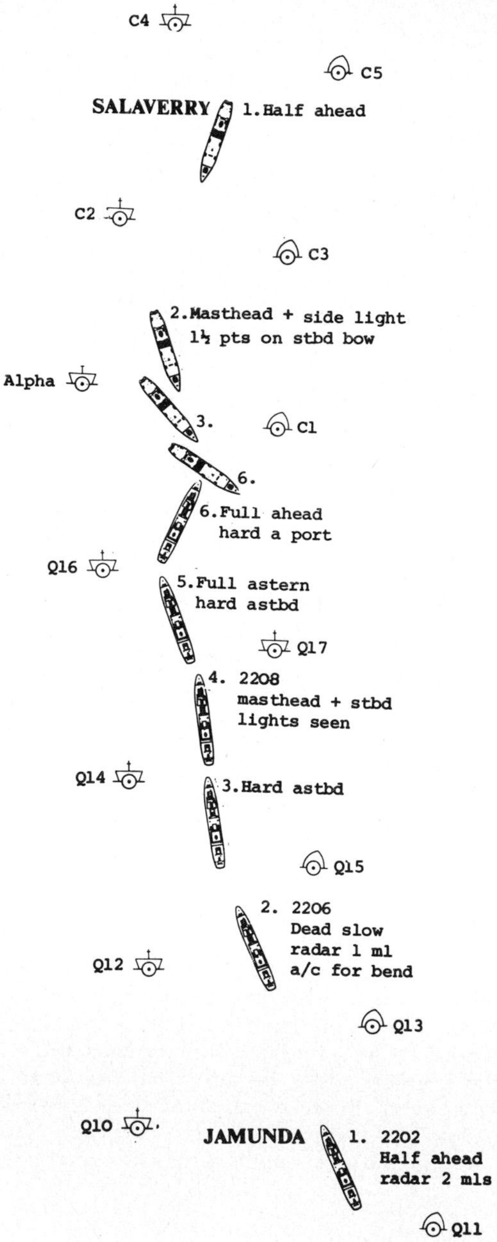

C4

C5

SALAVERRY 1.Half ahead

C2

C3

2.Masthead + side light
1½ pts on stbd bow

Alpha

3.

C1

6.

6.Full ahead
hard a port

Q16

5.Full astern
hard astbd

Q17

4. 2208
masthead + stbd
lights seen

Q14

3.Hard astbd

Q15

2. 2206
Dead slow
radar 1 ml
a/c for bend

Q12

Q13

Q10

JAMUNDA 1. 2202
Half ahead
radar 2 mls

Q11

was proceeding at excessive speed on her wrong side of channel.

It was held, by Brandon, J., that *Jamunda* was to blame (a) for bad look-out (i) in not watching echo of *Salaverry*; and (ii) in not hearing *Salaverry's* fog signals; (b) in proceeding at excessive speed in fog (three knots would have been a proper speed); (c) in not keeping to her starboard side of channel (she took bend in channel too wide); (d) in not taking proper action on sighting (she delayed one minute before reversing her engines); that *Salaverry* was to blame (a) for bad look-out (i) she should have seen *Jamunda* on her radar and kept careful watch on her; and (ii) she should have heard fog signals of *Jamunda* before sighting; and that in the result she was not aware of *Jamunda* until sighting; (b) in failing to navigate on her starboard side of channel (pilot was cutting corner in belief that nothing was coming up channel); (c) in proceeding at excessive speed in fog (a proper speed would have been three knots); (d) in taking wrong emergency action after sighting (she should have gone hard-a-starboard and full astern immediately).

Apportionment of blame: *Jamunda* one-third; *Salaverry* two-thirds.

In *The "Linde"*[1], a collision occurred between *Aristos* and *Linde*, in fog, in the English Channel. *Aristos's* case was that she was proceeding on course of 243 deg. (true) at stand-by half ahead (6.5 knots) and was sounding fog signals. Echo of *Linde* was observed distant just under 4 miles and bearing about 10 deg. on starboard bow. *Linde* appeared to be on opposite and parallel course shaping to pass starboard to starboard at about ¾ mile. Thereafter echo of *Linde* disappeared in clutter on radar screen which extended to range of about ¾ mile. One prolonged blast was heard from *Linde*, close on starboard beam. Engines of *Aristos* were stopped. Afterwards *Aristos* sounded 2 prolonged blasts. Thereafter masthead and green lights of *Linde* were seen emerging from fog just abaft starboard beam. *Linde* came on and with her stem struck starboard side of *Aristos* at a right angle. *Aristos* subsequently sank. *Linde's* case was that she was on course of 078 deg. (true) at full ahead (12 knots) and was sounding fog signals. Echo of *Aristos* was observed distant 12 miles and bearing about 6 deg. on port bow. *Aristos* appeared to be on opposite and parallel course. Bearing of echo broadened. When echo was distant 4 miles bearing 15 deg. to 20 deg. on port bow, *Aristos* appeared to alter course to port. *Linde's* engines were stopped. No signals were heard from *Aristos*. *Aristos* came into sight showing masthead and green lights, distant about ¾ mile bearing about 30 deg. on port bow, apparently heading 200 deg. (true) but

1. (1969) 2 Lloyd's Rep. 556.

swinging to port. *Linde's* engines were put full astern and helm hard-a-starboard. *Aristos* continued to swing to port and brought her starboard side into contact with stem of *Linde* at angle of 70 deg. leading forward on *Aristos*. Both vessels contended that the other was negligent in (*inter alia*) failing to make proper use of radar, proceeding at excessive speed and altering course at an improper time.

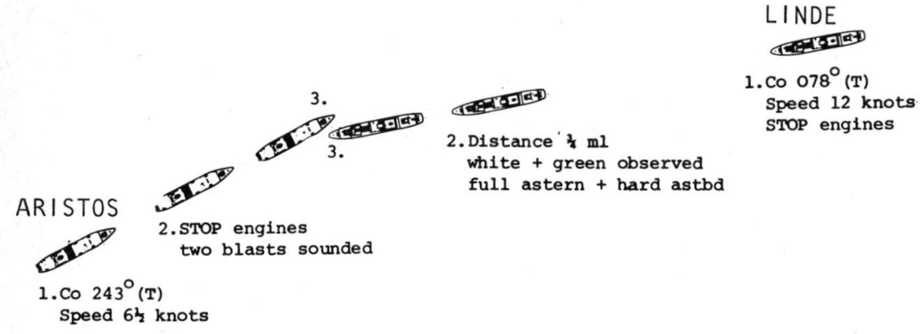

It was held by, Brandon, J. that both vessels were at fault in respect of radar look-out and appreciation. They were also proceeding at an excessive speed. The Court said that:[2]

"The fault on both sides was the same, namely, assuming that the approaching ship was on an opposite and parallel course, when the taking of bearings of the echo at proper intervals would have shown that she was on a crossing course.

As regards alteration of course, I have found that both ships altered about the same time and about the same amount. It was argued for the defendants that the *Linde* was in better case because she altered to starboard rather than to port. I cannot see this. I have been advised by the Elder Brethren that any alteration of course at the time made, namely, before sighting, and without the course of the other ship having been properly ascertained, was unseamanlike. It was an alteration blind, in their view. I accept that advice. I cannot see that there is any significant difference between the two ships in this respect."

---

1. Ibid., at p.568.

Rule 8 - *Action to avoid Collision*

(a) Any action taken to avoid collision shall, if the circumstances of the case admit, be positive, made in ample time and with due regard to the observance of good seamanship.

(b) Any alteration of course and/or speed to avoid collision shall if the circumstances of the case admit, be large enough to be readily apparent to another vessel observing visually or by radar; a succession of small alterations of course and/or speed should be avoided.

(c) If there is sufficient sea room, alteration of course alone may be the most effective action to avoid a close-quarters situation provided that it is made in good time, is substantial and does not result in another close-quarters situation.

(d) Action taken to avoid collision with another vessel shall be such as to result in passing at a safe distance. The effectiveness of the action shall be carefully checked until the other vessel is finally past and clear.

(e) If necessary to avoid collision or allow more time to assess the situation, a vessel shall slacken her speed or take all way off by stopping or reversing her means of propulsion.

As mentioned before, the rule of ordinary care and prudence applies to all vessels, irrespective of their size or the nature of their employment. When a course of action has been determined, it should be taken decisively and without any hesitation. Such course[1] must also be effective.

The "Bonifaz"[2] is a good illustration of a collision which was caused by a series of errors which could have been avoided. In this case, a collision occurred between the *Fabiola* and the *Bonifaz* in fog off Cape Finisterre. *Fabiola* was proceeding at full speed (16•2 knots) on course of 2 deg. (true) in visibility of five miles. At 20 20 hours radar was switched on and at 20 40 hours course was changed to North (true). At 21 40 hours, as dusk fell, "stand by" was ordered. At 21 54 hours, echo of *Bonifaz* was plotted by *Fabiola's* first officer as bearing 4 deg. (true) at eight miles. At 22 00 hours *Bonifaz* was plotted as bearing 7 deg. (true) at 4•9 miles, approaching at an estimated speed of 13 knots. At 22 06 hours, *Bonifaz* was plotted as bearing 14 deg. at 2 miles. Master of *Fabiola* ordered engines to be

---

1. Course does not mean "course by compass, but the action of the vessel". See *The Bellanoch* (1907) P. 170 at p.182.
2. (1967) 1 Lloyd's Rep. 321.

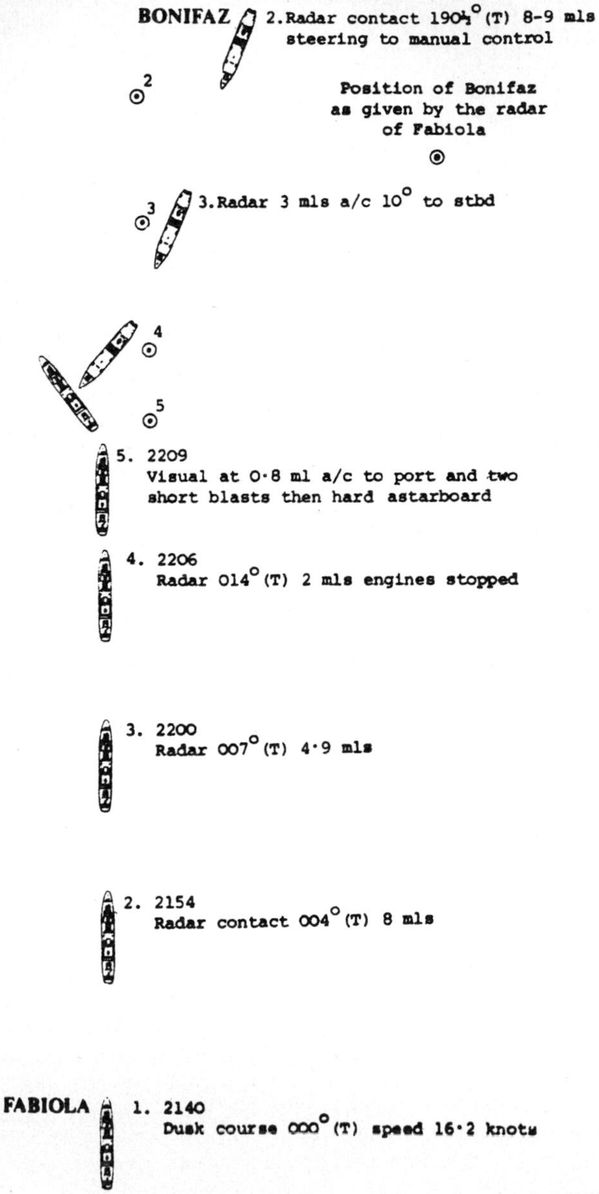

BONIFAZ

2. Radar contact 190½$^\circ$(T) 8-9 mls
steering to manual control

2

Position of Bonifaz
as given by the radar
of Fabiola

3

3. Radar 3 mls a/c 10° to stbd

4

5

5. 2209
Visual at 0·8 ml a/c to port and two
short blasts then hard astarboard

4. 2206
Radar 014°(T) 2 mls engines stopped

3. 2200
Radar 007°(T) 4·9 mls

2. 2154
Radar contact 004°(T) 8 mls

FABIOLA

1. 2140
Dusk course 000°(T) speed 16·2 knots

stopped but made no change of course. Shortly before 22 09 hours, first officer reported that *Bonifaz* was at just over a mile range and falling to starboard. At 22 09 hours, *Fabiola* sighted *Bonifaz* at range of 8 cables. *Fabiola* altered course to port, sounding two short blasts and receiving reply of one short blast from *Bonifaz*. Very shortly afterwards, *Fabiola's* master ordered hard-a-starboard. Collision occurred between stem of *Bonifaz* and starboard side of *Fabiola* at about a right angle. The *Bonifaz* case was that she was proceeding on a course of 196 deg. At 19 30 hours visibility deteriorated and radar was switched on. Echo of *Fabiola* was first observed at 8 to 9 miles bearing 5 to 6 deg. to port, and *Bonifaz's* steering was changed from automatic to manual. At three miles range, *Bonifaz* altered course 10 deg. to starboard. Speed of *Bonifaz* was reduced a few minutes before collision.

It was held, by Cumming-Bruce, J. that both vessels were to blame. The master of *Bonifaz*: (1) although relying on radar was not using it properly; (2) that he was proceeding at excessive speed in limited visibility; (3) that his alteration to starboard at 3 miles range was likely to mislead and materially contributed to dangerous situation; (4) that that alteration was also dangerous in that it was across bows of *Fabiola* and was due to master's failure to plot radar observation; and (5) that it would be a narrow view to focus much attention on terminal stage of a collision which was caused by error of navigation over a period of time.

Fabiola's master was negligent in not reducing speed or altering course to port during the period from 22 00 hours to 22 06 hours. He also made a serious error of navigation by turning to port and even though that error was made in an unexpected situation, which was itself partly caused by his own error.

Apportionment of blame: *Bonifaz* three-fifths and *Fabiola* two-fifths.

In *The "Martin Fierro"*[1], a collision occurred between the *Joaquin Ponte Naya* and the *Martin Fierro* in the River Parana. At about 19 10 when the vessels were 1400 metres apart, the order "hard to starboard" was given by those on board *Joaquin Ponte Naya*. At about the same time those on board *Martin Fierro* first saw her green light in addition to her red. At about 19 11½, when the vessels were about 700 metres apart, those on board *Martin Fierro* having lost sight of the red light of *Joaquin Ponte Naya*, and

---

1. (1974) 2 Lloyd's Rep. 203.

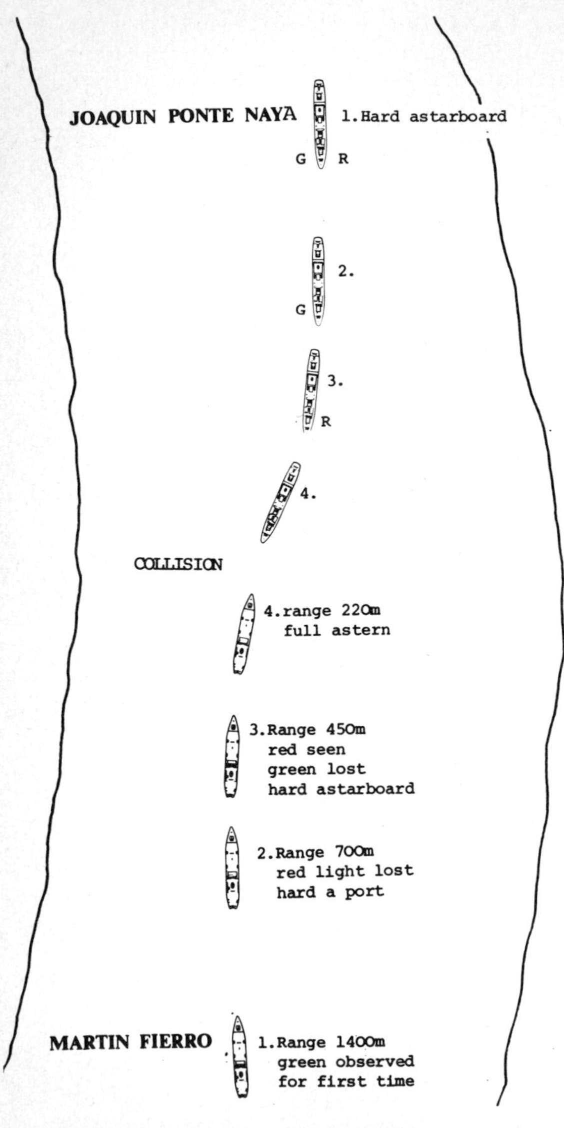

being able to see only her green, gave the order "hard to port" and sounded two short blasts. At 19 12 when the vessels were 400 to 500 metres apart, those on board *Martin Fierro*, having seen the red light of *Joaquin Ponte Naya* open again and the green light shut in, gave the order "hard to starboard" and sounded a signal of one short blast. At 19 12½, when the vessels were about 200 to 250 metres apart, those on board *Martin Fierro* gave the orders "wheel amidships" and "full astern". A collision occurred at 19 13, when *Joaquin Ponte Naya's* speed through the water was 6 knots, whilst that of *Martin Fierro* was 8 to 9 knots. The stem and port bow of *Martin Fierro* struck the port side of *Joaquin Ponte Naya* at an angle of 35 degrees leading aft.

It was held by Q.B.D. (Adm.Ct.) (Brandon, J.) that:

(1) *Joaquin Ponte Naya* was at fault in (i) navigating on the wrong side of the channel contrary to the local rules of navigation and the Collision Rules; and (ii) failing to sound one short blast when altering course to starboard.

(2) *Martin Fierro* was at fault in (i) not reducing speed as a situation of increasing danger developed ahead of her; and

(ii) putting her wheel hard to port in the face of an up coming vessel without sufficient evidence of her intentions; and although it had not been shown that a collision could have been avoided, it was possible that it would have been if *Martin Fierro* had taken the necessary action.

(3) *Joaquin Ponte Naya* was very much more at fault than *Martin Fierro*.

Apportionment of blame: *Joaquin Ponte Naya* 85 per cent.; *Martin Fierro* 15 per cent[1].

The British Aviator[2] is a case well known for actions which would have avoided the collision. In this case, a collision occurred between the *Crystal Jewel* and the *British Aviator*, in fog, in the English Channel.

Crystal Jewel's case was that while she was proceeding at half speed (7 knots) on course of 060 deg. (true), she observed *British Aviator* and other vessels on her radar. She then altered course, 5 deg. to starboard, and when bearing of *British Aviator* narrowed to 10 deg. she altered her course a further 5 deg. to starboard. At the range of 3½ miles, further alterations of course amounting to 15 deg. to starboard were made and *Crystal Jewel* was then heading 085 deg. The echo of *British Aviator* disappeared at the range of 3 miles, 8 deg. on port bow. Fog signals were heard on the port beam of *Crystal Jewel* which maintained her course and speed. When *British Aviator* was sighted at a distance of 300 to 400 ft. and 80 to 90 deg. on port bow, avoiding actions were taken but they were unsuccessful.

British Aviator's case was that she was proceeding on course of 229 deg. (true) at half speed (9½ knots). She observed *Crystal Jewel* on her radar at a distance of 10 miles, bearing 9 deg. on starboard bow. The first mate reported that *Crystal Jewel* was 30 deg. on starboard bow at a range of 2 miles. Fog signals were heard. Louder fog signals were again heard and a hard-a-port wheel action was ordered. 30 seconds later, *Crystal Jewel* was

---

1. Appeal by the Owners of Martin Fierro and a cross-appeal by the Owners of *Joaquin Ponte Naya* were dismissed, (1975) 2 Lloyd's Rep. 130. The Court of Appeal said that in addition to the faults found by the trial Judge, *Joaquin Ponte Naya* was at fault: in deviating to port; and in going hard to starboard. *Martin Fierro* was at fault for failing to alter course to starboard before *Joaquin Ponte Naya* opened her green light.
2. (1964) 2 Lloyd's Rep. 403.

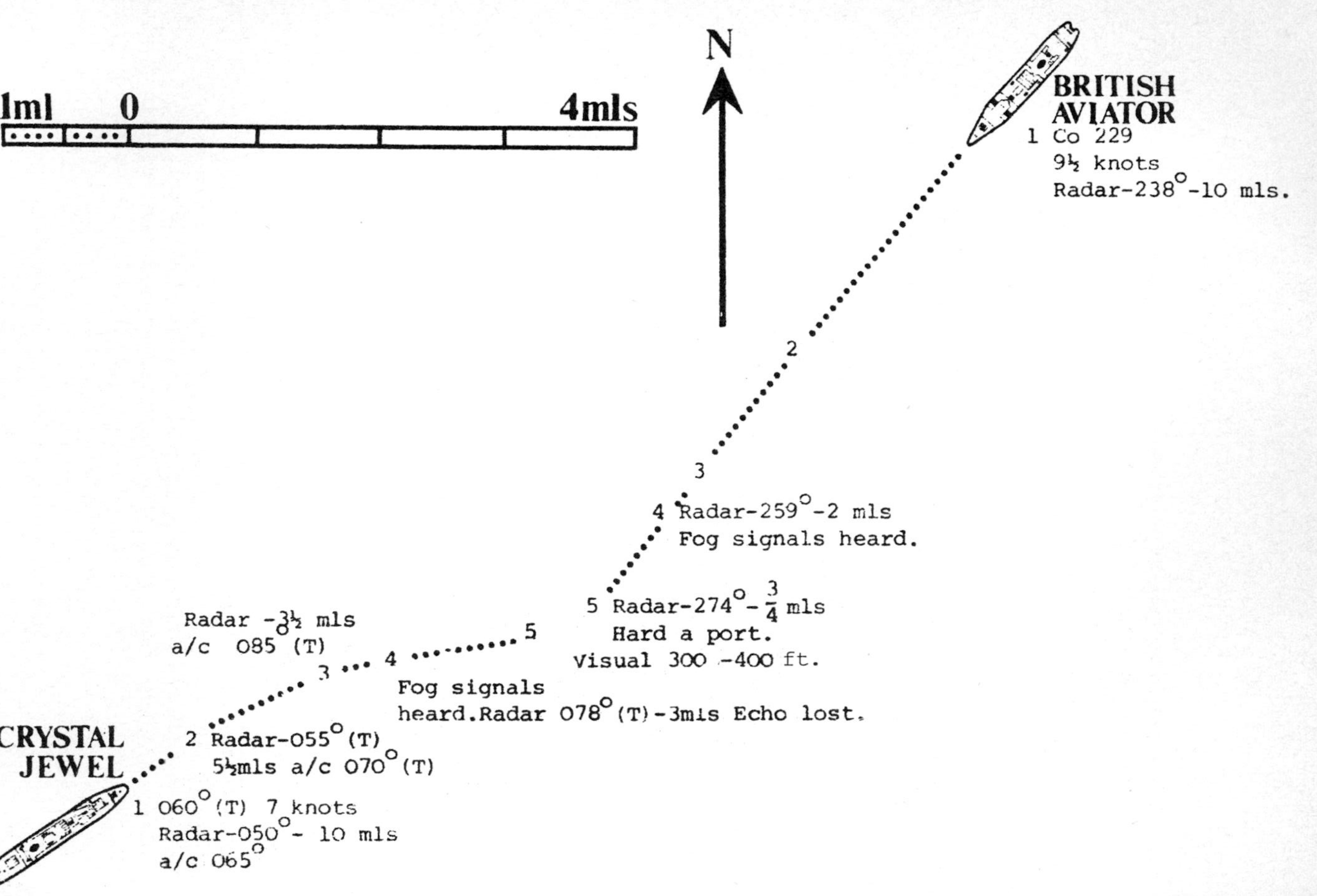
1ml
0
4mls
N
BRITISH AVIATOR
1 Co 229
9½ knots
Radar-238°-10 mls.
2
3
4 Radar-259°-2 mls
Fog signals heard.
5 Radar-274°-¾ mls
Hard a port.
Visual 300 -400 ft.
Radar -3½° mls
a/c 085 (T)
3
4
5
Fog signals
heard.Radar 078°(T)-3mls Echo lost.
CRYSTAL JEWEL
2 Radar-055°(T)
5½mls a/c 070°(T)
1 060°(T) 7 knots
Radar-050°- 10 mls
a/c 065°

sighted 60 ft. from the stem of the *British Aviator* and the collision occurred at about a right angle.

It was held by Cairns, J. that both vessels were in breach of principles of good seamanship and they were to blame in that they used the radar information as if it were visual information and as an excuse for maintaining speed. The alterations of course by *Crystal Jewel* were bad navigation, but *British Aviator* was more seriously negligent in altering course to port.

Apportionment of blame: *Crystal Jewel,* two-fifths; *British Aviator,* three-fifths.

On appeal, the Court held[1]:

(1) that, in addition to faults, common to both vessels, found by the trial Judge, there was the further fault of bad look-out in that neither vessel was interpreting correctly her radar information;

(2) that the *Crystal Jewel's* alteration of course was not only more blameworthy than Judge thought, but also had more causative effect in bringing about collision than any other single factor; that there was no good ground for differentiating between vessels; and that, therefore, liability should be apportioned equally.

Again, in *The Nassau*[2], a collision occurred in the Atlantic Ocean off New Jersey, at night, in a blizzard with limited visibility, between *Brott* and *Nassau*. Both vessels were using their radars; the first on an 8-mile ranger and the latter on a 3-mile range.

The *Haminella* was first seen ahead on *Brott's* radar at a distance of two miles on starboard bow and then visually seen at a distance of about ¾ mile, 5 deg. on starboard bow. The *Haminella* successfully passed, although no signal was sounded. *Nassau* was sighted by *Brott* at a distance of 100 yards heading for her bridge.

Nassau contended that when the green light of *Brott* was sighted 60 deg. on port bow, it was realised that *Brott* was starboarding.

The Court held that *Brott* was to blame for her failure to manoeuvre in relation to *Nassau* and for her excessive starboarding without signal. *Nassau* was also to blame for excessive speed, in particular as she was on short-range scale on the radar and

1. (1965) 1 Lloyd's Rep. 271.
2. (1964) 2 Lloyd's Rep. 509.

for inadequate look-out.

Apportionment of blame: *Brott*, two-fifths and *Nassau*, three-fifths.

Rule 8 in fact stresses that an alteration of course[1], when there is sufficient sea room, may be the most effective action to avoid a close quarters situation. Such alteration must be made in good time, substantial and would not result in another close quarters situation.

Close quarters situation

It is very difficult to define a close quarters situation. However, its existence[2] depends on many factors, such as the weather conditions, state of visibility, type of vessel, manoeuvrability and whether observations are carried out by visual means or by radar. In *The "Rattray Head"/"Tillerman"*[3], the Court of Inquiry said: "When vessels are approaching each other in restricted visibility in circumstances similar to those of this case and in which an exact appreciation of the course of an approaching vessel has not been made before it is desired to take action to avoid a close quarters situation, an alteration of course of 20° cannot be regarded as substantial action to avoid a close quarters situation ... The court does not feel that it would be advisable to try to lay down any specific figure which would be regarded as substantial in all circumstances ... because such circumstances inevitably vary, but in circumstances similar to those of this case, any alteration of course made under this Rule must be very much greater than 20°. It follows from this that if because of lack of sea room, the presence of other vessels, or any other reason an alteration of the necessary degree cannot safely be made, the echo of the approaching vessel must be closely watched, plots should be made and any person necessary to assist in this must be summoned to the bridge...".

The "Anneliese"[4] is another good illustration of manoeuvres which

---

1. Thus, an alteration of course is generally more effective than an alteration in speed, since it is quick to take effect; and is easily observed both visually and on radar.
2. A close quarters situation may arise when it becomes no longer possible for one ship, acting alone, to avoid the other ship by making a substantial alteration of course.
3. The findings of the Court of Inquiry were published by the Mercantile Marine Service Association, June 1970.
4. (1969) 2 Lloyd's Rep. 78; on Appeal (1970) 1 Lloyd's Rep. 355. See also *The Verena* (1960) 2 Lloyd's Rep. 386; C.A. (1961) 2 Lloyd's Rep. 127.

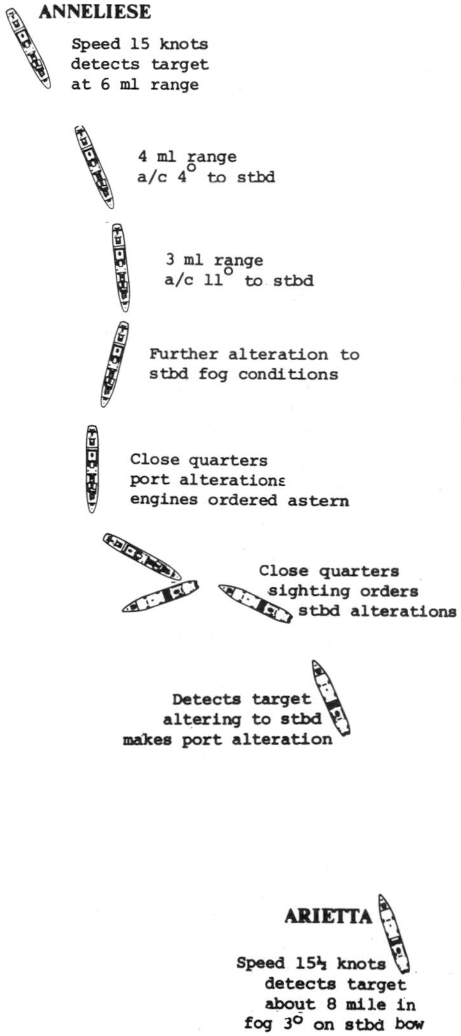

led to a close quarters situation. In this case, a collision occurred in the English Channel between *Arietta* and *Anneliese*. *Arietta's* case was that visibility was restricted by fog to three-quarters to one mile and she was sounding regulation signals. Her relative motion radar was on eight miles range and the echo of *Anneliese* was seen distant about eight miles bearing 5 deg. on the starboard bow. A little later, when *Arietta* saw that *Anneliese* had altered to starboard, *Arietta's* wheel was put hard-a-port. *Arietta* saw *Anneliese* visually distant a quarter to one half of a mile bearing 60 deg. on starboard bow, and sounded two two-short blasts signals. *Arietta's* wheel was ordered hard-a-starboard, but collision occurred between stem of *Anneliese* and starboard quarter of *Arietta* at angle of about 59 deg. leading forward on *Arietta*.

Anneliese was on a course of 235 deg. (true) with engines at full ahead (15 knots) when *Arietta* was sighted (visually and by radar) bearing ahead distant about six miles. *Arietta* was thereafter watched visually and by radar (true motion on six miles range). Four and a half minutes later *Anneliese* altered course to 239 deg. (true), bringing *Arietta* fine on port bow, distant about four

ANNELIESE
Speed 15 knots
detects target
at 6 ml range
4 ml range
a/c 4° to stbd
3 ml range
a/c 11° to stbd
Further alteration to
stbd fog conditions
Close quarters
port alterations
engines ordered astern
Close quarters
sighting orders
stbd alterations
Detects target
altering to stbd
makes port alteration
ARIETTA
Speed 15½ knots
detects target
about 8 mile in
fog 3° on stbd bow

miles. Three minutes later, visibility deteriorated and *Anneliese* altered course to 250 deg. (true) to increase passing distance between vessels. Half a minute later *Arietta* disappeared from view and *Anneliese* commenced fog signals. Two minutes later *Anneliese* altered to starboard over a period of about two minutes until on a course of 267 deg. (true). During this time, *Anneliese*, realizing from her radar that *Arietta* was altering to port, stopped her engines and, seeing *Arietta* visually distant half to a quarter of a mile, and bearing 45 deg. on the port bow, put her wheel hard-a-port and ordered engines emergency full astern, sounding a two-short-blasts signal and then a three-short-blasts signal.

It was held by Brandon, J.:

(1) that *Anneliese* was at fault in failing to reduce speed as soon as visibility deteriorated and in making a succession of small alterations to starboard after visibility had deteriorated. She was also at fault in her delay in realizing that *Arietta* was porting and in taking the appropriate avoiding action.

(2) That *Arietta* was at fault for (i) failure to keep a good visual look-out; (ii) failure to reduce speed as visibility deteriorated; (iii) failure to keep a good radar look-out (she should have appreciated more easily that *Anneliese* was starboarding if her radar had been switched to a closer range than eight miles); (iv) porting when she realized that *Anneliese* had altered course to starboard.

(3) As there was no clear preponderance of blame, therefore blame should be apportioned equally.

Appeal by *Anneliese*[1] was allowed on the grounds that:

(1) *Anneliese* was not at fault in making a succession of alterations to starboard;

(2) *Anneliese* was not at fault in failing to react more promptly to *Arietta's* turn to port; and

(3) it was possible to distinguish between the degrees in which each vessel was at fault.

Consequently, the Court of Appeal apportioned the blame: *Arietta*, two-thirds; *Anneliese*, one-third.

A very good illustration of a close-quarters situation is *The "Ercole"*[2], where a collision occurred in the South China Sea

---

1. (1970) 1 Lloyd's Rep. 355.
2. (1977) 1 Lloyd's Rep. 516.

between the *Embiricos* and the *Ercole*. The ship's were approaching each other on nearly opposite courses, but following alterations of course by the *Ercole* to starboard and the *Embiricos* to port, came into collision with the stem of the *Ercole* striking the starboard side aft of the *Embiricos* at an angle of 50 deg. leading forward on the *Embiricos*, causing substantial damage to both vessels.

Each ship was observed by the other on the radar during the approach period. The *Ercole* was steering 230 deg. and substantially making good that course at 13 knots. The *Embiricos* was on a course of 040 deg. doing about 15 knots. The visibility was restricted. The second officer, on watch on the *Embiricos*, first saw the *Ercole* at 18 miles some 2 to 3 deg. on the starboard bow. The *Ercole* then changed slowly to 6 deg. at eight miles and to 8 deg. at five miles, when she ceased to be visible because of rain. The second officer estimated that if the two ships maintained their courses they would pass each other on parallel courses at about ½ mile and switched from automatic to manual steeering. Meanwhile the master of *Ercole* first saw the *Embiricos* on radar on the 24 mile range bearing 6 deg. at 20 miles on her port bow. As she approached he changed to the 12 mile range and when the *Embiricos* was some three miles distant, her echo disappeared into the clutter round the centre of the radar screen and he formed the view that the two ships would pass port to port at 1½ to two miles. He altered course 10 deg. to starboard when some three miles distant. He next saw a group of white lights from the *Embiricos*, but before seeing her side lights he put the *Ercole* hard to starboard. The *Embiricos'* wheel was put hard to port and the collision then took place.

It was held by Brandon, J. (Adm.Ct.) that:

(1) assuming the course and speeds of the two ships were as set out above, if a proper radar look-out had been kept during the approach period, it should have been appreciated that a close-quarters situation with risk of collision was developing;

(2) when the *Ercole* ceased to be visible because of reduction of visibility and when the echo of the *Embiricos* disappeared into the clutter at four miles, the *Embiricos* should have put her engines slow ahead, so as to reduce her speed to about six to eight knots, and the *Ercole* should have stopped her engines and then navigated with caution;

(3) the alteration of course of 10 deg. by the *Ercole* when the *Embiricos* disappeared into the clutter, was not made in accordance with good seamanship in that it was too small and the *Ercole* should either have kept her course,or, if she was going to alter to starboard at all, should have made a much larger alteration than 10 deg;

(4) when the *Embiricos* saw, from the change in the lights of the *Ercole* that she was turning to starboard, the danger of some kind of collision being then imminent, the *Embiricos* had not erred in putting her wheel to port.

Apportionment of blame: *Embiricos* 40 per cent and the *Ercole* 60 per cent.

Rule 9 - *Narrow Channels*

(a) A vessel proceeding along the course of a narrow channel or fairway shall keep as near to the outer limit of the channel or fairway which lies on her starboard side as is safe and practicable.

(b) A vessel of less than 20 metres in length or a sailing vessel shall not impede the passage of a vessel which can safely navigate only within a narrow channel or fairway.

(c) A vessel engaged in fishing shall not impede the passage of any other vessel navigating within a narrow channel or fairway.

(d) A vessel shall not cross a narrow channel or fairway if such crossing impedes the passage of a vessel which can safely navigate only within such channel or fairway. The latter vessel may use the sound signal prescribed in Rule 34 (d) if in doubt as to the intention of the crossing vessel.

(e) (i) In a narrow channel or fairway when overtaking can take place only if the vessel to be overtaken has to take action to permit safe passing, the vessel intending to overtake shall indicate her intention by sounding the appropriate signal prescribed in Rule 34 (c) (i). The vessel to be overtaken shall, if in agreement, sound the appropriate signal prescribed in Rule 34 (c) (ii) and take steps to permit safe passing. If in doubt she may sound the signals prescribed in Rule 34 (d).

(ii) This Rule does not relieve the overtaking vessel of her obligation under Rule 13.

(f) A vessel nearing a bend or an area of a narrow channel or fairway where other vessels may be obscured by an intervening obstruction shall navigate with particular alertness and caution and shall sound the appropriate signal prescribed in Rule 34 (e).

(g) Any vessel shall, if the circumstances of the case admit, avoid anchoring in a narrow channel.

Rule 9 (a) differs from Rule 25 (a) of the 1960 Rules in that it extends the application of the narrow channel provisions to all vessels where previously, they were limited to power-driven vessels only.

Under paragraph (a) vessels are required to keep as near as possible to the outer limit of the channel or fairway so as not to impede the passage of vessels able to use only the deep water, or vessels overtaking.

Willmer, J. in *The Mersey No. 30*[1] said that "each vessel shall keep to her own starboard side of the channel". Obviously, a ship which is outside a fairway should not enter it at such a time or place as would cause danger or difficulty to other ships already in the fairway and proceeding up or down it.

Paragraph (d) prohibits vessels from crossing narrow channels or fairways if they will impede the passage of vessels, confined for navigational reasons to such channels or fairways. In the "*Troll River*"[2], the vessel left Nagoya for New Orleans with a pilot on board and proceeded down the fairway. When she approached the entrance to the harbour, she put her engines dead slow ahead to allow the pilot to disembark. The *Shavit* also stopped her engines and worked dead slow ahead in order to maintain steerage way whilst she was waiting to pick up the same pilot. Suddenly, *Shavit* moved forward into the fairway and went across *Troll River's* bows. *Troll River* starboarded, but her bow struck *Shavit's* port side at an angle of about 55 deg. leading aft on *Shavit*.

It was held, by Q.B.D. (Adm.Ct.) (Brandon, J.) that:

(1) *Shavit* was at fault in entering the fairway and trying to cross ahead of *Troll River*. The master of *Shavit* was misled

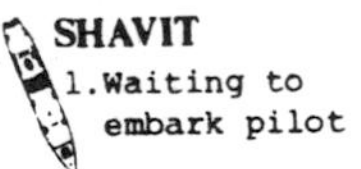

2.Increased speed
to enter fairway

TROLL RIVER

2.Hard
astarboard

1.Preparing to
disembark pilot

1. (1952) 2 Lloyd's Rep. 183, at p.190.
2. (1974) 2 Lloyd's Rep. 181.

about the extent of the fairway by having an out-of-date chart.

(2) *Troll River* had failed to keep a good aural look-out and should have heard the signals of one short blast sounded by *Shavit*. However, as no causative fault of navigation had been proved against *Troll River*, *Shavit* was alone to blame.

It must be noted that paragraph (e) (i) refers to Rule 34 (c). As this Rule opens with the words "when in sight of one another in a narrow channel or fairway", overtaking would normally take place when the vessels are in sight. The Rules make no provision for overtaking in a narrow channel in restricted visibility.

Meaning of "narrow channel" and "fairway"

In *The Stelling* and *The Ferranti*[1], Langton, J. held in relation to Erith and Halfway reaches of the River Thames and the bend between them, that the word "fairway" meant the whole area of navigable water between lines joining the buoys on either side and that "mid-channel" meant the centre line of that area. He considered "channel" as synonymous to "fairway" and as covering the whole area of navigable water as marked out by buoys. In *The Crackshot*[2] Willmer, J. construing Rule 38 of the Thames By-Laws, not having Justice Langton's decision nor any other earlier authority cited to him, held that the "fairway" or "mid-channel" was not the whole of the navigable water but was the dredged area indicated by pecked lines on a chart. He thought that it was unlikely that the Port of London Authority, having dredged a channel, would intend to refer to a different area as the fairway.

In *The American Jurist*[3], Willmer, J. drew attention to the discrepancy between his own earlier decision and that of Mr. Justice Langton but did not find it necessary either to revise his opinion or to re-affirm it[4].

---

1. (1942) 72 Ll.L.Rep. 177. See also *Smith* v. *Voss* (1857) 2 H. & N. 97, where at the trial of a collision action it had been left to the jury to consider what part of the River Thames was the "fairway" or "mid-channel". The jury found that the vessel was not in the fairway or mid-channel, having decided that those words did not mean the whole navigable width.
2. (1949) 82 Ll.L.Rep. 594.
3. (1958) 1 Lloyd's Rep. 423, at p.434.
4. Willmer, J. remarked that the following cases cited to him: *The Jaroslaw Dabrowski* (1952) 2 Lloyd's Rep. 20; *The Mersey No. 30* (1952) 2 Lloyd's Rep. 183; and *The British Tenacity* (1963) 2 Lloyd's Rep. 1, did not seem to throw any light on the particular problem with which he was faced.

More recently in *The "Koningin Juliana"*[1] a collision occurred at night, in good weather, between the *Thuroklint* and the *Koningin Juliana* in Harwich Harbour about 1½ cables S.S.W. of the Felixstowe Buoy.

Thuroklint changed pilots in the dredged channel about 1½ cables N.N.W. of the North Shelf buoy while *Koningin Juliana* approached her. The stem of *Koningin Juliana* struck the port side of *Thuroklint* in way of the forward part of her hold at an angle of about 70 deg. leading forward on *Thuroklint*. *Thuroklint's* heading at the time of collision was about 020 deg. (true) whereas that of *Koningin Juliana* was 090 deg. (true).

It must be noted that in the area relevant to this case the extent of the navigable water is marked by buoys placed on each side. The width of this navigable water is roughly three cables at its maximum. However, within this area, there is a dredged channel, maintained to a depth of 23½ ft., and approximately one cable in width. This dredged channel, which is conveniently indicated by pecked lines on the Admiralty chart, by no means follows the centre of the available navigable water.

The dispute between the parties centred on the meaning of the phrase "the fairway or mid-channel" and Brandon, J. had the following to say[2]: "It does not follow, however, because the expression 'narrow channel' means the whole area of navigable water, that the word 'mid-channel' means the centre line of that area without regard to the existence and position within that area of the dredged channel. On the contrary, it seems to me, as a matter of common sense, that the centre of the dredged channel must be regarded as mid-channel, not only in relation to the dredged channel itself, but also in relation to the wider navigable areas as a whole. I say 'as a matter of common sense', because it seems to me essential that rule 25 (a) should be applied uniformly to all ships navigating up and down the river, irrespective of their draught and whatever the state of the tide may be." Accordingly, his Lordship held that the expression 'narrow channel' meant the whole of the navigable water marked by buoys and the expression 'mid-channel' meant the centre of the dredged channel marked by pecked lines on the chart.

Appeal[3] by *Thuroklint* was allowed and Lord Denning, M.R. said[4]: "We hold that the line of division is the middle line of the

1. (1973) 2 Lloyd's Rep. 308.
2. Ibid., at pp.313, 314.
3. (1974) 2 Lloyd's Rep. 353.
4. Ibid., at pp.354, 355.

dredged channel, it is the 'fairway'; where there is no dredged channel, the 'mid-channel' of the navigable water. I would only add this: the regulation applies not only to the dredged channel itself, but also to the stretches of water on either side of it right up to the shore. If a vessel is proceeding along those stretches of water, it must keep to its proper side, i.e. to that side of the mid-line of the dredged channel which lies on the starboard side of the vessel."

Lord Justice Cairns concurred when he stated[1]: "It seems to me that the only way in which a sensible meaning can be extracted is by construing the By-law in the way suggested, namely, as referring to the channel dredged and maintained by the port authority."

This view was shared by Sir Gordon Willmer[2] who pointed out: "Approaching the problem de novo, and bearing in mind the emphatic opinion expressed by our Assessors, I think it is wrong, as argued on behalf of the appellants, to treat the word 'fairway' as wholly synonymous with 'channel'. Effect should be given to the fact that those responsible for drafting the rule saw fit to use two separate words. It seems to me that they must have had in mind that within any 'narrow channel' there may well be a defined 'fairway'. If there is a 'fairway' within the narrow channel, the requirement is that a vessel must keep to that side of such 'fairway' which lies on her starboard side. In the relatively rare case of a channel that does not include a defined fairway, the requirement is to keep to starboard of the middle of the channel as a whole. At all events I agree with the view expressed by my Lords, and by the Assessors who advise us, that in the entrance to Harwich harbour the requirement is that each vessel shall keep to starboard of the middle line of the 'fairway' as depicted by the pecked lines on the Admiralty chart."

It is interesting to note that on appeal by the *Koningin Juliana*, the House of Lords[3] reversed the decision of the Court of Appeal on the ground that the latter ought not to disturb the trial Judge's apportionment.

Some cases on collisions in narrow channels

There are many cases on collision which occurred in narrow

---

1. Ibid., at p.358.
2. Ibid., at p.362.
3. (1975) 2 Lloyd's Rep. 111.

channels[1]. In *The "British Patrol"*[2], the collision occurred in the River Thames at night. *Finnwood* was proceeding at full speed (12 knots) and departed from her starboard side of channel to pass to northward of Mid Barrow Light-vessel (in accordance with common practice). She then set course to get to her own side. *British Patrol* was proceeding at 13 knots, altering course slightly to avoid other vessels. Both vessels sighted each other at about four miles, before *Finnwood* passed light-vessel. After *Finnwood* passed light-vessel, vessels were approaching on almost opposite courses, and lights presented by each vessel to the other varied. *British Patrol* altered course to port. *Finnwood* altered course to starboard, and collision occurred about 1¾ miles from light-vessel at about a right angle.

It was held by Karminski, J. that although *British Patrol* was disconerted by *Finnwood's* passing to north of light-vessel when

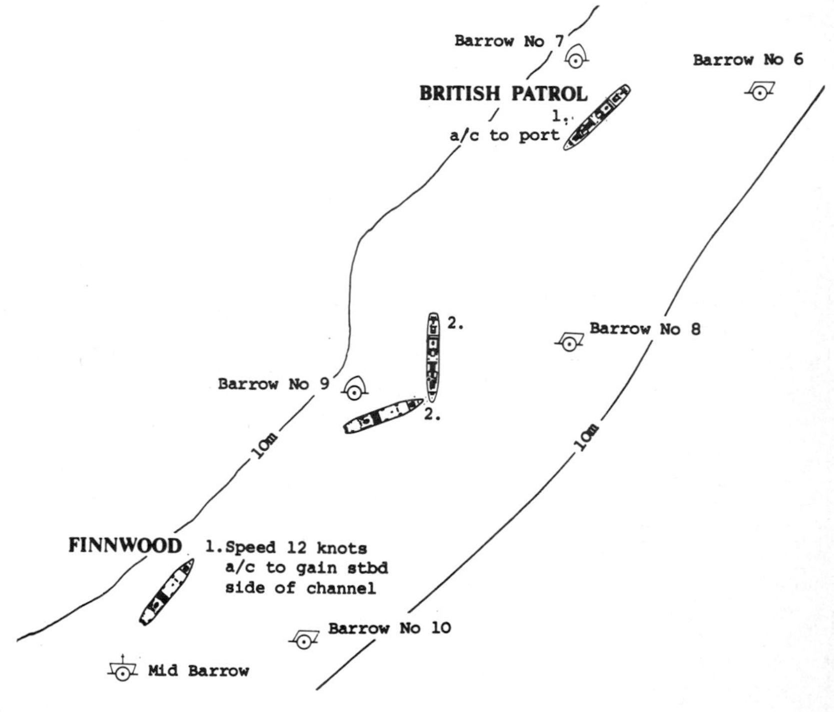

1. *The "Salaverry"* (1968) 1 Lloyd's Rep. 53; *The Marimar* (1968) 2 Lloyd's Rep. 165; *The "Hermes"* (1969) 1 Lloyd's Rep. 425 (Canada Ex. Ct.); *The Bovenkerk* (1973) 1 Lloyd's Rep. 63; *The "Martin Fierro"* (1974) 2 Lloyd's Rep. 203.
2. (1967) 2 Lloyd's Rep. 16.

Finnwood was clear, *British Patrol* was in no doubt as to *Finnwood's* action; that the position of difficulty was not created by *Finnwood*, but by *British Patrol's* standing on her course and at last moment going to port; that a slight alteration of course by vessels would have avoided collision; and that, therefore, both vessels were to blame.

Apportionment of blame: *Finnwood*, 25 per cent.; *British Patrol*, 75 per cent.

Appeal by *British Patrol* was allowed[1]. The Court held:

(1) that what immediately precipitated the collision was the fact of the *British Patrol* altering her course violently under hard-a-port wheel; but the trial Judge did not direct his mind to the vital fact that *Finnwood* was at all material times proceeding down on her wrong side of the channel;

(2) that there would have been nothing unsafe or impracticable in *Finnwood* passing to southward of Mid Barrow Light-vessel;

(3) that it was no answer to say that what *Finnwood* was doing was perfectly obvious to *British Patrol*;

(4) that dangerous position was created in first instance by *Finnwood's* persistence in holding her course on wrong side of channel and it was that which led *British Patrol* to take action which ultimately precipitated collision; and that, accordingly, the trial Judge misdirected himself by overlooking the vital importance of the observance of Rule 25 of the 1960 Rules;

(5) that both vessels contributed by their navigation to bringing about the dangerous end-on position, and both held on much too long in the face of obvious and mounting danger due to poor look-out; that it was impossible to distinguish between two vessels and that, therefore, they should be held equally to blame.

In *The "Sabine"*[2], the *Ore Prince* went aground in the channel in the River Schelde, and thirteen tugs assembled to assist her in refloating. In the meantime, the *Sabine* which was suffering from steering gear trouble, took emergency measures by letting go the port anchor some six cables up river from the place where *Ore Prince* was lying. The tugs assisting *Ore Prince* refloated her and she proceeded up river.

Meanwhile tugs assisting *Sabine* caused her to swing athwart the river facing upstream when the tide ebbed. At the time when *Ore Prince* refloated, *Sabine* had swung at least 15 deg. from a down-

---

1. (1968) 1 Lloyd's Rep. 117.
2. (1974) 1 Lloyd's Rep. 465.

river heading, and when *Ore Prince* put her engines to dead slow ahead, *Sabine* was angled about 45 deg. across the channel. A collision occurred at the port bow of *Ore Prince* striking the port side of *Sabine's* stern at an angle of 80 deg. leading aft on *Sabine*.

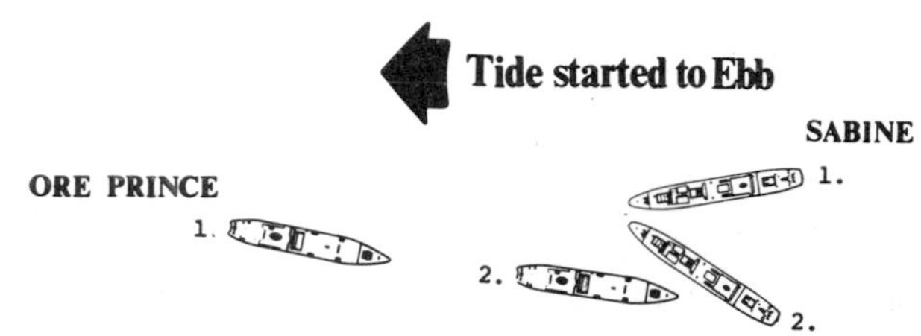

It was held, by Brandon, J. that:

(1) *Ore Prince* was at fault for (i) those on board her paid no attention to *Sabine* until after they had begun to proceed up river, and accordingly had not kept a proper look-out; (ii) putting her engines ahead and proceeding up river at a time when *Sabine* was already angled half athwart the channel; and (iii) continuing up river and not holding back, and these faults were causative but the first fault should be regarded as leading to the second fault, and the third fault as an aggravation of the second fault, rather than as separate and independent faults in either case.

(2) *Sabine* was not at fault for commencing her swing at the time she did or in continuing to swing, but she was at fault in (i) not keeping a proper look-out in that no one on board paid any attention to *Ore Prince* until about a minute before the collision; (ii) not sounding a warning signal for in the circumstances it was necessary or desirable to do so to attract attention in order to avoid a collision; and (iii) not using her engines or not using them sufficiently to take her as far towards the northern edge of the channel as possible, and the first fault led to the second and third faults and could not be regarded as a separate fault; and while the third fault was causative the second fault was not.

(3) It would not be right to regard either vessel as more to blame than the other, and the liability for the collision would be divided equally between them.

In *The "Esso Wandsworth"*[1], a collision occurred in the Lower Hope Reach in the River Thames, in thick fog.

The *Moerdyk*, with her sea pilot on board, was proceeding down river in Gravesend Reach on 087½ deg. (true) at manoeuvring full speed ahead in good visibility. When Tilbury buoy was abeam to port, *Moerdyk* swung to 064 deg. (true). Half a minute later she swung to 025 deg. (true) and steadied. As she ran into fog, her

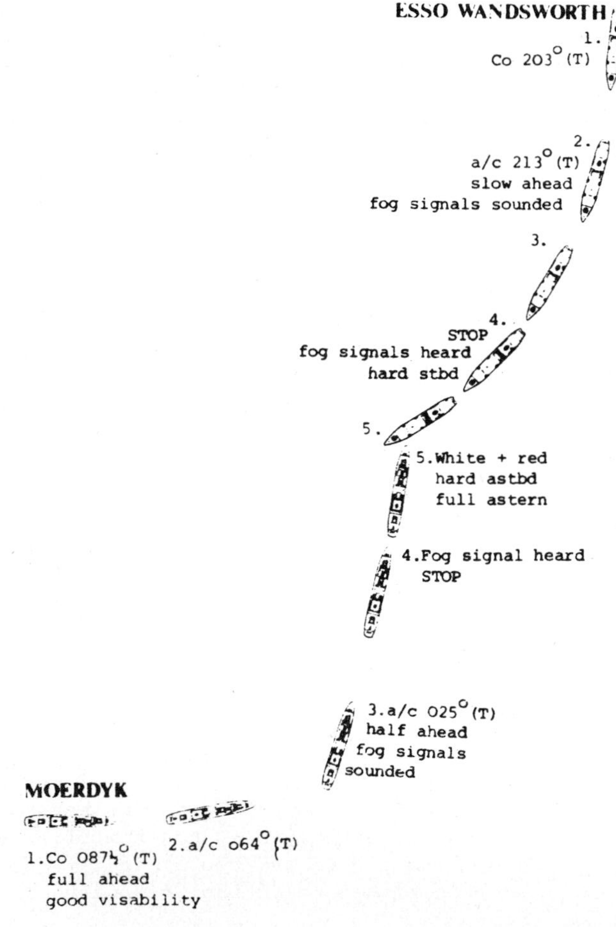

1. (1970) 2 Lloyd's Rep. 303.

engines were put half ahead and she began sounding fog signals. Shortly afterwards, the fog signal of the *Esso Wandsworth* was heard ahead and she was observed on *Moerdyk's* radar. *Moerdyk's* engines were ordered "dead slow ahead" and then "stop". The white lights and red of the *Esso Wandsworth* were seen ahead, distant about a cable, crossing from starboard to port. *Moerdyk's* pilot ordered "hard-a-starboard" and "full astern", but a collision occurred between the stem of *Moerdyk* and port side of *Esso Wandsworth* at an angle of 50 deg. leading aft on *Esso Wandsworth*.

The *Esso Wandsworth's* case was that she was proceeding up river in Lower Hope Reach and, five minutes before the collision, had altered to 203 deg. (true). 2½ minutes before the collision the *Esso Wandsworth* altered to 213 deg. (true) and, half a minute later, due to fog, her engines were put slow ahead and she commenced sounding fog signals. One minute before collision the *Moerdyk's* fog signal was heard ahead and she was observed on radar. The *Esso Wandsworth* stopped her engines, her wheel was put hard-a-starboard and then her port engine full ahead. She had altered to 255 deg. (true) when the collision occurred.

It was held, by Brandon, J.:

(1) that the *Moerdyk* was to blame for (i) defective radar and visual look-out; (ii) not keeping to her own starboard side; (iii) failure to reduce speed more or earlier; and (iv) failure to starboard to avoid collision; and that those faults were causative;

(2) that the *Esso Wandsworth* was at fault (i) in not reducing speed; (ii) in navigating on her wrong side of channel until very shortly before the collision; and that those faults were causative;

(3) that the *Moerdyk* was more to blame in that the main cause of the collision was the *Moerdyk* being on the wrong side and her speed at collision was very much greater.

Another example is the case of *The "Adolf Leonhardt"*[1], where a collision occurred in the River Maas in the port of Rotterdam. The wind was light, the weather was fine and clear, and the tide was ebbing with a force of two knots.

City of Capetown's case was that she was proceeding on the normal up-river course above Eeemhaven of 070 deg. (true) on her own starboard side of mid-channel. Her engines were at dead slow ahead. Her pilot attempted to contact *Adolf Leonhardt* on the

---

1. (1973) 2 Lloyd's Rep. 318.

V.H.F. radio without success. *Adolf Leonhardt* which was now distant about ½ mile bearing about ½ point on *City of Capetown's* starboard bow opened her red side light and closed her green side light. *City of Capetown's* engines were then stopped. *Adolf Leonhardt* sounded a signal of two short blasts. *City of Capetown's* engines were immediately put to full speed astern. *Adolf Leonhardt* bore down on *City of Capetown* and with her port bow struck the stem and port bow of *City of Capetown* at an angle of about 15 deg. leading aft on *Adolf Leonhardt* causing damage.

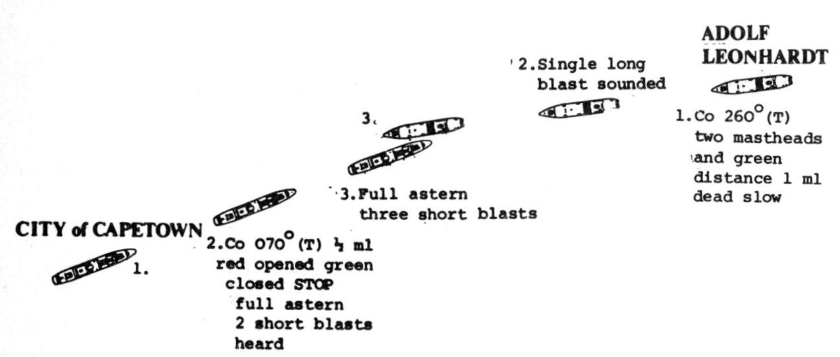

Adolf Leonhardt's case was that she left Waalhaven and was heading about 250 deg. (true) through the water. *City of Capetown's* two white masthead lights and green side light were first observed distant about one mile heading slightly to port of an up-channel course. *Adolf Leonhardt's* engines were put dead slow ahead and her course altered to 260 deg. (true). *Adolf Leonhardt* sounded one long blast on her whistle and reports were made to two shore radar stations that she intended to keep to starboard. *City of Capetown* came on maintaining her course across the river. Further signals of one long blast were sounded by *Adolf Leonhardt*. *Adolf Leonhardt's* engines were put to stop and immediately to emergency full astern. Three short blasts were sounded on her whistle. *City of Capetown* came on and with her stern struck the port bow of *Adolf Leonhardt* at an angle of 15 deg. leading aft causing damage.

It was held by Brandon, J. that:

(1) *Adolt Leonhardt* was to blame for failing to get and remain on her own starboard side of the channel, contrary to the Collision Rules and the local rules of navigation.

(2) *City of Capetown* was to blame for (i) she should have reduced

her speed more and earlier; and (ii) she should have edged further to starboard so as to give *Adolt Loonhardt* as much room as possible.

Apportionment of blame: *Adolf Leonhardt*, two-thirds; *City of Capetown*, one-third.

Again in *The "Ballylesson"*[1], the Court found that the *Ballylesson* was in breach of both the Mersey Channel Rules and the Rule on head-on situations, (Rule 14). In this case, the collision occurred at night in the River Mersey.

At 06 02 hours *Ballylesson*, which had crossed from her starboard side of channel, was making for entrance to Garston Channel when masthead lights (in line) and side lights of *Belgulf Union* were sighted bearing ahead distant about 1¼ miles. At 06 03 hours *Ballylesson's* master ordered port wheel, engines full ahead and sounded a two-short-blasts signal (not heard by *Belgulf Union*) (*Ballylesson* then had Pluckington Bank Buoy abeam to port at 500 ft.). At 06 04½ hours *Ballylesson's* engines were put slow ahead. At 06 05 hours one-short-blast signal by *Belgulf Union* was heard by *Ballylesson* and her master ordered hard-a-starboard, and gave one-short-blast signal (not heard by *Belgulf Union*). At 06 05½ hours he ordered engines full ahead. *Ballylesson* then heard three-short-blasts signal by *Belgulf Union* and saw her alteration to port. The master of *Ballylesson* put his engines full astern and sounded three-short-blasts. At 06 06½ hours pilot of *Belgulf Union* ordered emergency full speed astern and sounded three-short-blasts signal. Collision occurred about half a minute later between the stem of *Belgulf Union* and port side aft of *Ballylesson* at angle of about 60 deg. leading aft on *Ballylesson*.

It was held,by Brandon, J. that: *Belgulf Union* was at fault in:

(1) not seeing *Ballylesson* earlier and appreciating that she might be making for Garston Channel;

(2) as a result of (1) maintaining full speed too long;

(3) not hearing the signals of *Ballylesson*;

(4) sounding one-short-blast signal and inviting a port-to-port passing;

(5) not altering to starboard thereafter.

Ballylesson was in breach of the local rules of navigation and the head-on rule.

---

1. (1968) 1 Lloyd's Rep. 69.

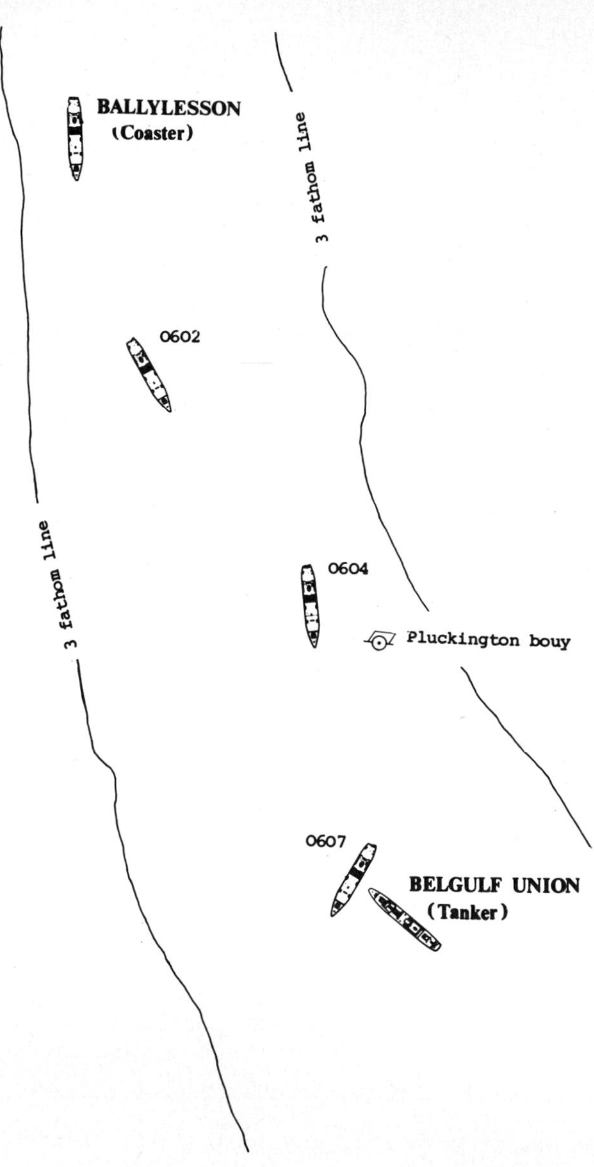
BALLYLESSON
(Coaster)
3 fathom line
0602
3 fathom line
0604
Pluckington bouy
0607
BELGULF UNION
(Tanker)

Apportionment of blame: *Belgulf Union*, two-thirds; *Ballylesson*, one-third.

Rule 10 - *Traffic Separation Schemes*[1]

(a) This Rule applies to traffic separation schemes adopted by the Organization.

(b) A vessel using a traffic separation scheme shall:

(i) proceed in the appropriate traffic lane in the general direction of traffic flow for that lane;

(ii) so far as practicable keep clear of a traffic separation line or separation zone;

(iii) normally join or leave a traffic lane at the termination of the lane, but when joining or leaving from the side shall do so at as small an angle to the general direction of traffic flow as practicable.

(c) A vessel shall so far as practicable avoid crossing traffic lanes, but if obliged to do so shall cross as nearly as practicable at right angles to the general direction of traffic flow.

(d) Inshore traffic zones shall not normally be used by through traffic which can safely use the appropriate traffic lane within the adjacent traffic separation scheme.

(e) A vessel, other than a crossing vessel, shall not normally enter a separation zone or cross a separation line except:

(i) in cases of emergency to avoid immediate danger;

(ii) to engage in fishing within a separation zone.

(f) A vessel navigating in areas near the terminations of traffic separation schemes shall do so with particular caution.

(g) A vessel shall so far as practicable avoid anchoring in a traffic separation scheme or in areas near its terminations.

(h) A vessel not using a traffic separation scheme shall avoid it by as wide a margin as is practicable.

(i) A vessel engaged in fishing shall not impede the passage of any vessel following a traffic lane.

(j) A vessel of less than 20 metres in length or a sailing vessel shall not impede the safe passage of a power-driven vessel following a traffic lane.

---

1. The title in the draft was "Conduct of vessels in or near a traffic separation scheme". See CR/CONF/3, p.73.

Since 1898, shipowners operating passenger ships in the North Atlantic adopted recommended routes. A reference to this practice was made in the International Convention for the Safety of Life at Sea, 1960, where the Contracting Governments undertook the responsibility of using their influence to induce the owners of all passenger ships crossing the Atlantic to follow the recognized routes, and to do everything in their power to ensure adherence to such routes in converging areas by all ships, so far as circumstances permit.

The density of traffic has increased substantially over the years. This is due to the use of larger and higher speed vessels, increased percentage of seatime, and greater concentration of ship movements on a limited number of trade routes. Consequently, there was a need for the adoption of certain measures to regulate navigation in order to reduce the risk of collision. Therefore, the Inter-Governmental Maritime Consultative Organisation (IMCO)[1] sought to recommend traffic separation schemes in many areas throughout the world. These schemes were adopted by IMCO, at the beginning, on a recommendatory basis.

Aim of the traffic separation schemes

IMCO states[2] that the aim of these schemes is "to produce an orderly flow of traffic for the purpose of reducing the risk of collision and for strandings, mainly in areas of converging routes on high traffic density".

Brandon, J. in *The "Genimar"*[3] said: "The purpose of the traffic separation scheme is to reduce the chances of risk of collision arising in waters where heavy concentrations of traffic proceeding in opposite directions are to be expected. That risk is especially great in fog, and, while every case must be decided on its own particular facts, I should in general have little hesitation, in the case of a collision in fog, in holding that a contravention of the scheme by one of the colliding ships contributed to the collision. Even in clear weather, however, the presence of several ships in the same vicinity may make navigation more difficult that when only two ships are involved, and it

---

1. IMCO is a Specialized Agency of the United Nations and its main objective is to facilitate co-operation among governments on technical matters affecting shipping. IMCO has no supervisory powers and as its name indicates, its functions are purely consultative and advisory. It is a forum where its Member States can consult and exchange information without any legal obligation to follow its recommendations.
2. See Ships' Routeing, IMCO Publication, 1973, p.5.
3. (1977) 2 Lloyd's Rep. 17, at p.25.

seems to me that this is also a risk which the scheme is intended to minimise."

Factors to be considered for a separation scheme

In deciding whether or not to adopt a traffic separation scheme, IMCO will consider:

"(a) whether the aids to navigation proposed will enable mariners to determine their position with sufficient accuracy to navigate in the scheme in accordance with the principles regarding the use of Routeing Schemes;

(b) whether or not the scheme complies with the established Methods of Routeing"[1].

The methods used for a separation scheme

When establishing routeing systems, the following are among the methods to be used:

"(a) separation of traffic by separation zones or lines;

(b) separation of traffic by natural obstacles and geographically defined objects;

(c) separation of traffic by inshore traffic zones intended for keeping coastal traffic away from traffic separation schemes;

(d) separation of traffic by sectors at approaches to focal points;

(e) separation of traffic by roundabouts intended to facilitate navigation at focal points, where traffic separation schemes meet;

(f) routeing of traffic by deep water routes, two-way routes or tracks for ships proceeding in specific directions"[2].

Routeing schemes became mandatory

The recent surveys indicated that conditions of traffic in congested areas have been substantially ameliorated by the implementation of separation and routeing measures. Therefore, the IMCO Assembly by Resolution A.228 (VII) has decided that the observance of traffic separation schemes should be mandatory, and recommended that member Governments should make it an offence for

---

1. Ships' Routeing, p.8.
2. Ibid., p.12. At present approximately seventy traffic separation schemes have been adopted by IMCO and recommended to member Governments for observance. These schemes are located all over the world, almost exclusively in areas of congested or converging traffic.

ships of their flag which use any traffic separation scheme to proceed against the established direction of traffic flow[1]. This is all that IMCO can do. There will, however, be no powers to proceed against delinquent ships of States non-party to the Rules, nor for any State to perform police functions on the high seas. The most a State can do towards enforcement of the schemes will be to report the miscreant master to the State of the flag.

The traffic schemes and the Rules

The principles of navigation within the traffic separation schemes have been revised by IMCO in order to bring them into line with those adopted in the Rules. Rule 10 makes it clear that the Rules apply to navigation in routeing systems[2]. IMCO keeps the subject of ships' routeing under continuous review in order to adopt new schemes or to amend and update schemes already in operation. These new schemes may modify Rule 10 and other Steering and Sailing Rules[3]. Therefore, the relevant volume of Sailing Directions

---

1. Resolution A. 205 (VII) was adopted to amend Regulation 8 of Chapter V of the International Convention for the Safety of Life at Sea, 1960. The Resolution states that where the Organisation has adopted traffic separation schemes which specify one-way traffic lanes, ships crossing these lanes shall proceed in the specified direction of traffic flow. Ships crossing the lanes shall do so as far as practicable at right-angles.
2. It must be noted that the observation made by Brandon, J. in *The "Genimar"* (1972) 2 Lloyd's Rep. 17 was in respect of the 1960 Rules and not the 1972 Rules. His Lordship said (at p.25): "The scheme, however, cannot and does not override the Collision Regulations which continue to regulate the duties and obligations of two ships as between one another whether they are navigating in accordance with the scheme or in contravention of it."
3. M. 793.

and up to date charts, should be consulted with the Collision Rules.

It must be noted that navigation in the wrong direction of the scheme may not necessarily be the cause of the collision. In *The "Estrella"*[1], a collision occurred between *Setubal* and *Estrella* off Capt St. Vincent. *Setubal* was within the traffic separation zone and navigating wrongly in the north-bound traffic lane. Brandon, J. said[2]: "There may well be cases where a fault of that kind could be regarded as causative of a subsequent collision. In this case, however, there were no other ships about, the two ships concerned were able to see each other and did see each other at a distance of several miles, and the only requirement for avoiding a collision was that each should comply with the crossing rules. In these circumstances, while but for this first fault there would have been no collision, I do not consider that the collision was caused by it."

Again in *The "Genimar"*[3], a collision occurred between the *Larry L* and the *Genimar* approximately 4·1 miles, 129 deg. from the East Goodwin light-vessel in the Dover Strait. A well known traffic separation scheme exists in this area. The lane on the English side is for traffic proceeding in a south-westerly direction and the lane on the French side is for traffic proceeding in a north-easterly direction.

As the collision took place on the English side of the Strait, the *Genimar* was navigating in contravention of the scheme. Brandon, J. said[4]: "I do not think it would be right to regard the contravention of the scheme by the *Genimar* as being in no way causative of the collision. On the contrary, I think that such contravention should be regarded as a contributory cause, although, because of the ample later opportunities which both ships, and particularly the *Larry L* had of avoiding a collision, its causative effect should be treated as relatively small."

Location of the traffic separation schemes

IMCO maintains that its competence over high seas routeing schemes is exclusive to the extent that it will not recommend any arrangement operated by national authorities until it has been looked at by its Navigation Sub-Committee[5]. As some of the

1. (1977) 1 Lloyd's Rep. 525.
2. Ibid., at p.535.
3. (1977) 2 Lloyd's Rep. 17.
4. Ibid., at p.26.
5. IMCO accepts that a Government may establish a routeing system partly within international waters for local requirements provided that the scheme will be later adopted by its Navigation Sub-Committee. See Ships' Routeing, IMCO Publication, 1973, p.8.

schemes are not on the high seas, the legal regime of the scheme will depend on its location.

On the high seas: Whether it is an offence for a ship to proceed against the established direction of traffic flow in, or through traffic separation schemes, on the high seas, depends on whether the Government of the flag of the ship is party to the Rules or not[1]. If the Government for whom the ship flies its flag is not party to the Rules, no offences would be committed by the ship.

In the territorial waters: Where the traffic separation schemes are wholly within the territorial waters of a State which is party to the Rules, she will be required by Rule 10 to observe these schemes. As the coastal State exercises sovereign rights on its territorial waters, foreign vessels, even if they fly flags of non-party States to the Rules, must comply with the laws and regulations enacted by the coastal State[2].

In case the coastal State is not party to the Rules, or did not accept IMCO recommendation for making the scheme compulsory, it is difficult to see how IMCO could impose any routeing scheme. Undoubtedly, foreign ships have the right of innocent passage. However, this right refers to the right of foreign ships to enter the territorial waters and navigate through it, so long as the passage is not prejudicial to the main interests of the coastal State. Thus, other questions related to the general regime of navigation may arise; e.g. the powers of the coastal State to regulate the passage and the conditions for passage for ships with special characteristics. It must be remembered that a routeing scheme, even if located within the territorial waters

---

1. The fundamental rule which governs the effect of conventions upon third States is that a convention applies only between contracting parties, and parties to a treaty cannot impose an obligation on a third State. This rule appears to have been derived from Roman Law in the form of the well-known "*maxim pacta tertiis nec nocent posunt*" (agreements neither impose obligations nor confer benefits upon third parties). Traditionally the justification of this rule rests on the principle of the sovereignty of states. It seems, however, more appropriate today to regard it as a rule of customary international law.
2. Brandon, J. in *The "Genimar"* (1977) 2 Lloyd's Rep. 17 said in an *obiter dictum* (at p.24): "Compliance with the scheme, so far as foreign ships are concerned, is not compulsory by law. Good seamanship, however, requires that ships should, in general, comply with the scheme, so that failure by any ship to comply with it may well amount to negligent navigation on her part."

of a State, should be protected because it is established in the general interest of international maritime navigation. Nevertheless, International Law empowers the coastal State to prescribe within its territorial waters the condition under which navigation of foreign ships should be carried out.

If the routeing scheme is partly in the high seas and partly in the territorial water of a State, the situation could be very complicated. For instance, the westbound lane of a scheme lies in the territorial waters while the eastbound lane is on the high seas. In such a case IMCO would have to get the agreement of the coastal State.

Added to this is the difficulty in establishing the position of collision with certainty. In *The "Genimar"*[1], Brandon, J. was faced with this difficulty. He said[2]: "There are two main approaches to the problem. One approach is to take the position of the *Genimar* at 04 35 as observed and plotted by the Coastguard officers, and continue her track for a further 3½ minutes on the basis of her further navigation as found by me. The other approach is to continue the track of the *Larry L* onward from the 04 25 position, again on the basis of her subsequent navigation as I have found it to have been. Making use of both these approaches, and bearing in mind that neither the 03 35 position for the *Genimar*, not the 04 25 position for the *Larry L*, are necessarily completely accurate, I find that the approximate place of collision was 4·1 miles 129 deg. true from the East Goodwin light vessel. I stress, however, that this finding is, and can be, approximate only."

(II) CONDUCT OF VESSELS IN SIGHT OF ONE ANOTHER

Rule 11 - *Application*

Rules in this Section apply to vessels in sight of one another.

As mentioned earlier, Rule 3 (k) defines the words "in sight of one another" as "one can be observed visually from the other". In *The "Lucile Bloomfield"*[3], Karminski, J. said[4]: The words 'in sight' mean precisely what they say... 'In sight', in my view, means something which is visible if you take the trouble to keep a look-out."

---

1. (1977) 2 Lloyd's Rep. 17.
2. Ibid., at p.22.
3. (1966) 2 Lloyd's Rep. 239.
4. Ibid., at p.245.

"In sight of one another" occurs at some specific moment in time. In fact, it is difficult to envisage a situation where one vessel claims that she is in sight of another and the latter denies this. An element of reciprocity exists in such a situation.

Rule 12 - *Sailing Vessels*

(a) When two sailing vessels are approaching one another, so as to involve risk of collision, one of them shall keep out of the way of the other as follows:

(i) when each has the wind on a different side, the vessel which has the wind on the port side shall keep out of the way of the other;

(ii) when both have the wind on the same side, the vessel which is to windward shall keep out of the way of the vessel which is to leeward;

(iii) if a vessel with the wind on the port side sees a vessel to windward and cannot determine with certainty whether the other vessel has the wind on the port or on the starboard side, she shall keep out of the way of the other.

(b) For the purposes of this Rule the windward side shall be deemed to be the side opposite to that on which the mainsail is carried or, in the case of a square-rigged vessel, the side opposite to that on which the largest fore-and-aft sail is carried.

As mentioned earlier, Rule 3 (c) defines a sailing vessel as a vessel under sail provided that propelling machinery, if fitted, is not used. This definition applies to all sailing vessels regardless of their types or their capacity for manoeuvring[1].

Rule 12 stipulates the rules to be followed by two sailing vessels and states which one should keep out of the way of the other. If a sailing vessel is approaching a power driven vessel, Rule 18 would be applicable[2].

Rule 12 follows the same basic principles contained in the International Yacht Racing Rules[3] and thus brought changes to the rules on sailing vessels as provided for in the 1960 Regulations. Under those Regulations, there was a duty on the sailing vessel

1. A schooner is usually more capable to manoeuvre than a square-rigged vessel.
2. If in a traffic separation scheme, Rule 10 (j) would apply and if in a narrow channel, Rule 9 (b) would apply.
3. These Rules came into force on April 1, 1977.

which was running free to keep out of the way of the one which was close-hauled. Rule 12, in fact, overcomes the difficulties which arise when the master of a sailing ship at night discovers an approaching vessel, but is not able to tell from her lights or other factors whether she is close-hauled or is running free.

It must be noted that Rule 12[1] should be read with Rule 13 on overtaking. Racing between yachts will be governed by the International Yacht Racing Rules. However, when these yachts meet other vessels, the Collision Rules and in particular Rule 12 applies.

Rule 13 - *Overtaking*

(a) Notwithstanding anything contained in the Rules of this Section any vessel overtaking any other shall keep out of the way of the vessel being overtaken.

(b) A vessel shall be deemed to be overtaking when coming up with another vessel from a direction more than 22·5 degrees abaft her beam, that is, in such a position with reference to the vessel she is overtaking, that at night she would be able to see only the sternlight of that vessel but neither of her sidelights.

(c) When a vessel is in any doubt as to whether she is overtaking another, she shall assume that this is the case and act accordingly.

(d) Any subsequent alteration of the bearing between the two vessels shall not make the overtaking vessel a crossing vessel within the meaning of these Rules or relieve her of the duty of keeping clear of the overtaken vessel until she is finally past and clear[2].

The test adopted by the courts for a long time of whether a vessel is overtaking or crossing another is whether "the hinder ship"

---

1. Paragraph (iii) of Rule 12 (a) was proposed by the Netherlands delegation and they suggested that (b) of the same Rule would be omitted as the term "windward side" is well known to mariners. See CR/CONF/3, p.88.
2. Willmer, L.J. in *The "Tojo Maru"* (1968) 1 Lloyd's Rep. 365 said (at p.377): "It seems to me that no vessel is entitled, in face of another vessel seen to be approaching, to put herself deliberately on a crossing course in the position of a stand-on vessel, so as to force that other vessel to keep out of her way. I should certainly regard it as wrong to adopt any such manoeuvre at a late moment when the vessels are within a short range of each other."

can "see any part of the side lights of the forward ship"[1]. If so, it is a crossing situation, otherwise it would be an overtaking one. Thus, paragraph (b) of Rule 13 states that a ship is considered to be an "overtaking" ship when she is coming up[2] with another vessel from a direction more than 22·5 degrees abaft her beam, that is, in a position from which, at night, she cannot see the other's sidelights but only the sternlight. In other words, Rule 13 will start to be applicable as soon as the vessel sights and determines to overtake another vessel ahead[3]. In case of doubt, the vessel shall assume that she is an overtaking vessel and keep out of the way.

Rule 13 continues to apply until all danger of collision is over. It is not enough that the overtaking vessel has got slightly in the lead, but the Rule applies until the overtaking vessel is past and clear.

It must be noted that the overtaking vessel bears all the risks inherent in passing the other vessel. However, it would appear that there is no liability on the overtaking vessel if the risks are due to the negligence of a third vessel and this could not be reasonably foreseen.

Duty of overtaking vessel

The duty of the overtaking vessel is set out in paragraph (a) mainly to keep out of the way of the vessel being overtaken. No special signals are required except in a narrow channel[4].

---

1. *The Franconia* (1876) 2 Prob. Div. 8, 3 Asp. 295.
2. In *The "Auriga"* (1977) 1 Lloyd's Rep. 384, Brandon, J. said (at p.394): "The expression 'coming up with another vessel' appears to me to involve, in the ordinary and natural meaning of the words used, the concept of a certain degree of proximity between the two ships concerned in terms of either space or time or both, so that the navigation of each ship impinges, or may reasonably be expected to impinge, in the normal course of things, on the navigation of the other."
3. In this respect, Brandon, J. said that: "when ship A is coming up with ship B from a direction more than two points abaft her beam at night, the only visual indication to those on board ship A of the presence of ship B will be the stern light of the latter vessel. It seems to me a reasonable inference from the fact that the rules do not require a stern light to be visible at a distance of more than two miles, that they do not contemplate, in general at any rate, the existence of an overtaking situation ... when the two ships concerned are appreciably more than that distance apart from one another." Ibid., at pp.394, 395.
3. See Rule 34 (c) (i) and (ii).

Cases on overtaking

The following are some of the cases on overtaking. In *The "Cadans"*[1], a collision occurred between the *Firle* and the *Cadans* in Long Reach, River Thames.

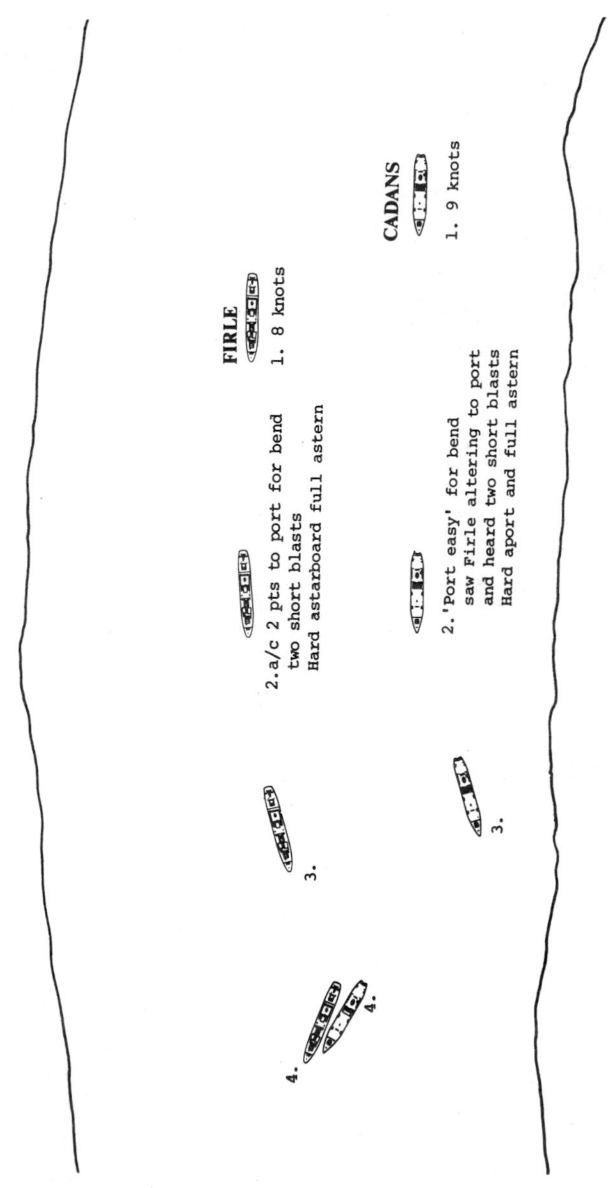

1. (1967) 2 Lloyd's Rep. 147.

Firle's case was that she was proceeding up river at eight knots on her starboard side of the channel. *Cadans* was sighted coming up astern and gaining slowly. As vessels approached a port hand bend at top of Long Reach, *Cadans'* bow drew level with stern of *Firle* on port side at lateral distance of about 200 ft. When the bridge of *Cadans* was level with the bridge of *Firle*, *Cadans* began altering course to starboard. *Firle* put her wheel hard-a-starboard, sounded emergency signal of series of short blasts, and put her engines full astern. *Cadans* continued to alter to starboard and *Cadans'* stem struck *Firle's* port side at a right angle, on north edge of channel. *Cadans* argued that as she was proceeding at nine knots, she was gaining on *Firle* up Long Reach. As vessels approached port hand bend, the pilot of *Cadans* ordered "port easy" for bend. Pilot then saw *Firle* shaping to cross his bow and heard two short blasts. Pilot ordered "hard-a-port" and "full astern" (causing *Cadans* to cant to starboard) but collision at angle of six or seven points occurred half way between mid-channel and northern edge.

It was held, by Brandon, J.:

(1) that *Cadans* was negligent in not keeping out of *Firle's* way or altering to port substantially at an earlier stage or dropping back astern;

(2) that, although *Firle* should have ported less, her alteration of two points to port was not negligent;

(3) that although *Cadans* should have stopped her engines, she was not negligent in going full astern; and

(4) that *Firle* was not negligent in failing to take evading action.

Cadans found solely to blame.

In *The "Fogo"*[1], a collision occurred between the *Trentbank* and the *Fogo* in the Mediterranean Sea in clear weather. Plaintiff's case was that *Trentbank* (on automatic steering) was on course of 288 deg. (true) at speed of 14·25 knots when *Fogo* was observed distant about 2½ miles fine on starboard bow. As *Trentbank* overtook *Fogo*, *Trentbank's* course was altered 2 deg. to port and

---

1. (1967) 2 Lloyd's Rep. 208.

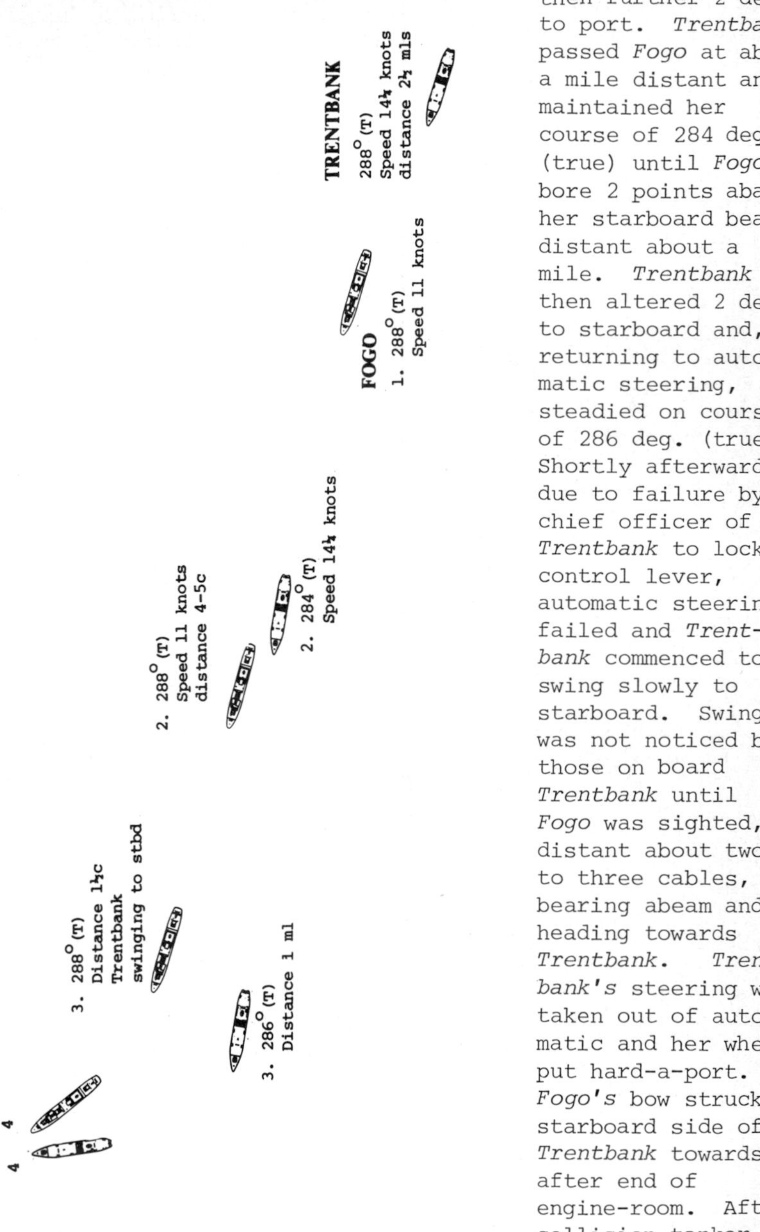

then further 2 deg. to port. *Trentbank* passed *Fogo* at about a mile distant and maintained her course of 284 deg. (true) until *Fogo* bore 2 points abaft her starboard beam, distant about a mile. *Trentbank* then altered 2 deg. to starboard and, returning to automatic steering, steadied on course of 286 deg. (true). Shortly afterwards, due to failure by chief officer of *Trentbank* to lock control lever, automatic steering failed and *Trentbank* commenced to swing slowly to starboard. Swing was not noticed by those on board *Trentbank* until *Fogo* was sighted, distant about two to three cables, bearing abeam and heading towards *Trentbank*. *Trentbank's* steering was taken out of automatic and her wheel put hard-a-port. *Fogo's* bow struck starboard side of *Trentbank* towards after end of engine-room. After collision tanker *Harold H. Helm* took *Trentbank* in tow, but on Sept. 24, 1964, *Trentbank* sank in vicinity of Port Said before she could be beached. Defendants' case was that *Fogo* (on automatic steering) was proceeding on course of 288 deg. (true) at speed of 11 knots when

Trentbank was observed overhauling *Fogo*, distant about four to five cables about one point on port quarter. When *Trentbank* was 20 to 30 deg. forward of *Fogo's* beam, distant about 1½ cables, *Trentbank* altered course rapidly to starboard. *Fogo* took hard-a-starboard wheel action, keeping her engines full ahead but collision occurred.

It was held, by Cairns, J.:

(1) that when the unexplained alteration of *Trentbank's* heading occurred while she was on automatic steering it was not improbable that something had gone wrong with apparatus;

(2) that, because of previous breakdowns, it was incumbent on those navigating *Trentbank* to place no undue reliance on gyro compass and automatic steering until they had been overhauled;

(3) that, at passing, distance between vessels was between 1½ and 2 cables; and that chief officer of *Trentbank* was negligent in passing, with no look-out, so close to *Fogo*;

(4) that chief officer of *Fogo* was not negligent in (a) failing to give warning signal or to turn to starboard before *Trentbank* veered to starboard; (b) failing to get *Fogo* moving to starboard earlier; or (c) failing to order engines full astern; and that, therefore, *Trentbank* was wholly to blame for collision;

(5) (*obiter*) that plaintiffs should have arranged for tug to be in attendance on *Trentbank* on her arrival at Port Said; that if tugs had been present *Trentbank* could have been beached; that that failure to beach resulted in the sinking; and that, therefore, that negligence by plaintiffs was a *novus actus interveniens*, and *Fogo* was not liable.

Judgment for defendants[1].

In *The "Frosta"*[2], a collision occurred in the Indian Ocean between *Fotini Carras* and *Frosta*. The *Frosta* was overtaking *Fotini Carras*, leaving a distance of only 2 cables between them. *Frosta's* steering gear jammed and she went to starboard. She sounded whistles of one short blast and exhibited not-under-command lights, but failed to extinguish her masthead lights. *Fotini Carras* starboarded but a collision occurred between the starboard

1. Per Cairns, J. (at p.221): "Automatic steering is a most valuable invention if properly used. It can lead to disaster when it is left to look after itself while vigilance is relaxed. It is on men that safety at sea depends and they cannot make a greater mistake than to suppose that machines can do all their work for them."
2. (1973) 2 Lloyd's Rep. 348.

bow of *Frosta* and the port side forward of *Fotini Carras* at a fairly narrow angle. A second collision occurred between the starboard side aft of *Frosta* and the port side aft of *Fotini Carras*.

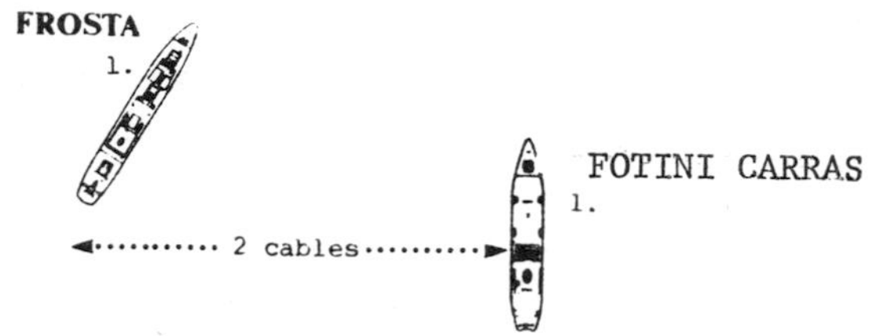

It was held, by Brandon, J. that:

(1) *Frosta* was to blame for (i) she was the overtaking vessel and had failed to keep out of the way of *Fotini Carras*; (ii) she had overtaken *Fotini Carras* too close; and (iii) she had failed to stop her engines as soon as the steering gear defect became apparent and thereafter to keep them stopped; and all these faults were causative of the collision;

(2) *Fotini Carras* was at fault for not switching from automatic to manual steering earlier than she did but this would not have prevented the collision;

(3) *Fotini Carras*, however, was not at fault (i) in failing to alter course to starboard earlier for (a) the chief officer did not hear *Frosta's* signals of one short blast because he was sounding *Fotini Carras'* warning signals simultaneously, and (b) he did not see the not-under-command lights because the masthead lights on *Frosta* had not been switched off; and (ii) in failing to reverse her engines, for such an order could not have been executed immediately in the engine-room unless an order to stand-by had been given 20 to 30 minutes earlier, and no one could have reasonably anticipated that in the open sea such an order would be required;

(4) Accordingly, *Frosta* was solely to blame for the collision.

Interaction

In certain circumstances, when a vessel is in close proximity to another, and enters into a sheer or swerve, interaction may cause or contribute to the collision. In *The Queen Mary*[1], Lord Porter said: "No doubt the effect of the forces of interaction are very imperfectly known, and one cannot impude to the captains of the two ships any expert or exact knowledge of them, but I should have expected some allowance to have been made for their coming into play, in the sense that the ships should not have been allowed to approach so near to one another as to run a risk of their coming into action."

Rule 14 - *Head-on Situation*

(a) When two power-driven vessels are meeting on reciprocal or nearly reciprocal courses so as to involve risk of collision each shall alter her course to starboard so that each shall pass on the port side of the other.

(b) Such a situation shall be deemed to exist when a vessel sees the other ahead or nearly ahead and by night she could see the masthead lights of the other in a line or nearly in a line and/or both sidelights and by day she observes the corresponding aspect of the other vessel.

(c) When a vessel is in any doubt as to whether such a situation exists she shall assume that it does exist and act accordingly.

The words "so as to involve risk of collision', which are repeated in other parts of the Rules, were held not to refer to an existing risk of collision, but to refer to an earlier time where there will be a risk if nothing is done to prevent it[2]. The alteration of course required by paragraph (a) must be timely and sufficient to give safe clearance and it would be a serious fault to turn to port.

Again the words "so that each shall pass on the port side of the other" are self-explanatory. This rule may be modified through special circumstances, such as the one provided for in Rule 9 (b) that: "A vessel of less than 20 metres in length ... shall not impede the passage of a vessel which can safely navigate only

---

1. (1949) 82 Ll.L.Rep. 303.
2. *The Bellanoch* (1907) P. 170 at p.192 which applied *The Beryl* (1884) 9 P.D. 137.

within a narrow channel or fairway."

Paragraph (c) was added to eliminate the possibility of conflicting manoeuvres when two vessels are meeting end on. The Dutch delegation proposed[1] that the alteration of course would be to starboard. This proposal was not approved and it was felt that the words "act accordingly" are preferable.

It must be noted that Rule 14 will generally be superceded in the following situations:

(1) where each vessel is already clear to pass the other port to port or starboard to starboard; and

(2) where by night, both sidelights of the other vessel are seen anywhere but ahead.

Sometimes it is not easy to say with any degree of certainty[2] whether the vessels are in a head-on situation governed by Rule 14, or a crossing situation subject to Rule 15. The following two situations may be cited:

(1) when the courses on which the vessels will pass are not exactly parallel, but are at an angle with one another and will intersect as the vessels advance.

(2) when two vessels are meeting from opposite directions and one of them changes her course and directs it across that of the other.

Rule 15 - *Crossing Situation*

When two power-driven vessels are crossing so as to involve risk of collision, the vessel which has the other on her own starboard side shall keep out of the way and shall, if the circumstances of the case admit, avoid crossing ahead of the other vessel.

In a crossing situation, the duty of the ship, having the other

---

1. The proposed text was as follows: "(c) when a vessel is in any doubt as to whether she is meeting another vessel on a nearly reciprocal course or is crossing within the meaning of the Rules of this Section. She shall assume that she is meeting at a nearly reciprocal course and shall when possible make a substantial alteration of course to starboard." See CR/CONF/3, p.91.
2. For the application of the rule on head-on in a narrow channel, see *The "Ballylesson"* (1968) 1 Lloyd's Rep. 69.

on her starboard side, is to keep clear of the other ship and, if practicable, to avoid crossing ahead of her. She would keep clear without crossing ahead in three ways:

(1) by altering course to starboard so as to pass astern of the other ship;

(2) by reducing speed, allowing the other ship to cross ahead; or

(3) by altering to port and turning through some 360 deg.

Whichever action is adopted, it should be carried out early and positively. On the other hand, the duty of the other ship is to keep her course and speed subject to the provisions of Rule 17 relating to action by stand-on vessel.

The "Aracelio Iglesias"[1] is a good illustration of the duties imposed by Rule 15. In fact, in this case if both vessels had maintained their courses and speeds a collision would have occurred. In an attempt to avoid a collision, the stand-on vessel departed from her course. The collision, in this case, occurred in Panama Bay, in moonlight between *Nidareid* and *Aracelio Iglesias*. *Nidareid* saw *Aracelio Iglesias* leaving the Canal and showing her green light. Her engines, which were at full ahead were ordered to stand-by. At 19 02 hours her engines were put to slow ahead and were stopped at 19 05 hours. *Aracelio Iglesias* was then 20 deg. on port bow of *Nidareid*. When vessels were half a mile apart, *Nidareid* went hard-a-starboard and gave one-short-blast signal. No reply was heard from *Aracelio Iglesias*, and *Nidareid's* engines were put full astern. Collision occurred between stem of *Nidareid* and starboard side of *Aracelio Iglesias*, at angle of 60 deg. leading aft on *Aracelio Inglesias*.

It was held, by Karminski, J. that:

(1) *Nidareid*, the stand-on vessel, acted correctly in goind to starboard and putting engines astern when the vessels were half a mile apart;

(2) *Nidareid* was not at fault in not going to port;

(3) *Nidareid* was right to assume risk of collision and to depart from her course; and

(4) *Aracelio Iglesias* was solely to blame.

---

1. (1968) 1 Lloyd's Rep. 131. Appeal by *Aracelio Iglesias* (1968) 2 Lloyd's Rep. 7, was dismissed.

ARACELIO INGLESIAS

1. 137°(T) full ahead
+ working up speed

2.a/c 5° to port for
bouy heard one short
blast replied with five

3.

4.Five short blasts
hard a port

5.

Speeds about 7 knots

5.

4.
alterd to starboard
and gave one short
blast and went full
astern

3.STOP

2.Slow ahead

NIDAREID 1.Slowing down

Crossing Rules - When to Apply

One of the difficult questions which arises in the mind of many Masters is when there is a crossing situation and, consequently, when Rule 15 is applicable. Two cases recently attempted to lay down certain principles in this respect. The first is *"Alonso de Ojeda"* (Owners) v. *"Sestriere"* (Owners), *(The "Sestriere")*[1] where a collision occurred between the *Alonso* and *Sestriere* in the River Plate. Both vessels had Buenos Aires pilots on board, whom they were due to drop near the Intersection Pontoon. *Alonso* proceeded faster than *Sestriere*, which had left first, and overtook her on *Sestriere's* starboard side.

At 19 48 *Alonso* was turning to a northerly heading to approach the Pontoon and *Sestriere* observed that manoeuvre. After *Alonso* completed her turn, she stopped her engines. *Sestriere* was still approaching and *Alonso* saw the possibility of a collision. *Alonso* sounded a series of short blasts as a warning. *Sestriere* also sounded short blasts but neither signal was heard on board the other ship. *Alonso* put her engines full ahead and turned hard to starboard. The ships converged and collision occurred.

Brandon, J. clearly stated when the crossing rules apply by saying: "for the crossing rules to apply, it was necessary that the stand-on ship should be on a clearly defined course, apparent to the other ship." His Lordship held in this case that *Alonso* was manoeuvring to drop her pilot and for this purpose was proceeding slowly ahead on a northerly heading. While performing this operation, she was free to adjust and to change her heading as she might wish. In these circumstances, she was not on a sufficiently settled course to bring the crossing rules into operation.

The second case is *The "Savina"*[2], where a collision occurred between *Forest Hill* and *Savina* in the roadstead of Ras Tanura. *Forest Hill* was proceeding from an anchorage in the southern part of the roadstead to the sea on a northerly course. *Savina* was proceeding from the south pier to an anchorage in the northern part of the roadstead on an easterly course. The stem and starboard bow of *Savina* struck the port side aft of *Forest Hill* in the way of her nos. 8 and 9 cargo tanks at an angle of about 75 deg. leading forward on *Forest Hill*.

Brandon, J. held that from the time that *Forest Hill* steadied on a course of 350 deg. (T) at or shortly before C-8, there was a

---

1. (1976) 1 Lloyd's Rep. 125. See also *The Alcoa Rambler* (1949) A.C. 236; (1949) 82 Ll.L.Rep. 359.
2. (1974) 2 Lloyd's Rep. 317.

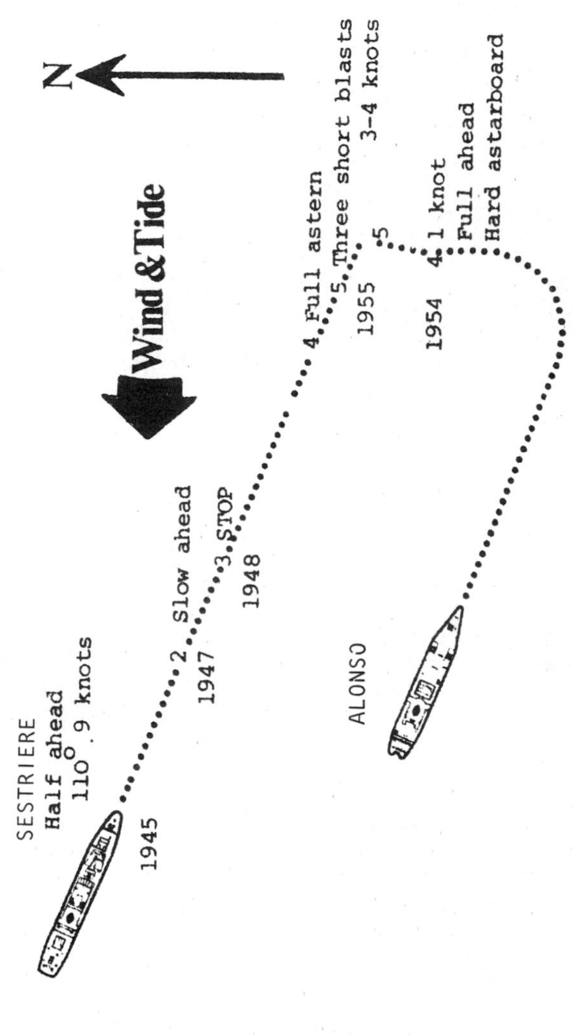
N
Wind & Tide
SESTRIERE
Half ahead
110° 9 knots
1945
2 Slow ahead
1947
3 STOP
1948
4 Full astern
5 Three short blasts
3-4 knots
1955
ALONSO
1954
4 1 knot
Full ahead
Hard astarboard
5

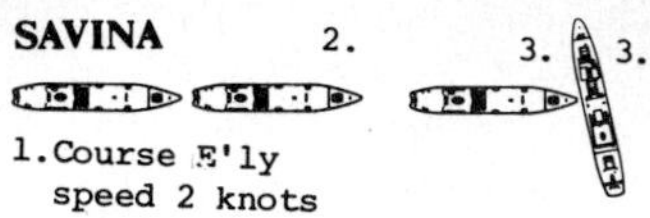

crossing situation, but not at any earlier time because, until C-8, *Forest Hill* was not on a definite course at all. The Appeal Court[1] reversed the apportionment and said that: "it could not be precisely determined as a matter of law when a 'course' was established for the purpose of the crossing rules; but in the present case *Forest Hill* was not on a course until she had steadied on 350 deg. (T), and, consequently, it was only from that time that the crossing rules applied"[2].

---

1. (1975) 2 Lloyd's Rep. 141.
2. In fact both Mr. Justice Brandon and the Court of Appeal are in agreement. The situation in *The Savina* was by definition a crossing situation. It is also true that in other situations, it would be rather difficult to determine as a matter of law which 'course' will bring the crossing rules into operation.

Crossing Rules - When to Cease

In *Orduna* (Owners) v. *Shipping Controller*[1], it was unsuccessfully argued on behalf of the *Orduna* that the crossing rules had ceased to apply and that at the critical time the ships were no longer crossing ships. In his speech, Viscount Finlay said: "These conditions (crossing) continue to subsist until the vessels have definitely passed out of the phase of crossing ships. It was far too soon to conclude that the vessels had passed when the green light of the *Konakry* got ahead of the *Orduna*. The operation of

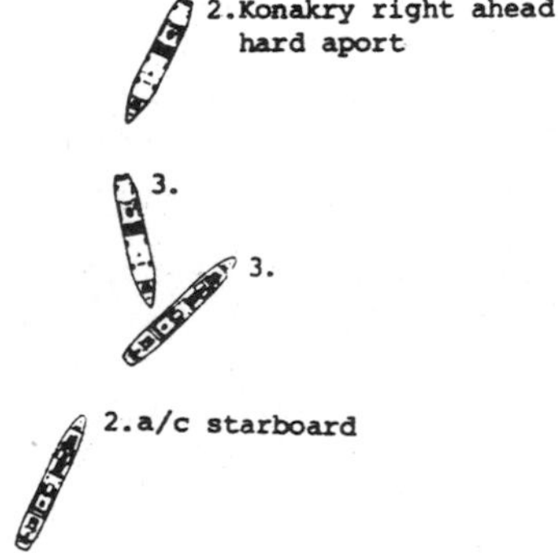

1. (1920) 5 Ll.L.Rep. 241; (1921) 1 A.C. 250.

passing was not yet completed, and it would lead to danger and collision in very many cases if such a state of matters should be considered to constitute the position of passed ships so as to absolve either of them from further attention to the regulations for crossing."

Failure to Observe the Crossing Rules

It is frequently found that a failure to observe Rule 15 together with breaches of other rules, especially bad look-out and bad appreciation of the situation, lead to a collision. In *The Toni*[1], a collision occurred at night, in good visibility between the *Cardo* and the *Toni*, off the south-east coast of Africa.

Cardo was on a course of 056 deg. (true) with engines at full speed ahead (15½ knots) and exhibiting the regulation lights. *Toni* was on a course of 221 deg. (true) and with engines at full speed ahead (10 knots) and exhibiting the regulation lights. *Cardo's* radar was operating on the 40-mile range. Two masthead lights of *Toni* were sighted bearing about 10 deg. on the port bow and at a distance of 14 miles. *Toni* was heading across *Cardo's* bows. The radar was switched to the 16-mile range and *Toni* was carefully watched. When *Toni* had closed to a distance of 4·7 miles with her green visible, *Cardo* altered course to 061 deg. (true). When *Toni* was 2·3 miles distant, it appeared that she had altered to port as if to cross ahead of *Cardo*. *Cardo* altered to 089 deg. (true). When *Toni* was seen broad on the port bow and distant about 1·1 miles still apparently altering her course to port, *Cardo's* helm was put hard-a-starboard. Shortly afterwards *Cardo* sounded five short blasts followed by one short blast, put her engines to "standby" and thereafter "stop". *Cardo's* helm was put hard-a-port as *Toni* came on at speed, and with her stem and starboard bow struck *Cardo's* port side just above the bridge superstructure at an angle of about 50 deg. leading forward on *Cardo*.

The Court held that:

(1) *Toni* was to blame for (i) she had not kept a proper look-out and had failed to appreciate that the vessels were on crossing courses and to observe until a very late stage that *Cardo* altered course to starboard; (ii) she had taken no early positive action to keep out of *Cardo's* way; (iii) she had kept her course which involved her in trying to cross ahead of *Cardo*; (iv) she had altered course to port instead of to starboard; and (v) she had failed to signal the alteration of course to port by sounding two short blasts.

---

1. (1973) 1 Lloyd's Rep. 79. On appeal (1974) 1 Lloyd's Rep. 489.

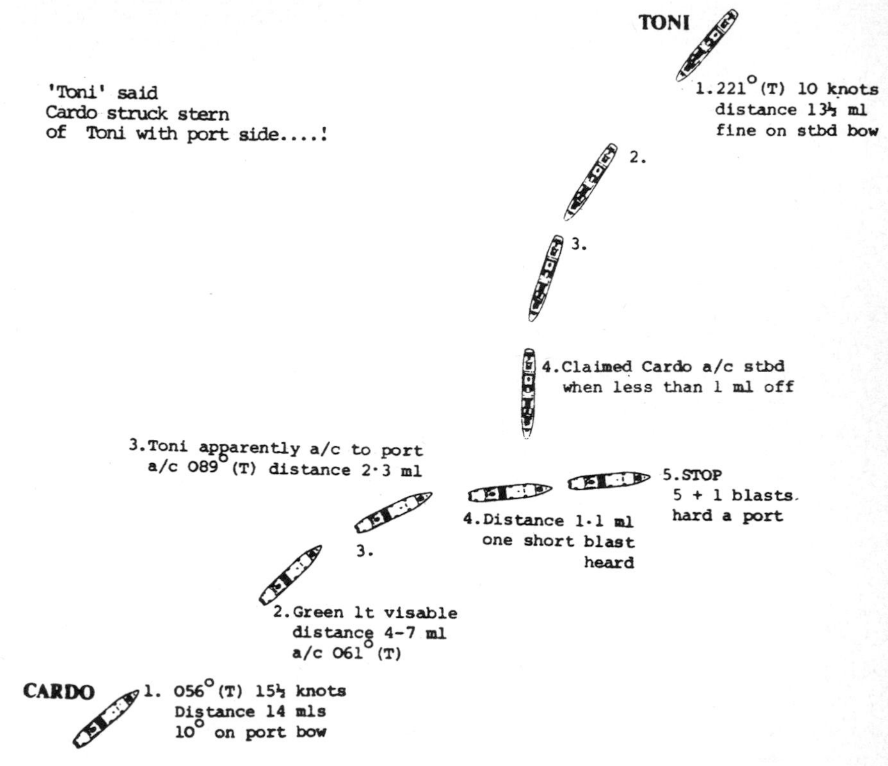

(2) *Cardo* was also at fault for (i) she had not kept her course and speed, in that she had made a succession of alterations of course to starboard; and (ii) she had not sounded a signal of one short blast when the second and third alterations of course to starboard were made.

In "*The Forest Lake*"[1], the give-way vessel failed to observe her duty as she should have waited for *Forest Lake* to pass ahead. In this case, a collision occurred in daylight between *Janet Quinn* and *Forest Lake* in Suez Bay.

Janet Quinn was anchored about a quarter of a mile astern of *Harpula* (also anchored), heading of north and preparing to continue her voyage to India. *Forest Lake* was proceeding north-westerly

1. (1967) 1 Lloyd's Rep. 171.

to anchorage to north of *Janet Quinn* prior to navigating through the Suez Canal and, sighting *Janet Quinn*, exhibiting black anchor ball, decided to proceed between *Janet Quinn* and *Harpula*. *Janet Quinn* weighed anchor and proceeded slowly to sea, heading north-east. One long blast was sounded by *Forest Lake*, and the vessels continued to approach on crossing courses. *Janet Quinn* lowered the black ball. *Forest Lake* sounded three short blasts and went full astern (her head falling off to starboard). The stem of *Forest Lake* struck the starboard side of *Janet Quinn* a little aft of amidships, with the result that the *Janet Quinn* had to be beached.

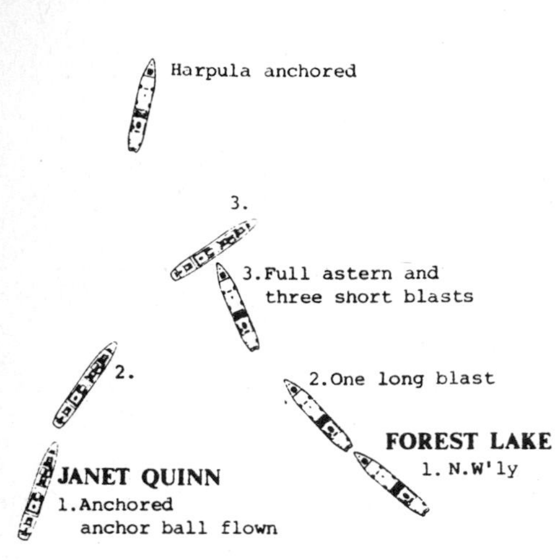

It was held that:

(1) *Janet Quinn* was to blame for (i) she ought to have waited for *Forest Lake* to pass ahead; (ii) she lowered her anchor ball just before *Forest Lake* sounded three short blasts; and (iii) in getting under way before her anchor ball was down.

(2) *Forest Lake* was not to blame for not appreciating *Janet Quinn* was under way or for setting course between *Janet Quinn* and *Harpula*.

Therefore, *Janet Quinn* was solely to blame[1].

---

1. The learned Judge made the following observation on vessels at anchor: "It seems to me that a mariner seeing two ships at anchor both with anchor balls hoisted is entitled to assume that they are both anchored as the signs indicate. If the anchor ball is dropped, then of course great care must be taken. Again I have taken advice on it from the Elder Brethren, and they agree with my view that there is no burden on an oncoming ship to watch the other ship against the land, which is not very far away here, and then to judge after a good deal of worry whether that ship is moving at all." Ibid., at p.178.

In *The "Statue of Liberty"*[1] a collision occurred between *Andulo* and *Statue of Liberty* in good visibility off Capt St. Vincent. The main causative fault was that the *Statue of Liberty* failed, in a crossing situation, to take early and positive action to get out of the other vessel's way.

The *Andulo* was proceeding on a course of 172 deg. (true) at 14 knots when the masthead lights and green light of the *Statue of Liberty* were seen bearing 20 deg. on the port bow, distant about 5 to 6½ miles; about 5 minutes later the bearing narrowed to about 10 deg. on the port bow. When the *Statue of Liberty's* green light was just starboard of the foremast and about 7 cables distant, the *Andulo* altered course to 161 deg. (true) (merely to get on her course to Casablanca); during that alteration, the *Statue of Liberty* altered to starboard; the *Andulo* took further port wheel action and then hard-a-port action. The vessels continued to swing and the *Statue of Liberty* collided with the starboard side of the *Andulo*.

It was held by Brandon, J. that:

(1) The *Statue of Liberty* was at fault for her bad look-out; not taking early and positive action to get out of the *Andulo's* way; and for her failure to signal her alterations to starboard.

(2) The *Andulo* was at fault for her failure to take compass bearings and not keeping her course.

Apportionment of blame: *Statue of Liberty* 70 per cent; *Andulo* 30 per cent.

The Court of Appeal found that the *Andulo's* failure to take compass bearings was not a causative fault or any fault of proper navigation. Consequently, it varied the apportionment and held that the *Statue of Liberty* was 85 per cent to blame, and the *Andulo* 15 per cent.

On appeal by the *Andulo* and cross-appeal by the *Statue of Liberty*, the House of Lords[2] held that the *Andulo* was not justified in assuming that no further alteration of course would be made by the *Statue of Liberty* even if the green light of the *Statue of Liberty* was ahead. Further, the *Statue of Liberty's* failure to give way earlier was the most causative fault. Consequently, the appeal and the cross-appeal were dismissed.

---

1. (1970) 2 Lloyd's Rep. 151.
2. (1971) 2 Lloyd's Rep. 277.

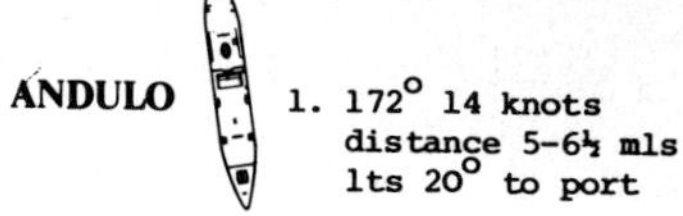
ANDULO
1. 172° 14 knots
distance 5-6½ mls
lts 20° to port

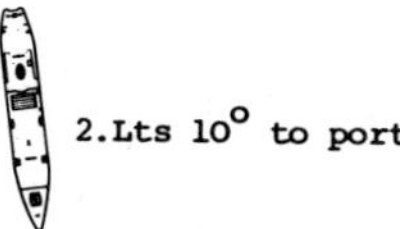
2.Lts 10° to port

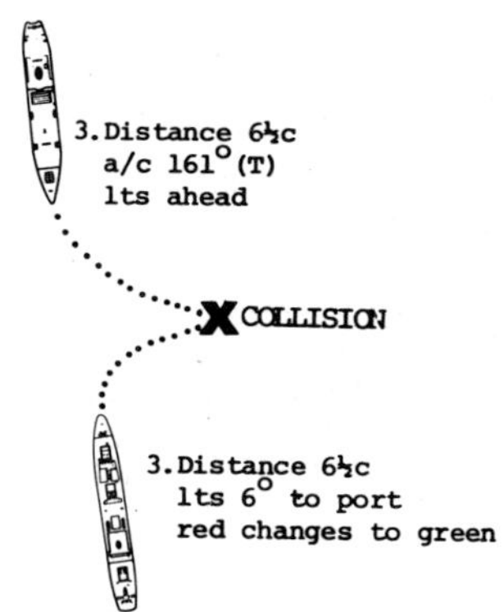
3.Distance 6½c
a/c 161°(T)
lts ahead
COLLISION
3.Distance 6½c
lts 6° to port
red changes to green

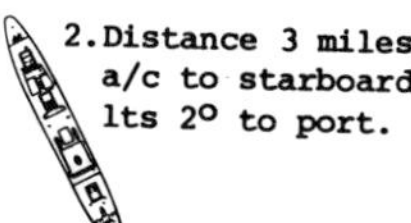
2.Distance 3 miles
a/c to starboard
lts 2° to port.

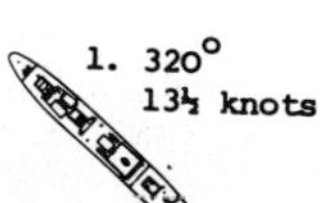
STATUE of LIBERTY
1. 320°
13½ knots

Crossing Situations in Approaching a Pilot Station and in Narrow Channel

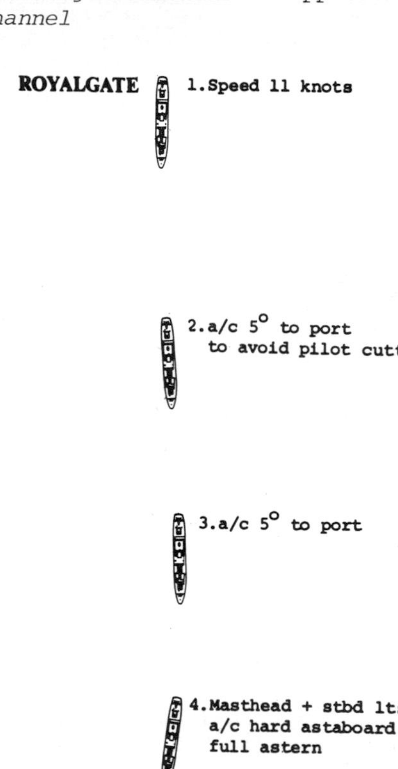

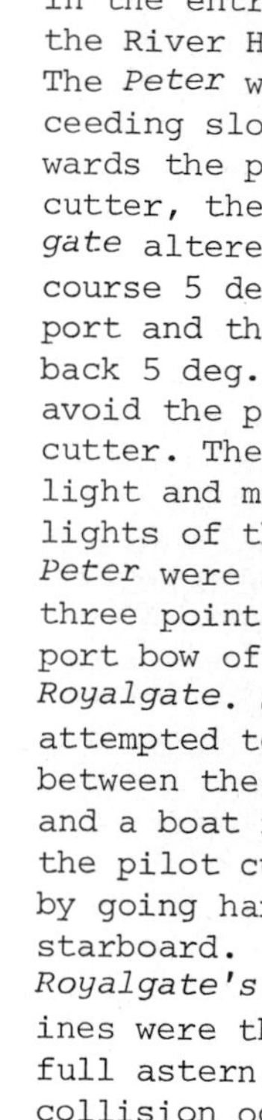

A crossing situation may occur when a vessel is approaching a pilot station to take a pilot on board. In *The "Royalgate"*[1], a collision occurred between the *Peter* and the *Royalgate* at night, in the entrance to the River Humber. The *Peter* was proceeding slowly towards the pilot cutter, the *Royalgate* altered course 5 deg. to port and then came back 5 deg. to avoid the pilot cutter. The green light and masthead lights of the *Peter* were seen three points on port bow of the *Royalgate*. She attempted to go between the *Peter* and a boat from the pilot cutter by going hard-a-starboard. The *Royalgate's* engines were then put full astern, but collision occurred.

Karminski, J. said[2]: The position, as I find it

1. (1967) 1 Lloyd's Rep. 352.
2. Ibid., at p.358.

was this. The *Royalgate* had ahead of her a pilot vessel and also the *Peter*. By this time, astern of the *Peter*, were the tug and tow. The *Royalgate* was in this position, that she rightly expected the *Peter*, the give-way vessel, to get out of her way. It is in my view clear that the initial fault here was on the *Peter*, which took no steps as she approached the pilot vessel to keep clear of the *Royalgate* until the very last moment."

The learned Judge held that the two vessels were on crossing courses. The *Peter* was at fault in not giving way to the *Royalgate*. On the other hand, the *Royalgate* was at fault (i) for her bad look-out in that she ought to have kept clear of the pilot cutter and reduced her speed; and (ii) she starboarded too late[1].

The "Santander"[2] shows how the crossing rules apply in a narrow channel. In this case, collision occurred in the River Mersey, at night, in restricted visibility and at flood tide. *Naess Tern* was proceeding at manoeuvring full speed (11 knots) on course of 325 deg. when she saw deck lights of *Santander*; distant one mile and stationary right ahead. The course of *Naess Tern* was altered to 335 deg. and then to 345 deg. in order to go down river on her own starboard side. The engines of *Naess Tern* were reduced to slow ahead at 21 39 hours when the lights of *Santander* (or one of her tugs) were sighted by *Naess Tern*. The engines of *Naess Tern* were stopped; her wheel put hard-a-starboard, and one short

---

1. See also *"Alonso de Ojeda"* (Owners) v. *"Sestriere"* (Owners), *The "Sestriere"* (1976) 1 Lloyd's Rep. 125.
2. (1966) 2 Lloyd's Rep. 77.

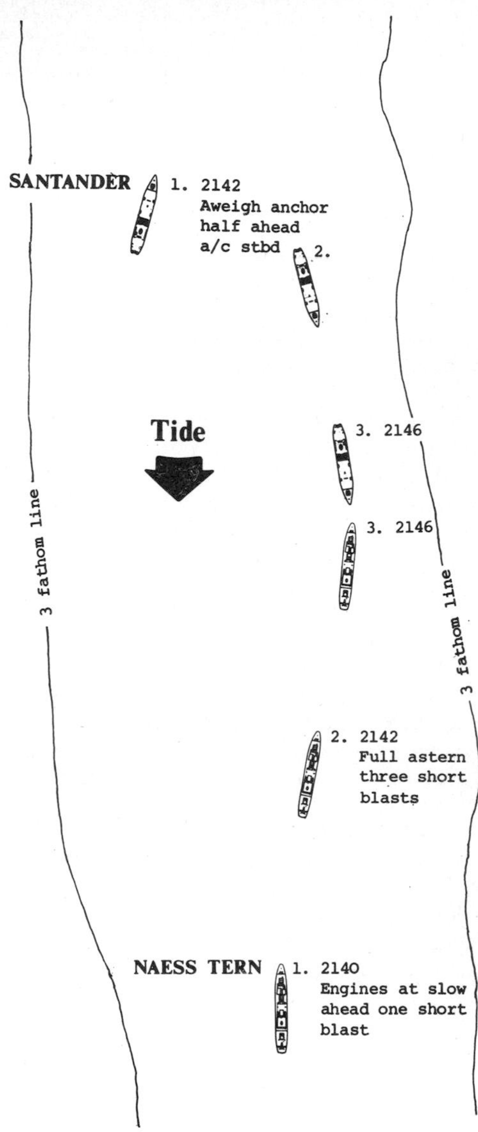

blast was sounded (21 40 hours). The engines of *Naess Tern* were put full astern and three short blasts were sounded (21 42 hours). However, collision occurred between port bow of *Naess Tern* and the starboard bow of *Santander* at angle of three points at 21 46 hours.

The Court found that the collision was between a down-going vessel and a crossing vessel. In such a situation it was the duty of the crossing vessel not to interfere with the down-going vessel. Also the *Santander* commenced crossing at an improper time, due to bad look-out and the pilot's belief that *Naess Tern* would pass to westward. After discussing the faults on each vessel the Court apportioned the blame: *Santander*, two-thirds; *Naess Tern*, one-third.

Distinction Between Overtaking and Crossing Situations

Perhaps the most difficult situation is the one where the master is faced with the dilemma of whether the situation is crossing or overtaking. In *The Main*[1], Lord Herschell, presiding in the Court of Appeal, approved *The Franconia*[2], and said[3]: "It has been contended on behalf of the defendants that a ship is being overtaken by another, within the meaning of this article when a ship is approaching another in a position in which she is unable to see the lights of the vessel which is ahead of her, and which she is approaching. On the other hand, it has been contended for the plaintiffs that a vessel is only being overtaken when the course of the overtaking ship is such that if it be left unchanged a collision will ensue. The latter is, I think, certainly too narrow a construction."

However, in *The Banshee*[4], Lord Esher, M.R. said: "Now, at what period of time is it that the Regulations begin to apply to two ships? It cannot be said that they are applicable however far off the ships may be. Nobody could seriously contend that, if two ships are six miles apart, the Regulations for Preventing Collisions are applicable to them. They only apply at a time when, if either of them does anything contrary to the Regulations, it will cause danger of collision. None of the Regulations apply unless that period of time has arrived. It follows that anything done before the time arrives at which the Regulations apply is immaterial, because anything done before that time cannot produce risk of collision within the meaning of the Regulations[5].

More recently, in *The "Nowy Sacz"*[6], a collision occurred in the Atlantic Ocean south of Cape St. Vincent between *Olympian* and the *Nowy Sacz*. Both vessels were proceeding on about parallel

---

1. (1886) 11 P.D. 132.
2. (1876) 2 P.D. 12.
3. (1886) 11 P.D. 132, at p.135.
4. (1887) 6 Asp. Mar. Law Cas. 220.
5. Sir Boyd Merriman P., followed *The Banshee* in *The Manchester Regiment* (1938) 60 Ll.L.Rep. 279; (1938) P. 117.
6. (1976) 2 Lloyd's Rep. 682.

courses in a northerly direction. The night was clear and the visibility good. At about 02 45, when the *Olympian* was bearing about 25 deg. to 30 deg. abaft the starboard beam of the *Nowy Sacz*, the second officer of the *Nowy Sacz* was seeing the masthead lights of the *Olympian*, but not then her red light some three miles away. At the same time the second officer of the *Olympian* had not yet observed any lights of the *Nowy Sacz*.

By 03 00, when the bearing of the *Olympian* from the *Nowy Sacz* ceased to be more than two points abaft the beam, the second officer was seeing the red light of the *Olympian* as well as her masthead lights. The second officer of the *Olympian* also saw the masthead lights and green light of the *Nowy Sacz*.

Owing to the relative courses and speeds of the two ships - the closing speed being between 2 and 2½ knots - the time at which risk of collision arose was about 03 30, when the *Nowy Sacz* was on the *Olympian's* port beam and appeared to be closing on a crossing course from port to starboard at an angle of 25 deg. to 30 deg. At the same time the *Olympian's* master sounded one long blast of 20 to 30 seconds, to which there was no response.

At 03 50 the second officer of the *Nowy Sacz* gave a warning signal of five short flashes on the signalling lamp. There was no response and shortly afterwards the *Nowy Sacz* reduced speed and stopped her engines. On hearing a signal of one short blast from the *Olympian*, which was then about 1-2 cables away, the second officer of *Nowy Sacz* put her engines first half, then full astern and sounded three short blasts. The *Olympian's* master put her engines to stand-by, ordered one short blast, and put her wheel hard to starboard. Shortly afterwards at 03 57 a collision occurred between the stem of the *Nowy Sacz* and the port quarter of the *Olympian* at an angle of about 10 deg.

The owners of the *Olympian* contended that the situation was a crossing one and consequently *Nowy Sacz* was under a duty to keep out of the way of the *Olympian*. On the other hand, the owners of the *Nowy Sacz* argued that the situation was an overtaking one and it was the duty of the *Olympian*, as the overtaking ship, to keep out of the way of the *Nowy Sacz*, the ship being overtaken.

Brandon, J. rejected the contention that the situation was an overtaking one and said[1]: "It is clear that the overtaking rules would only have been applicable in the present case if, before about 03 00, when the *Olympian* was still bearing more than two points abaft the beam of the *Nowy Sacz*, two conditions were fulfilled: firstly, that the two ships were by then already in

---

1. Ibid., at p.694.

sight of one another; and secondly, that risk of collision between them had by then already arisen"[1].

His Lordship held that it was a crossing situation. The *Nowy Sacz* should have kept out of the way of the *Olympian*. The latter as the stand-on vessel should have kept her course and speed. Accordingly, *Nowy Sacz* was three-quarters to blame and the *Olympian* one-quarter[2].

On appeal by the owners of *Nowy Sacz*, the Court of Appeal[3] referred to the old authorities and said that it appears that *The Banshee*[4] is in conflict with *The Main*[5] and it followed *The Main*. The Appeal Court added that the overtaking rule applies before there is a risk of collision. However, this does not mean that it necessarily comes into effect as soon as the vessels are in sight of one another. The overtaking rules begin to operate as soon as it could properly be said that the overtaking ship was coming up[6] with the overtaken ship. When exactly that will be may not always be easy to determine but we see no reason to suppose that it will be any more difficult than the decision as to when the situation involves a risk of collision[7]. Although the Court of Appeal approved Brandon, J. that the risk of collision arose in this case at about 03 30, it considered the situation as overtaking. *Nowy Sacz* was the stand-on ship and the *Olympian* was the give-way ship. It apportioned the blame: *Nowy Sacz* one-quarter and the *Olympian* three-quarters.

In *The "Auriga"*[8], a collision occurred in the Atlantic Ocean off the west coast of Spain between the *Manuel Campos* and the *Auriga*. Both vessels were proceeding in a southerly direction at the respective speeds of between 11 and 12½ and 14 knots.

At 19 08, when *Manuel Campos* reached a position in which she had Cape Villano light abeam to port distant 10½ miles by radar, she

---

1. It seems that the second condition was also fulfilled because collision would have happened if the two vessels had continued on their respective courses.
2. Ibid., at p.695.
3. (1977) 2 Lloyd's Rep. 91.
4. (1887) 6 Asp. Mar. Law Cas. 220.
5. (1886) 11 P.D. 132.
6. In *The Auriga* (1977) 1 Lloyd's Rep. 384, Brandon, J. said that the words "coming up with" another involve an element of proximity in space or time between the ships.
7. (1977) 2 Lloyd's Rep. 91, at p.98.
8. (1977) 1 Lloyd's Rep. 384.

altered course from 239 deg. to 205 deg. After steadying on her new course, the master noticed the two white masthead lights and red side light of *Auriga* bearing about 10 deg. off the starboard quarter and distant about three miles and it was assumed that *Auriga* was overtaking.

Auriga was proceeding at full speed on a course of 212 deg. and the courses of the two vessels were diverging at an angle of 7 deg. while *Auriga* was gaining on *Manuel Campos* at the rate of 2-2½ knots. At about 19 22 or 19 23 G.M.T., *Auriga* altered course to 181 deg. and by the time the alteration had been made the bearing of *Auriga* abaft the starboard beam of *Manuel Campos* was less than two points abaft and her distance a little over 2¼ miles. The courses of the two vessels were now converging at an angle of 24 deg. with a risk of collision if the courses were maintained.

At about 19 46 G.M.T., the forward masthead light of *Manuel Campos* was bearing 122 deg. indicating that the bearing of *Auriga* from the bridge of *Manuel Campos* was then only one-half point abaft the beam. Neither of the vessels took any effective avoiding action nor did they keep a continual and careful observation. Shortly afterwards the collision occurred causing substantial damage to both vessels.

The *Manuel Campos* argued that since the *Auriga* was bearing two points abaft her beam and was proceeding faster than her, she was an overtaking vessel. Further, the fact that the bearing of the *Auriga* later altered, so that it ceased to be more than two points abaft her beam, made no difference because of the principle "once an overtaking vessel always an overtaking vessel".

The Court rejected this argument as the courses of the two ships were diverging and the distances[1] between them at every stage were too great for a risk of collision to exist. The Court added that as an overtaking situation did not exist, it must follow that, in the latter stages of the two ships' approach to one another, when their courses were converging at an angle of 24 deg-

---

1. In fact, an overtaking situation existed prior to 19 08 and the distances between the two ships were irrelevant.

rees, there was a crossing situation[1].

Rule 16 - *Action by Give-way Vessel*

Every vessel which is directed to keep out of the way of another vessel shall, so far as possible, take early and substantial action to keep well clear.

There are three situations where risk of collision exist namely: overtaking (Rule 13)[2]; head-on (Rule 14); and crossing (Rule 15). In both overtaking and crossing, one vessel would be the stand-on vessel and the other the give-way vessel. In a head-on situation, both vessels would be give-way vessels. Rule 16 deals with action by give-way vessel while Rule 17 concerns with action by stand-on vessel.

Under Rule 16, the give-way vessel may take different actions such as reducing her speed, stopping or reversing. Whatever action she takes must be in accordance with the practice of good seamanship, timely and substantial, so as to leave the stand-on ship in no possible doubt as to what she is doing. In *The Billings Victory*[3], Willmer, J., after stating the duty of the give-way vessel to take timely action to keep clear, said[4]: "Moreover, it is her duty to act, if I may use the expression, handsomely, so as to leave the

---

1. Brandon, J. said that the overtaking rules "only apply when the relationship between the two ships concerned is such that risk of collision between them exists. In determining whether such risk exists in any particular case it is necessary to take all the relevant circumstances into consideration. Of these the most important will normally be the distance between the two ships, the speed at which the one is gaining on the other, and the lateral distance at which the faster ship is shaping to pass the slower ship. In connection with the last of these matters, it will be material to know, among other things, whether the courses of the two ships are diverging, converging or substantially parallel." Ibid., at p.383.
   With respect, this observation is not compatible with Rule 7 (d) (i) and Rule 13 (d).
2. *The Banshee* (1887) 6 Asp.Mar.Law Cas. 221; *The Manchester Regiment* (1938) 60 Ll.L.Rep. 279; *The Nowy Sacz* (1976) 2 Lloyd's Rep. 682.
3. (1949) 82 Ll.L.Rep. 877.
4. Ibid., at p.881.

stand-on vessel in no possible doubt as to what the give-way vessel is doing. If her method of giving way is to alter course, she ought to make a substantial alteration."

In *The "Toni"*[1], the Court found that the officer of the watch of the *Cardo* "at fault in not sounding a signal of one short blast when he made his second and third alterations of course to starboard. If such signals had been sounded, they might have alerted those on board the *Toni* to what was happening"[2].

Again, in *The "Genimar"*[3], a collision occurred in the Dover Strait between the *Larry L* and the *Genimar*. Both ships were fitted with radar and visibility was variable from three to four miles.

Larry L was on a south-westerly course of 235 deg. at a speed of 16 knots while the *Genimar* was on a north-easterly course of 058 deg. at a speed of between 8 and 8½ knots.

At about 04 20 while using the radar on the eight mile range, the chief officer of *Larry L* first observed the echo of *Genimar* bearing fine on the starboard bow and distant about seven miles. Between 04 21 and 04 22 *Larry L* altered course 3½ deg. to port from 255 deg. to 231½ deg. and between 04 30½ and 04 33 a further alteration of 4 deg. to port from 231½ deg. to 227½ deg. was made.

Shortly after 04 30 *Genimar*, having altered course from 058 deg. to 068 deg. saw the two white masthead lights and green side light of *Larry L* bearing fine on the port bow. It appeared that *Larry L* was shaping to cross the course of *Genimar* from port to starboard at a narrow angle and *Genimar* therefore altered course 10 deg. to starboard from 068 deg. to 078 deg.

Just after 04 33 the chief officer of *Larry L* saw the two white masthead lights and red side light of *Genimar* bearing fine on the starboard bow distant about two miles and appreciated that she was on a course crossing that of *Larry L* from starboard to port. After watching the light of *Genimar* for a few minutes during which her distance closed while her bearing of 078 deg. remained the same, a signal of five short blasts was sounded by *Larry L*. When *Genimar* was less than a mile away, *Larry L* altered course 9½ deg. to starboard and almost immediately reversed the action by putting her wheel hard to port. At the same time as *Larry L*

---

1. (1973) 1 Lloyd's Rep. 79, at p.85.
2. See also *The "Anneliese"* (1969) 2 Lloyd's Rep. 78; *The "Savina"* (1974) 2 Lloyd's Rep. 317.
3. (1977) 2 Lloyd's Rep. 17.

was turning to port, *Genimar* having sounded a signal of one short blast, was turning rapidly to starboard and soon after the collision occurred.

It was held, by Q.B. (Adm.Ct.), Brandon, J. that:

(1) *Larry L* was at fault in failing to keep out of the way of the *Genimar* and in putting her wheel hard to port at the last moment;

(2) *Genimar* was at fault in failing to keep her course and in navigating in the wrong lane of the traffic separation scheme.

As the faults of *Larry L* were serious in respect of both culpability and causative effect, the Court held that *Larry L* was two-thirds to blame, and *Genimar* was one-third.

Rule 17 - *Action by Stand-on Vessel*

(a) (i) Where by any of these Rules one of two vessels is to keep out of the way the other shall keep her course and speed.

(ii) The latter vessel may however take action to avoid collision by her manoeuvre alone, as soon as it becomes apparent to her that the vessel required to keep out of the way is not taking appropriate action in compliance with these Rules.

(b) When, from any cause, the vessel required to keep her course and speed finds herself so close that collision cannot be avoided by the action of the give-way vessel alone, she shall take such action as will best aid to avoid collision.

(c) A power-driven vessel which takes action in a crossing situation in accordance with sub-paragraph (a) (ii) of this Rule to avoid collision with another power-driven vessel shall, if the circumstances of the case admit, not alter course to port for a vessel on her own port side.

(d) This Rule does not relieve the give-way vessel of her obligation to keep out of the way.

Course and speed in (a) (i) and (b)

In the leading case, *The Reanoke*[1], Lord Alverstone, C.J. said that "course and speed" mean "course and speed in following the nautical manoeuvre in which, to the knowledge of the other vessel, the vessel is at the time engaged.... The 'course' certainly does not mean the actual compass direction of the heading of the vessel at the time the other is sighted... A vessel bound to keep her course and speed may be obliged to reduce her speed to avoid some danger of navigation, and the question must be in each case, 'Is the manoeuvre in which the vessel is engaged an ordinary and proper manoeuvre in the course of navigation which will require an alteration of course and speed; ought the other vessel to be aware of the manoeuvre which is being attempted to be carried out'? ".

Lord Justice Kennedy, in the same case, referred to the criterion of good seamanship and added[2]: "It would be a strange thing if a vessel, in order successfully and in the ordinary and proper way to perform a proper nautical manoeuvre, must alter her speed... such alteration if it takes place at a time when she is being approached by another vessel, which is either overtaking her... or is a crossing steamship which has her on the starboard side... although the manoeuvre in which she is engaged, and the necessity of altering speed which the manoeuvre involves, are perfectly obvious to the overtaking or crossing vessel, and although the alteration in speed in no way prevents such overtaking or crossing vessel, if properly navigated, from keeping out of her way. It seems to me that this cannot be the right interpretation of the injunction to keep her speed. It would introduce into navigation not infrequently a probable source of danger. A steamer approaching her landing place for goods or passengers, or drawing up to an anchorage, must often either reduce her speed or abandon

---

1. (1908) P. 231 at p.239. In that case the ship, which was the stand-on ship in a crossing situation, reduced her speed to pick up a pilot. It was held that, where a stand-on ship was, to the knowledge of the give-way ship, properly engaged in an ordinary nautical manoeuvre of that kind, she was entitled to carry it out, even though it involved a reduction of speed. See also *The Cederic* (1924) P. 215; (1924) 19 Ll.L.Rep. 391. In that case a ship, which was being overtaken by another ship in a river, had, before the overtaking situation arose, put her engines from half ahead to full ahead. As a result, after the overtaking situation had arisen, her speed through the water increased gradually from six knots to 7½ or eight knots as she worked up to her full speed. It was held that this was not a breach of her duty to keep her speed.
2. Ibid., at p.246.

her object... "

In *The Taunton*[1], a collision occurred between a steamship, which was proceeding seawards down the Bristol Channel with a strong tide behind her, and a sailing vessel, a ketch, which was engaged in crossing the Channel from south to north. It was the duty of the steamship to keep clear of the sailing vessel, and there was a corresponding duty on the sailing vessel to keep her course. However, because she was proceeding across a strong tide the sailing vessel had to make repeated alterations of helm in order to maintain her position. It was argued that she was not complying with the Rules in that she was not keeping her course, but the Court had no difficulty in rejecting this argument.

Another classic case on the duty of the stand-on vessel is to be found in *The Otranto*[2], where Lord Buckmaster said[3]: "The ship that is bound to keep her course is not entitled to alter it at a moment when there is ample time for the ship that is bound to give way to discharge her duty, for that ship is entitled to rely upon obedience to the rule by the ship that has to keep her course. But, acknowledging to the full the vital consequences of strict obedience, there still remains the fact that these rules were made for the guidance of mariners and not of mathematicians, and that it is not right, by an elaborate process of calculation after the event, to decide that the ship that was bound to keep her course acted a little before the moment that in fact she need have done."

In *The "Aracelio Iglesias"*[4], Karminski, J. said[5]: "... the Regulations presumably were in the hands of the master of the *Aracelio* and to anybody looking at a ship coming up at that hour and steering as she was it must have been perfectly apparent why she was going in that direction and that in order to anchor in the anchorage ground, which was an extensive one, sooner or later she must reduce speed."

Brandon, J. in *The "Toni"*[6] found that the *Cardo* was at fault in failing to keep her course and speed because she made a succession of alterations of course to starboard. The reason she did so was that the officer of the watch formed a firm view early on that the ships would pass each other port to port, and that it would, therefore, be heopful for him to alter course to starboard

---

1. (1928) 31 Ll.L.Rep. 119.
2. (1931) A.C. 194; (1930) 38 Ll.L.Rep. 204.
3. Ibid., at p.208.
4. (1968) 1 Lloyd's Rep. 131.
5. Ibid., at p.139.
6. (1973) 1 Lloyd's Rep. 79.

to give more room. The other ship, the *Toni*, being the give-way ship, failed to give way and instead tried to cross ahead[1].

In *The "Homer"*[2], a collision occurred in the Thames Estuary between the *Elisa F* and the *Homer*.

Elisa F (drawing 37 ft. fore and aft), was proceeding in the middle of the Yantlet Channel with engines at manoeuvring full ahead. She altered course half a mile off no. 1 Sea Reach buoy from 086 deg. (true) to 090 deg. (true). The mast lights and red side light of the inward-bound *Homer* were sighted distant about two miles and bearing about 15 deg. on the starboard bow. *Homer* was on a course of 290 deg. (true) and with her engines at manoeuvring full ahead was making about 12 knots through the water.

Soon afterwards, *Elisa F* altered course to 095 deg. (true) to pass no. 1 Sea Reach buoy to port. At the same time *Homer's* pilot first noticed *Elisa F's* lights and green side light, distant about one mile bearing fine on the port bow. He formed the view, mistakenly, that *Elisa F* was navigating to the north of the channel.

Elisa F reached no. 1 Sea Reach buoy and passed it close on her port side, putting her engines half ahead (making about 8 to 9 knots through the water). As her stern cleared the buoy, her wheel was put hard-a-starboard (with the intention of passing *Homer* port to port) and one short blast was sounded. However, that signal was not heard on *Homer*. *Elisa F* began to swing slowly to starboard and sounded a second one short blast. This was not noticed on board *Homer*, which, believing that *Elisa F* was continuing on an easterly course, altered course from 290 deg. (true) to 285 deg. (true) and sent a V.H.F. message to *Elisa F.*: "I am altering course to port to let you go to the north." *Elisa F's* pilot promptly ordered wheel hard-a-port and sounded two short blasts, replying on V.H.F.: "I am altering course to port now." However, *Elisa F* continued to swing to starboard and the pilot of *Homer* became aware for the first time of *Elisa F's* alteration to starboard. Accordingly, *Homer's* wheel was ordered hard-a-starboard and one short blast was sounded. By this time the *Elisa F* had checked her swing to starboard and begun to swing back to port. Although *Homer* ordered port wheel action, and in spite of full astern orders on both vessels, the vessels continued to swing together and a collision took place between the stem of *Homer* and starboard bow of *Elisa F*.

Brandon, J. held that the *Homer* was at fault because she should have kept her course and speed. Her alteration from 290 deg. to

---

1. Ibid., at pp.84, 85.
2. (1972) 1 Lloyd's Rep. 429; On appeal (1973) 1 Lloyd's Rep.501.

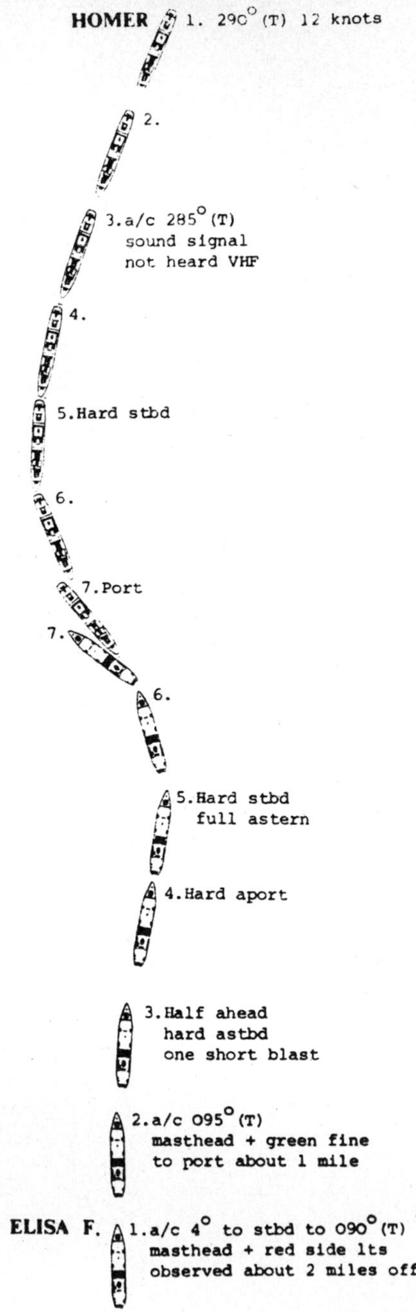
HOMER
1. 290° (T) 12 knots
2.
3. a/c 285° (T)
sound signal
not heard VHF
4.
5. Hard stbd
6.
7. Port
7.
6.
5. Hard stbd
full astern
4. Hard aport
3. Half ahead
hard astbd
one short blast
2. a/c 095° (T)
masthead + green fine
to port about 1 mile
ELISA F.
1. a/c 4° to stbd to 090° (T)
masthead + red side lts
observed about 2 miles off

285 deg. was wrong. However, her most causative fault was her bad aural and visual look-out. The *Elisa F* was not at fault in (1) keeping close to the centre line of the channel; (2) altering to starboard; (3) failing to reduce speed earlier; and (4) altering to port after the *Homer* had done so. The *Homer* was alone to blame.

The course shall be maintained until the last safe moment. Lord Buckmaster, in *The Otranto*[1], explained this rule by stating: "What that safe moment is, must depend primarily upon the judgment of a competent sailor, forming his opinion with knowledge of the necessity of obedience to the rule and in face of all the existing facts. Subsequent examination may show that his judgment could not properly have been formed, in which case the rule has been broken without excuse, but the ultimate decision is not to be settled merely by exact calculations made after the event, but by considering these facts as they presented themselves to a skilled man at the time."

In many cases[2], it was held that the stand-on vessel is entitled to be judged with some degree of leniency if she does take the wrong action when put in such a position of difficulty.

Take action para. (a) (ii)

Sub-paragraph (ii) of (a)[3] gives the stand-on vessel freedom to take action at an early stage to avoid a collision. This liberalization of the duty of the stand-on vessel is an innovation which allows a mariner in the stand-on vessel who encounters a vessel in a potential collision situation to avoid it by an early evasive manoeuvre. The time of action and whether it is too soon or too late depends on the circumstances. In *The "Alletta" and the "England"*[4], a collision occurred at night in the River Thames. The Court of Appeal held that both vessels were to blame. The *England* was free of blame up to the time when the green light of *Alletta* was opened. After this, the situation was altered and the *England* should have taken drastic action at short notice, namely,

---

1. (1931) A.C. 194, at p.201; (1930) 38 Ll.L.Rep. 204, at p.208.
2. See for example *The Billings Victory* (1949) 82 Ll.L.Rep. 877.
3. This is new
4. (1966) 1 Lloyd's Rep. 573.

she should have gone full astern[1].

In *The "Ek"*[2], a collision occurred between *Debalzevo* and the tanker *Ek* in the North Sea. *Debalzevo* was proceeding on course of 190 deg. (true) at full speed (14 knots) and *Ek* was proceeding on course of 152 deg. (true) at full speed (12½ knots) about one mile to starboard of *Debalzevo* and on bearing of 260 deg. Both vessels thought that they were on parallel courses. Four minutes before collision, *Ek* was seen by *Debalzevo* to be apparently turning to port, and the engines of *Debalzevo* were stopped. 1½ minutes before collision, the distance between the vessels was two to three cables and the vessels were closing rapidly. *Debalzevo*

---

1. Per Willmer, L.J. (at p.581): "In a situation of this nature I think that it can seldom be wrong to take off way, and the best method of taking off way is to reverse the engines. Taking off way increases the time available for both vessels to manoeuvre; it also reduces the amount of the damage if a collision does happen to take place. Whatever the *Alletta* was engaged in doing, and whatever her intention may have been, it seems to me that putting the engines of the *England* full speed astern could not possibly do any harm."
2. (1966) 1 Lloyd's Rep. 440. See also *The Otranto* (1931) A.C. 194; (1930) 38 Ll.L.Rep. 204, where Lord Buckmaster said: "It is never an easy decision for the man in charge of a stand-on ship. The question which is posed is one which is not to be solved by exact mathematical calculations *ex post facto*. The duty of the Court is to look at the circumstances as they would have presented themselves to the officer in charge of the ship which is called upon to act." See also Lord Merriman, P. in *The Sparto* (1956) 1 Lloyd's Rep. 400, where he stated (at p.407): "(This Rule) is perhaps the most difficult of all the Regulations for seamen to adhere to. It must always be a matter of difficulty for the officer in charge of the vessel which has to keep her course and speed to determine when the time has arrived to take action, for if he acts too soon, he may disconcert any action which the other vessel may be about to take to avoid his vessel, and be blamed for so doing, and yet the time may come when he must take action. The precise point when he should cease to keep his course and speed is difficult to determine, and some latitude is allowed him in determining this."

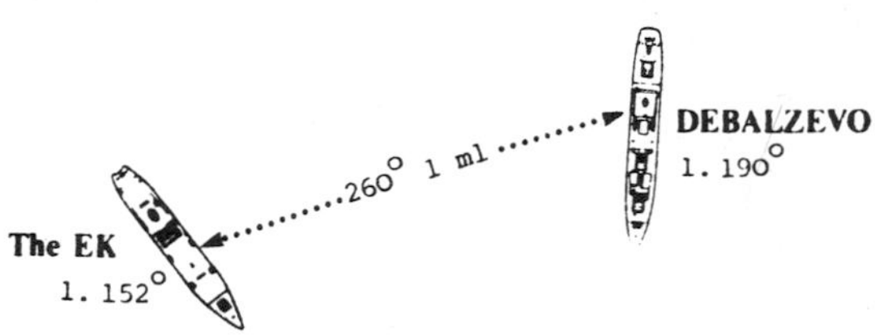

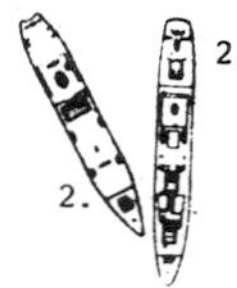

then put her wheel hard-a-port. When the vessels were 100 metres apart, *Ek* realized that collision was imminent and her engines were put to stand by, then to half speed, and her wheel was put hard-a-starboard. Port bow of *Ek* struck the starboard side of *Debalzevo* at angle of 20 deg. leading forward on *Debalzevo*.

It was held, by Cairns, J.:

(1) that *Ek* did not alter course to port and *Debalzevo* could have avoided collision by starboarding under stern of *Ek*, and, when it was too late for that, she could have turned to port (and that was the more necessary when she thought, wrongly, that *Ek* was turning to port), but she maintained her course; and that, therefore, she was to blame;

(2) that *Ek* should have realized that collision was imminent when vessels were three or four cables apart and should then have turned to starboard; that to allow vessels to close to 50 or 60 metres without doing anything was quite wrong; that *Ek's* failure to sound five-short-blasts signal did not contribute to damage in that *Debalzevo* would not have acted differently.

Apportionment of blame: *Debalzevo* three-quarters; *Ek* one-quarter.

Debalzevo awarded all her costs[1].

In *The "Estrella"*[2], a collision occurred off Capt St. Vincent between the *Setubal* and the *Estrella*. At about 23 00 the *Setubal* had Cape St. Vincent abeam to port about two miles, i.e. she was within the traffic separation zone and navigating wrongly in a northbound traffic lane. Her radar was on and her master was using automatic steering. She was making full speed about 12½ knots on a course of 135 deg. The *Estrella* was making 13½ knots on a course of 302 deg. and at 23 00 saw the mast headlights of the *Setubal*, and before either ship altered course for the other, the *Setubal* was bearing fine on the starboard bow of the *Estrella* and the *Estrella* was bearing fine on the port bow of the *Setubal*, both vessels' navigation lights being on at the time. At that stage the vessels were crossing so as to involve risk of collision.

Some seven minutes before the collision the *Setubal* had made a gradual alteration to port from 135 to 125 deg. when the *Estrella* was three miles distant showing her green light fine on her port bow, and 2½ minutes before the collision the *Setubal* made a more rapid alteration to port from 125 deg. to 085 deg. when the *Estrella* was little more than a mile way. The *Estrella* meanwhile some eight minutes before the collision altered to starboard on seeing the lights of the *Setubal* and continued on a slow and gradual alteration to starboard until two minutes before the collision altering 24 deg. from her original course of 302 deg. to a heading of 326 deg. which was the result of the second officer of the *Estrella* applying 15 deg. of starboard rudder in order to give way to the *Setubal* under the crossing rules. The second officer of the *Estrella* put her rudder hard to starboard on seeing from the lights of the *Setubal* that she had altered course to port, a minute before the collision and half a minute before collision seeing that collision was imminent the rudder of the *Estrella* was put hard to port. The stem of the *Estrella* struck the starboard side of the *Setubal* at nearly a right angle when both ships were proceeding at nearly their full speeds. The *Setubal* was badly holed and later sank; the bow of the *Estrella* was damaged.

Brandon, J. said[3]: "It seems to me that the primary cause of the collision was that the *Setubal*, being the stand-on ship in a crossing situation, failed to keep her course, and instead made successive alterations to port, first of 10 deg. when the ships were still a substantial distance apart, and then a further 40 deg. or so as they approached closer to each other. The failure

---

1. See also *The "Tojo Maru"* (1968) 1 Lloyd's Rep. 365; *The "Savina"* (1974) 2 Lloyd's Rep. 317.
2. (1977) 1 Lloyd's Rep. 525.
3. Ibid., at p.525.

of the *Estrella* to take more positive action to give way in ample time was also a serious fault. Two points can, however, be made in mitigation of it. First, the *Estrella* did at least appreciate that a crossing situation existed, and took action which was in principle proper action, namely altering to starboard, in fulfilment of her obligation to keep out of the way of the *Setubal*. Second, the alteration to starboard which she made, though not sufficiently large or rapid...was nevertheless enough to have enabled the two ships to pass safely port to port, and so to have avoided a collision, provided only that the *Setubal* had also played her part by keeping her course. As regards the later faults of the *Estrella* in not putting her engines astern a little earlier, and in checking her starboard swing at the last, I think that these errors occurred in a situation of urgent danger brought about largely by the negligence of the *Setubal*, and that in those circumstances not too much weight should be given to them.

Having considered carefully the culpability and causative effect of the faults on either side, I have come to the conclusion that the *Setubal* was considerably more to blame than the *Estrella*, and that a fair division of responsibility is *Estrella* three-eighths and *Setubal* five-eighths."

Sub-paragraphs (c) and (d)

Sub-paragraphs (c) and (d) are new. Sub-paragraph (c) requires that a power driven vessel, taking action in accordance with sub-paragraph (a) (ii) shall not normally alter course to port for a vessel on her port side.

Sub-paragraph (d) reminds the give-way vessel of her obligation under rule 16.

Rule 18 - *Responsibilities between Vessels*

Except where Rules 9, 10 and 13 otherwise require:

(a) A power-driven vessel underway shall keep out of the way of:

(i) a vessel not under command;

(ii) a vessel restricted in her ability to manoeuvre;

(iii) a vessel engaged in fishing;

(iv) a sailing vessel.

(b) A sailing vessel underway shall keep out of the way of:

(i) a vessel not under command;

(ii) a vessel restricted in her ability to manoeuvre;

(iii) a vessel engaged in fishing.

(c) A vessel engaged in fishing when underway shall, so far as possible, keep out of the way of:

(i) a vessel not under command;

(ii) a vessel restricted in her ability to manoeuvre;

(d) (i) Any vessel other than a vessel not under command or a vessel restricted in her ability to manoeuvre shall, if the circumstances of the case admit, avoid impeding the safe passage of a vessel constrained by her draught, exhibiting the signals in Rule 28.

(ii) A vessel constrained by her draught shall navigate with particular caution having full regard to her special condition.

(e) A seaplane on the water shall, in general, keep well clear of all vessels and avoid impeding their navigation. In circumstances, however, where risk of collision exists, she shall comply with the Rules of this Part.

Rule 18 on "Responsibilities between Vessels" opens by stating that it does not apply in three situations, namely, in a narrow channel (Rule 9), separation scheme (Rule 10) and overtaking (Rule 13). All other situations are subject to it. Consequently, in a crossing situation, involving say a vessel constrained by her draught, the crossing rule does not apply.

In fact, the draftsmen of the Rules felt that the mutual responsibilities of the different categories of vessels would be better illustrated if they were listed in one rule and Rule 18 spells out these responsibilities. Manoeuvrability is the test for priority[1] among the various categories of vessels.

The "Carebeka 1"[2] is a good illustration of the responsibilities between a fishing and a power-driven vessel. In this case, a collision occurred in the English channel between the fishing vessel *Robin John* and the m.v. *Carebeka 1*. *Robin John*, carrying regulation lights, was trawling southward at two to three knots along Decca Lane Green C. 42. *Carebeka 1's* masthead light and red were sighted distant four to five miles on the starboard beam. *Carebeka 1* continued to close and when she was half a mile distant *Robin John* opened her throttle to full, put her wheel hard-

1. The order of priority is reversed in a narrow channel. See Rule 9 (b), (c).
2. (1973) 1 Lloyd's Rep. 396.

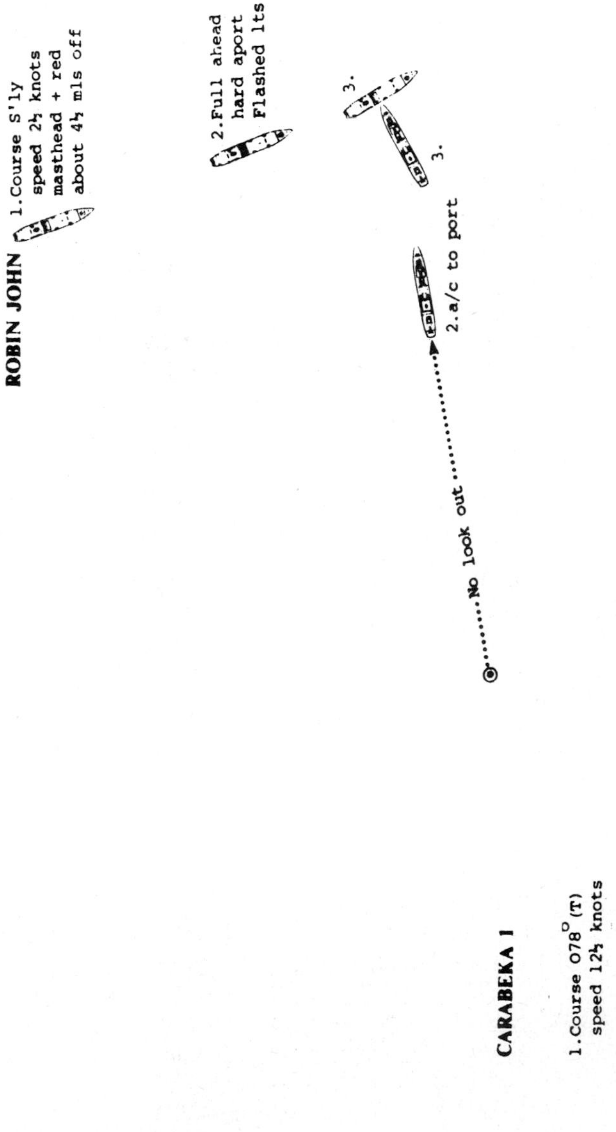

ROBIN JOHN

1.Course S'ly
speed 2½ knots
masthead + red
about 4½ mls off

2.Full ahead
hard aport
Flashed lts

3.

3.

2.a/c to port

No look out

CARABEKA I

1.Course 078° (T)
speed 12½ knots

a-port, flashed deck and navigation lights on and off, blew one or two two-short-blast signals and then a one-long-blast signal. A collision occurred between *Carebeka 1's* bow and the starboard side of *Robin John*.

It was held, by Brandon, J. that the intention of the Collision Regulations was that a ship not engaged in fishing was under a duty to keep clear of a ship which was so engaged; that *Robin John* was not negligent in failing to ease or stop her engines since she could not be certain what *Carebeka 1* might do; that even though *Robin John* might not have appreciated the bearing and heading of *Carebeka 1*, that was not a cause of the collision and even if *Robin John* were under a duty to sound signals earlier there was no look-out on the other vessel.

Paragraph (d)

It is not clear whether paragraph (d) (i) grants a privilege to a "vessel constrained by her draught"[1] or merely provides for an "identification signal" in order to warn other vessels of her limitation in manoeuvring. The second part of this paragraph (ii) which states that "a vessel constrained by her draught shall navigate with particular caution", negates the idea of a privilege as such a vessel would be treated as any other power-driven vessel. However, it is clear from the preparatory works of the Rules that some privilege is given to a vessel constrained by her draught subject to five limitations:

(1) A vessel constrained by her draught must manoeuvre when she encounters a vessel with a superior privilege[2].

(2) As mentioned before, no privilege could be claimed in a narrow

---

1. For the meaning of "a vessel constrained by her draught", see Rule 3 (h).
2. The Netherlands delegation stated in a working paper: "A vessel constrained by her draught should not obtain a full privilege by a provision in the Rules which prescribes that other vessels have to get out of the way of a vessel constrained by her draught. The Rules should contain a restricted privilege by a provision which prescribes that other vessels should not impede the safe navigation of a vessel constrained by her draught. This last privilege accorded to a vessel constrained by her draught, still gives such a vessel the responsibility to comply with the steering and sailing rules as much as possible." Conference Committee II, W.P. 1 at pp.5, 6.
   It is not clear, however, whether a vessel constrained by her draught has the duty of a stand-on vessel or a give-way vessel when the privileges conflict or when she encounters another vessel in a similar condition.

channel, separation scheme and overtaking situations.

(3) The privilege cannot be claimed unless the signals in Rule 28 are exhibited.

(4) The privilege cannot be accepted if it would lead to a dangerous or unseamanlike situation. This is clear from the use of the words "if the circumstances of the case admit" in (i).

(5) The second paragraph of (d) states that: "A vessel constrained by her draught shall navigate with particular caution having full regard to her special condition." This means that in spite of the privilege granted to a vessel constrained by her draught, she is still under a duty to navigate with caution. This duty should be observed by a vessel constrained by her draught whether she is exhibiting the signals in Rule 28 or not.

In brief, a vessel constrained by her draught enjoys a qualified privilege when exhibiting the signals in Rule 28. Other vessels with lesser privileges would be under a duty to avoid impeding her safe passage, if the circumstances of the case admit.

(III) CONDUCT OF VESSELS IN RESTRICTED VISIBILITY

Rule 19 - *Conduct of Vessels in Restricted Visibility*

(a) This Rule applies to vessels not in sight of one another when navigating in or near an area of restricted visibility.

(b) Every vessel shall proceed at a safe speed adapted to the prevailing circumstances and conditions of restricted visibility. A power-driven vessel shall have her engines ready for immediate manoeuvre.

(c) Every vessel shall have due regard to the prevailing circumstances and conditions of restricted visibility when complying with the Rules of Section I of this Part.

(d) A vessel which detects by radar alone the presence of another vessel shall determine if a close-quarters situation is developing and/or risk of collision exists. If so, she shall take avoiding action in ample time, provided that when such action consists of an alteration of course, so far as possible the following shall be avoided:

(i) an alteration of course to port for a vessel forward of the beam, other than for a vessel being overtaken;

(ii) an alteration of course towards a vessel abeam or abaft the beam.

(e) Except where it has been determined that a risk of collision does not exist, every vessel which hears apparently forward of

her beam the fog signal of another vessel, or which cannot avoid a close-quarters situation with another vessel forward of her beam, shall reduce her speed to the minimum at which she can be kept on her course. She shall if necessary take all her way off and in any event navigate with extreme caution until danger of collision is over.

Rule 19 applies when vessels are navigating in or near an area of restricted visibility. The word "navigating" should be noted and therefore this Rule would not apply to a ship lying dead in the water, with her engines stopped[1].

Paragraph (b) refers to safe speed as provided for in Rule 6 which applies in any kind of visibility. It also reaffirms that restricted visibility has to be taken into consideration when determining the safe speed. The second part of paragraph (b) requires that engines should be ready for immediate manoeuvre and perhaps if necessary with engineers in immediate attendance.

Paragraph (c) refers to Section 1, namely Rules 5 to 10.

Paragraph (d) requires a vessel which detects by radar alone[2] another vessel, to use the radar for determining if a close-quarters situation is developing and/or risk of collision is likely. The information gained from the radar would assist in taking any avoiding action. This paragraph also states that the following two actions should be avoided:

(1) alteration of course to port for a vessel forward of the beam; and

(2) alteration of course towards a vessel which is abeam or

---

1. However, a vessel which stops in the water, e.g. in a busy traffic lane, would not necessarily be considered innocent if a collision followed.
2. The Court of Appeal in *The Lady Gweldolen* (1965) P. 294 said that although much discretion must be left to the master, it is the duty of shipowners: (a) to appreciate the navigational problems posed by the use of radar in fog; (b) to impress the urgency of those problems upon the masters of their ships; and (c) to take steps to ensure so far as they reasonably can that their ships are navigated safely in fog. This last duty involves some measure of supervision and control of masters and officers by shipowners and their responsible shore based staff such as marine superintendents.

abaft the beam[1].

Finally, paragraph (e) states that this section of the rules of conduct should be followed by every vessel in restricted visibility[2].

---

1. The Court of Inquiry in *The Rattray Head/Tillerman* collision said:
   "(i) That when the range of visibility has reduced to between 3 and 2½ miles, the master should be informed of the situation so that he can judge whether or not his presence on the bridge is desirable.
   (ii) That when visibility has reduced to 2 miles, fog signals ought to be sounded, certainly if the radar screen shows echoes in any direction.
   (iii) That when visibility has reduced to 2 miles and the radar screen shows echoes ahead with any risk of a close-quarters situation arising, speed must be reduced and the master called to the bridge if he is not already there. To leave this, as some witnesses suggested, to 1½ or even one mile does not give the master sufficient time to assess the situation and to act at speeds at which the vessels are likely to be approaching each other if they are still navigating at their full speed. If each ship is navigating at 10 knots, one mile will be covered in three minutes. Whenever their initial speeds are greater or the observations of speed of approach of a radar echo shows that they may be greater (and with the tendency towards faster vessels a closing speed of 30 knots is not uncommon), precautions need to be taken correspondingly earlier.
   (iv) When no echoes are visible on the radar screen and the vessel is in open water not approaching any river or harbour entrance, it may be justifiable to maintain full speed with a good radar look-out in somewhat more restricted visibility. But if visibility is less than one mile and the vessel is proceeding on a coastal route round the British Isles, this Court would not condone a failure to reduce speed even for coasting vessels of the nature concerned in this case, still less for larger or faster vessels, which may have to reduce speed at greater visibilities, even if no echoes are visible."
   The findings of the Court of Inquiry are published in a brochure issued by The Mercantile Marine Service Association in June 1970.
2. A difficult situation arises when some vessels are in sight while others, including "another" vessel in paras. (d) and (e) are not.

Cases which have a bearing upon Rule 19

The "Almizar"[1] is the best illustration for the application of both paragraphs (b) and (d). In this case, a collision occurred in fog, between *John C. Pappas* and *Almizar* in the Arabian Sea. *John C. Pappas,* with engines at slow ahead, was on course of 203 deg. (true) and sounding fog signals. She was equipped with radar but it was out of order. She heard one long blast from *Almizar* on the starboard bow whereupon *John C. Pappas* stopped her engines and sounded one long blast. *John C. Pappas* then put her engines emergency full astern and sounded three short blasts. She sounded two long blasts when she thought she was stopped (her master considering that fog would clear), and, hearing one long blast from *Almizar* close by, sounded second two-long-blasts signal. Single white light of *Almizar* was observed approaching from two points on starboard bow and *John C. Pappas* sounded warning short blasts, but collision occurred between her starboard side and stem of *Almizar.*

It was held, by Karminski, J.:

(1) that *John C. Pappas* was at fault in that she maintained her speed on encountering fog; should have reduced speed much earlier; took no special precaution by way of extra look-outs; altered to port; was not stopped in water when she sounded two long blasts; and wrongly assumed that she would get out of fog quickly;

(2) that *Almizar* was at fault in that her speed was too high and should have been reduced earlier; she was guilty of a poor radar look-out and should have realized radar echo was of a large vessel on a steady course; and she should have stopped engines and not altered course to starboard.

Apportionment of blame: *Almizar,* 60 per cent.; *John C. Pappas,* 40 per cent.

On appeal by *Almizar*[2], the Court of Appeal held that:

(1) *John C. Pappas* was at fault in failing to proceed at moderate speed in fog; to hear the signal forward of her beam; and in altering her course to port.

(2) *Almizar* was not at fault in altering course to starboard.

(3) The most serious fault was the failure of *John C. Pappas* to reduce her speed on entering the fog.

Apportionment of blame: *Almizar,* 40 per cent.; *John C. Pappas,* 60 per cent.

---

1. (1969) 1 Lloyd's Rep. 1.
2. (1970) 1 Lloyd's Rep. 67.

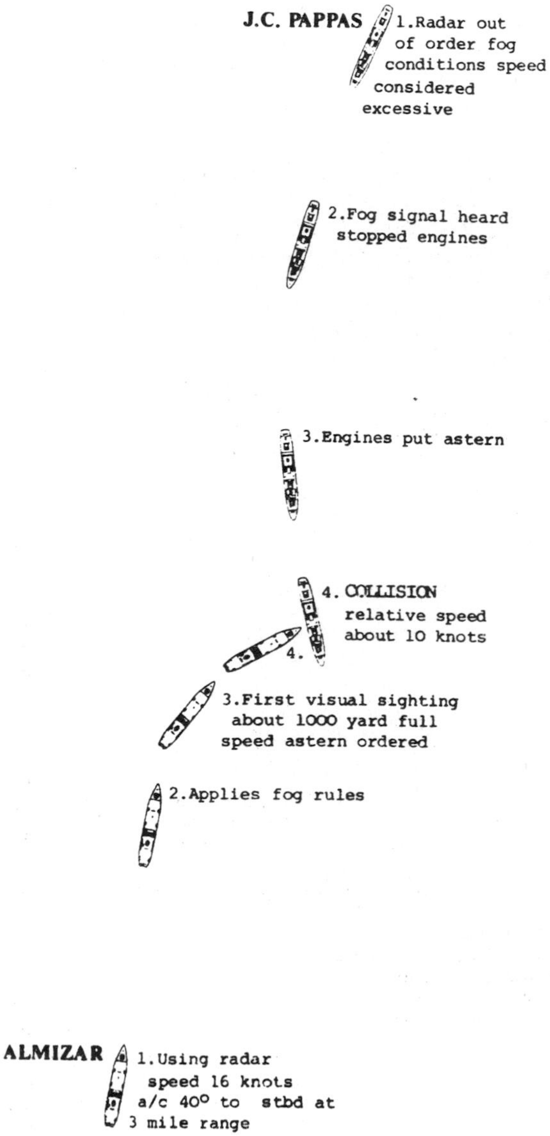

J.C. PAPPAS

1. Radar out of order fog conditions speed considered excessive

2. Fog signal heard stopped engines

3. Engines put astern

4. COLLISION relative speed about 10 knots

4.

3. First visual sighting about 1000 yard full speed astern ordered

2. Applies fog rules

ALMIZAR

1. Using radar speed 16 knots a/c 40° to stbd at 3 mile range

On appeal by *John C. Pappas* and cross-appeal by *Almizar*, the House of Lords[1] held that the porting of *John C. Pappas* was far more blameworthy and was more potent causatively than that of the *Almizar*. Consequently, the appeal was dismissed and the cross-appeal was allowed in part.

Apportionment of blame: *Almizar*, 30 per cent.; *John C. Pappas*, 70 per cent.

The excessive speed (seven to eight knots) of *The "Elazig"*[2] and her failure to reduce it after hearing the fog signal was one of the causes which contributed to the collision. In this case, a collision occurred in fog between *Linda* and *Elazig* near the entrance of the Bosphorous.

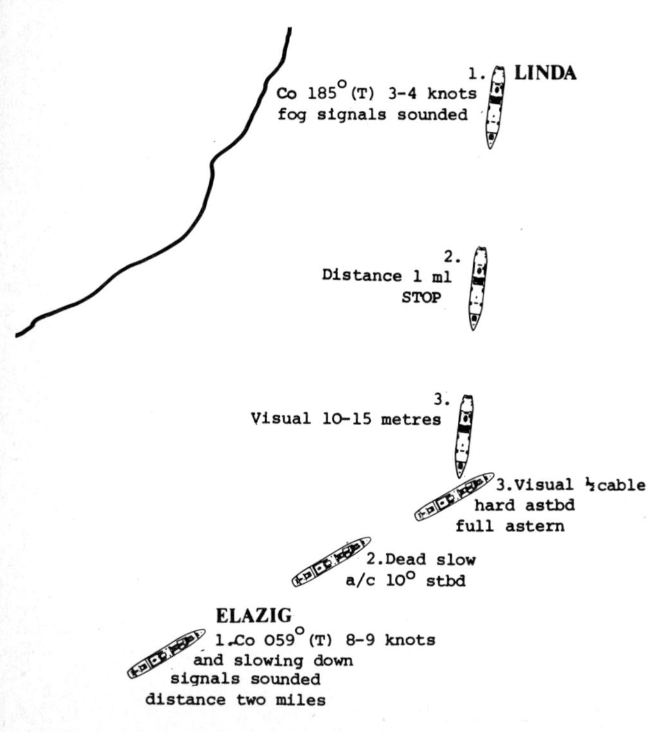

Linda was on a course of 185, with her engines at dead slow ahead and was making about 3 to 4 knots through the water. *Elazig* was on a course of 059, with her engines at slow ahead and was making about 8 to 9 knots.

Linda was sounding fog signals and her radar was in use on the 3-mile range scale. *Elazig* was first observed at a distance of about 1 mile bearing about 32 deg. on the starboard bow.

---

1. (1971) 2 Lloyd's Rep. 277.
2. (1972) 1 Lloyd's Rep. 355.

Linda stopped engines and increased the frequency of her fog signals. One prolonged blast was heard from *Elazig*, whose bows came into sight distant about 10 to 15 metres, bearing broad on *Linda's* starboard bow. *Linda* rang "full astern". *Elazig* continued on and before *Linda's* engines could be worked astern, *Elazig's* stem and starboard bow struck *Linda's* starboard side in way of the forward end of no. 6 hold at an angle of about 85 deg. leading aft on *Linda*.

It was held, by Brandon, J. that:

(1) *Elazig* was to blame for (i) she had not kept a proper radar look-out, and her appreciation was bad; (ii) keeping a speed of 9 knots until much too late, and not stopping her engines; (iii) not going full astern at once; and (iv) for taking a wrong action in altering course to starboard and in going full ahead.

(2) *Linda* was at fault in (i) not keeping a proper look-out and not making a proper appreciation; (ii) proceeding at an excessive speed (3 to 4 knots); (iii) not stopping on seeing the echo of *Elazig* at one mile; and (iv) not going full astern when *Elazig* was half a mile away or less.

Apportionment of blame: *Elazig*, 60 per cent.; *Linda*, 40 per cent.

The "Osprey"[1] is a good example of the application of Rule 19 in a narrow channel. In this case, a collision occurred between *Lokoja Palm* and *Osprey* in fog, in the River Oder. The *Lokoja Palm* was navigating by radar in dense fog and was proceeding at dead slow ahead on her starboard side of channel on course of 176 deg. (true), when she observed echo of *Osprey* on her radar, bearing about ahead, at a little under one mile, and heard fog signal. She altered course to 180 deg. (true) to follow river, bringing echo on to port bow. White lights of *Osprey* were sighted ahead at 200 metres and *Lokoja Palm's* wheel was put hard-a-starboard, but port bows of vessels collided. *Osprey* was proceeding down channel in visibility of two miles, at five knots, when she sighted masthead lights of *Lokoja Palm* about ahead, at distance of one mile. She appreciated that visibility down channel was worse and heard fog signals. Pilot set his course by leading lights astern. When *Lokoja Palm* altered course to starboard, both side lights of *Lokoja Palm* were seen momentarily by *Osprey*. *Osprey* mistakenly thought that *Lokoja Palm* was altering course back to port and put her wheel hard-a-starboard but it had no effect and vessels collided.

---

1. (1967) 1 Lloyd's Rep. 76.

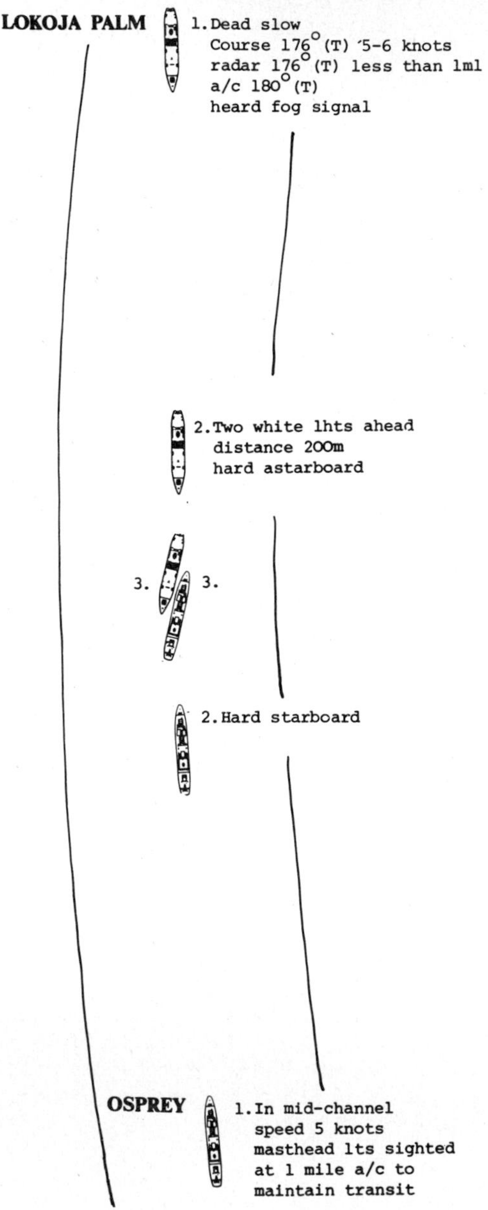
LOKOJA PALM
1. Dead slow
Course 176°(T) 5-6 knots
radar 176°(T) less than 1ml
a/c 180°(T)
heard fog signal
2. Two white lhts ahead
distance 200m
hard astarboard
3.
3.
2. Hard starboard
OSPREY
1. In mid-channel
speed 5 knots
masthead lts sighted
at 1 mile a/c to
maintain transit

It was held, by Brandon, J. that:

(1) *Lokoja Palm* was at fault (i) in proceeding at excessive speed in dense fog; (ii) in not reducing her speed after the radar sighting; and (iii) for allowing herself to get on to her port side of the channel before the radar sighting.

(2) *Osprey* was at fault (i) in maintaining her speed after sighting *Lokoja Palm*; and (ii) in failing after sighting to take wheel action to get to her starboard side of the channel.

Apportionment of blame: *Lokoja Palm* three-fifths; *Osprey* two-fifths.

In *The "Marimar"*[1], the *Scotland* collided with the *Marimar* in fog in the Downs. Both vessels were in charge of pilots. The *Scotland* was proceeding in buoyed channel at stand by full ahead (11 knots).

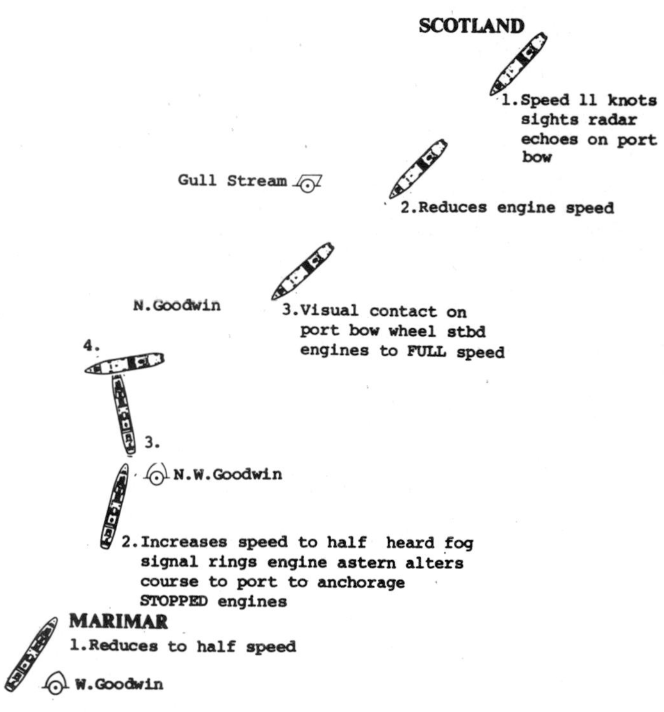

1. (1968) 2 Lloyd's Rep. 165.

After passing Elbow Buoy, the visibility deteriorated and *Scotland* commenced sounding fog signals. As the *Scotland* approached Gull Stream Buoy the pilot saw echoes of two ships ahead on starboard. *Scotland* altered 5 deg. to starboard on to course of 227 deg., bringing echoes of two vessels on to port bow. *Scotland* reduced to slow ahead off Gull Stream Buoy. When *Scotland* was abreast of North Goodwin Buoy her master and mate left radar unattended to look visually for the other two ships. *Marimar* was sighted four points on *Scotland's* port bow heading across *Scotland's* course. *Scotland's* wheel was put hard-a-starboard and the engines full ahead. One-short-blast signal was sounded. Answer of three short blasts was heard from *Marimar*. *Scotland's* wheel was put hard-a-port. The collision occurred between stem of *Marimar* and port side of *Scotland*.

It was held, by Cairns, J.:

(1) that *Scotland* was at fault in proceeding at too high a speed in the conditions of fog;

(2) that there was misjudgment on the part of *Marimar's* pilot in deciding to cross channel and that that misjudgment amounted to a fault; but that having decided to cross he was not negligent in proceeding at half speed; and that order for full astern on *Marimar* was not a wrong one in the special circumstances that existed;

(3) that *Marimar* was not keeping a good look-out;

(4) that *Scotland* was to blame in failing to attend continuously to her radar.

Apportionment of blame: *Scotland* 60 per cent; *Marimar* 40 per cent.

Chapter 6

LIGHTS, SHAPES; SOUND, LIGHT SIGNALS; AND EXEMPTIONS

There are few cases on lights, shapes and sound.

(I) LIGHTS AND SHAPES

Rule 20 - *Application*

(a) Rules in this Part shall be complied with in all weathers.

(b) The Rules concerning lights shall be complied with from sunset to sunrise, and during such times no other lights shall be exhibited, except such lights as cannot be mistaken for the lights specified in these Rules or do not impair their visibility or distinctive character, or interfere with the keeping of a proper look-out.

(c) The lights prescribed by these Rules shall, if carried, also be exhibited from sunrise to sunset in restricted visibility and may be exhibited in all other circumstances when it is deemed necessary.

(d) The Rules concerning shapes shall be complied with by day.

(e) The lights and shapes specified in these Rules shall comply with the provisions of Annex I to these Regulations.

Paragraph (a) provides that lights and shapes shall be complied with in all weather conditions. Consequently, the ship is required to exhibit her navigational lights from sunset to sunrise even if the weather is fine and clear but not dark.

In *The "Tojo Maru"*[1], the Court found that although the lights which *Fina Italia* was exhibiting were contrary to the Rules, her navigational lights would still have been visible up to a mile away to anybody keeping a good look-out.

"No other lights" paragraph (b)

The use of other lights is permitted provided they cannot be mistaken or do not impair their visibility or interfere with the navigational lights. The working lights of fishing vessels may

---

1. (1968) 1 Lloyd's Rep. 365.

give rise to difficulties as they may interfere with the navigational lights[1]. Further, a proper look-out could be affected by the working lights.

It must be noted that in paragraph (b) the words "from sunset to sunrise" are used, while paragraph (d) refers to the word "day" and not from sunrise to sunet.

Rule 21 - *Definitions*

(a) "Masthead light" means a white light placed over the fore and aft centreline of the vessel showing an unbroken light over an arc of the horizon of 225 degrees and so fixed as to show the light from right ahead to 22·5 degrees abaft the beam on either side of the vessel.

(b) "Sidelights" means a green light on the starboard side and a red light on the port side each showing an unbroken light over an arc of the horizon of 112·5 degrees and so fixed as to show the light from right ahead to 22·5 degrees abaft the beam on its respective side. In a vessel of less than 20 metres in length the sidelights may be combined in one lantern carried on the fore and aft centreline of the vessel.

(c) "Sternlight" means a white light placed as nearly as practicable at the stern showing an unbroken light over an arc of the horizon of 135 degrees and so fixed as to show the light 67·5 degrees from right aft on each side of the vessel.

(d) "Towing light" means a yellow light having the same characteristics as the "sternlight" defined in paragraph (c) of this Rule.

(e) "All-round light" means a light showing an unbroken light over an arc of the horizon of 360 degrees.

(f) "Flashing light" means a light flashing at regular intervals at a frequency of 120 flashes or more per minute.

Paragraph (c) defines the sternlight as a white light placed as nearly as practicable at the stern, and this position was agreed so as to make it possible for tugs and supply ships to comply with the Rules.

Both paragraphs (d) and (f) are new and the latter paragraph was made in accordance with the International Association of Lighthouse Authorities (IALA) recommendations.

---

1. The same remark applies to supply vessels, oil and gas rigs.

Rule 22 - *Visibility of Lights*

The lights prescribed in these Rules shall have an intensity as specified in Section 8 of Annex I to these Regulations so as to be visible at the following minimum ranges:

(a) In vessels of 50 metres or more in length:

- *a masthead light, 6 miles;*
- *a sidelight, 3 miles;*
- *a sternlight, 3 miles;*
- *a towing light, 3 miles;*
- *a white, red, green or yellow all-round light, 3 miles.*

(b) In vessels of 12 metres or more in length but less than 50 metres in length:

- *a masthead light, 5 miles; except that where the length of the vessel is less than 20 metres, 3 miles;*
- *a sidelight, 2 miles;*
- *a sternlight, 2 miles;*
- *a towing light, 2 miles;*
- *a white, red, green or yellow all-round light, 2 miles.*

(c) In vessels of less than 12 metres in length:

- *a masthead light, 2 miles;*
- *a sidelight, 1 mile;*
- *a sternlight, 2 miles;*
- *a towing light, 2 miles;*
- *a white, red, green or yellow all-round light, 2 miles.*

Rule 22 provides for the minimum visibility ranges for the various categories of vessels[1] and the distance at which the lights are to be visible is stated in nautical miles. It should be noted that this Rule is considered as a practical guide to the ranges of visibility and the more technical details are contained in the Annex.

---

1. The Netherlands note stated that the range of the lights have little bearing upon the operation of the Rules and therefore it suggested that it should be included in Annex I. See CR/CONF/3, p.144. Notes from the governments of the United Kingdom, United States of America, Federal Republic of Germany and the Netherlands expressed great concern on the relaxation provided by Rule 22 for lights for small power-driven vessels and small sailing vessels. CR/CONF/WP. 17.

Rule 23 - *Power-driven Vessels Underway*

(a) A power-driven vessel underway shall exhibit:

(i) a masthead light forward;

(ii) a second masthead light abaft of and higher than the forward one; except that a vessel of less than 50 metres in length shall not be obliged to exhibit such light but may do so;

(iii) sidelights;

(iv) a sternlight.

(b) An air-cushion vessel when operating in the non-displacement mode shall, in addition to the lights prescribed in paragraph (a) of this Rule, exhibit an all-round flashing yellow light.

(c) A power-driven vessel of less than 7 metres in length and whose maximum speed does not exceed 7 knots may, in lieu of the lights prescribed in paragraph (a) of this Rule, exhibit an all-round white light. Such vessel shall, if practicable, also exhibit sidelights.

Paragraph (b) aims to identify an air-cushion vehicle operating in the non-displacement mode, while paragraph (c) covers small power-driven vessels which may not have enough power to comply with it[1].

---

1. In the note of the Union of Soviet Socialist Republics, it was stated that the requirement for exhibiting lights should not be based on the speed of the vessel. CR/CONF/3, p.147. Notes from the governments of the United Kingdom, United States of America, Federal Republic of Germany and the Netherlands pointed out that paragraph (c) allows all vessels of less than 7 metres in length to exhibit only an all-round white light. This one white light will certainly create an element of great uncertainty which is highly undesirable and dangerous. They added: "imagine a week-end night in a crowded port entrance and harbour where all small vessels are exhibiting only white lights, no sidelights." CR/CONF/WP. p.17. For this reason paragraph (c) states that such vessels shall also exhibit sidelights if practicable, thus allowing the case where there is no place for fitting the lights.

Rule 24 - *Towing and Pushing*

(a) A power-driven vessel when towing shall exhibit:

(i) instead of the light prescribed in Rule 23 (a) (i), two masthead lights forward in a vertical line. When the length of the tow, measuring from the stern of the towing vessel to the after end of the tow exceeds 200 metres, three such lights in a vertical line;

(ii) sidelights;

(iii) a sternlight;

(iv) a towing light in a vertical line above the sternlight;

(v) when the length of the tow exceeds 200 metres, a diamond shape where it can best be seen.

(b) When a pushing vessel and a vessel being pushed ahead are rigidly connected in a composite unit they shall be regarded as a power-driven vessel and exhibit the lights prescribed in Rule 23.

(c) A power-driven vessel when pushing ahead or towing alongside, except in the case of a composite unit, shall exhibit:

(i) instead of the light prescribed in Rule 23 (a) (i), two masthead lights forward in a vertical line;

(ii) sidelights;

(iii) a sternlight.

(d) A power-driven vessel to which paragraphs (a) and (c) of this Rule apply shall also comply with Rule 23 (a) (ii).

(e) A vessel or object being towed shall exhibit:

(i) sidelights;

(ii) a sternlight;

(iii) when the length of the tow exceeds 200 metres, a diamond shape where it can best be seen.

(f) Provided that any number of vessels being towed or pushed in a group shall be lighted as one vessel,

(i) a vessel being pushed ahead, not being part of a composite unit, shall exhibit at the forward end, sidelights;

(ii) a vessel being towed alongside shall exhibit a sternlight and at the forward end, sidelights.

(g) Where from any sufficient cause it is impracticable for a vessel or object being towed to exhibit the lights prescribed in paragraph (e) of this Rule, all possible measures shall be taken to light the vessel or object towed or at least to indicate the

presence of the unlighted vessel or object.

The distinguishing lights of the tug in the case of towing and pushing are "for the purpose of warning all approaching vessels that she is not in all respect mistress of her movements"[1] and to show that she is encumbered.

Paragraph (b) provides that when a pushing vessel and a vessel being pushed are rigidly connected together, they will be considered, for the purpose of lighting, as one unit and, therefore, only the lights required by Rule 23 shall be exhibited.

The purpose of paragraph (d) is to give some indication of the length of a towing vessel and this could be important if the tow is not carrying any lights.

Paragraph (g) applies only to vessels being towed and not to vessels being pushed ahead or towed alongside.

Rule 25 - *Sailing Vessels Underway and Vessels under Oars*

(a) A sailing vessel underway shall exhibit:

(i) sidelights;

(ii) a sternlight.

(b) In a sailing vessel of less than 12 metres in length the lights prescribed in paragraph (a) of this Rule may be combined in one lantern carried at or near the top of the mast where it can best be seen.

(c) A sailing vessel underway may, in addition to the lights prescribed in paragraph (a) of this Rule, exhibit at or near the top of the mast, where they can best be seen, two all-round lights in a vertical line, the upper being red and the lower green, but these lights shall not be exhibited in conjunction with the combined lantern permitted by paragraph (b) of this Rule.

(d) (i) A sailing vessel of less than 7 metres in length shall, if practicable, exhibit the lights prescribed in paragraph (a) or (b) of this Rule, but if she does not, she shall have ready at hand an electric torch or lighted lantern showing a white light which shall be exhibited in sufficient time to prevent collision.

---

1. *The American* and *The Syria* (1874) L.R. 6 P.C. 127, at p.131.

(ii) *A vessel under oars may exhibit the lights prescribed in this Rule for sailing vessels, but if she does not, she shall have ready at hand an electric torch or lighted lantern showing a white light which shall be exhibited in sufficient time to prevent collision.*

(e) A vessel proceeding under sail when also being propelled by machinery shall exhibit forward where it can best be seen a conical shape, apex downwards.

There is little change in the lights required for sailing vessels underway and vessels under oars. Paragraph (b) provides that, in a sailing vessel of less than 12 metres in length, the sternlight may be combined with the sidelights into one lantern. Paragraph (c) states that the red over green identification lights are all round lights and this is quite different from the old Rules.

The difference in the wording of paragraph (d) is noteworthy. Sub-paragraph (i) uses the word "shall", while sub-paragraph (ii) tends towards a permissive form and uses the word "may". Again, in sub-paragraph (i), the words "if practicable" are used and perhaps they mean "if it is physically practicable", or "if the officer in charge should reasonably think that it is practicable".

Rule 26 - *Fishing Vessels*

(a) A vessel engaged in fishing, whether underway or at anchor, shall exhibit only the lights and shapes prescribed in this Rule.

(b) A vessel when engaged in trawling, by which is meant the dragging through the water of a dredge net or other apparatus used as a fishing appliance, shall exhibit:

(i) *two all-round lights in a vertical line, the upper being green and the lower white, or a shape consisting of two cones with their apexes together in a vertical line one above the other; a vessel of less than 20 metres in length may instead of this shape exhibit a basket;*

(ii) *a masthead light abaft of and higher than the all-round green light; a vessel of less than 50 metres in length shall not be obliged to exhibit such a light but may do so;*

(iii) *when making way through the water, in addition to the lights prescribed in this paragraph, sidelights and a sternlight.*

(c) A vessel engaged in fishing, other than trawling, shall exhibit:

(i) *two all-round lights in a vertical line, the upper being red and the lower white, or a shape consisting of two cones with apexes together in a vertical line one above the other; a vessel of less than 20 metres in length may instead of this shape exhibit a basket;*

(ii) *when there is outlying gear extending more than 150 metres horizontally from the vessel, an all-round white light or a cone apex upwards in the direction of the gear;*

(iii) *when making way through the water, in addition to the lights prescribed in this paragraph, sidelights and a sternlight.*

(d) A vessel engaged in fishing in close proximity to other vessels may exhibit the additional signals described in Annex II to these Regulations.

(e) A vessel when not engaged in fishing shall not exhibit the lights or shapes prescribed in this Rule, but only those prescribed for a vessel of her length.

Sub-paragraph (b) (ii) and paragraph (d) are new. Sub-paragraph (b) (ii) brought radical changes from the old Rules and requires that the masthead light should be carried above and abaft the green light provided for in sub-paragraph (b) (i) in all fishing vessels of 50 metres or more engaged in trawling. This is not required for fishing vessels less than 50 metres but they may do so. The aim of paragraph (d) and Annex II is to assist in identifying fishing vessels engaged in special fishing operations.

Rule 27 - *Vessels not under Command or Restricted in their Ability to Manoeuvre*

(a) A vessel not under command shall exhibit:

(i) *two all-round red lights in a vertical line where they can best be seen;*

(ii) *two balls or similar shapes in a vertical line where they can best be seen;*

(iii) *when making way through the water, in addition to the lights prescribed in this paragraph, sidelights and a sternlight.*

(b) A vessel restricted in her ability to manoeuvre, except a vessel engaged in minesweeping operations, shall exhibit:

(i) *three all-round lights in a vertical line where they can best be seen. The highest and lowest of these lights shall be red and the middle light shall be white;*

(ii) three shapes in a vertical line where they can best be seen. The highest and lowest of these shapes shall be balls and the middle one a diamond;

(iii) when making way through the water, masthead lights, sidelights and a sternlight, in addition to the lights prescribed in sub-paragraph (i);

(iv) when at anchor, in addition to the lights or shapes prescribed in sub-paragraphs (i) and (ii), the light, lights or shape prescribed in Rule 30.

(c) A vessel engaged in a towing operation such as renders her unable to deviate from her course shall, in addition to the lights or shapes prescribed in sub-paragraphs (b) (i) and (ii) of this Rule, exhibit the lights or shape prescribed in Rule 24 (a).

(d) A vessel engaged in dredging or underwater operations, when restricted in her ability to manoeuvre, shall exhibit the lights and shapes prescribed in paragraph (b) of this Rule and shall in addition, when an obstruction exists, exhibit:

(i) two all-round red lights or two balls in a vertical line to indicate the side on which the obstruction exists;

(ii) two all-round green lights or two diamonds in a vertical line to indicate the side on which another vessel may pass;

(iii) when making way through the water, in addition to the lights prescribed in this paragraph, masthead lights, sidelights and a sternlight;

(iv) a vessel to which this paragraph applies when at anchor shall exhibit the lights or shapes prescribed in sub-paragraphs (i) and (ii) instead of the lights or shape prescribed in Rule 30.

(e) Whenever the size of a vessel engaged in diving operations makes it impracticable to exhibit the shapes prescribed in paragraph (d) of this Rule, a rigid replica of the International Code flag "A" not less than 1 metre in height shall be exhibited. Measures shall be taken to ensure all-round visibility.

(f) A vessel engaged in minesweeping operations shall, in addition to the lights prescribed for a power-driven vessel in Rule 23, exhibit three all-round green lights or three balls. One of these lights or shapes shall be exhibited at or near the foremast head and one at each end of the fore yard. These lights or shapes indicate that it is dangerous for another vessel to approach closer than 1,000 metres astern or 500 metres on either side of the minesweeper.

(g) Vessels of less than 7 metres in length shall not be required to exhibit the lights prescribed in this Rule.

(h) The signals prescribed in this Rule are not signals of vessels in distress and requiring assistance. Such signals are contained in Annex IV to these Regulations.

Rule 27 has brought little changes; the most important are paragraphs (d) and (e). Paragraph (d) prescribes special signals for vessels engaged in dredging or underwater operations when restricted in their ability to manoeuvre. Sub-paragraph (iv) states that vessels subject to this paragraph when at anchor, are not to exhibit the anchor lights prescribed by Rule 30. Paragraph (e) is new.

Rule 28 - *Vessels constrained by their Draught*

A vessel constrained by her draught may, in addition to the lights prescribed for power-driven vessels in Rule 23, exhibit where they can best be seen three all-round red lights in a vertical line, or a cylinder.

This is a new Rule. A substantial minority at the IMCO meeting was in favour of including a second sub-paragraph, which reads as follows: "in addition to the black cylinder, by day, an all-round flashing yellow light"[1]. However, this proposal was not accepted.

Rule 29 - *Pilot Vessels*

(a) A vessel engaged on pilotage duty shall exhibit:

(i) at or near the masthead, two all-round lights in a vertical line, the upper being white and the lower red;

(ii) when underway, in addition, sidelights and a sternlight;

(iii) when at anchor, in addition to the lights prescribed in sub-paragraph (i), the anchor light, lights or shape.

(b) A pilot vessel when not engaged on pilotage duty shall exhibit the lights or shapes prescribed for a similar vessel of her length.

---

1. CR/CONF/3, p.183.

The lights required by Rule 29 apply whether the pilot vessel is a power-driven or a sailing vessel. The flare-up light is no longer required.

Rule 30 - *Anchored Vessels and Vessels Aground*

(a) A vessel at anchor shall exhibit where it can best be seen:

(i) in the fore part, an all-round white light or one ball;

(ii) at or near the stern and at a lower level than the light prescribed in sub-paragraph (i), an all-round white light.

(b) A vessel of less than 50 metres in length may exhibit an all-round white light where it can best be seen instead of the lights prescribed in paragraph (a) of this Rule.

(c) A vessel at anchor may, and a vessel of 100 metres and more in length shall, also use the available working or equivalent lights to illuminate her decks.

(d) A vessel aground shall exhibit the lights prescribed in paragraph (a) or (b) of this Rule and in addition, where they can best be seen:

(i) two all-round red lights in a vertical line;

(ii) three balls in a vertical line.

(e) A vessel of less than 7 metres in length, when at anchor or aground, not in or near a narrow channel, fairway or anchorage, or where other vessels normally navigate, shall not be required to exhibit the lights or shapes prescribed in paragraphs (a), (b) or (d) of this Rule.

The words "at anchor" have been the subject of litigation in many cases and they mean that the vessel is in fact being held by an anchor[1]. As for the meaning of the word "aground", it was held that a vessel dragging through mud is not "aground"[2].

The lights required by Rule 30 shall be exhibited where they can best be seen, and not in the fore part of the vessel. In *The West and Others* v. *Ritchie and Others (The "Convallaria")*[3], a fishing vessel, *May Lily*, was anchored at a fishing anchorage. Another fishing vessel, "*Convallaria*", collided with her while

---

1. *The Esk* and *The Gitana* (1869) L.R. 2 A. & E.
2. *The Turquoise* (1908) P. 184.
3. (1969) 1 Lloyd's Rep. 511.

making for anchorage and going at a speed of about eight knots. The owners of *Convallaria* contended that *May Lily* was to blame because she failed to display a white all-round anchor light.

It was held, by the Court of Session, that the master of *Convallaria* was at fault in not keeping a proper look-out and in proceeding at excessive speed into anchorage. The Court also blamed the master of the *May Lily* for his failure to exhibit a white all-round anchor light.

With regard to the lights of *May Lily*, the Court said[1]: "circumstances are both averred and proved by the defenders which would have led a reasonably careful skipper in charge of the *May Lily* to exhibit a white all-round anchor light from the time when she anchored at least until the time when the collision occurred. In the conditions of weather and light which prevailed, it would in my opinion have been reasonable to take such a precaution, bearing in mind that the *May Lily* was, as I have said, lying at anchor at or near by the western edge of the anchored fleet and presenting a stern-on silhouette to any vessel approaching the anchorage from seaward. Moreover, the skipper of the *May Lily* should have been aware that other fishing vessels might seek an anchorage in the bay before it was full daylight. Indeed he was well aware that the *Convallaria* had been at sea fishing and still with about 10 nets to haul, when he himself had proceeded up Loch Broom, and he should therefore have foreseen that she would almost certainly follow into the anchorage later. If an all-round white anchor light had been exhibited by the *May Lily* at the material time, I am of opinion that it would probably have been picked up by the skipper of the *Convallaria* in time for him to take avoiding action, since in conditions of gloomy twilight it would have been more conspicuous and more likely to attract attention than either the outline of the *May Lily* or the glow of the light showing from her galley."

Rule 31 - *Seaplanes*

Where it is impracticable for a seaplane to exhibit lights and shapes of the characteristics or in the positions prescribed in the Rules of this Part she shall exhibit lights and shapes as closely similar in characteristics and position as is possible.

The permissive form of this Rule is noteworthy. However, it provides that lights and shapes shall be as closely similar in character and position as possible.

---

1. Ibid., at p.514.

(II) SOUND AND LIGHT SIGNALS

Rule 32 - *Definitions*

(a) The word "whistle" means any sound signalling appliance capable of producing the prescribed blasts and which complies with the specifications in Annex III to these Regulations.

(b) The term "short blast" means a blast of about one second's duration.

(c) The term "prolonged blast" means a blast of from four to six seconds' duration.

Rule 33 - *Equipment for Sound Signals*

(a) A vessel of 12 metres or more in length shall be provided with a whistle and a bell and a vessel of 100 metres or more in length shall, in addition, be provided with a gong, the tone and sound of which cannot be confused with that of the bell. The whistle, bell and gong shall comply with the specifications in Annex III to these Regulations. The bell or gong or both may be replaced by other equipment having the same respective sound characteristics, provided that manual sounding of the required signals shall always be possible.

(b) A vessel of less than 12 metres in length shall not be obliged to carry the sound signalling appliances prescribed in paragraph (a) of this Rule but if she does not, she shall be provided with some other means of making an efficient sound signal.

The general principle is that sound and light signals are not considered as an invitation for actions, but they are regarded as an indication of deliberate movements[1]. Paragraph (a) provides that vessels of 12 metres or more in length should have a whistle and a bell and vessels of 100 metres in length should also have a gong. The bell or gong may be replaced by other equipment which must comply with the specifications prescribed in Annex III of these Rules.

There are many tugs which are less than 12 metres in length and which are engaged in towing barges of considerable size. These tugs, although they are relieved from carrying the sound signalling appliances prescribed in paragraph (a), they, nevertheless, must have other efficient means of sound signal devices.

---

1. *The Firston* (1963) 1 Lloyd's Rep. 74.

Rule 34 - *Manoeuvring and Warning Signals*

(a) When vessels are in sight of one another, a power-driven vessel underway, when manoeuvring as authorized or required by these Rules, shall indicate that manoeuvre by the following signals on her whistle:

- *one short blast to mean "I am altering my course to starboard";*
- *two short blasts to mean "I am altering my course to port";*
- *three short blasts to mean "I am operating astern propulsion".*

(b) Any vessel may supplement the whistle signals prescribed in paragraph (a) of this Rule by light signals, repeated as appropriate, whilst the manoeuvre is being carried out:

(i) these light signals shall have the following significance:

- *one flash to mean "I am altering my course to starboard";*
- *two flashes to mean "I am altering my course to port";*
- *three flashes to mean "I am operating astern propulsion";*

(ii) the duration of each flash shall be about one second, the interval between flashes shall be about one second, and the inverval between successive signals shall be not less than ten seconds;

(iii) the light used for this signal shall, if fitted, be an all-round white light, visible at a minimum range of 5 miles, and shall comply with the provisions of Annex 1.

(c) When in sight of one another in a narrow channel or fairway:

(i) a vessel intending to overtake another shall in compliance with Rule 9 (e) (i) indicate her intention by the following signals on her whistle:

- *two prolonged blasts followed by one short blast to mean "I intend to overtake you on your starboard side";*
- *two prolonged blasts followed by two short blasts to mean "I intend to overtake you on your port side";*

(ii) the vessel about to be overtaken when acting in accordance with Rule 9 (e) (i) shall indicate her agreement by the following signal on her whistle:

- *one prolonged, one short, one prolonged and one short blast, in that order.*

(d) When vessels in sight of one another are approaching each other and from any cause either vessel fails to understand the

intentions or actions of the other, or is in doubt whether sufficient action is being taken by the other to avoid collision, the vessel in doubt shall immediately indicate such doubt by giving at least five short and rapid blasts on the whistle. Such signal may be supplemented by a light signal of at least five short and rapid flashes.

(e) A vessel nearing a bend or an area of a channel or fairway where other vessels may be obscured by an intervening obstruction shall sound one prolonged blast. Such signal shall be answered with a prolonged blast by any approaching vessel that may be within hearing around the bend or behind the intervening obstruction.

(f) If whistles are fitted on a vessel at a distance apart of more than 100 metres, one whistle only shall be used for giving manoeuvring and warning signals.

The warning signals in Rule 34 mean nothing more than the vessel is directing her course to one side or the other. The words "in sight of one another" mean "when one (vessel) can be observed visually by the other"[1]. In *The "Lucile Bloomfield"*[2], a collision occurred between *Ronda* and *Lucile Bloomfield* in the approaches to Le Havre, at night, in fair visibility. Wind was westerly, force 6; and the tide was starting to ebb in easterly direction.

At 22 10 hours *Ronda* was proceeding at full speed on course of 114 deg., for L.H. 2 Buoy, where pilot vessel was stationed. Green light and then white light of *Lucile Bloomfield* were seen broadening on starboard bow of *Ronda*. *Lucile Bloomfield* was proceeding westerly from Le Havre towards the pilot vessel at 15 knots. The speed of *Ronda* was reduced to pick up the pilot and her course was altered (without sounding signal) to give lee to pilot launch. At 22 20 hours her engines were stopped, but were given a kick ahead to keep steerage way. At 22 21 hours red light of *Lucile Bloomfield* was sighted by *Ronda* and one short blast was heard. *Ronda* sounded two short blasts, receiving reply of three short blasts from *Lucile Bloomfield*. *Ronda* went full astern at 22 22 hours and bows of *Lucile Bloomfield* struck starboard side of *Ronda* at 22 23 hours. *Ronda* went into Le Havre, where she sank next day.

It was held, by Karminski, J. that after initial sighting by

1. Rule 3 (k).
2. (1966) 2 Lloyd's Rep. 239. Appeal by *Lucile Bloomfield* was dismissed (1967) 1 Lloyd's Rep. 341.

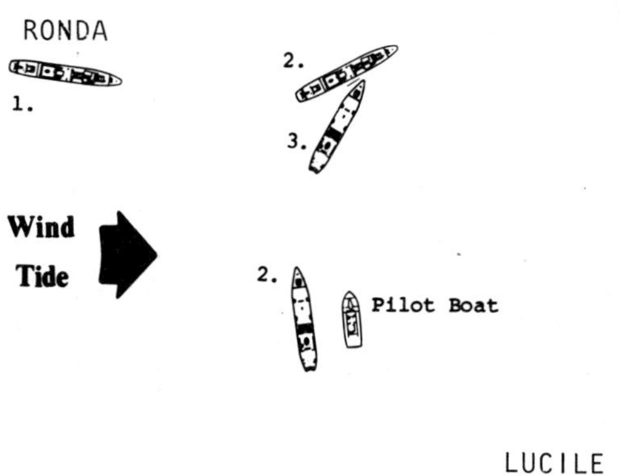

Ronda, neither vessel saw the other until they were 300 yards apart. Both vessels failed to sound the appropriate signal when they altered their course and they were equally to blame.

In *The "Alletta"* and *The "England"*[1], a collision occurred between *England* and *Alletta* at night in the River Thames. *England* was proceeding at full speed (11½ knots) on her starboard (southward) side of mid-channel. Stern light and deck lights of *Alletta*, which was apparently moving down jetty, were sighted at distance of five cables about 15 deg. on port bow of *England*. The engines of *England* were reduced to slow and one short blast was sounded (to indicate that *England* was keeping to south side of channel) when *Alletta's* green light opened at distance of two cables. One-short blast signal was repeated by *England*, which starboarded. *Alletta* continued slowly across river. Long warning blast was sounded by *England* and her engines stopped. Within half a minute, engines of *England* were put to emergency full astern and three short blasts were sounded (*Alletta* was then half a cable distant). Stem of *England* collided with starboard side of *Alletta* at about a right angle, on southern edge of channel.

The Court went on to specify the faults of *Alletta*. She failed

1. (1966) 1 Lloyd's Rep. 573.

to sound the signal before her three-short blasts signal when she put her engines astern. Further, she proceeded at about two to three knots on a curved course and by the time of collision she had reached a heading appreciably up river of athwart. This gradual movement was difficult to detect by a following ship.

Rule 35 - *Sound Signals in Restricted Visibility*[1]

In or near an area of restricted visibility, whether by day or night, the signals prescribed in this Rule shall be used as follows:

(a) A power-driven vessel making way through the water shall sound at intervals of not more than 2 minutes one prolonged blast.

(b) A power-driven vessel underway but stopped and making no way through the water shall sound at intervals of not more than 2 minutes two prolonged blasts in succession with an interval of about 2 seconds between them.

(c) A vessel not under command, a vessel restricted in her ability to manoeuvre, a vessel constrained by her draught, a sailing vessel, a vessel engaged in fishing and a vessel engaged in towing or pushing another vessel shall, instead of the signals prescribed in paragraphs (a) or (b) of this Rule, sound at intervals or not more than 2 minutes three blasts in succession, namely one prolonged followed by two short blasts.

(d) A vessel towed or if more than one vessel is towed the last vessel of the tow, if manned, shall at intervals of not more than 2 minutes sound four blasts in succession, namely one prolonged followed by three short blasts. When practicable, this signal shall be made immediately after the signal made by the towing vessel.

(e) When a pushing vessel and a vessel being pushed ahead are rigidly connected in a composite unit they shall be regarded as a power-driven vessel and shall give the signals prescribed in paragraphs (a) or (b) of this Rule.

(f) A vessel at anchor shall at intervals of not more than one minute ring the bell rapidly for about 5 seconds. In a vessel

1. In the original draft the opening of Rule 35 ran as follows: "In or near an area of fog, mist, falling snow, heavy rainstorms, sandstorms or any other conditions similarly restricting visibility, whether by day or night, the signals.....". However, it was felt that as article 3 (L) gives the definition of the term "restricted visibility", there is no need for repeating this definition in Rule 35. See CR/CONF/3, p.208.

of 100 metres or more in length the bell shall be sounded in the forepart of the vessel and immediately after the ringing of the bell the gong shall be sounded rapidly for about 5 seconds in the after part of the vessel. A vessel at anchor may in addition sound three blasts in succession, namely one short, one prolonged and one short blast, to give warning of her position and of the possibility of collision to an approaching vessel.

(g) A vessel aground shall give the bell signal and if required the gong signal prescribed in paragraph (f) of this Rule and shall, in addition, give three separate and distinct strokes on the bell immediately before and after the rapid ringing of the bell. A vessel aground may in addition sound an appropriate whistle signal.

(h) A vessel of less than 12 metres in length shall not be obliged to give the above-mentioned signals but, if she does not, shall make some other efficient sound signal at intervals of not more than 2 minutes.

(i) A pilot vessel when engaged on pilotage duty may in addition to the signals prescribed in paragraphs (a), (b) or (f) of this Rule sound an identity signal consisting of four short blasts.

Rule 35 resolves, to some extent, the doubt on what amount of restricted visibility must exist to make the use of the signals prescribed in it necessary, by adding the words "near an area of restricted visibility". This is a reasonable precaution[1].

All whistle signals in this Rule are sounded at intervals of not more than 2 minutes.

In *The Gannet*"[2], Karminski, J. said[3]: "So far as the fog signals are concerned, it is clear, as I find, that the *Gannet*, which had been in fog for some time, was sounding regularly. The *Katharina*, on the other hand, coming into the fog only sounded once. I am quite clear that she ought to have sounded earlier. Whether in the conditions prevailing anybody would have heard the other's fog signals remains a matter of conjecture. I have consulted the Elder Brethren about this and they advise me, and

---

1. The International Chamber of Shipping made the following comments on paragraph (d) of Rule 35: "This signal would warn other vessels of the need, particularly in conditions of restricted visibility, to keep much further away than they might do for the sound signal of one long blast followed by two short blasts. See CR/CONF/3, p.212.
2. (1967) 1 Lloyd's Rep. 97.
3. Ibid., at p.101.

I accept their advice, that the optimum range for hearing a fog signal would probably be not above two miles and might well be less. It depends upon a number of imponderables. It may be in some cases that the fog muffles sound, and this was a thick fog. I have to consider, too, as they advise me, that there are usually noises on board ship, one of which comes from outside, namely, water noises against the hull and, at a speed of 10 knots, noises which can be quite considerable. Last but by no means least is the noise caused on board ship by the modern diesel engine, no doubt a very effective means of locomotion, but, in general, a noisy one. Certainly the *Gannet* had nothing to hear except the one possible signal, and the *Katharina* heard practically nothing except, I think, just before the collision. The *Katharina*, as I find, was in fault in not sounding her signals, but I cannot find in the circumstances that I have set out any sort of evidence which would enable me to conclude that her failure to sound her fog signals had any effect at all on this collision."

In "*Dalhanna*" and "*Staxton Wyke*"[1], the Court of Inquiry said that: "the Mate of the *Staxton Wyke* was in charge of the navigation until very shortly before the collision. In continuously proceeding at full speed in the dense fog he was following the example set by the Skipper. In failing to sound fog signals he was again following the example of the Skipper, whose practice was to sound only when he saw a concentration of shipping on the radar screen."

Rule 36 - *Signals to attract Attention*

If necessary to attract the attention of another vessel any vessel may make light or sound signals that cannot be mistaken for any signal authorized elsewhere in these Rules, or may direct the beam of her searchlight in the direction of the danger, in such a way as not to embarrass any vessel.

In *The "Sabine"*[2], the plaintiffs argued *inter alia* that it was the duty of the *Sabine* to sound either a signal of four short blasts under the local regulations or a signal to attract attention. The Court found that the four short blasts signal in the local regulations relates to a ship unable to manoeuvre. As the *Sabine* had the use of her engines, some use of her helm, and the assistance of six tugs, the above mentioned argument was not accepted. The Court held that the *Sabine* was at fault in not giving

---

1. Merchant Navy Journal, April-June, 1960, p.20.
2. (1974) 1 Lloyd's Rep. 465.

a warning signal, which is necessary to attract attention in order to avoid a collision[1].

Rule 37 - *Distress Signals*

When a vessel is in distress and requires assistance she shall use or exhibit the signals prescribed in Annex IV to these Regulations.

(III) EXEMPTIONS

Rule 38 - *Exemptions*

Any vessel (or class of vessel) provided that she complies with the requirements of the International Regulations for Preventing Collisions at Sea, 1960, the keel of which is laid or which is at a corresponding stage of construction before the entry into force of these Regulations may be exempted from compliance therewith as follows:

(a) The installation of lights with ranges prescribed in Rule 22, until four years after the date of entry into force of these Regulations.

(b) The installation of lights with colour specifications as prescribed in Section 7 of Annex I to these Regulations, until four years after the date of entry into force of these Regulations.

(c) The repositioning of lights as a result of conversion from Imperial to metric units and rounding off measurement figures, permanent exemption.

(d) (i) The repositioning of masthead lights on vessels of less than 150 metres in length, resulting from the prescriptions of Section 3 (a) of Annex I, permanent exemption.

(ii) The repositioning of masthead lights on vessels of 150 metres or more in length, resulting from the prescriptions of Section 3 (a) of Annex I to these Regulations, until nine years after the date of entry into force of these Regulations.

(e) The repositioning of masthead lights resulting from the prescriptions of Section 2 (b) of Annex I, until nine years after the date of entry into force of these Regulations.

---

1. See also *The "Kathy K"* (1972) 2 Lloyd's Rep. 36 (Canada Ex.Ct.).

(f) the repositioning of sidelights resulting from the prescriptions of Section 3 (b) of Annex I, until nine years after the date of entry into force of these Regulations.

(g) The requirements for sound signal appliances prescribed in Annex III, until nine years after the date of entry into force of these Regulations.

Obviously, all vessels built after 15th July 1977, must comply with the lights prescribed in the Rules. However, the difficulty arises for the existing vessels or vessels under construction. In order to solve this difficulty, Rule 38 provides for exemptions during transitional periods.

Appendix I

The Convention on the International Regulations for Preventing Collisions at Sea, 1972, is printed with comments in chapters 4, 5 and 6.

ANNEX I

Positioning and technical details of lights and shapes

1. *Definition*

The term "height above the hull" means height above the uppermost continuous deck.

2. *Vertical positioning and spacing of lights*

(a) On a power-driven vessel of 20 metres or more in length the masthead lights shall be placed as follows:

(i) the forward masthead light, or if only one masthead light is carried, then that light, at a height above the hull of not less than 6 metres, and, if the breadth of the vessel exceeds 6 metres, then at a height above the hull not less than such breadth, so however that the light need not be placed at a greater height above the hull than 12 metres;

(ii) when two masthead lights are carried the after one shall be at least 4·5 metres vertically higher than the forward one.

(b) The vertical separation of masthead lights of power-driven vessels shall be such that in all normal conditions of trim the after light will be seen over and separate from the forward light at a distance of 1,000 metres from the stem when viewed from sea level.

(c) The masthead light of a power-driven vessel of 12 metres but less than 20 metres in length shall be placed at a height above the gunwale of not less than 2·5 metres.

(d) a power-driven vessel of less than 12 metres in length may carry the uppermost light at a height of less than 2·5 metres above the gunwale. When however a masthead light is carried in addition to sidelights and a sternlight, then such masthead light shall be carried at least 1 metre higher than the sidelights.

(e) One of the two or three masthead lights prescribed for a power-driven vessel when engaged in towing or pushing another vessel shall be placed in the same position as the forward masthead light of a power-driven vessel.

(f) In all circumstances the masthead light or lights shall be so placed as to be above and clear of all other lights and obstructions.

(g) The sidelights of a power-driven vessel shall be placed at a height above the hull not greater than three-quarters of that of the forward masthead light. They shall not be so low as to be interfered with by deck lights.

(h) The sidelights, if in a combined lantern and carried on a power-driven vessel of less than 20 metres in length, shall be placed not less than 1 metre below the masthead light.

(i) When the Rules prescribe two or three lights to be carried in a vertical line, they shall be spaced as follows:

(i) on a vessel of 20 metres in length or more such lights shall be spaced not less than 2 metres apart, and the lowest of these lights shall, except where a towing light is required, not be less than 4 metres above the hull;

(ii) on a vessel of less than 20 metres in length such lights shall be spaced not less than 1 metre apart and the lowest of these lights shall, except where a towing light is required, not be less than 2 metres above the gunwale;

(iii) when three lights are carried they shall be equally spaced.

(j) The lower of the two all-round lights prescribed for a fishing vessel when engaged in fishing shall be at a height above the sidelights not less than twice the distance between the two vertical lights.

(k) The forward anchor light, when two are carried, shall not be less than 4·5 metres above the after one. On a vessel of 50 metres or more in length this forward anchor light shall not be less than 6 metres above the hull.

3. *Horizontal positioning and spacing of lights*

(a) When two masthead lights are prescribed for a power-driven vessel, the horizontal distance between them shall not be less than one half of the length of the vessel but need not be more than 100 metres. The forward light shall be placed not more than one quarter of the length of the vessel from the stem.

(b) On a vessel of 20 metres or more in length the sidelights shall not be placed in front of the forward masthead lights. They shall be placed at or near the side of the vessel.

4. *Details of location of direction-indicating lights for fishing vessels, dredgers and vessels engaged in underwater operations*

(a) The light indicating the direction of the outlying gear from a vessel engaged in fishing as prescribed in Rule 26 (c) (ii) shall be placed at a horizontal distance of not less than 2 metres and not more than 6 metres away from the two all-round red and white lights. This light shall be placed not higher than the all-round white light prescribed in Rule 26 (c) (i) and not lower than the sidelights.

(b) The lights and shapes on a vessel engaged in dredging or underwater operations to indicate the obstructed side and/or the side on which it is safe to pass, as prescribed in Rule 27 (d) (i) and (ii), shall be placed at the maximum practical horizontal distance, but in no case less than 2 metres, from the lights or shapes prescribed in Rule 27 (b) (i) and (ii). In no case shall the upper of these lights or shapes be at a greater height than the lower of the three lights or shapes prescribed in Rule 27 (b) (i) and (ii).

5. *Screens for sidelights*

The sidelights shall be fitted with inboard screens painted matt black, and meeting the requirements of Section 9 of this Annex. With a combined lantern, using a single vertical filament and a very narrow division between the green and red sections, external screens need not be fitted.

6. *Shapes*

(a) Shapes shall be black and of the following sizes:

(i) a ball shall have a diameter of not less than 0·6 metre;

(ii) a cone shall have a base diameter of not less than 0·6 metre and a height equal to its diameter;

(iii) a cylinder shall have a diameter of at least 0·6 metre and a height of twice its diameter;

(iv) a diamond shape shall consist of two cones as defined in (ii) above having a common base.

(b) The vertical distance between shapes shall be at least 1·5 metres.

(c) In a vessel of less than 20 metres in length shapes of lesser dimensions but commensurate with the size of the vessel may be used and the distance apart may be correspondingly reduced.

7. *Colour specification of lights*

The chromaticity of all navigation lights shall conform to the following standards, which lie within the boundaries of the area of the diagram specified for each colour by the International Commission on illumination (CIE).

The boundaries of the area for each colour are given by indicating the corner co-ordinates, which are as follows:

(i) *White*

x	0·525	0·525	0·452	0·310	0·310	0·443
y	0·382	0·440	0·440	0·348	0·283	0·382

(ii) *Green*

x	0·028	0·009	0·300	0·203
y	0·385	0·723	0·511	0·356

(iii) *Red*

x	0·680	0·660	0·735	0·721
y	0·320	0·320	0·265	0·259

(iv) *Yellow*

x	0·612	0·618	0·575	0·575
y	0·382	0·382	0·425	0·406

8. *Intensity of lights*

(a) The minimum luminous intensity of lights shall be calculated by using the formula:

$$1 = 3{\cdot}43 \times 10^{6} \times T \times D^{2} \times K^{-D}$$

where 1 is luminous intensity in candelas under service conditions,

T is threshold factor 2×10^{-7} lux,

D is range of visibility (luminous range) of the light in nautical miles,

K is atmospheric transmissivity.

For prescribed lights the value of K shall be 0·8 corresponding to a meteorological visibility of approximately 13 nautical miles.

(b) A selection of figures derived from the formula is given in the following table:

Range of visibility (luminous range) of light in nautical miles *D*	Luminous intensity of light in candelas for K = 0·8 *I*
1	0·9
2	4·3
3	12
4	27
5	52
6	94

Note: The maximum luminous intensity of navigation lights should be limited to avoid undue glare.

9. *Horizontal sectors*

(a) (i) In the forward direction, sidelights as fitted on the vessel must show the minimum required intensities. The intensities must decrease to reach practical cut-off between 1 degree and 3 degrees outside the prescribed sectors.

(ii) For sternlights and masthead lights and at 22·5 degrees abaft the beam for sidelights, the minimum required intensities shall be maintained over the arc of the horizon up to 5 degrees within the limits of the sectors prescribed in Rule 21. From 5 degrees within the prescribed sectors the intensity may decrease by 50 per cent up to the prescribed limits; it shall decrease steadily to reach practical cut-off at not more than 5 degrees outside the prescribed limits.

(b) All-round lights shall be so located as not to be obscured by masts, topmasts or structures within angular sectors of more than 6 degrees, except anchor lights, which need not be placed at an impracticable height above the hull.

10. *Vertical sectors*

(a) The vertical sectors of electric lights, with the exception of lights on sailing vessels shall ensure that:

(i) at least the required minimum intensity is maintained at all angles from 5 degrees above to 5 degrees below the horizontal;

(ii) at least 60 per cent of the required minimum intensity is maintained from 7·5 degrees above to 7·5 degrees below the horizontal.

(b) In the case of sailing vessels the vertical sectors of electric lights shall ensure that:

(i) at least the required minimum intensity is maintained at all angles from 5 degrees above to 5 degrees below the horizontal;

(ii) at least 50 per cent of the required minimum intensity is maintained from 25 degrees above to 25 degrees below the horizontal.

(c) In the case of lights other than electric these specifications shall be met as closely as possible.

11. *Intensity of non-electric lights*

Non-electric lights shall so far as practicable comply with the minimum intensities, as specified in the Table given in Section 8 of this Annex.

12. *Manoeuvring light*

Notwithstanding the provisions of paragraph 2 (f) of this Annex the manoeuvring light described in Rule 34 (b) shall be placed in the same fore and aft vertical plane as the masthead light or lights and, where practicable, at a minimum height of 2 metres vertically above the forward masthead light, provided that it shall be carried not less than 2 metres vertically above or below the after masthead light. On a vessel where only one masthead light is carried the manoeuvring light, if fitted, shall be carried where it can best be seen, not less than 2 metres vertically apart from the masthead light.

13. *Approval*

The construction of lanterns and shapes and the installation of lanterns on board the vessel shall be to the satisfaction of the appropriate authority of the State where the vessel is registered.

ANNEX II

Additional signals for fishing vessels fishing in close proximity

1. *General*

The lights mentioned herein shall, if exhibited in pursuance of Rule 26 (d), be placed where they can best be seen. They shall be at least 0·9 metre apart but at a lower level than lights prescribed in Rule 26 (b) (i) and (c) (i). The lights shall be visible all round the horizon at a distance of at least 1 mile but at a lesser distance than the lights prescribed by these Rules for fishing vessels.

2. *Signals for trawlers*

(a) Vessels when engaged in trawling, whether using demersal or pelagic gear, may exhibit:

(i) when shooting their nets:
two white lights in a vertical line;

(ii) when hauling their nets:
one white light over one red light in a vertical line;

(iii) when the net has come fast upon an obstruction:
two red lights in a vertical line.

(b) Each vessel engaged in pair trawling may exhibit:

(i) by night, a searchlight directed forward and in the direction of the other vessel of the pair;

(ii) when shooting or hauling their nets or when their nets have come fast upon an obstruction, the lights prescribed in 2 (a) above.

3. *Signals for purse seiners*

Vessels engaged in fishing with purse seine gear may exhibit two yellow lights in a vertical line. These lights shall flash alternately every second and with equal light and occultation duration. These lights may be exhibited only when the vessel is hampered by its fishing gear.

ANNEX III

Technical details of sound signal appliances

1. *Whistles*

(a) *Frequency and range of audibility*

The fundamental frequency of the signal shall lie within the range 70-700 Hz.

The range of audibility of the signal from a whistle shall be determined by those frequencies, which may include the fundamental and/or one or more higher frequencies, which lie within the range 180-700 Hz (± 1 per cent) and which provide the sound pressure levels specified in paragraph 1 (c) below.

(b) *Limits of fundamental frequencies*

To ensure a wide variety of whistle characteristics, the fundamental frequency of a whistle shall be between the following limits:

(i) 70-200 Hz, for a vessel 200 metres or more in length;

(ii) 130-350 Hz, for a vessel 75 metres but less than 200 metres in length;

(iii) 250-700 Hz, for a vessel less than 75 metres in length.

(c) *Sound signal intensity and range of audibility*

A whistle fitted in a vessel shall provide, in the direction of maximum intensity of the whistle and at a distance of 1 metre from it, a sound pressure level in at least one 1/3rd-octave band within the range of frequencies 180-700 Hz (± 1 per cent) of not less than the appropriate figure given in the table below.

Length of vessel in metres	1/3rd-octave band level at 1 metre in dB referred to 2×10^{-5} N/m^2	Audibility range in nautical miles
200 or more	143	2
75 but less than 200	138	1·5
20 but less than 75	130	1
Less than 20	120	0·5

The range of audibility in the table above is for information and is approximately the range at which a whistle may be heard on its forward axis with 90 per cent probability in conditions of still air on board a vessel having average background noise level at the listening posts (taken to be 68 dB in the octave band centred on 250 Hz and 63 dB in the octave band centred on 500 Hz).

In practice the range at which a whistle may be heard is extremely variable and depends critically on weather conditions; the values given can be regarded as typical but under conditions of strong wind or high ambient noise level at the listening post the range may be much reduced.

(d) *Directional properties*

The sound pressure level of a directional whistle shall be not more than 4 dB below the sound pressure level on the axis at any direction in the horizontal plane within ± 45 degrees of the axis. The sound pressure level at any other direction in the horizontal plane shall be not more than 10 dB below the sound pressure level on the axis, so that the range in any direction will be at least half the range on the forward axis. The sound pressure level shall be measured in that 1/3rd-octave band which determines the audibility range.

(e) *Positioning of whistles*

When a directional whistle is to be used as the only whistle on a vessel, it shall be installed with its maximum intensity directed straight ahead.

A whistle shall be placed as high as practicable on a vessel, in order to reduce interception of the emitted sound by obstructions and also to minimize hearing damage risk to personnel. The sound pressure level of the vessel's own signal at listening posts shall not exceed 110 dB (A) and so far as practicable should not exceed 100 dB (A).

(f) *Fitting of more than one whistle*

If whistles are fitted at a distance apart of more than 100 metres, it shall be so arranged that they are not sounded simultaneously.

(g) *Combined whistle systems*

If due to the presence of obstructions the sound field of a single whistle or of one of the whistles referred to in paragraph 1 (f) above is likely to have a zone of greatly reduced signal level, it is recommended that a combined whistle system be fitted so as to overcome this reduction. For the purposes of the Rules a combined whistle system is to be regarded as a single whistle.

The whistles of a combined system shall be located at a distance apart of not more than 100 metres and arranged to be sounded simultaneously. The frequency of any one whistle shall differ from those of the others by at least 10 Hz.

2. *Bell or gong*

(a) *Intensity of signal*

A bell or gong, or other device having similar sound characteristics shall produce a sound pressure level of not less than 110 dB at 1 metre.

(b) *Construction*

Bells and gongs shall be made of corrosion-resistant material and designed to give a clear tone. The diameter of the mouth of the bell shall be not less than 300 mm for vessels of more than 20 metres in length, and shall be not less than 200 mm for vessels of 12 to 20 metres in length. Where practicable, a power-driven bell striker is recommended to ensure constant force but manual operation shall be possible. The mass of the striker shall be not less than 3 per cent of the mass of the bell.

3. *Approval*

The construction of sound signal appliances, their performance and their installation on board the vessel shall be to the satisfaction of the appropriate authority of the State where the vessel is registered.

ANNEX IV

Distress Signals

1. The following signals, used or exhibited either together or separately, indicate distress and need of assistance:

(a) a gun or other explosive signal fired at intervals of about a minute;

(b) a continuous sounding with any fog-signalling apparatus;

(c) rockets or shells, throwing red stars fired one at a time at short intervals;

(d) a signal made by radiotelegraphy or by any other signalling method consisting of the group ... _ _ _ ... (SOS) in the Morse Code;

(e) a signal sent by radiotelephony consisting of the spoken word "Mayday";

(f) the International Code Signal of distress indicated by N.C.;

(g) a signal consisting of a square flag having above or below it a ball or anything resembling a ball;

(h) flames on the vessel (as from a burning tar barrel, oil barrel, etc.);

(i) a rocket parachute flare or a hand flare showing a red light;

(j) a smoke signal giving off orange-coloured smoke;

(k) slowly and repeatedly raising and lowering arms outstretched to each side;

(l) the radiotelegraph alarm signal;

(m) the radiotelephone alarm signal;

(n) signals transmitted by emergency position-indicating radio beacons.

2. The use or exhibition of any of the foregoing signals except for the purpose of indicating distress and need of assistance and the use of other signals which may be confused with any of the above signals is prohibited.

3. Attention is drawn to the relevant sections of the internat-ional Code of Signals, the Merchant Ship Search and Rescue Manual and the following signals:

(a) a piece of orange-coloured canvas with either a black square and circle or other appropriate symbol (for identification from the air);
(b) a dye marker.

Appendix II

LIST OF THE STATES WHICH RATIFIED THE COLLISION REGULATIONS, 1972 *

Contracting States

	Date of signature or deposit of Instrument	Date of entry into force
India (signature)	30 May 1973	15 July 1977
USSR (accession) 1/	9 November 1973	"
Ghana (ratification)	7 December 1973	"
Liberia (accession)	28 December 1973	"
Nigeria (accession)	17 January 1974	"
Denmark (ratification)	24 January 1974	"
France (approval)	10 May 1974	"
Spain (accession)	31 May 1974	"
United Kingdom (acceptance)	28 June 1974	"
Norway (ratification)	13 August 1974	"
Brazil (ratification)	26 November 1974	"
Greece (ratification)	17 December 1974	"
Canada (accession) 1/	7 March 1975	"
Romania (accession) 1/	27 March 1975	"
Iceland (ratification)	21 April 1975	"
Sweden (ratification)	28 April 1975	"
Bulgaria (ratification)	29 April 1975	"
German Democratic Republic (accession) 1/	15 May 1975	"
Belgium (ratification)	22 December 1975	"
Switzerland (ratification)	30 December 1975	"
Netherlands (accession)	4 February 1976	"

---

* This list is reproduced by the permission of IMCO in June, 1977.

1/ With declaration/statement.

	Date of signature or deposit of Instrument	Date of entry into force
Syrian Arab Republic (accession)1/	16 February 1976	15 July 1977
Yugoslavia (accession)	23 March 1976	"
Mexico (accession)	8 April 1976	"
Papua New Guinea (accession)	18 May 1976	"
Germany, Federal Republic of (ratification) 1/	14 July 1976	"
Bahamas (accession)	22 July 1976	"
Algeria (accession)	4 October 1976	"
United States (acceptance)	23 November 1976	"
New Zealand (ratification)	26 November 1976	"
Poland (ratification)	14 December 1976	"
Hungary (accession)1/	15 December 1976	"
South Africa (accession)	20 December 1976	"
Monaco (accession)	18 January 1977	"
Zaire (accession)	10 February 1977	"
Finland (ratification)	16 February 1977	"
Czechoslovakia (accession)1/	7 April 1977	"
Tonga (accession)	12 April 1977	"
Morocco (accession)	27 April 1977	"
Cape Verde (accession)	28 April 1977	"
Singapore (accession)	29 April 1977	"
Argentina (accession)	11 May 1977	"
Austria (accession)	8 June 1977	"
Japan (accession)	21 June 1977	"
Israel (accession)	24 June 1977	"

The Convention will be effective in respect of the following territories:

Hong Kong	30 October 1974	15 July 1977

1/ With declaration/statement.

	Date of signature or deposit of Instrument	Date of entry into force
Puerto Rico, Guam, The Canal Zone, The Virgin Islands of the United States, American Samoa, the trust territory of the Pacific Islands, Midway, Wake, Johnston Islands, Palmyra Island, Kingman Reef, Howland Island, Baker Island, Jarvis Island and Navassa Island	1 April 1977	15 July 1977

Appendix III

1977 No. 982

MERCHANT SHIPPING

SAFETY

CIVIL AVIATION

The Collision Regulations and Distress Signals Order 1977

Whereas -

(1) by virtue of sections 418, 424 and 738 of the Merchant Shipping Act 1894 (hereinafter referred to as "the 1894 Act"), as amended by section 52(1) of the Civil Aviation Act 1949, and of that Act as extended to the Isle of Man and the Channel Islands, Her Majesty may by Order in Council, on the joint recommendation of the Secretary of State for Defence and the Secretary of State for Trade, make regulations for the prevention of collisions at sea (referred to in those Acts as "the Collision Regulations") and may, if it appears to Her Majesty that the government of any foreign country is willing that those regulations should apply to vessels of that country while beyond the limits of British jurisdiction, direct that they shall so apply:

(2) section 59(2) of the Civil Aviation Act 1949, and of that Act as extended as aforesaid, makes provision for the extension by Order in Council of the extra-territorial operation of the Collision Regulations to British aircraft registered in any country or territory referred to in section 66(1) of that Act or registered in the Isle of Man or the Channel Islands:

(3) by virtue of section 21 of the Merchant Shipping (Safety Convention) Act 1949 (hereinafter referred to as "the 1949 Act") and section 734 of the 1894 Act, Her Majesty may by Order in Council prescribe what signals may be used by vessels as signals of distress and may, if the government of a foreign country so desires, extend the application of that section to vessels of that country which are not locally within the jurisdiction of that country:

(4) the afore-mentioned Secretaries of State have recommended Her Majesty to give effect to the International Regulations for Preventing Collisions at Sea 1972 (hereinafter referred to as "the International Regulations"):

(5) it appears to Her Majesty that the governments of the foreign countries specified in Schedule 2 to this Order are willing that those Regulations should apply to vessels, other than hovercraft,

of their respective countries while beyond the limits of British jurisdiction and are desirous that the provisions of section 21 of the 1949 Act should apply to such vessels while not locally within their respective jurisdictions:

Now, therefore, Her Majesty, in exercise of the above-mentioned powers and of all other powers enabling Her in that behalf, is pleased, by and with the advice of Her Privy Council, to order, and it is hereby ordered, as follows:

Citation, commencement, interpretation and revocation

1. (1) This Order may be cited as the Collision Regulations and Distress Signals Order 1977 and shall come into operation on 15th July 1977:

Provided that it shall not come into operation in relation to any vessel until noon on that date by the zone time in the area in which the vessel is situated.

(2) For the purposes of this Order:

(a) "appropriate authority" means in relation to the United Kingdom, the Secretary of State for Trade, and in relation to any other country the authority responsible under the law of that country for promoting the safety of life at sea and the avoidance of collisions;

"the Organization" means the Inter-governmental Maritime Consultative Organization;

references to "vessels" in this Order shall have the same meaning as in Rule 3(a) of Schedule 1 hereto;

(b) the traffic separation schemes adopted by the Organization and referred to in Rules 1(d) and 10(a) in Schedule 1 hereto shall be the schemes specified as so adopted in Notice No. 17 of 1977 of Admiralty Notices to Mariners published by the Hydrographer of the Navy;

(c) the diagram mentioned in paragraph 7 of Annex I to the International Regulations shall be the diagram specified in the Chromaticity Chart (1975) published by the International Commission on Illumination (CIE);

(d) the International Code of Signals mentioned in paragraph 3 of Annex IV to the International Regulations shall be the International Code of Signals (1969) published by Her Majesty's Stationery Office, and the Merchant Ship Search and Rescue Manual mentioned in that paragraph shall be the manual of that name published in 1970 by the Organization.

(3) The Interpretation Act 1889 shall apply for the interpret-

ation of this Order as it applies for the interpretation of an Act of Parliament and as if this Order and the Orders hereby revoked were Acts of Parliament.

(4) The following Orders are hereby revoked (except in so far as they relate to hovercraft):

(a) the Collision Regulations (Ships and Seaplanes on the Water) and Signals of Distress (Ships) Order 1965;

(b) the Collision Regulations (Traffic Separation Schemes) Order 1972;

(c) the Collision Regulations (Traffic Separation Schemes) (Amendment) Order 1974.

Collision Regulations and Distress Signals

2. (1) Subject to the provisions of this Order, the International Regulations as set out in Schedule 1 hereto shall, with the exception of Annex IV thereto (distress signals), have effect (except in so far as they relate to hovercraft) as the Collision Regulations for the purposes of the 1894 Act, as amended by the Civil Aviation Act 1949 and by that Act as extended to the Isle of Man and the Channel Islands.

(2) The signals specified in Annex IV to the International Regulations (set out in Schedule 1 hereto) are hereby prescribed for the purposes of section 21 of the 1949 Act as signals which shall be used by vessels (other than seaplanes and hovercraft) as signals of distress.

3. (1) The Collision Regulations shall apply to:-

(a) British seaplanes on the surface of the water which are registered in any country or territory mentioned in section 66(1) of the Civil Aviation Act 1949, or in the Isle of Man or the Channel Islands, wherever such seaplanes may be;

(b) to all vessels (other than hovercraft) of the foreign countries specified in Schedule 2 to this Order, whether such vessels are within British jurisdiction or not and such vessels shall, for the purposes of the Collision Regulations, be treated as if they were British vessels.

(2) The provisions of section 21 of the 1949 Act (distress signals) shall apply to vessels (other than seaplanes and hovercraft) of the foreign countries specified in Schedule 2 of this Order, whether such vessels are within British jurisdiction or not, as if those vessels were British vessels.

4. Nothing in the foregoing provisions of this Order shall be taken to authorise the prosecution of the master or owner of a foreign vessel, for any offence consisting only of an act or omission outside British jurisdiction.

1977 No. 1301

MERCHANT SHIPPING

SAFETY

CIVIL AVIATION

The Collision Regulations and Distress Signals (Amendment) Order 1977

Her Majesty, in exercise of the powers conferred upon Her by sections 418, 424 and 738 of the Merchant Shipping Act 1894 and all other powers enabling Her in that behalf, on the joint recommendation of the Secretary of State for Defence and the Secretary of State for Trade, is pleased, by and with the advice of Her Privy Council, to order, and it is hereby ordered, as follows:-

1. This Order may be cited as the Collision Regulations and Distress Signals (Amendment) Order 1977 and shall come into operation on 2nd August 1977.

2. The Collision Regulations and Distress Signals Order 1977 shall be amended as follows:

(1) At the end of Article 3(1) there shall be added the following proviso:
"Provided that nothing in this Order shall be taken to require compliance by any vessel or class of vessels which, by virtue of Rule 38 of the Collision Regulations, may be exempted from compliance therewith, with any of the provisions of the said Regulations specified in paragraphs (a) to (g) inclusive of that Rule, at any time when, by virtue of that Rule, that vessel or class of vessels may be exempted from that provision."

(2) In Schedule 2 there shall be inserted in the list of foreign countries, in the appropriate alphabetical order, the following:

Argentina
Austria
Israel
Japan

Appendix IV

IMCO RECOMMENDATION ON BASIC PRINCIPLES AND OPERATIONAL GUIDANCE RELATING TO NAVIGATIONAL WATCHKEEPING

Section I

BASIC PRINCIPLES TO BE OBSERVED IN KEEPING A NAVIGATIONAL WATCH

Introduction

1. The master of every ship is bound to ensure that the watchkeeping arrangements are adequate for maintaining a safe navigational watch. Under his general direction, the officers of the watch are responsible for navigating the ship safely during their periods of duty when they will be particularly concerned to avoid collision and stranding.

2. This Section includes the basic principles which shall at least be taken into account by all ships.

Watch arrangements

3. The composition of the watch, including the requirement for look-out(s), shall at all times be adequate and appropriate to the prevailing circumstances and conditions.

4. When deciding the composition of the watch on the bridge the following points are among those to be taken into account:

(a) at no time shall the bridge be left unattended;

(b) the weather conditions, visibility and whether there is daylight or darkness;

(c) the proximity of navigational hazards which may make it necessary for the officer in charge to carry out additional navigational duties;

(d) the use and operational condition of navigational aids such as radar or electronic position-indicating devices and any other equipment affecting the safe navigation of the ship;

(e) whether the ship is fitted with automatic steering;

(f) any additional demands on the navigational watch that may arise as a result of special operational circumstances.

Fitness for duty

5. The watch system shall be such that the efficiency of the watchkeeping members of the crew is not impaired by fatigue. Accordingly, the duties shall be so organized that the first watch at the commencement of a voyage and the subsequent relieving watches are sufficiently rested and otherwise fit when going on duty.

Navigation

6. The intended voyage shall be planned in advance taking into consideration all pertinent information and any course laid down shall be checked.

7. On taking over the watch the ship's estimated or true position, intended track, course and speed shall be confirmed; any navigational hazard expected to be encountered during the watch shall be noted.

8. During the watch the course steered, position and speed shall be checked at sufficiently frequent intervals using any available navigational aids necessary to ensure that the ship follows the planned course.

9. The safety and navigational equipment with which the ship is provided and the manner of its operation shall be clearly understood; in addition its operational condition shall be fully taken into account.

10. Whoever is in charge of a navigational watch shall not be assigned to undertake any duties which would interfere with the safe navigation of the ship.

Look-out

11. Every ship shall at all times maintain a proper look-out by sight and hearing as well as by all available means appropriate in the prevailing circumstances and conditions so as to make a full appraisal of the situation and of the risk of collision, stranding and other hazards to navigation. Additionally, the duties of the look-out shall include the detection of ships or aircraft in distress, shipwrecked persons, wrecks and debris. In applying these principles the following shall be observed:

(a) whoever is keeping a look-out must be able to give full attention to that task and no duties shall be assigned or undertaken which would interfere with the keeping of a proper look-out;

(b) the duties of the person on look-out and helmsman are separate and the helmsman should not be considered the person on look-out while steering; except in small vessels where an unobstructed all round view is provided at the steering position and there is no impairment of night vision or other impediment to the keeping of a proper look-out;

(c) there may be circumstances in which the officer of the watch can safely be the sole look-out in daylight. However, this practice shall only be followed after the situation has been carefully assessed on each occasion and it has been established without doubt that it is safe to do so. Full account shall be taken of all relevant factors including but not limited to the state of weather, conditions of visibility, traffic density, proximity of navigational hazards and if navigating in or near a traffic separation scheme.

Navigation with pilot embarked

12. Despite the duties and obligations of a pilot, his presence on board does not relieve the master or officer in charge of the watch from their duties and obligations for the safety of the ship. The master and the pilot shall exchange information regarding navigation procedures, local conditions and the ship's characteristics.

Protection of the marine environment

13. The master and officer in charge of the watch shall be aware of the serious effects of operational or accidental pollution of the marine environment and shall take all possible precautions to prevent such pollution particularly within the existing framework of existing international regulations.

Section II

OPERATIONAL GUIDANCE FOR OFFICERS IN CHARGE OF A NAVIGATIONAL WATCH

Introduction

1. This Section contains operational guidance of general application for officers in charge of a navigational watch, which masters are expected to supplement as appropriate. It is essential that officers of the watch appreciate that the efficient performance of their duties is necessary in the interest of safety of

life and property at sea and the avoidance of pollution of the marine environment.

General

2. The officer of the watch is the master's representative and his primary responsibility at all times is the safe navigation of the vessel. He must at all times comply with the applicable regulations for preventing collisions at sea (see also paragraphs 23 and 24).

3. The officer of the watch should keep his watch on the bridge which he should in no circumstances leave until properly relieved. It is of especial importance that at all times the officer of the watch ensures that an efficient look-out is maintained. In a vessel with a separate chart room the officer of the watch may visit this, when essential, for a short period for the necessary performance of his navigational duties, but he should previously satisfy himself that it is safe to do so and ensure than an efficient look-out is maintained.

4. There may be circumstances in which the officer of the watch can safely be the sole look-out in daylight. However, this practice shall only be followed after the situation has been carefully assessed on each occasion and it has been established without doubt that it is safe to do so. Full account shall be taken of all relevant factors including but not limited to the state of weather, conditions of visibility, traffic density, proximity of navigational hazards and if navigating in or near a traffic separation scheme.

When the officer of the watch is acting as the sole look-out he must not hesitate to summon assistance to the bridge, and when for any reason he is unable to give his undivided attention to the look-out such assistance must be immediately available.

5. The officer of the watch should bear in mind that the engines are at his disposal and he should not hesitate to use them in case of need. However, timely notice of intended variations of engine speed should be given when possible. He should also keep prominently in mind the manoeuvring capabilities of his ship including its stopping distance.

6. The officer of the watch should also bear in mind that the sound signalling apparatus is at his disposal and he should not hesitate to use it in accordance with the applicable regulations for preventing collisions at sea.

7. The officer of the watch continues to be responsible for the safe navigation of the vessel despite the presence of the master on the bridge until the master informs him specifically that he

has assumed responsibility and this is mutually understood.

Taking over the watch

8. The officer of the watch should not hand over the watch to the relieving officer if he has any reason to believe that the latter is apparently under any disability which would preclude him from carrying out his duties effectively. If in doubt, the officer of the watch should inform the master accordingly. The relieving officer of the watch should ensure that members of his watch are apparently fully capable of performing their duties and in particular the adjustment to night vision.

9. The relieving officer should not take over the watch until his vision is fully adjusted to the light conditions and he has personally satisfied himself regarding:

(a) standing orders and other special instructions of the master relating to the navigation of the vessel;

(b) the position, course, speed and draught of the vessel;

(c) prevailing and predicted tides, currents, weather, visibility and the effect of these factors upon course and speed;

(d) the navigational situation including but not limited to the following:

(i) the operational condition of all navigational and safety equipment being used or likely to be used during the watch;

(ii) errors of gyro and magnetic compasses;

(iii) the presence and movement of vessels in sight or known to be in the vicinity;

(iv) conditions and hazards likely to be encountered during his watch;

(v) the possible effects of heel, trim, water density and squat on underkeel clearance.

10. If at the time the officer of the watch is to be relieved a manoeuvre or other action to avoid any hazard is taking place, the relief of the officer should be deferred until such action is completed.

Periodic checks of navigational equipment

11. The officer of the watch should make regular checks to ensure that:

(a) the helmsman or the automatic pilot is steering the correct course;

(b) the standard compass error is established at least once a watch and when possible, after any major alteration of course. The standard and the gyro compasses should be frequently compared; repeaters should be synchronized with their master compass;

(c) the automatic pilot is tested in the manual position at least once a watch;

(d) the navigation and signal lights and other navigational equipment are functioning properly.

Automatic pilot

12. Officers of the watch should bear in mind the need to station the helmsman and to put the steering into manual control in good time to allow any potentially hazardous situation to be dealt with in a safe manner. With a vessel under automatic steering it is highly dangerous to allow a situation to develop to the point where the officer of the watch is without assistance and has to break the continuity of the look-out in order to take emergency action. The change-over from automatic to manual steering and vice versa should be made by, or under the supervision of, a responsible officer.

Electronic navigational aids

13. The officer of the watch should be thoroughly familiar with the use of electronic navigational aids carried, including their capabilities and limitations.

Echo sounder

14. The echo-sounder is a valuable navigational aid and should be used whenever appropriate.

Navigational records

15. A proper record of the movements and activities of the vessel should be kept during the watch.

Radar

16. The officer of the watch should use the radar when appropriate and whenever restricted visibility is encountered or expected and at all times in congested waters having due regard to its limitations.

17. Whenever radar is in use, the officer of the watch should select an appropriate range scale, observe the display carefully and plot effectively.

18. The officer of the watch should ensure that range scales employed are changed at sufficiently frequent intervals so that echoes are detected as early as possible and that small or poor echoes do not escape detection.

19. The officer of the watch should ensure that plotting or systematic analysis is commenced in ample time, remembering that sufficient time can be made available by reducing speed if necessary.

20. In clear weather, whenever possible, the officer of the watch should carry out radar practice.

Navigation in coastal waters

21. The largest scale chart on board, suitable for the area and corrected with the latest available information, should be used. Fixes should be taken at frequent intervals; whenever circumstances allow, fixing should be carried out by more than one method.

22. The officer of the watch should positively identify all relevant navigation marks.

Clear weather

23. The officer of the watch should take frequent and accurate compass bearings of approaching vessels as a means of early detection of risk of collision; such risk may sometimes exist even when an appreciable bearing change is evident, particularly when approaching a very large vessel or a tow or when approaching a vessel at close range. He should also take early and positive action in compliance with the applicable regulations for preventing collisions at sea and subsequently check that such action is having the desired effect.

Restricted visibility

24. When restricted visibility is encountered or suspected, the first responsibility of the officer of the watch is to comply with the relevant rules of the applicable regulations for preventing collisions at sea, with particular regard to the sounding of fog signals, proceeding at a moderate speed and he shall have the engines ready for immediate manoeuvres. In addition, he should:

(a) inform the master (see paragraph 25);

(b) post look-out(s) and helmsman and, in congested waters, revert to hand steering immediately;

(c) exhibit navigation lights;

(d) operate and use the radar.

It is important that the officer of the watch should have the manoeuvring capabilities including the "stopping distance" of his own vessel prominently in mind.

Calling the master

25. The officer of the watch should notify the master immediately under the following circumstances:

(a) if restricted visibility is encountered or suspected;

(b) if the traffic conditions or the movements of other vessels are causing concern;

(c) if difficulty is experienced in maintaining course;

(d) on failure to sight land, a navigation mark or to obtain soundings by the expected time;

(e) if land or a navigation mark is sighted or a change in soundings occurs unexpectedly;

(f) on the breakdown of the engines, steering gear or any essential navigational equipment;

(g) in heavy weather if in any doubt about the possibility of weather damage;

(h) in any other emergency or situation in which he is in any doubt.

Despite the requirement to notify the master immediately in the foregoing circumstances, the officer of the watch should in addition not hesitate to take immediate action for the safety of the ship, where circumstances so require.

Navigation with pilot embarked

26. Despite the duties and obligations of a pilot, his presence on board does not relieve the officer of the watch from his duties and obligations for the safety of the ship. He should co-operate closely with the pilot and maintain an accurate check on the vessel's positions and movements. If he is in any doubt as to the pilot's actions or intentions, he should seek clarification from the pilot and if doubt still exists he should notify the master immediately and take whatever action is necessary before the master arrives.

The watchkeeping personnel

27. The officer of the watch should give the watchkeeping personnel all appropriate instructions and information which will ensure the keeping of a safe watch including an appropriate look-out.

Ship at anchor

28. If the master considers it necessary a continuous navigational watch should be maintained. In all circumstances, however, the officer of the watch should

(a) determine and plot the ship's position on the appropriate chart as soon as practicable and at sufficiently frequent intervals check when circumstances permit by taking bearings of fixed navigational marks of readily identifiable shore objects, whether the ship is remaining securely at anchor;

(b) ensure that an efficient look-out is maintained;

(c) ensure that inspection rounds of the vessel are made periodically;

(d) observe meteorological and tidal conditions and the state of the sea;

(e) notify the master and undertake all necessary measures if the vessel drags the anchor;

(f) ensure that the state of readiness of the main engines and other machinery is in accordance with the master's instructions;

(g) if visibility deteriorates notify the master and comply with the applicable regulations for preventing collisions at sea;

(h) ensure that the vessel exhibits the appropriate lights and shapes and that appropriate sound signals are made at all times;

(i) take measures to protect the environment from pollution by the ship and comply with the applicable pollution regulations.

Appendix V

Merchant Shipping Notice No. M.685

KEEPING A SAFE NAVIGATIONAL WATCH

Notice to Shipowners, Masters, Skippers and Navigating Officers

1. The Inter-Governmental Maritime Consultative Organization (IMCO) has adopted Resolution A.285 (VIII) "Recommendation on basic principles and operational guidance relating to navigational watchkeeping", relating to the principles to be observed in order to ensure that a safe navigational watch is maintained.

2. The relevant recommendations on:

(i) Basic principles to be observed in keeping a navigational watch; and

(ii) Operational guidance for officers in charge of a navigational watch are to be published by IMCO as saleable documents.

3. These recommended measures, as detailed in Appendices A and B to this Notice for advance information, are in amplification of those promulgated in Notice M.621.

4. Candidates for all deck officer certificates of competency appearing for oral examination after 1 September 1974 will be expected to have a thorough knowledge of the contents of the Appendices to this Notice.

No. M.708

KEEPING A SAFE NAVIGATIONAL WATCH

Notice to Shipowners, Masters, Skippers and Navigating Officers

In line with an amendment to IMCO Resolution A.285 (VIII) M Notice No. M.685 should be amended by the addition of the following sentence to sub-paragraph (b) (iv) (3) of Appendix A:

> "Assistance must be summoned to the bridge when any change in the situation necessitates this and such assistance must be immediately available."

Appendix VI

Merchant Shipping Notice No. M.517

THE USE OF RADAR

Collisions have been caused far too frequently by failure to make proper use of radar; by altering course on insufficient information and by maintaining too high a speed particularly when a close quarters situation is developing or is likely to develop. It cannot be emphasised too strongly that navigation in restricted visibility is difficult and great care is needed even though all the information which can be obtained from radar observation is available. Where continuous radar watchkeeping and plotting cannot be maintained even greater caution must be exercised.

Recommendations on the use of radar, agreed at the 1960 Safety of Life at Sea Conference, have been printed as an Annex to the international collision regulations. These are contained in Statutory Instrument 1965 no. 1525, The Collision Regulations (Ships and Seaplanes on the Water) and Signals of Distress (Ships) Order 1965. This Annex, besides giving some internationally agreed recommendations on the use of radar as an aid to avoid collisions at sea, also clarified the interpretation of Rule 16 in the radar context. The present Notice consists of some notes which it is hoped will help mariners to obtain the utmost benefit from their radar equipment.

Clear weather practice

Whether or not radar training courses have been taken it is important that shipmasters and others using radar should gain and maintain experience in radar observation and appreciation by practice at sea in clear weather. In these conditions radar observations can be checked visually and misinterpretation of the radar display or false appreciation of the situation should not be potentially dangerous. Only by making and keeping themselves familiar with the process of systematic radar observation, and with the relationship between the radar information and the actual situation, will officers be able to deal rapidly and competently with the problems which will confront them in restricted visibility.

Interpretation

(a) It is essential for the observer to be aware of the

current quality of performance of the radar set (which can be most easily ascertained by a performance monitor) and to take account of the possibility that small vessels, small icebergs and similar floating objects may escape detection.

(b) Echoes may be obscured by sea or rain clutter. Adjustment of controls to suit the circumstances will help, but will not completely remove this possibility.

(c) Masts and other obstructions may cause shadow sectors on the display. Merchant Shipping Notice No. M.535 on the fitting of radar sets makes provision for the measurement and recording of such sectors.

Plotting

To estimate the degree of risk of collision with another vessel it is necessary to forecast her nearest approach distance. Choice of appropriate avoiding action is facilitated by knowledge of the other vessel's course and speed, and one of the simplest methods of estimating these factors is by plotting. This invokes knowledge of own ship's course and distance run during the plotting interval.

Appreciation

(a) A single observation of the range and bearing of an echo can give no indication of the course and speed of a vessel in relation to one's own. To estimate this a succession of observations at known time intervals must be made.

(b) Estimation of the other ship's course and speed is only valid up to the time of the last observation and the situation must be kept constantly under review, for the other vessel, which may or may not be on radar watch, may alter her course or speed. Such alterations in course or speed will take time to become apparent to a radar observer.

(c) It should not be assumed that because the relative bearing is changing there is no risk of collision. Alteration of course by one's own ship will alter the relative bearing. A changing compass bearing is more to be relied upon. However, this has to be judged in relation to range, and even with a changing compass bearing a close quarters situation with risk of collision may develop.

Operation

(a) If weather conditions by day or night are such that visibility may deteriorate, the radar should be running, or on "standby". This latter permits operation in less than one minute, whilst it normally takes up to five minutes to operate from switching on). At night, in areas where fogbanks or small craft or unlighted obstructions such as icebergs are likely to be encountered, the radar set should be left permanently running. This is particularly important when there is any danger of occasional fogbanks, so that other vessels can be detected before entering the fogbank.

(b) The life of components, and hence the reliability of the radar set, will be far less affected by continuous running than by frequent switching on and off, so that in periods of uncertain visibility it is better to leave the radar either in full operation or on standby.

Radar watchkeeping

In restricted visibility it is always best to have the radar set running and the display observed, the frequency of observation depending upon the prevailing circumstances, such as the speed of one's own ship and the type of craft or other floating object likely to be encountered.

Radar training

It is essential for a radar observer to have sufficient knowledge and ability to recognise when the radar set he is using is unsatisfactory, giving poor performance or inaccurate information. This knowledge and ability can only be obtained by a full and proper training; experience alone or inadequate training can be dangerous and lead to collision or stranding through failure to detect the presence of other vessels or through misinterpretation of the radar picture.

Radar training courses have been established at a number of centres in the United Kingdom.

The Radar Observer Course is open to shipmasters, deck officers and intending deck officers of the Merchant Navy and those concerned with navigation in the Fishing Fleet. This course enables the mariner to obtain training in the operation and use of marine radar.

The Radar Simulator Course, open to shipmasters and senior deck officers, enables those officers to practise ship manoeuvring and collision avoidance on radar information. Considerable experience of realistic radar observation, interpretation and collision avoidance manoeuvres can be obtained during the five days of this course.

Appendix VII

Merchant Shipping Notice No. M.626

THE USE OF RADAR FOR COLLISION AVOIDANCE

Investigations of recent casualties involving the use of radar have indicated that some such collisions may have been avoided if more advanced warning of the approach of other ships had been obtained by the users of radar equipment.

General advice on the use of radar is contained in Merchant Shipping Notice No. M.517. In the context of early warning of other ships two aspects should be stressed:

(i) *Performance of the radar*

The ability of the radar to display echoes at their maximum detection range is dependent on the overall quality of performance of the radar equipment. Users of radar are reminded that frequent checks of the radar performance should be made to ensure that it has not deteriorated.

(ii) *Choice of range scales*

Although the choice of range scales for observation and plotting is dependent on several factors such as traffic density, speed of the observing ship and the frequency of observation it is not generally advisable to commence plotting on short range scales. In any case advance warning of the approach of other vessels, or changes in traffic density, should be obtained by occasional use of the longer range scales. This advice applies particularly when approaching areas of expected high density when information obtained from the use of the longer range scales may be an important factor in deciding a safe speed.

Appendix VIII

Merchant Shipping Notice No.M.535

RADAR IN MERCHANT SHIPS: SITING PRECAUTIONS

General

This Notice, is issued for information and guidance when radar is to be installed in merchant ships. For new ships, much of the advice is worth considering at the time when the ship is being designed, rather than at the stage of building.

It is the practice of the Department of Trade and Industry, after consultation with representatives of the users and manufacturers of radar equipment, to set down performance standards and a performance specification which, in their opinion, an efficient general purpose radar equipment should meet. These standards and specifications are subject to revision from time to time. The Department undertakes to test a specimen model of a type of radar equipment and to compare its performance with the standards and the specification. Where the performance of the specimen model is found to comply with requirements, a Certificate of Type-Testing is granted to the manufacturers.

In this Notice, the phrase "type-tested set" is used to denote a set which has satisfactorily passed the Department's type-test and has received a Certificate of Type-Testing.

Precautions to be taken before fitting

1. *Compasses*

1.1 It is most important that units of radar sets that contain magnetic material should not be sited too close to magnetic compasses. Many units of radar sets contain enough magnetic material to make the minimum separation distances quoted in paragraph 12 and Appendix II of Notice No. M.616 insufficient. In accordance with the requirements of the Department's Specification each unit of a type-tested set is tested by the Admiralty Compass Observatory to determine the minimum "safe distances" at which it should be installed from both steering and standard magnetic compasses in order not to affect the accuracy of those compasses, and such safe distances are indicated on a tally plate on the unit concerned. A "safe distance" takes account of both the constant effect on a magnetic compass due to the presence of magnetic material and also any variable effect due, for example, to electrical circuits or to opening or closing of drawers. Thus, provided a unit is not placed in a position nearer the centre of the bowl of a magnetic compass than the prescribed safe distance, the unit may be installed or removed without any need for adjustment of that compass.

1.2 If, in installing a radar equipment in a particular ship, it should prove impracticable to site any particular unit of the equipment outside the tested safe distance as indicated on the unit concerned, a Department Surveyor should be consulted. He will advise whether it is possible to site the unit concerned in a position nearer to the compasses than the indicated safe distance where the effect of such siting on the compasses will be stable and can be allowed for by compass adjustment.

1.3 Whenever a unit is fitted nearer a magnetic compass than the safe distance that compass should be adequately checked and, if necessary, adjusted. This should also be done whenever such a unit is removed, replaced or modified. Shipowners and masters are warned that these changes may seriously affect the compasses and disregard of this precaution may have dangerous consequences. It should also be noted that any maintenance that involves more extensive movements of parts of the set than can be brought about by finger pressure on the handles or catches may have an abnormal effect on the compasses while it is in progress.

1.4 Permanent structures such as masts that support units of the radar equipment housed above deck and huts that house equipment or parts of equipment will normally be considered as part of the ship's structure and will not be marked with "safe distances". After the installation of such items near a magnetic compass, the same precautions with regard to the accuracy of that compass should be taken as are taken after any other structural alteration.

1.5 In determining "safe distances" no account is taken of magnetic material other than that in the unit under test. If steel parts of a ship's structure are so situated that they form either a magnetic link or a magnetic screen between the compass and the radar set, they may increase or decrease the separation necessary. If any such complication is suspected, a Department Surveyor should be consulted.

1.6 If the radar set to be fitted is of a type that has not yet, or has only recently, been type-tested, the compass "safe distances" may not at the time of fitting be marked on it. The manufacturers of the equipment and the Department's surveyors should be consulted as to the possible effects of the units of the equipment on the compasses and ample allowance should be made for these effects in siting the units.

1.7 Certain radar spares - particularly spare magnetrons - may seriously affect magnetic compasses. Such spares should normally be stored at least 30 feet from magnetic compasses; but if, being spares for a type-tested set, they are housed in a compartment or receptacle that has been designed by the manufacturer of the radar equipment for their storage and is marked with a "safe distance" allotted by the Admiralty Compass Observatory they may be stored within 30 feet of the compasses but no nearer than the indicated "safe distance".

2. *Effect on other radio installations including D/F*

2.1 *Radio interference.* Whilst direct radio interference from the units of a type-tested radar equipment should not be excessive, it is advisable that all such units - and particularly that containing the modulator - should not be sited within 20 feet of leads from the loop of the direction-finder or from other radio aerials.

2.2 *Effect on D/F.* Bearing errors may be introduced into a direction-finder if metallic masses, parts of which are higher than the base of the loop, are sited within 6 feet of the loop. In siting radar aerials or radar cabins account should be taken of this important limitation.

3. *Siting of aerial unit*

3.1 Experience has shown that an aerial height of between 40 and 60 feet offers the best overall radar performance. Increased aerial height will increase the maximum target detection range of the equipment but will at the same time increase the amplitude and extent of "sea clutter" thus rendering the echoes of buoys and small craft within this area of sea clutter less conspicuous. The aerial should be mounted on a rigid structure which will not twist and give rise to bearing errors.

3.2 Any part of the ship's structure that is at about the same height as the radar aerial may produce a "shadow sector" on the display, i.e. a sector on the radar screen in which targets may not be seen. The angular width of a shadow sector is determined by the width of the obstruction that causes it and the nearness of that obstruction to the aerial. It is highly desirable so to site the aerial as to avoid shadow sectors, or, if this is not possible, to ensure that such shadow sectors as exist will be as narrow as possible and will occur in sectors where they will detract least from the value of the radar as a navigational instrument. Raising the aerial so that it looks over obstructions may be an acceptable measure provided the limitations mentioned in para. 3.1 above are borne in mind. In ships that frequently navigate astern, the need to avoid shadow sectors astern should not be forgotten.

3.3 Reception of signals not directly from the target but by reflection from a part of the ship's structure that causes a shadow sector may result in false echoes appearing on the display within that shadow sector. False echoes may also be caused by parts of the ship's structure which whilst they do not cause shadow sectors, are so disposed as to deflect into the radar aerial energy returning from a target. In each case the false echo will appear to emanate from the relative bearing along which the reflecting object lies. Such false echoes may be eliminated by attaching to the reflecting object a flat metal sheet so placed that its surface reflects radar energy upwards, or a sheet of corrugated metal that will scatter the radar energy, or fitting Radar Absorbent Material (RAM) which will absorb it. These measures will not, of course, remove a shadow sector.

3.4 The needs of servicing in all weathers should be taken into account. If the transmitter is housed immediately below the aerial, some form of platform is desirable so that adjustments may be carried out in situ.

3.5 The aerial unit should be mounted where there is least danger of its being fouled by ropes, bunting, derricks, etc., or of its constituting a hazard to personnel working near it.

4. *Siting of the display unit*

4.1 Display units may be sited in the wheelhouse, in the chartroom or in both. The following are some of the factors that should be borne in mind in selecting the most convenient site for the unit:

(i) *Magnetic safe distances*. The permissible separation of the unit from magnetic compasses may dictate the site.

(ii) *Lighting*. The small amount of light issuing from the display unit may be enough to interfere with visual lookout when the wheelhouse is blacked out; and there will be occasions when additional light is needed at the display unit either for comparison of the display with a chart or for running repairs to the unit. Conversely, there will be times when ambient light in the wheelhouse is too strong for effective viewing of the display. Difficulties such as the foregoing may be overcome either by siting the display in the chartroom or by screening it with curtains if it is sited in the wheelhouse.

(iii) *Comparison of radar information with other information.* A radar observer will wish to compare his radar display with his charts and with what is seen visually from the wheelhouse. In deciding whether the balance of advantage lies in siting the display in the wheelhouse or the chartroom, the complement of watch-keeping officers available will be an important factor for it is essential that where only one watchkeeper is on duty he should be able to refer to the radar display and at the same time be immediately available for visual lookout.

A site in the wheelhouse for the display unit is also convenient for reference by the master or pilot.

(iv) *Viewing facilities.* It should be possible for two officers to view a display simultaneously and for one officer to observe for long periods. The height and angle of the display may be such as to make the provision of a seat desirable.

(v) *Direction of view.* Navigators have evinced a strong preference for the display unit to be so sited that the observer faces forward when viewing it.

(vi) It may be advantageous to provide a communication link between the display unit and the transceiver where these units are widely separated.

5. *Performance monitor*

When a performance monitor carries a permanent echo on the display, the echo should fall in an existing shadow sector or on a bearing of minor importance. Preferably, the performance monitor should be of a type which does not exhibit an echo when it is not activated.

6. *Exposed and protected equipment*

6.1 Manufacturers of type-tested sets are required to mark each unit of a set as "Class X" (suitable for fitting in an open space or exposed position) or "Class B" (for use below deck or in a deckhouse). No units of "Class B" should be mounted in an open space.

6.2 If a ship is to be fitted with a non-type-tested set, the manufacturer should be asked to state which items have been designed for siting in an exposed position and all units not so designed should be sited below deck or in a deckhouse.

6.3 Care should be taken in siting radar equipment to avoid an environment of excessive heat, fumes or vibration.

7. *Lengths of wave-guide and cable runs*

When a set is type-tested, the manufacturer is required to provide lengths of cable and wave-guide equal to the maximum lengths that will be employed in a normal installation. If these lengths are exceeded, the performance of the set may be impaired.

Manufacturers should therefore be consulted as to the length of wave-guide and cable runs for which a set was designed and the units should be so sited that these lengths are not exceeded.

8. *Accident prevention*

High voltage circuits

Type-tested sets are so designed that there are safeguards that deny ready access to high voltages. Each unit of a non-type-tested set should be so installed as not to constitute a danger either by physical contact or by electric shock to those who handle it.

9. *Motor alternators or inverters*

9.1 *Noise.* Though the mechanical noise from units of a type-tested radar equipment will have been reduced to a minimum care should be taken in the siting of a motor alternator unit to ensure that the noise from it will not interfere with the crew either on or off duty.

9.2 *Heat and/or fumes. Motor alternators or inverters should not be installed in positions where excessive heat, fumes or vibration will cause failure in a relatively short period.*

Precautions to be taken after fitting

10. *Alignment of heading marker*

10.1 A marine radar of a type that has been granted the Department's Certificate of Type-Testing should be capable of measuring the bearing of an object whose echo appears near the edge of the PPI display with an error of no more than 1°. If, however, the commencement of the PPI trace is not correctly centred *with the bearing scale,* or the heading marker is not accurately aligned with the *ship's fore and aft line,* additional *bearing* errors will be introduced. It is therefore important that the equipment be correctly set up in these two respects when installed and that its accuracy should be periodically checked. When the heading marker is accurately aligned, a bearing taken by radar should be substantially the same as that obtained visually.

10.2 The following procedures are recommended:

(a) centring the trace

Each time the radar is switched on, and at the commencement of each watch when the radar is used continuously and whenever bearings are to be measured, the observer should check that the trace is rotating about the centre of the display and should, if necessary, adjust it (*the centre of the display is the centre of rotation of the bearing scale cursor*).

(b) aligning the heading marker and *radar aerial*

Visually aligning the *radar aerial* along what appears to be the *ship's fore and aft line* is not a sufficiently accurate method of alignment. The following procedure is recommended for accurate alignment:

(i) adjust accurately the centre of rotation of the trace. Switch off azimuth stabilisation;

(ii) on equipments possessing the appropriate controls, rotate the PPI picture so that the heading marker lies at 0° on the bearing scale;

(iii) select an object which is conspicuous but small visually and whose echo is small and distinct and lies as nearly as possible at a maximum range of the range scale in use. Measure simultaneously the relative visual bearing of this object and the angle on the PPI that its echo makes with the heading marker; it is important that the visual bearing should be measured from a position near the radar scanner in plan. Repeat these measurements twice at least and calculate the mean difference between bearings obtained visually and by radar;

(iv) if an error exists, adjust the heading marker contacts in the scanner assembly to correct the position of the heading marker by moving it an amount equal to the mean difference calculated in (iii) above;

(v) rotate the PPI picture to return the heading marker to 0° on the bearing scale;

(vi) take simultaneous visual and radar bearings as in (iii) above to check the accuracy of alignment. *Alignment of the heading marker or correcting the alignment on a ship berthed in a dock or harbour, or using bearings of a target that has not been identified with certainty both by radar and visually can introduce serious bearing errors. The procedure for alignment of heading marker should be carried out on clearly identified targets clear of a confusion of target echoes. The alignment should be checked at the earliest opportunity.*

10.3 Checking heading marker alignment. It is recommended that checks should be made periodically in the manner laid down in (b) (i), (ii) and (iii) above to ensure that correct alignment is maintained. (Care should be taken to centre the trace accurately beforehand). If adjustment of the heading marker contacts is required but cannot be carried out immediately, a notice should be displayed prominently calling attention to the existence of an error in heading marker alignment, and in operating the radar due allowance should be made for this error. The alignment should be adjusted at the first opportunity.

11. *Measurement of shadow sectors*

11.1 The angular width and bearing of any shadow sectors should be determined. For a new vessel, this should be done during trials. In other ships it should be done at the first opportunity after fitting the radar set. When determined, the particulars should be recorded on a tally plate fixed near each display unit of the set.

11.2 Two methods of determining the angular width of a shadow sector are:

(a) observation of the behaviour of the echo of a small isolated object, such as a *buoy* not fitted with a corner reflector or a beacon post, when the ship is turned slowly through 360 degrees at a distance of a mile or so from the object. The display unit should be carefully watched, and the bearings between which the echo from the buoy disappears and reappears taken as indicating the shadow sector or sectors. The sea should be calm so that the echo is not lost in the sea clutter or submerged or hidden by waves from time to time, or in the case of a buoy or other floating object the echo fading temporarily due to any rolling motion.

(b) observation of the shadow sector against a background of sea clutter.

Note

A shadow sector cannot be fairly estimated in heavy clutter, as echoes from either side of the sector may spread into it and give an illusion that objects in the sector are being observed. Nor can it be satisfactorily determined in confined waters, because of the probability of indirect, false or multiple echoes being produced from nearby buildings or other vessels.

11.3 Calculation of a shadow sector's width and position from a knowledge of the width of the mast or other object causing the shadow and its distance and bearing from the centre of the radar aerial is a useful guide to the shadow sector's expected appearance on the plan display.

11.4 If derricks are found to cause shadow sectors, the effect of their being stowed in more than one position should be observed.

11.5 A change in trim may alter shadow sectors. If visual inspection of the objects causing or likely to cause shadow sectors shows that this is likely, the sectors should be measured under various conditions of trim as opportunity permits.

12. *D/F apparatus and compasses*

The calibration of D/F apparatus on the ship should be checked as soon as *practicable* after installation of radar equipment; if necessary the apparatus should be re-calibrated.

The accuracy of compass deviation corrections should be checked as soon as *practicable* after installation of radar equipment even if all units of the equipment are sited outside their prescribed "safe distances"; if necessary the compass should be adjusted.

If any unit has been sited nearer to a compass than the safe distance, checking the compass should be regarded as essential (see paragraphs 1.2 and 1.3).

13. *Mutual interference between radio and radar*

Tests should be made with radio receivers and transmitters, working on all frequencies likely to be used, for possible mutual interference between the radar and radio installations.

Further advice on siting precautions in particular installations can be obtained from the Department of Trade and Industry, Marine Navigational Aids Branch, or from the Marine Surveyors at the ports.

Appendix IX

Merchant Shipping Notice No. M.767

INTRODUCTION

Only the letter spelling table as contained in Chapter X of the International Code of Signals and in the Radio Regulations to be used on any occasion when spelling is necessary.

This vocabulary has been compiled:

to assist in the greater safety of navigation and of the conduct of ships;
to standardise the language used in communication for navigation at sea, in port-approaches, in waterways and harbours.

These phrases are not intended to supplant or contradict the International Regulations for Preventing Collisions at Sea or special local Rules or Recommendations made by IMCO concerning ships' routeing schemes. Neither are they intended to supersede the International Code of Signals and the Radio Regulations nor to supplant normal Radiotelephone practice as set out in the ITU Regulations.

It is not intended that use of the vocabulary shall be mandatory, but rather through constant repetition in ships and in training establishments ashore, that the phrases and terms used will become those normally accepted and commonplace among seamen. Use of the contents of the vocabulary should be made as often as possible in preference to other wording of similar meaning.

In this way it is intended to become an acceptable "language", using the English tongue, for the interchange of intelligence between individuals of all maritime nations on the many and varied occasions when precise meanings and translations are in doubt, increasingly evident under modern conditions at sea.

The typographic conventions used throughout most of this vocabulary are as follows:

( ) brackets indicate that the part of the message enclosed within the brackets may be added where it is relevant.

/ oblique stroke indicates that the items on either side of the stroke are alternatives.

... dots indicate that the relevant information is to be filled in where the dots occur.

1. *Procedure*

Should it be necessary to indicate that phrases in this vocabulary are to be used the following message may be sent:

"*Please use/I will use* the Standard Marine Vocabulary"

2. *Standard Verbs*

Where possible sentences should be introduced by one of the following verb forms:

Imperative
Always to be used when mandatory orders are being given

You must	Do Not	Must I?
Indicative	*Negative*	*Interrogative*[2]
I require	I do not require	
I am	I am not	Do I require?
You are	You are not	Am I?
I have	I do not have	Are you?
I can	I cannot	Do you have?
		Can I?) (Is it
		Can you?) possible?)
I wish to	I do not wish to	Do you wish to?
I will (future)	I will not (future)	
You may	You need not	May I? (permission)
Advise[1]	Advise not[1]	
There is	There is not	Is there?
		What/where/when is?
		What/where/when are?

Note 1: "Advise", "Advise not" are to be used when recommendations are being given.
Note 2: The interrogative may be preceded by the use of the word "question".

3. *Responses*

Where the answer to a questions is in the affirmative say:
"YES" followed by the appropriate phrase in full.
Where the answer to a question is in the negative say:
"NO" followed by the appropriate phrase in full.
Where the information is not immediately available but soon will be say:
"STAND BY".
Where the information cannot be obtained say:
"NO INFORMATION".
Where a message is not properly heard say:
"SAY AGAIN".
Where a message is not understood say:
"MESSAGE NOT UNDERSTOOD".

4. *Urgent Messages*

MAYDAY PAN SECURITE	are to be used to prefix Distress, Urgency and Safety signals respectively, in accordance with Radio Regulations

ATTENTION .... Repeated if necessary, may be used at the beginning of an urgent message.

5. *Miscellaneous Phrases*

5.1 What is your name (and call sign)?

5.2 How do you read me?

5.3 I read you	bad/1	with signal strength	1/barely perceptible
	poor/2		2/weak
	fair/3		3/fairly good
	good/4		4/good
	excellent/5		5/very good

5.4 Stand by on channel ......

5.5 Change to channel ....

5.6 I cannot read you. *(Pass your message through vessel ....)/ (Advise try channel .....).*

5.7 I cannot understand you. Please use the *Standard Marine Vocabulary/International Code of Signals.*

5.8 I am passing a message for vessel .....

5.9 Correction .....

5.10 I am *ready/not ready* to receive your message.

5.11 I do not have channel .... Please use channel ....

6. *Repetition*

If any parts of the message are considered sufficiently important to need safeguarding, use the word "repeat", e.g. "You will load 163 repeat 163 tons bunkers,"
"Do not repeat do not overtake".

7. *Position*

When latitude and longitude are used, these shall be expressed in degrees and minutes (and decimals of a minute if necessary), North or South of the Equator and East or West of Greenwich.

When the position is related to a mark, the mark shall be a well-defined charted object. The bearing shall be in the 360 degree notation from True North and shall be that of the position *FROM* the mark.

Examples: "THERE ARE SALVAGE OPERATIONS IN POSITION 15 DEGREES 34 MINUTES NORTH 61 DEGREES 29 MINUTES WEST",

"YOUR POSITION IS 137 DEGREES TWO POINT FOUR MILES *FROM* BARR HEAD LIGHTHOUSE".

8. *Courses*

Always to be expressed in 360° notation from North (true North unless otherwise stated). Whether this is *to* or *from* a mark can be stated.

9. *Bearings*

The bearing of the mark or vessel concerned, is the bearing in the 360° notation from North (true North unless otherwise stated), except in the case of relative bearings.

However, bearings may be either FROM the mark or FROM the vessel,

Examples: "The Pilot boat is bearing 215° from you".
"Your bearing is 127° from the signal station".

Note: Vessels reporting their position should always quote their bearing *FROM* the mark, as described in paragraph 7.

Relative Bearings

Relative bearings can be expressed in degrees relative to the ship's head/bow. More frequently this is in relation to the port or starboard bow,

Example: "The buoy is 030° on your port bow".
(However relative, DF bearings are more commonly expressed in the 360° notation).

10. *Distances*

Preferably to be expressed in nautical miles or cables (tenths of a mile) otherwise in kilometres or metres, the unit always to be stated.

11. *Speed*

To be expressed in knots
(a) without further notation meaning speed through the water; or
(g) "ground speed" meaning speed over the ground.

12. *Numbers*

Numbers are to be spoken thus "One-Five-Zero" for 150. "Two point five" for 2·5.

13. *Geographical Names*

Place names used should be those on the chart or Sailing Directions in use. Should these not be understood latitude and longitude should be given.

14. *Time*

Times should be expressed in the 24 hour notation indicating whether GMT, zonetime or local shoretime is being used.

Note: In cases not covered by the above phraseology normal R/T practice will prevail.

(This is followed by sections on Glossary and Phrase vocabulary).

Appendix X

MARITIME BUOYAGE - Harmonization of Systems in North-West Europe

(1) The International Association of Lighthouse Authorities (I.A.L.A.) has informed the Inter-Governmental Maritime Consultative Organisation (I.M.C.O.) of plans to introduce a new system of maritime buoyage in North-West Europe, commencing in the English Channel in April 1977.

(2) As a preliminary notification to mariners, and others who will be affected by the proposed changes, the I.A.L.A. Note to I.M.C.O. is reproduced below, together with the I.A.L.A. rules entitled "Maritime Buoyage Systems - System 'A' (February 1976)". As stated in paragraph 8 of the Note, "an intensive educational and information programme about the system" will be undertaken by I.A.L.A.

(3) Attention is also drawn to paragraph 5 which explains that implementation of the proposed changes will be subject to certain factors, including "charting considerations". In the Hydrographic Department, the I.A.L.A. statement has been studied to determine the implications for Admiralty Charts and other navigational publications. A detailed chart amendment programme cannot be prepared until a full list of changes to existing buoyage, and the implementation schedule, are available. However, it seems likely that promulgation by Hydrographer of the Navy will be in several stages, as follows:-

(a) Publication of a booklet, setting out the details of the new buoyage system 'A', with explanatory diagrams and other relevant information concerning chart symbols and abbreviations, etc. It is unlikely that this new navigational publication will be available for issue before late summer 1976.

(b) Three or four months prior to each stage in the change-over of buoyage, the details of the proposed alterations will be announced in a Preliminary Notice to Mariners. Consideration is being given to the possibility of making the full list of proposed changes available as a separate publication, provided that each year's changes are notified in their entirety, sufficiently in advance.

(c) Amendments to individual charts affected will be promulgated through the normal channels, using the most appropriate method in each case, i.e. New Edition, N.M. Block, Notice to Mariners or Revised Reprint. As far as is practicable, the issue of these amendments will be co-ordinated with the change-over schedule of the buoyage authorities.

(d) Confirmation that the changes in specific areas have been carried out will be announced in Radio Navigational Warnings. It is unlikely that strict co-ordination of buoyage changes and issue of amended charts will always be achieved and mariners may find it necessary to carry out hand corrections to existing charts on the basis of the advance information promulgated in the Preliminary Notices to Mariners (see sub paragraph (3b) above).

(4) This Notice has been issued to give, as early as possible, a warning of the I.A.L.A. intentions and to indicate the likely implications for charts and other navigational publications. Further information will be published in Notices to Mariners in due course. However, there may be some organisations or publishers whose need to prepare for the proposed changes in 1977 and in subsequent years, will be met more effectively by procurement of information and data direct from the members of I.A.L.A. In the United Kingdom, requests for such assistance should be addressed to:-

Trinity House Lighthouse Service,
Trinity House, Tower Hill, London EC3N 4DH.

Appendix XI

RECOMMENDATIONS APPLICABLE TO NUCLEAR SHIPS

NOTE: Throughout the following Recommendations, "the present Convention" means the International Convention for the Safety of Life at Sea, 1974.
Attention is drawn to the Regulations concerning nuclear ships in Chapter VIII of the present Convention.

1. *General Safety of Nuclear Ships*

(a) Since a casualty involving the non-nuclear features of a nuclear ship, such as a steering gear failure, fire or collision, and so forth, could endanger the nuclear power plant, it is desirable that these features should provide for the maximum practicable safety. A nuclear ship should comply with the relevant requirements of the present Convention, the Administration and a recognized Classification Society. Components and systems such as watertight subdivision, fire protection, bilge pumping arrangements, fire-extinguishing arrangements, electrical installations, steering gear, astern power, stability and navigational aids should receive special consideration to ensure that adequate protection is given to the ship to minimize the hazards peculiar to the nuclear power plant. Consideration should be given to the results of past marine casualties involving similar size ships with the intent of preventing the dangerous uncontrolled release of radioactive or toxic materials in the event of similar casualties.

(b) Special attention should be given to general structural strength of nuclear ships and to the local strength of structures in and around the reactor compartment.

(c) A nuclear ship should remain afloat and have sufficient stability when not less than any two adjacent main watertight compartments are flooded, in all anticipated conditions of loading.

(d) Fire protection systems and the watertight integrity should be at least equivalent to the highest standards of the present Convention.

2. *General Requirements of Nuclear Power Plant*

(a) It should be demonstrated by calculation and experiment that the properties of the plant and the nature of the enclosure provide the maximum practicable protection against accidents or failures resulting in unreasonable radiation at sea or in port, to the crew, passengers or public, or to the waterways or food or water resources.

(b) The reactor installation should be designed to prevent an uncontrolled chain reaction under all foreseeable operational and accident conditions including sinking of the ship.

(c) A nuclear ship equipped with a single-reactor nuclear power plant, the dependability of which has not been proven, should be provided with an emergency propulsion plant capable of propelling the ship at a navigable speed. Such emergency propulsion plant should be in a state of readiness whenever the ship is navigating in territorial waters.

(d) The nuclear power plant should be such as to ensure manoeuvrability equivalent to that of a similar conventional ship.

(e) Requirements for standby emergency components for the conventional portions of the nuclear power plant should be in accordance with those for a similar conventional ship. Standby and emergency nuclear components should be considered and developed in relation to the type of nuclear power plant used.

(f) Where standby systems are essential to the safe operation of the reactor installation, they should be so separated from the main systems as to give maximum protection in the event of an accident.

(g) An emergency source of power should be provided which is capable of furnishing power to the components necessary for safely shutting down the reactor installation and retaining it in a safe condition.

(h) The reactor compartment should contain no inflammable materials other than those necessary for use in the reactor installation.

(i) Reactor materials which are chemically reactive with air or water to a dangerous degree should not be used unless it can be shown that adequate safeguards are incorporated in the particular system.

(j) The machinery and reactor installation should be designed to operate satisfactorily under seagoing conditions having regard to the ship's attitude, accelerations and vibrations.

(k) Reactor cooling systems should provide for the same removal of decay heat from the reactor and should prevent excessive temperature conditions under all foreseeable operational and accident conditions at angles of heel and list within the stability range. Failure of decay heat removal facilities should not result in the release of hazardous amounts of radioactive or toxic materials from the enclosure of the reactor installation.

(l) Adequate reactor controls, protective devices and instrumentation should be provided.

(m) Necessary controls and instrumentation should be arranged to permit control of the reactor installation from outside its enclosure.

3. *Protection and Enclosure of Reactor Installation*

(a) The reactor installation should be so arranged, protected and securely fastened as to minimize the probability of its damage in the event of a ship accident.

(b) The reactor installation should be provided with enclosures, systems, or arrangements which in the event of damage to its components will prevent the release of hazardous amounts of radioactive or toxic materials into service and accommodation spaces and the ship's environment. These outer enclosures, systems, or arrangements should be subjected to suitable tests to demonstrate satisfactory performance under all foreseeable conditions of accident.

(c) The enclosures, systems or arrangements should be located in such a manner as to minimize damage in the event of collision or grounding. In construction, arrangements should be made, if practicable, to facilitate the possible salvage of the reactor or of its essential parts from the vessel in the event of shipwreck, without adversely affecting the safety of the reactor installation under normal conditions.

(d) Facilities should be provided to ensure that fires within and without the reactor installation do not impair the integrity of the enclosures, systems, or arrangements provided, or the arrangements provided for safely shutting down the reactor installation and retaining it in a safe condition.

4. *Shielding and Radiation Safety*

(a) A nuclear power plant should be provided with reliable biological shielding to protect persons on board ship or within the immediate vicinity of the ship against hazardous effect of radiation under normal and accident conditions. Maximum permissible levels of radiation in accommodation and service spaces should be in accordance with international levels when established.

(b) Maintenance and operation instructions in regard to appropriate radiation protection should be worked out for every nuclear ship. Knowledge of these instructions by the nuclear power plant personnel should be periodically checked by the Administration.

(c) Radiation monitoring instruments should be installed at appropriate locations. These should give warning in the event of any radiation exceeding a predetermined safe level.

5. *Radioactive Wastes*

(a) Special arrangements should be provided for the safe temporary storage, where necessary, and for the safe disposal of solid, liquid and gaseous radioactive wastes.

(b) Monitoring devices should be provided for these waste disposal systems. These should give warning and, if necessary, take action in the event of any radiation exceeding a predetermined safe level.

(c) The maximum permissible levels of radiation for waste disposal on the high seas should be in accordance with international levels when established.

6. *Fuelling and Maintenance*

(a) Reactor fuelling should be carried out exclusively at locations suitably equipped for this purpose.

(b) Arrangements should be provided to ensure that de-fuelling, re-fuelling, servicing and maintenance can be carried out without unacceptable exposure of personnel to radiation and without hazardous release of radioactive or toxic materials to the environment.

7. *Manning*

The master, officers and members of the crew of a nuclear ship should possess qualifications and have undergone proper training appropriate to their responsibilities and duties in accordance with arrangements provided by the Administration. Such personnel should also be instructed as to the precautions to be taken in the matter of radiological protection.

8. *Operating Manual*

The Operating Manual should provide detailed operating procedures for the various equipment and systems under normal and accident conditions, as well as provide for the maintenance of adequate records of operation, radiation levels, waste disposal, and tests and inspections pertinent to the safety of the reactor installation.

9. *Safety Assessment*

(a) The Safety Assessment should include sufficiently detailed information to permit qualified personnel to assess the safety of the ship and its power plant, including standards and procedures followed, and to determine whether initial and continued performance will be safe. Typical items which the safety assessment should include are a description of the ship; propulsion and reactor systems; a discussion of the operation under normal sea, port and emergency conditions; a description of reactor control; protection and enclosure; radiation protection; radioactive waste disposal; fuelling; standby and emergency components; test procedures; manning and training requirements; and an evaluation of credible accidents which indicates that the hazards are minimized. The Safety Assessment should indicate that the reactor installation does not constitute an undue hazard, to the crew, passengers or the public, or to the waterways, or food or water resources.

(b) The content of the Safety Assessment should not be considered limited to the information suggested herein, and such additional specific data as necessary should be made available. The complete Safety Assessment should be prepared for the first installation of a reactor type in a ship type. For second and following generation reactor and ship types where performance and safety have been demonstrated, acceptance may be based on an analysis of deviations from the previous design.

10. *Publication of Requirements*

The Contracting Governments should publish any special requirements which they make regarding the approach, entry into, or stay in their ports of a nuclear ship.

11. *Special Control*

After the safety of the nuclear ship and its nuclear power plant has been properly established, the following actions should, in general, be adequate to determine their safe operational conditions.

(a) Examination of the daily log of the behaviour of the nuclear power plant and equipment, covering a reasonable period of between one week to one month including the stay in the last port.

(b) Determination that the nuclear power plant is properly certified and that any periodic checks required by the Operating Manual have been complied with.

(c) Determination that radiation levels in areas within the ship and in the vicinity of the ship which are accessible to shore personnel are not in excess of maximum permissible levels specified by the Operating Manual to be determined by examination of the ship's records or by independent measurement.

(d) Determination of the quantity and activity of radioactive waste stored aboard the ship by examination of the ship's records or by independent measurement, and of the procedures and programme for any disposal.

(e) Determination that the reactor installation protection and enclosure is intact, and that any programme involving a breach of its integrity complies with the requirements of the Operating Manual.

(f) Determination that conventional and emergency arrangements and equipment, the reliability of which is essential when navigating in narrow waters, are in efficient operating condition.

Appendix XII

INTERNATIONAL CONVENTION FOR THE UNIFICATION OF CERTAIN RULES OF LAW WITH RESPECT TO COLLISION BETWEEN VESSELS

(Brussels, September 23rd, 1910)

(*Translation*)

Having recognized the desirability of determining by mutual agreement certain uniform rules of law with respect to collisions. Have decided to conclude a convention to that end, and have appointed as their Plenipotentiaries, namely:

(*Follows the list of Plenipotentiaries*)

Who, having been duly authorized to that effect, have agreed as follows:

Article 1

Where a collision occurs between sea-going vessels or between sea-going vessels and vessels of inland navigation, the compensation due for damages caused to the vessels, or to any things or persons on board thereof, shall be settled in accordance with the following provisions, in whatever waters the collision takes place.

Article 2

If the collision is accidental, if it is caused by *force majeure*, or if the causes of the collision is left in doubt, the damages are borne by those who have suffered them.

This provision is applicable notwithstanding the fact that the vessels, or any one of them, may be at anchor (or otherwise made fast) at the time of the casualty.

Article 3

If the collision is caused by the fault of one of the vessels, liability to make good the damages attaches to the one which has committed the fault.

Article 4

If two or more vessels are in fault the liability of each vessel is in proportion to the degree of the faults respectively committed. Provided that if, having regard to the circumstances, it is not possible to establish the degree of the respective faults, or if it appears that the faults are equal, the liability is apportioned equally.

The damages caused, either to the vessels or to their cargoes,or to the effects or other property of the crews, passengers, or other persons on board, are borne by the vessels in fault in the above proportion, and even to third parties a vessel is not liable for more than such proportion of such damages.

In respect of damages caused by death or personal injuries, the vessels in fault are jointly as well as severally liable to third parties, without prejudice however to the right of the vessel which has paid a larger part than that which, in accordance with the provisions of the first paragraph of this Article, she ought ultimately to bear, to obtain a contribution from the other vessel or vessels in fault.

It is left to the law of each country to determine, as regards such right to obtain contribution, the meaning and effect of any contract or provision of law which limits the liability of the owners of a vessel towards persons on board.

Article 5

The liability imposed by the preceding Articles attaches in cases where the collision is caused by the fault of a pilot even when the pilot is carried by compulsion of law.

Article 6

The right of action for the recovery of damages resulting from a collision is not conditional upon the entering of a protest or the fulfilment of any other special formality.

All legal presumptions of fault in regard to liability for collision are abolished.

Article 7

Actions for the recovery of damages are barred after an interval of two years from the date of the casualty.

The period within which an action must be instituted for enforcing the right to obtain contribution permitted by paragraph 3 of Article 4 is one year from the date of payment.

The grounds upon which the said periods of limitation may be suspended or interrupted are determined by the law of the court where the case is tried.

The High Contracting Parties reserve to themselves the right to provide, by legislation in their respective countries, that the said periods shall be extended in cases where it has not been possible to arrest the defendant vessel in the territorial waters of the State in which the plaintiff has his domicile or principal place of business.

Article 8

After a collision, the master of each of the vessels in collision is bound, so far as he can do so without serious danger to his vessel, her crew and her passengers, to render assistance to the other vessel, her crew and her passengers.

He is likewise bound so far as possible to make known to the other vessel the name of his vessel and the port to which she belongs, and also the names of the ports from which she comes and to which she is bound.

A breach of the above provisions does not of itself impose any liability on the owner of a vessel.

Article 9

The High Contracting Parties whose legislation does not forbid infringements of the preceding Article bind themselves to take or to propose to their respective Legislatures the measures necessary for the prevention of such infringements.

The High Contracting Parties will communicate to one another as soon as possible the laws or regulations which have already been or may be hereafter promulgated in their States for giving effect to the above undertaking.

Article 10

Without prejudice to any conventions which may hereafter be made, the provisions of this Convention do not affect in any way the law in force in each country with regard to the limitation of shipowners' liability, nor do they alter legal obligations arising from contracts of carriage or from any other contracts.

Article 11

This Convention does not apply to ships of war or to Government ships appropriated exclusively to a public service.

Article 12

The provisions of this Convention shall be applied as regards all persons interested when all the vessels concerned in any action belong to States of the High Contracting Parties, and in any other cases for which the national laws provide.

Provided always that:

1. As regards persons interested who belong to a non-contracting State, the application of the above provisions may be made by each of the contracting States conditional upon reciprocity.

2. Where all the persons interested belong to the same State as the court trying the case, the provisions of the national law and not of the Convention are applicable.

Article 13

This Convention extends to the making good of damages which a vessel, or to goods or persons on board either vessel, either by the execution or non-execution of a manoeuvre or by the non-observance of the regulations, even if no collision had actually taken place.

(Follows the articles on coming into force, accession, ratification and denunciation of the Convention).

Appendix XIII

INTERNATIONAL CONVENTION ON CERTAIN RULES CONCERNING CIVIL JURISDICTION IN MATTERS OF COLLISION

(Brussels, May 10th, 1952)

The High Contracting Parties,

Having recognized the advisability of establishing by agreement certain uniform rules relating to civil jurisdiction in matters of collision;

Having decided to conclude a convention for this purpose and thereto have agreed as follows:

Article 1

1. An action for collision occurring between seagoing vessels, or between seagoing vessels and inland navigation craft, can only be introduced:

   (a) either before the Court where the defendant has his habitual residence or a place of business;

   (b) or before the Court of the place where arrest has been effected of the defendant ship or of any other ship belonging to the defendant which can be lawfully arrested, or where arrest could have been effected and bail or other security has been furnished;

   (c) or before the Court of the place of collision when the collision has occurred within the limits of a port or inland waters.

2. It shall be for the plaintiff to decide in which of the Courts referred to in (1) of this Article the action shall be instituted.

3. A claimant shall not be allowed to bring a further action against the same defendant on the same facts in another jurisdiction, without discontinuing an action already instituted.

Article 2

The provisions of Article 1 shall not in any way prejudice the right of the Parties to bring an action in respect of a collision before a Court they have chosen by agreement or to refer it to arbitration.

Article 3

1. Counterclaims arising out of the same collision can be brought before the Court having jurisdiction over the principal action in accordance with the provisions of Article 1.

2. In the event of there being several claimants, any claimant may bring his action before the Court previously seized of an action against the same party arising out of the same collision.

3. In the case of a collision or collisions in which two or more vessels are involved nothing in this Convention shall prevent any Court seized of an action by reason of the provisions of this Convention, from exercising jurisdiction under its national laws in further actions arising out of the same incident.

Article 4

This Convention shall also apply to an action for damage caused by one ship to another or to the property of persons on board such ships through the carrying out of or the omission to carry out a manoeuvre or through non-compliance with regulations even when there has been no actual collision.

Article 5

Nothing contained in this Convention shall modify the rules of law now or hereafter in force in the various Contracting States in regard to collisions involving warships or vessels owned by or in the service of a State.

Article 6

This Convention does not affect claims arising from contracts of carriage or from any other contracts.

Article 7

This Convention shall not apply in cases covered by the provisions of the revised Rhine Navigation Convention of 17 October 1868.

Article 8

The provisions of this Convention shall be applied as regards all persons interested when all the vessels concerned in any action belong to States of the High Contracting Parties.

Provided always that:

1. As regards persons interested who belong to a non-contracting State, the application of the above provisions may be made by each of the Contracting States conditional upon reciprocity.

2. Where all the persons interested belong to the same State as the Court trying the case, the provisions of the national law and not of the Convention are applicable.

Article 9

The High Contracting Parties undertake to submit to arbitration any disputes between States arising out of the interpretation or application of this Convention, but this shall be without prejudice to the obligations of those High Contracting Parties who have agreed to submit their disputes to the International Court of Justice.

(Follows the articles on coming into force, accession, ratification, reversion and denunciation of the Convention).

Appendix XIV

INTERNATIONAL CONVENTION FOR THE UNIFICATION OF CERTAIN RULES RELATING TO PENAL JURISDICTION IN MATTERS OF COLLISION OR OTHER INCIDENTS OF NAVIGATION

(Brussels, May 10th, 1952)

The High Contracting Parties,

Having recognized the advisability of establishing by agreement certain uniform rules relating to penal jurisdiction in matters of collision or other incidents of navigation.

Have decided to conclude a convention for this purpose and thereto have agreed as follows:

Article 1

In the event of a collision or any other incident of navigation concerning a sea-going ship and involving the penal or disciplinary responsibility of the master or of any other person in the service of the ship, criminal or disciplinary proceedings may be instituted only before the judicial or administrative authorities of the State of which the ship was flying the flag at the time of the collision or other incident of navigation.

Article 2

In the case provided for in the preceding Article, no arrest or detention of the vessel shall be ordered, even as a measure of investigation, by any authorities other than those whose flag the ship was flying.

Article 3

Nothing contained in this Convention shall prevent any State from permitting its own authorities, in cases of collision or other incidents of navigation, to take any action in respect of certificates of competence or licences issued by that State or to prosecute its own nationals for offences committed while on board a ship flying the flag of another State.

Article 4

This Convention does not apply to collisions or other incidents of navigation occurring within the limits of a port or in inland waters.

Furthermore the High Contracting Parties shall be at liberty at the time of signature, ratification or accession to the Convention, to reserve to themselves the right to take proceedings in respect of offences committed within their own territorial waters.

Article 5

The High Contracting Parties undertake to submit to arbitration any disputes between States arising out of the interpretation or application of this Convention, but this shall be without prejudice to the obligations of those High Contracting Parties who have agreed to submit their disputes to the International Court of Justice.

(Follows the articles on coming into force, accession, ratification, reversion and denunciation of the Convention).

Appendix XV

INTERNATIONAL CONVENTION FOR THE UNIFICATION OF CERTAIN RULES RELATING TO THE ARREST OF SEA-GOING SHIPS

(Brussels, May 10th, 1952)

The High Contracting Parties,

Having recognized the desirability of determining by agreement certain uniform rules of law relating to the arrest of sea-going ships.

Have decided to conclude a convention for this purpose and thereto have agreed as follows:

Article 1

In this Convention the following words shall have the meanings hereby assigned to them:

1. *Maritime Claim* means a claim arising out of one or more of the following:

(a) damage caused by any ship either in collision or otherwise;

(b) loss of life or personal injury caused by any ship or occurring in connection with the operation of any ship;

(c) salvage;

(d) agreement relating to the use or hire of any ship whether by charter-party or otherwise;

(e) agreement relating to the carriage of goods in any ship whether by charter-party or otherwise;

(f) loss of or damage to goods including baggage carried in any ship;

(g) general average;

(h) bottomry;

(i) towage;

(j) pilotage;

(k) goods or materials wherever supplied to a ship for her operation or maintenance;

(l) construction, repair or equipment of any ship or dock charges and dues;

(m) wages of Masters, Officers, or crew;

(n) Master's disbursements, including disbursements made by shippers, charterers or agents on behalf of a ship or her owner;

(o) disputes as to the title or to ownership of any ship;

(p) disputes between co-owners of any ship as to the ownership, possession employment or earnings of that ship;

(q) the mortgage or hypothecation of any ship.

2. *Arrest* means the detention of a ship by judicial process to secure a maritime claim, but does not include the seizure of a ship in execution or satisfaction of a judgment.

3. *Person* includes individuals, partnerships and bodies corporate, Governments, their Departments and Public Authorities.

4. *Claimant* means a person who alleges that a maritime claim exists in his favour.

Article 2

A ship flying the flag of one of the contracting States may be arrested in the jurisdiction of any of the contracting States in respect of any maritime claim, but in respect of no other claim; but nothing in this Convention shall be deemed to extend or restrict any right or Powers vested in any Governments or their Departments, Public Authorities, or Dock or Harbour Authorities under their existing domestic laws or regulations to arrest, detain or otherwise prevent the sailing of vessels within their jurisdiction.

Article 3

1. Subject to the provisions of (4) of this Article and of Article 10, a claimant may arrest either the particular ship in respect of which the maritime claim arose, or any other ship which is owned by the person who was, at the time when the maritime claim arose, the owner of the particular ship, even though the ship arrested be ready to sail; but no ship, other than the particular ship in respect of which the claim arose, may be arrested in respect of any of the maritime claims enumerated in Article 1, 1(o), (p) or (q).

2. Ships shall be deemed to be in the same ownership when all the shares therein are owned by the same person or persons.

3. A ship shall not be arrested, nor shall bail or other security be given more than once in any one or more of the jurisdictions of any of the Contracting States in respect of the same maritime

claim by the same claimant and, if a ship has been arrested in any one of such jurisdictions, or bail or other security has been given in such jurisdiction either to release the ship or to avoid a threatened arrest, any subsequent arrest of the ship or of any ship in the same ownership by the same claimant for the same maritime claim shall be set aside, and the ship released by Court or other appropriate judicial authority of that State, unless the bail or other security had been finally released before the subsequent arrest or that there is other good cause for maintaining that arrest.

4. When in the case of a charter by demise of a ship the charterer and not the registered owner is liable in respect of a maritime claim relating to that ship, the claimant may arrest such ship or any other ship in the ownership of the charterer by demise, subject to the provisions of this Convention but no other ship in the ownership of the registed owner shall be liable to arrest in respect of such maritime claims.

The provisions of this paragraph shall apply to any case in which a person other than the registered owner of a ship is liable in respect of a maritime claim relating to that ship.

Article 4

A ship may only be arrested under the authority of a Court or of the appropriate judicial authority of the Contracting State in which the arrest is made.

Article 5

The Court or other appropriate judicial authority within whose jurisdiction the ship has been arrested shall permit the release of the ship upon sufficient bail or other security being furnished, save in cases in which a ship has been arrested in respect of any of the maritime claims enumerated in Article 1, 1(o) and (p). In such cases the Court or other appropriate judicial authority may permit the person in possession of the ship to continue trading the ship, upon such person furnishing sufficient bail or other security, or may otherwise deal with the operation of the ship during the period of the arrest.

In default of agreement between the Parties as to the sufficiency of the bail or other security, the Court or other appropriate judicial authority shall determine the nature and amount thereof.

The request to release the ship against such security shall not be construed as an acknowledgment of liability or as a waiver of the benefit of the legal limitation of liability of the owner of the ship.

Article 6

All questions whether in any case the claimant is liable in damages for the arrest of a ship or for the costs of the bail or other security furnished to release or prevent the arrest of a ship, shall be determined by the law of the Contracting State in whose jurisdiction the arrest was made or applied for.

The rules of procedure relating to the arrest of a ship to the application for obtaining the authority referred to in Article 4, and all matters of procedure which the arrest may entail, shall be governed by the law of the Contracting State in which the arrest was made or applied for.

Article 7

1. The Courts of the country in which the arrest was made shall have jurisdiction to determine the case upon its merits:

- if the domestic law of the country in which the arrest is made gives jurisdiction to such Courts;

- or in any of the following cases namely:

(a) if the claimant has his habitual residence or principal place of business in the country in which the arrest was made;

(b) if the claim arose in the country in which the arrest was made;

(c) if the claim concerns the voyage of the ship during which the arrest was made;

(d) if the claim arose out of a collision or in circumstances covered by Article 13 of the International Convention for the unification of certain rules of law with respect to collisions between vessels, signed at Brussels on 23rd September 1910;

(e) if the claim is for salvage;

(f) if the claim is upon a mortgage or hypothecation of the ship arrested.

2. If the Court within whose jurisdiction the ship was arrested has not jurisdiction to decide upon the merits, the bail or other security given in accordance with Article 5 to procure the release of the ship shall specifically provide that it is given as security for the satisfaction of any judgment which may eventually be pronounced by a Court having jurisdiction so to decide; and the Court or other appropriate judicial authority of the country in which the arrest is made shall fix the time within which the claimant shall bring an action before a Court having such jurisdiction.

3. If the parties have agreed to submit the dispute to the

jurisdiction of a particular Court other than that within whose jurisdiction the arrest was made or to arbitration, the Court or other appropriate judicial authority within whose jurisdiction the arrest was made may fix the time within which the claimant shall bring proceedings.

4. If, in any of the cases mentioned in the two preceding paragraphs, the action or proceedings are not brought within the time so fixed, the defendant may apply for the release of the ship or of the bail or other security.

5. This Article shall not apply in cases covered by the provisions of the revised Rhine Navigation Convention of 17 October 1868.

Article 8

1. The provisions of this Convention shall apply to any vessel flying the flag of a Contracting State in the jurisdiction of any Contracting State.

2. A ship flying the flag of a non-Contracting State may be arrested in the jurisdiction of any Contracting State in respect of any of the maritime claims enumerated in Article 1 or of any other claim for which the law of the Contracting State permits arrest.

3. Nevertheless any Contracting State shall be entitled wholly or partly to exclude from the benefits of this Convention any Government of a non-Contracting State or any person who has not, at the time of the arrest, his habitual residence or principal place of business in one of the Contracting States.

4. Nothing in this Convention shall modify or affect the rules of law in force in the respective Contracting States relating to the arrest of any ship within the jurisdiction of the State of her flag by a person who has his habitual residence or principal place of business in that State.

5. When a maritime claim is asserted by a third party other than the original claimant, whether by subrogation, assignment or otherwise, such third party shall, for the purpose of this Convention, be deemed to have the same habitual residence or principal place of business as the original claimant.

Article 9

Nothing in this Convention shall be construed as creating a right of action, which, apart from the provisions of this Convention, sould not arise under the law applied by the Court which had seisin of the case, nor as creating any maritime liens which do not exist under such law or under the Convention on Maritime Mortgages and Liens, if the latter is applicable.

Article 10

The High Contracting Parties may at the time of signature, deposit of ratification or accession, reserve

(a) the right not to apply this Convention to the arrest of a ship for any of the claims enumerated in paragraphs (o) and (p) of Article 1, but to apply their domestic laws to such claims;

(b) the right not to apply the first paragraph of Article 3 to the arrest of a ship, within their jurisdiction, for claims set out in Article 1, paragraph (q).

Article 11

The High Contracting Parties undertake to submit to arbitration any disputes between States arising out of the interpretation or application of this Convention, but this shall be without prejudice to the obligations of those High Contracting Parties who have agreed to submit their disputes to the International Court of Justice.

(Follows the articles on coming into force, accession, amendment and denunciation of the Convention).

Appendix XVI

CONVENTION RELATING TO THE UNIFICATION OF CERTAIN RULES CONCERNING COLLISIONS IN INLAND NAVIGATION, 1960

Article 1

1. This Convention shall govern compensation for damage caused by a collision between vessels of inland navigation in the waters of one of the Contracting Parties either to the vessels or to persons or objects on board.

2. This Convention shall also govern compensation for any damage caused by a vessel of inland navigation in the waters of one of the Contracting Parties, either to other vessels of inland navigation or to persons or objects on board such other vessels, through the carrying out of or failure to carry out a manoeuvre, or through failure to comply with regulations, even if no collision has taken place.

3. The fact that the vessels referred to in paragraphs 1 and 2 of this article belong to the same train shall not affect the application of this Convention.

4. For the purposes of this Convention,

(a) the term 'vessels' includes small craft;

(b) the term 'vessels' includes hydroplanes, rafts, ferryboats, movable sections of boat-bridges, dredgers, floating cranes, elevators, and all floating appliances or plant of a similar nature.

Article 2

1. The duty to compensate for damage shall arise only if the damage is due to a fault. There shall be no legal presumption of fault.

2. If the damage is accidental, if it is due to *force majeure*, or if its causes cannot be determined, it shall be borne by the persons suffering it.

3. Where vessels are in tow, a vessel forming part of the train shall be liable only if it has committed a fault.

Article 3

If the damage is caused by the fault of one vessel only, liability to compensate for the damage shall attach to that vessel.

Article 4

1. Where damage is due to faults committed by two or more vessels, these vessels shall be liable jointly and severally for the damage caused to persons and to the vessels which committed no fault and to objects on board such vessels, but severally for damage caused to other vessels and to objects on board such vessels.

2. Where there is no joint and several liability, each vessel which by its fault contributed to the damage shall be liable to the injured party or parties in proportion to the seriousness of the fault committed by it; but if in the circumstances the proportion cannot be determined or if the fault appear to be equally serious, then the liability shall be apportioned equally.

3. Where there is no joint and several liability, the liability for the sum payable to the claimant shall be apportioned in conformity with the shares in the fault attributed to the vessels under paragraph 2 of this article. If one defendant makes a payment in excess of the share which is due, that defendant shall have a right to recover the excess from the other defendants who have paid less than their share. If any of the joint defendants should be insolvent the consequential loss shall be shared among the other defendants in conformity with their proportionate shares in the fault as determined under paragraph 2 of this article.

Article 5

The liability imposed by the preceding articles shall attach notwithstanding that the damage is caused by the fault of a pilot, even if pilotage is compulsory.

Article 6

Actions for compensation for damage shall not be subject to the prior fulfilment of any special formality.

Article 7

1. Actions for compensation for damage must be brought within two years from the date of the occurrence.

2. Actions in exercise of the right of recourse must be brought within a period of one year. This period shall begin either on the date of a final judicial decision fixing the amount of the joint and several liability or, where there is no such decision, on the date of the payment giving rise to the right of recourse. With regard, however, to actions concerning the re-apportionment of the share of an insolvent joint defendant, the aforesaid period shall not begin until the claimant has become aware of the insolvency.

3. The interruption and suspension of these periods of limitation shall be governed by the relevant provisions of the law of the court in which the action is brought.

Article 8

1. Nothing in the provisions of this Convention shall be deemed to affect general limitations of the liability of owners or managers of ships or of carriers under international conventions or national law, such as limitations based on the tonnage of the ship, the horsepower of its engines or its value, or such as those resulting from the right of abandonment; nor shall anything in the provisions of this Convention be deemed to affect obligations arising out of transport or other contracts.

2. The provisions of this Convention shall not apply to compensation for damage which is occasioned by or results from the radioactive properties or a combination of radioactive properties with toxic, explosive or other hazardous properties of nuclear fuel or radioactive products or waste.

Article 9

Each Contracting Party may at the time of signing, ratifying or acceding to this Convention declare:

(a) that it reserves the right to provide by law or international agreement that the provisions of this Convention shall not apply to vessels exclusively employed by the public authorities;

(b) that it reserves the right to provide by law that the provisions of this Convention shall not apply on waterways reserved exclusively for its own shipping.

Article 10

1. This Convention is open to signature or accession by countries members of the Economic Commission for Europe and countries admitted to the Commission in a consultative capacity under paragraph 8 of the Commission's Terms of Reference.

2. Such countries as may participate in certain activities of the Economic Commission for Europe in accordance with paragraph 11 of the Commission's Terms of Reference may become Contracting Parties of this Convention by acceding thereto after its entry into force.

3. The Convention shall be open to signature until 15 June 1960 inclusive. Thereafter, it shall be open for accession.

4. This Convention shall be ratified.

5. Instruments of ratification or accession shall be deposited with the Secretary-General of the United Nations.

Article 11

1. This Convention shall come into force on the ninetieth day after five of the countries referred to in article 10, paragraph 1, have deposited their instruments of ratification or accession.

2. With respect to any country which ratifies the Convention or accedes to it after five countries have deposited their instruments of ratification or accession, this Convention shall enter into force on the ninetieth day after the said country has deposited its instruments of ratification or accession.

Article 12

1. Any Contracting Party may denounce this Convention by so notifying the Secretary-General of the United Nationa.

2. Denunciation shall take effect twelve months after the date of receipt by the Secretary-General of the notification of denunciation.

Article 13

If, after the entry into force of this Convention, the number of Contracting Parties is reduced, as a result of denunciations, to less than five, the Convention shall cease to be in force from the date on which the last of such denunciations takes effect.

Article 14

Any dispute between two or more Contracting Parties relating to the interpretation or application of this Convention which the Parties are unable to settle by negotiation or other means may, at the request of any one of the Contracting Parties concerned, be referred for settlement to the International Court of Justice.

Article 15

1. Any country may, at the time of signing this Convention or of depositing its instrument of ratification or accession, declare that it does not consider itself bound by article 14 of the Convention in so far as it concerns the referral of disputes to the International Court of Justice. Other Contracting Parties shall not be bound by article 14 with respect to any Contracting Party which has entered such a reservation.

2. Any Contracting Party which has entered a reservation under paragraph 1 may at any time withdraw the reservation by notifying the Secretary-General of the United Nations.

Article 16

Save for the reservations provided for in article 9, sub-paragraphs (a) and (b), and in article 15 of this Convention, no reservation to this Convention shall be admitted.

Article 17

1. After this Convention has been in force for three years, any Contracting Party may, by notification to the Secretary-General of the United Nations, request that a conference be convened for the purpose of reviewing the Convention. The Secretary-General shall notify all the Contracting Parties of the request and a review conference shall be convened by the Secretary-General if, within a period of four months following the date of notification by the Secretary-General, not less than one-fourth of the Contracting Parties notify him of their concurrence with the request.

2. If a conference is convened in accordance with the preceding paragraph, the Secretary-General shall notify all the Contracting Parties and invite them to submit within a period of three months such proposals as they may wish the conference to consider. The Secretary-General shall circulate to all Contracting Parties the provisional agenda for the conference, together with the texts of such proposals, at least three months before the date on which the conference is to meet.

3. The Secretary-General shall invite to any conference convened in accordance with this article all the countries referred to in article 10, paragraph 1, and the countries which have become Contracting Parties under article 10, paragraph 2.

Article 18

In addition to the notifications provided for in article 17, the Secretary-General of the United Nations shall notify the countries referred to in article 10, paragraph 1, and the countries which have become Contracting Parties under article 10, paragraph 2, of:

(a) declarations made in accordance with article 9, sub-paragraphs (a) and (b);

(b) ratifications and accessions under article 10;

(c) the dates of entry into force of this Convention in accordance with article 11;

(d) denunciations under article 12;

(e) the termination of this Convention in accordance with article 13;

(f) declarations and notifications received in accordance with article 15, paragraphs 1 and 2.

Article 19

This Convention is done in a single copy in French and Russian. Texts in English and German are attached thereto. At the time of signing this Convention or of depositing its instrument of ratification or accession any country may declare that it adopts the French, Russian, English or German text; in that case, the said text shall also be authoritative in the relations between the Contracting Parties which have exercised this right and adopted the same text. In all other cases, the French and Russian texts shall be authentic.

Article 20

After 15 June 1960, the original of this Convention and the attached English and German texts shall be deposited with the Secretary-General of the United Nations, who shall transmit to each of the countries mentioned in article 10, paragraphs 1 and 2, certified true copies of the original and of the English and German texts.

In witness whereof, the undersigned, being thereunto duly authorized, have signed this Convention done at Geneva this fifteenth day of March one thousand nine hundred and sixty.

LEG/CONF.5/10
19 November 1976

Appendix XVII

CONVENTION ON LIMITATION OF LIABILITY FOR MARITIME CLAIMS, 1976

The States Parties to this Convention,

Having recognized the desirability of determining by agreement certain uniform rules relating to the limitation of liability for maritime claims;

Have decided to conclude a Convention for this purpose and have thereto agreed as follows:

Chapter I - The Right of Limitation

Article 1

Persons entitled to limit liability

1. Shipowners and salvors, as hereinafter defined, may limit their liability in accordance with the rules of this Convention for claims set out in Article 2.

2. The term shipowner shall mean the owner, charterer, manager and operator of a sea-going ship.

3. Salvor shall mean any person rendering services in direct connection with salvage operations. Salvage operations shall also include operations referred to in Article 2, paragraph 1(d), (e) and (f).

4. If any claims set out in Article 2 are made against any person for whose act, neglect or default the shipowner or salvor is responsible, such person shall be entitled to avail himself of the limitation of liability provided for in this Convention.

5. In this Convention the liability of a shipowner shall include liability in an action brought against the vessel herself.

6. An insurer of liability for claims subject to limitation in accordance with the rules of this Convention shall be entitled to the benefits of this Convention to the same extent as the assured himself.

7. The act of invoking limitation of liability shall not constitute an admission of liability.

Article 2

Claims subject to limitation

1. Subject to Articles 3 and 4 the following claims, whatever the basis of liability may be, shall be subject to limitation of liability:

(a) claims in respect of loss of life or personal injury or loss of or damage to property (including damage to harbour works, basins and waterways and aids to navigation), occurring on board or in direct connection with the operation of the ship or with salvage operations, and consequential loss resulting therefrom;

(b) claims in respect of loss resulting from delay in the carriage by sea of cargo, passengers or their luggage;

(c) claims in respect of other loss resulting from infringement of rights other than contractual rights, occurring in direct connection with the operation of the ship or salvage operations;

(d) claims in respect of the raising, removal, destruction or the rendering harmless of a ship which is sunk, wrecked, stranded or abandoned, including anything that is or has been on board such ship;

(e) claims in respect of the removal, destruction or the rendering harmless of the cargo of the ship;

(f) claims of a person other than the person liable in respect of measures taken in order to avert or minimize loss for which the person liable may limit his liability in accordance with this Convention, and further loss caused by such measures.

2. Claims set out in paragraph 1 shall be subject to limitation of liability even if brought by way of recourse or for indemnity under a contract or otherwise. However, claims set out under paragraphs 1(d), (e) and (f) shall not be subject to limitation of liability to the extent that they relate to remuneration under a contract with the person liable.

Article 3

Claims excepted from limitation

The rules of this Convention shall not apply to:

(a) claims for salvage or contribution in general average;

(b) claims for oil pollution damage within the meaning of the International Convention on Civil Liability for Oil Pollution

Damage, dated 29 November 1969 or of any amendment or Protocol thereto which is in force;

(c) claims subject to any international convention or national legislation governing or prohibiting limitation of liability for nuclear damage;

(d) claims against the shipowner of a nuclear ship for nuclear damage;

(e) claims by servants of the shipowner or salvor whose duties are connected with the ship or the salvage operations, including claims of their heirs, dependants or other persons entitled to make such claims, if under the law governing the contract of service between the shipowner or salvor and such servants the shipowner or salvor is not entitled to limit his liability in respect of such claims, or if he is by such law only permitted to limit his liability to an amount greater than that provided for in Article 6.

Article 4

Conduct barring limitation

A person liable shall not be entitled to limit his liability if it is proved that the loss resulted from his personal act or omission, committed with the intent to cause such loss, or recklessly and with knowledge that such loss would probably result.

Article 5

Counterclaims

Where a person entitled to limitation of liability under the rules of this Convention has a claim against the claimant arising out of the same occurrence, their respective claims shall be set off against each other and the provisions of this Convention shall only apply to the balance, if any.

Article 6

The general limits

1. The limits of liability for claims other than those mentioned in Article 7, arising on any distinct occasion, shall be calculated as follows:

(a) in respect of claims for loss of life or personal injury,

(i) 333,000 Units of Account for a ship with a tonnage not exceeding 500 tons,

(ii) for a ship with a tonnage in excess thereof, the following amount in addition to that mentioned in (i):

for each ton from 501 to 3,000 tons, 500 Units of Account;
for each ton from 3,001 to 30,000 tons, 333 Units of Account;
for each ton from 30,001 to 70,000 tons, 250 Units of Account; and
for each ton in excess of 70,000 tons, 167 Units of Account;

(b) in respect of any other claims,

(i) 167,000 Units of Account for a ship with a tonnage not exceeding 500 tons;

(ii) for a ship with a tonnage in excess thereof the following amount in addition to that mentioned in (i):

for each ton from 501 to 30,000 tons, 167 Units of Account;
for each ton from 30,001 to 70,000 tons, 125 Units of Account; and
for each ton in excess of 70,000 tons, 83 Units of Account.

2. Where the amount calculated in accordance with paragraph 1(a) is insufficient to pay the claims mentioned therein in full, the amount calculated in accordance with paragraph 1(b) shall be available for payment of the unpaid balance of claims under paragraph 1(a) and such unpaid balance shall rank rateably with claims mentioned under paragraph 1(b).

3. However, without prejudice to the right of claims for loss of life or personal injury according to paragraph 2, a State Party may provide in its national law that claims in respect of damage to harbour works, basins and waterways and aids to navigation shall have such priority over other claims under paragraph 1(b) as is provided by that law.

4. The limits of liability for any salvor not operating from any ship or for any salvor operating solely on the ship to, or in respect of which he is rendering salvage services, shall be calculated according to a tonnage of 1,500 tons.

5. For the purpose of this Convention the ship's tonnage shall be the gross tonnage calculated in accordance with the tonnage measurement rules contained in Annex I of the International Convention on Tonnage Measurement of Ships, 1969.

Article 7

The limit for passenger claims

1. In respect of claims arising on any distinct occasion for loss of life or personal injury to passengers of a ship, the limit of liability of the shipowner thereof shall be an amount of 46,666 Units of Account multiplied by the number of passengers which the ship is authorized to carry according to the chip's certificate, but not exceeding 25 million Units of Account.

2. For the purpose of this Article "claims for loss of life or personal injury to passengers of a ship" shall mean any such claims brought by or on behalf of any person carried in that ship:

(a) under a contract of passenger carriage, or

(b) who, with the consent of the carrier, is accompanying a vehicle or live animals which are covered by a contract for the carriage of goods.

Article 8

Unit of Account

1. The Unit of Account referred to in Articles 6 and 7 is the Special Drawing Right as defined by the International Monetary Fund. The amounts mentioned in Articles 6 and 7 shall be converted into the national currency of the State in which limitation is sought, according to the value of that currency at the date the limitation fund shall have been constituted, payment is made, or security is given which under the law of that State is equivalent to such payment. The value of a national currency in terms of the Special Drawing Right, of a State Party which is a member of the International Monetary Fund, shall be calculated in accordance with the method of valuation applied by the International Monetary Fund in effect at the date in question for its operations and transactions. The value of a national currency in terms of the Special Drawing Right, of a State Party which is not a member of the International Monetary Fund, shall be calculated in a manner determined by that State Party.

2. Nevertheless, those States which are not members of the International Monetary Fund and whose law does not permit the application of the provisions of paragraph 1 may, at the time of signature without reservation as to ratification, acceptance or approval or at the time of ratification, acceptance, approval or accession or at any time thereafter, declare that the limits of liability provided for in this Convention to be applied in their territories shall be fixed as follows:

(a) in respect of Article 6, paragraph 1(a) at an amount of:

(i) 5 million monetary units for a ship with a tonnage not exceeding 500 tons;

(ii) for a ship with a tonnage in excess thereof, the following amount in addition to that mentioned in (i):

for each ton from 501 to 3,000 tons, 7,500 monetary units;
for each ton from 3,001 to 30,000 tons, 5,000 monetary units;
for each ton from 30,001 to 70,000 tons, 3,750 monetary units;
and for each ton in excess of 70,000 tons, 2,500 monetary units;

(b) in respect of Article 6, paragraph 1(b), at an amount of:

(i) 2·5 million monetary units for a ship with a tonnage not exceeding 500 tons;

(ii) for a ship with a tonnage in excess thereof, the following amount in addition to that mentioned in (i):

for each ton from 501 to 30,000 tons, 2,500 monetary units;
for each ton from 30,001 to 70,000 tons, 1,850 monetary units;
and for each ton in excess of 70,000 tons, 1,250 monetary units;

(c) in respect of Article 7, paragraph 1, at an amount of 700,000 monetary units multiplied by the number of passengers which the ship is authorized to carry according to its certificate, but not exceeding 375 million monetary units.

Paragraphs 2 and 3 of Article 6 apply correspondingly to sub-paragraphs (a) and (b) of this paragraph.

3. The monetary unit referred to in paragraph 2 corresponds to sixty-five and a half milligrammes of gold of millesimal fineness nine hundred. The conversion of the amounts referred to in paragraph 2 into the national currency shall be made according to the law of the State concerned.

4. The calculation mentioned in the last sentence of paragraph 1 and the conversion mentioned in paragraph 3 shall be made in such a manner as to express in the national currency of the State Party as far as possible the same real value for the amounts in Articles 6 and 7 as is expressed there in units of account. States Parties shall communicate to the depositary the manner of calculation pursuant to paragraph 1, or the result of the conversion in paragraph 3, as the case may be, at the time of the signature without reservation as to ratification, acceptance or approval, or when depositing an instrument referred to in Article 16 and whenever there is a change in either.

Article 9

Aggregation of claims

1. The limits of liability determined in accordance with Article 6 shall apply to the aggregate of all claims which arise on any distinct occasion:

(a) against the person or persons mentioned in paragraph 2 of Article 1 and any person for whose act, neglect or default he or they are responsible; or

(b) against the shipowner of a ship rendering salvage services from that ship and the salvor or salvors operating from such ship and any person for whose act, neglect or default he or they are responsible; or

(c) against the salvor or salvors who are not operating from a ship or who are operating solely on the ship to, or in respect of which, the salvage services are rendered and any person for whose act, neglect or default he or they are responsible.

2. The limits of liability determined in accordance with Article 7 shall apply to the aggregate of all claims subject thereto which may arise on any distinct occasion against the person or persons mentioned in paragraph 2 of Article 1 in respect of the ship referred to in Article 7 and any person for whose act, neglect or default he or they are responsible.

Article 10

Limitation of liability without constitution of a limitation fund

1. Limitation of liability may be invoked notwithstanding that a limitation fund as mentioned in Article 11 has not been constituted. However, a State Party may provide in its national law that, where an action is brought in its Courts to enforce a claim subject to limitation, a person liable may only invoke the right to limit liability if a limitation fund has been constituted in accordance with the provisions of this Convention or is constituted when the right to limit liability is invoked.

2. If limitation of liability is invoked without the constitution of a limitation fund, the provisions of Article 12 shall apply correspondingly.

3. Questions of procedure arising under the rules of this Article shall be decided in accordance with the national law of the State Party in which action is brought.

Chapter II - The Limitation Fund

Article 11

Constitution of the fund

1. Any person alleged to be liable may constitute a fund with the Court or other competent authority in any State Party in which legal proceedings are instituted in respect of claims subject to limitation. The fund shall be constituted in the sum of such of the amounts set out in Articles 6 and 7 as are applicable to claims for which that person may be liable, together with interest thereon from the date of the occurrence giving rise to the liability until the date of the constitution of the fund. Any fund thus constituted shall be available only for the payment of

claims in respect of which limitation of liability can be invoked.

2. A fund may be constituted, either by depositing the sum, or by producing a guarantee acceptable under the legislation of the State Party where the fund is constituted and considered to be adequate by the Court or other competent authority.

3. A fund constituted by one of the persons mentioned in paragraph 1(a), (b) or (c) or paragraph 2 of Article 9 or his insurer shall be deemed constituted by all persons mentioned in paragraph 1(a), (b) or (c) or paragraph 2, respectively.

Article 12

Distribution of the Fund

1. Subject to the provisions of paragraphs 1, 2 and 3 of Article 6 and of Article 7, the fund shall be distributed among the claimants in proportion to their established claims against the fund.

2. If, before the fund is distributed, the person liable, or his insurer, has settled a claim against the fund such person shall, up to the amount he has paid, acquire by subrogation the rights which the person so compensated would have enjoyed under this Convention.

3. The right of subrogation provided for in paragraph 2 may also be exercised by persons other than those therein mentioned in respect of any amount of compensation which they may have paid, but only to the extent that such subrogation is permitted under the applicable national law.

4. Where the person liable or any other person establishes that he may be compelled to pay, at a later date, in whole or in part any such amount of compensation with regard to which such person would have enjoyed a right of subrogation pursuant to paragraphs 2 and 3 had the compensation been paid before the fund was distributed, the Court or other competent authority of the State where the fund has been constituted may order that a sufficient sum shall be provisionally set aside to enable such person at such later date to enforce his claim against the fund.

Article 13

Bar to other actions

1. Where a limitation fund has been constituted in accordance with Article 11, any person having made a claim against the fund shall be barred from exercising any right in respect of such claim against any other assets of a person by or on behalf of whom the fund has been constituted.

2. After a limitation fund has been constituted in accordance with Article 11, any ship or other property, belonging to a person on behalf of whom the fund has been constituted, which has been arrested or attached within the jurisdiction of a State Party for a claim which may be raised against the fund, or any security given, may be released by order of the Court or other competent authority of such State. However, such release shall always be ordered if the limitation fund has been constituted:

(a) at the port where the occurrence took place, or, if it took place out of port, at the first port of call thereafter; or

(b) at the port of disembarkation in respect of claims for loss of life or personal injury; or

(c) at the port of discharge in respect of damage to cargo; or

(d) in the State where the arrest is made.

3. The rules of paragraphs 1 and 2 shall apply only if the claimant may bring a claim against the limitation fund before the Court administering that fund and the fund is actually available and freely transferable in respect of that claim.

Article 14

Governing law

Subject to the provisions of this Chapter the rules relating to the constitution and distribution of a limitation fund, and all rules of procedure in connection therewith, shall be governed by the law of the State Party in which the fund is constituted.

Chapter III - Scope of Application

Article 15

1. This Convention shall apply whenever any person referred to in Article 1 seeks to limit his liability before the Court of a State Party or seeks to procure the release of a ship or other property or the discharge of any security given within the jurisdiction of any such State. Nevertheless, each State Party may exclude wholly or partially from the application of this Convention any person referred to in Article 1, who at the time when the rules of this Convention are invoked before the Courts of that State does not have his habitual residence in a State Party, or does not have his principal place of business in a State Party or any ship in relation to which the right of limitation is invoked or whose release is sought and which does not at the time specified above fly the flag of a State Party.

2. A State Party may regulate by specific provisions of national law the system of limitation of liability to be applied to vessels which are:

(a) according to the law of that State, ships intended for navigation on inland waterways;

(b) ships of less than 300 tons.

A State Party which makes use of the option provided for in this paragraph shall inform the depositary of the limits of liability adopted in its national legislation or of the fact that there are none.

3. A State Party may regulate by specific provisions of national law the system of limitation of liability to be applied to claims arising in cases in which interests of persons who are nationals of other States Parties are in no way involved.

4. The Courts of a State Party shall not apply this Convention to ships constructed for, or adapted to, and engaged in, drilling:

(a) when that State has established under its national legislation a higher limit of liability than that otherwise provided for in Article 6; or

(b) when that State has become party to an international convention regulating the system of liability in respect of such ships.

In a case to which sub-paragraph (a) applies that State Party shall inform the depositary accordingly.

5. This Convention shall not apply to:

(a) air-cushion vehicles;

(b) floating platforms constructed for the purpose of exploring or exploiting the natural resources of the sea-bed or the subsoil thereof.

(Follows the articles on coming into force, accession and ratification of the Convention).

Appendix XVIII

LLOYD'S STANDARD FORM OF ARBITRATION AGREEMENT IN CASES OF COLLISION

(Approved and Published by the Committee of Lloyd's)

AN AGREEMENT made the day of 19 between the Owners of the ship or property of the first part and of the Owners of the ship or property of the second part.

Whereas it is alleged that on or about the day of 19 damage was caused by a collision or occurrence in which the said ship or property and the said ship or property were involved

NOW IT IS HEREBY AGREED as follows:-

1. All questions between the parties hereto with regard first to the liability of them and of the said ships or property in connection with the said collision or occurrence and secondly to the amount of such liability if any are (subject to as hereinafter provided) hereby referred to Arbitration in London by an Arbitrator to be appointed by the Committee of Lloyd's (hereinafter called "the Committee").

2. Each party agrees forthwith to give through the Committee or otherwise security to the other to an amount which the other shall reasonably require which security shall be enforceable only by the Committee or under their direction for the purpose of satisfying the claims (including costs) of the party or parties at whose request it was given and for carrying into effect the provisions of Clause 13(b). The security shall be given in such form as the Committee in their absolute discretion may think proper but the Committee shall not be in any way responsible for the sufficiency whether in amount or otherwise of any security nor for the default or insolvency of any person, firm or corporation giving the same.

3. The Committee shall not be bound to appoint an Arbitrator until such security shall have been given by each party as shall comply with Clause 2 hereof.

4. Until security which shall comply with Clause 2 hereof shall have been given to answer the claim of a party that party shall have the same rights and remedies as if this Agreement had not been made and shall accordingly in particular but without prejudice to the generality of the foregoing be entitled to arrest or detain any ship of the party failing to provide security in such manner as the law of the place where that ship for the time being is situated shall allow.

5. The parties to this Agreement hereby agree not to arrest or detain any ship of a party which has provided security in accordance with Clause 2 hereof so long as that security remains valid and they further agree that as soon as such security is provided they will take all proper steps to procure the release or annul the arrest or detention of any ship which they have arrested or detained or which they have taken steps to arrest or detain in order to obtain such security.

6. Within 14 days after notice of appointment of the Arbitrator the parties or any of them shall apply to the Arbitrator for directions. The Arbitrator shall have discretionary power to make any Order or Orders (which shall be binding on the parties and without right of appeal) as to any matters which he may consider proper in the circumstances of the case with regard to pleadings discovery and inspection of documents examination of witnesses survey costs security for costs copying and translation of documents and any other matter whatsoever relating to the conduct of the Arbitration. In the event of any party failing within a reasonable time to appoint a permanent agent as provided in Clause 15 hereof or failing to comply with any Orders made under the provisions of this Clause 6 the Arbitrator and Arbitrator or Arbitrators on Appeal hereinafter referred to and the Committee may proceed in all respects as though the said Clause 15 and Orders had been complied with.

7. The Arbitrator shall in the first instance make an Award (hereinafter called the "Award as to Liability") with reference to the question of liability if any and if necessary a later Award (hereinafter called "the Award as to Amount") with reference to the amount of damages sustained by a party or parties as a consequence of the said collision or occurrence. Both the Award as to Liability and the Award as to Amount shall be subject to Appeal as hereinafter provided. Unless the Arbitrator shall otherwise determine (such determination not being subject to Appeal) the Arbitrator shall not make the Award as to Amount or deal with any question of amount until (a) the party or parties held liable under the Award as to Liability agree in writing to the satisfaction of the Committee not to prosecute an Appeal from it or (b) the time for appealing against the Award as to Liability shall have expired without notice of Appeal having been given

or (c) the Appeal Award as to Liability hereinafter referred to shall have been made and published by the Committee.

8. Any party may appeal against the Award as to Liability and/or the Award as to Amount by giving written notice of Appeal within 30 days (or such longer period as the Committee may in their discretion either generally or in any particular case fix) from the publication by the Committee of the Award as to Liability or the Award as to Amount as the case may be. An Award as to Liability and an Award as to Amount by an Arbitrator who shall first deal with the matter shall be called an "Original Award" the Arbitrator who shall make such Award shall be called "Original Arbitrator" the Arbitrator or Arbitrators by whom an Appeal shall be heard shall be called "Appeal Arbitrator" or "Appeal Arbitrators" and an Award by an Appeal Arbitrator or Appeal Arbitrators shall be called "Award on Appeal". Any Award in respect of which no notice of Appeal shall have been given within the above stated time shall be final and binding on the parties. As soon as practicable after receipt of such notice of Appeal the Committee shall refer the Appeal to the hearing and determination of one or more Appeal Arbitrators selected by them. An Award on Appeal shall be final and binding on the parties. No evidence other than the documents put in on the Arbitration before the Original Arbitrator and his notes or the shorthand notes if any of the proceedings and evidence shall be used on an Appeal unless the Appeal Arbitrator or Appeal Arbitrators shall in his or their discretion call for other evidence.

9. Both the Original Arbitrator and the Appeal Arbitrator or Arbitrators shall be entitled to the assistance of nautical or mercantile assessors if they so desire and shall if any of the parties so desire arrange for such assistance. The said assessors shall be appointed by the Committee upon the nomination or request of the Arbitrator or Arbitrators.

10. The Original Arbitrator and (subject to Clause 8 hereof) the Arbitrator or Arbitrators on Appeal if there be any such Appeal or Appeals may receive and act upon such evidence whether oral or written and whether strictly admissible as evidence or not as he or they shall in his or their discretion think fit. Save as aforesaid the Arbitration or Arbitration to be conducted hereunder shall be conducted generally in accordance with English law and in particular with the law for the time being in force in England as to Arbitrations.

11. The costs of the Arbitration or Arbitrations and the Award or Awards shall be paid in accordance with the directions of the Original Arbitrator or (if there be an Appeal or Appeals) the Appeal Arbitrator or Appeal Arbitrators such costs including (if the Original Arbitrator or the Appeal Arbitrator or Arbitrators

shall think fit) any costs in relation to the provision of security the arrest of one or more ships and/or any other proceedings arising out of the said collision or occurrence. Costs shall be taxed by a Registrar or Assistant Registrar of the Probate Divorce and Admiralty Division of the High Court of Justice (Admiralty). The Original Arbitrator and the Appeal Arbitrator or Arbitrators may charge such fees as he or they may think reasonable and the Committee may in any event charge a reasonable fee for their services in connection with this Agreement whether or not an Arbitration or Arbitrations be conducted hereunder and such fee shall be treated as part of the costs. Interest at the rate of five per cent per annum shall be payable upon any sum and/or amount of costs awarded from such date or dates as may be specified in the Original Award as to Amount or the Appeal Award as to Amount if there be an Appeal as to Amount.

12. Subject to Clause 13 hereof as soon as all questions of liability and amount shall in the opinion of the Committee have been finally determined either by agreement by the parties or by the Original Arbitrator or by the Arbitrator or Arbitrators on Appeal the Committee shall realize and enforce or direct the realization and enforcement of the security provided hereunder and apply the same as may be agreed by the parties or in accordance with the provisions of the Award which shall finally determine the rights and liberties of the parties under this Agreement.

13. (a) Nothing in this Agreement shall prejudice the right of a party to commence proceedings in the High Court of Justice in England to limit liability in respect of the collision or occurrence concerning which this Agreement is made in accordance with the provisions of the Merchant Shipping Acts and if any party commences such proceedings any other party to this Agreement having a claim against that party hereby agrees to accept service of any writ or summons issued in such proceedings and to submit to the jurisdiction of the said High Court.

(b) If at any time before the Committee apply the security in accordance with Clause 12 hereof the party providing that security commences an action in the High Court to limit liability in respect of the collision or occurrence with reference to which his security has been provided the Committee will retain the said security unless and until the said party obtains a decree limiting his liability. If the said action fails the Committee will proceed as if no such action had been started. On the said party obtaining a decree limiting his liability under the Merchant Shipping Acts and on his paying into Court the amount ordered by the Court the Committee (subject to payment by the said party of such costs and fees in connection with this Agreement and the proceedings thereunder as the Committee may in its absolute jurisdiction fix) shall release the said security. If the said party desires to utilize the security which he has provided under this Agreement in order to make the above mentioned payment into Court and/or to provide for the costs of the said limitation proceedings out of the proceeds the Committee (subject to the payment of the above mentioned costs and fees) will do such things as may be necessary and be within their power to enable the said party so to do.

14. This Agreement is made subject in general to the law of England and in particular to the law of England as to Arbitrations and the parties hereto submit to the jurisdiction of the English Courts.

15. Each of the parties hereto shall appoint an agent in London for the service of all processes and notices required to be served or given hereunder or under any proceedings permitted hereby and shall as soon as practicable inform each of the other parties in writing of the name and address of such agent. Until such notification shall have been given any such notice to any party or process required to be served on any party shall be deemed to have been delivered to or served upon that party if left addressed to that party at the offices of the Committee of Lloyd's at Lloyd's Building Leadenhall Street London E.C.3. but neither the Society of Lloyd's nor the Committee shall be under any obligation to forward any such notice or process to the party to whom it is addressed.

16. Any notice authority order or other document signed by the Chairman or Deputy Chairman of Lloyd's or a Clerk to the Committee of Lloyd's on behalf of the Committee of Lloyd's shall be deemed to have been duly made or given by the Committee of Lloyd's and shall have the same force and effect in all respects as if it had been signed by every member of the Committee of Lloyd's.

17. In this Agreement the expression "collision or occurrence" shall include any casualty arising out of the management or navigation of a ship or vessel whereby damage or loss is caused to any ship vessel or other floating craft harbour dock wharf pier pontoon berth foreshore goods or other property whatsoever except in so far as such casualty causes loss or damage to cargo for which the owners of the said cargo seek to recover damages from the carrying ship or her owners.

IN WITNESS whereof the parties have caused this Agreement to be duly signed the day and year first above written.

Notes on the Use of Lloyd's Arbitration Agreement in Cases of Collision

The Agreement is to be signed only by principals, for example, the owners of the colliding ships or by Agents to whom special authority has been given for the purpose. Immediately after the Agreement has been signed it should be lodged with the Committee of Lloyd's, London, EC3M 7HA, and each party should appoint an Agent in London to represent their interests in regard to the arbitration and notify the name of that Agent to the other parties. Until such notification, notices to any party may be given to them at the offices of the Committee of Lloyd's who are, however, not bound to forward notices to the party concerned. It is essential, therefore, that in their own interests each party should appoint an Agent with the utmost speed and notify the appointment to the other parties. Each party should also notify the Committee of Lloyd's.

Each party should also at the earliest possible moment inform each other party the amount of security which that party requires, as the Committee of Lloyd's will not appoint an Arbitrator until they are satisfied that the security required by each party has been given. Security should be given on one of the forms provided by the Committee, and these forms include a Form of Undertaking by Solicitors for use in those cases where, as a temporary measure, it is desired to give security in this way.

As soon as security has been given the parties are bound to release all arrests of the opposing vessels and to discontinue all proceedings in Court which they may have commenced. The security given will be available for payment into Court should the party providing the security desire to limit liability on a tonnage basis under the Merchant Shipping Acts.

Appendix XIX

LLOYD'S

STANDARD FORM OF
SALVAGE AGREEMENT

(Approved and Published by The Committee of Lloyd's)

NO CURE - NO PAY

On board the
Dated 19

IT IS HEREBY AGREED between Captain for and on behalf of the Owners of the " " her cargo and freight and for and on behalf of (hereinafter called "the Contractor"):-

1. The Contractor agrees to use his best endeavours to salve the and/or her cargo and take them into or other place to be hereafter agreed. The services shall be rendered and accepted as salvage services upon the principle of "no cure - no pay". In case of arbitration being claimed the Contractor's remuneration in the event of success shall be fixed by arbitration in London in the manner hereinafter prescribed: and any difference arising out of this Agreement or the operations thereunder shall be referred to arbitration in the same way. In the event of the services referred to in this Agreement or any part of such services having been already rendered at the date of this Agreement by the Contractor to the said vessel and/or her cargo it is agreed that the provisions of this Agreement shall apply to such services.

2. The Contractor may make reasonable use of the vessel's gear anchors chains and other appurtenances during and for the purpose of the operations free of expense but shall not unecessaarily damage abandon or sacrifice the same or any other of the property the subject of this Agreement.

3. The Master or other person signing this Agreement on behalf of the property to be salved is not authorised to make or give and the Contractor shall not demand or take any payment draft or order for or on account of the remuneration.

Provisions as to Security

4. The Contractor shall immediately after the termination of the services or sooner notify the Committee of Lloyd's of the amount for which he requires security (inclusive of costs, expenses and interest) to be given. Unless otherwise agreed by the parties such security shall be given to the Committee of Lloyd's, and security so given shall be in a form approved by the Committee and shall be given by persons firms or corporations resident in the United Kingdom either satisfactory to the Committee of Lloyd's or agreed by the Contractor. The Committee of Lloyd's shall not be responsible for the sufficiency (whether in amount or otherwise) of any security which shall be given nor for the default or insolvency of any person firm or corporation giving the same.

5. Pending the completion of the security as aforesaid, the Contractor shall have a maritime lien on the property salved for his remuneration. The salved property shall not without the consent in writing of the Contractor be removed from the place of safety to which the property is taken by the Contractor on the completion of the salvage services until security has been given as aforesaid. The Contractor agrees not to arrest or detain the property salved unless the security be not given with 14 days (exclusive of Saturdays and Sundays or other days observed as general holidays at Lloyd's) of the termination of the services (the Committee of Lloyd's not being responsible for the failure of the parties concerned to provide the required security within the said 14 days) or the Contractor has reason to believe that the removal of the property salved is contemplated contrary to the above agreement. In the event of security not being provided as aforesaid or in the event of any attempt being made to remove the property salved contrary to this agreement or of the Contractor having reasonable grounds to suppose that such an attempt will be made the Contractor may take steps to enforce his aforesaid lien. The Arbitrator appointed under Clause 10 or the person or persons appointed under Clause 12 hereof shall have power in their absolute discretion to include in the amount awarded to the Contractor the whole or such part of the expenses incurred by the Contractor in enforcing or in taking reasonable steps to enforce his lien as they shall think fit.

Provisions as to Arbitration

6. Where security is given to the Committee of Lloyd's any claim for arbitration must be made in writing or by telegram or by telex and must be received by the Committee of Lloyd's within 42 days from the date of completion of such security. If such a claim is not made by any of the parties entitled or authorised to make a claim for arbitration in respect of the salved property on behalf of which security has been given, the Committee

of Lloyd's shall after the expiry of the said 42 days call upon the party or parties concerned to pay the amount thereof and in the event of non-payment shall realize or enforce the security and pay over the amount thereof to the Contractor. The receipt of the Contractor shall be a good discharge to the Committee of Lloyd's for any monies so paid and it shall incur no responsibility to any of the parties concerned for making such payment. No claim for arbitration shall be entertained or acted upon unless received by the Committee of Lloyd's within 42 days from the date of completion of the security.

7. Upon receipt of a written or telegraphic or telex notice of a claim for arbitration from any of the parties entitled or authorised to make such a claim the Committee of Lloyd's shall appoint an Arbitrator whether security has been given or not.

8. Any of the following parties may make a claim for arbitration viz: (1) The Owners of the ship. (2) The Owners of the cargo or any part thereof. (3) The Owners of any freight separately at risk or any part thereof. (4) The Contractor. (5) Any other person who is a party to this Agreement.

9. If the parties to any such Arbitration or any of them desire to be heard or to adduce evidence at the Arbitration they shall give notice to that effect to the Committee of Lloyd's and shall respectively nominate a person in the United Kingdom to represent them for all the purposes of the Arbitration and failing such notice and nomination being given the Arbitrator may proceed as if the parties failing to give the same had renounced their right to be heard or adduce evidence.

10. In case of arbitration being claimed the remuneration for the services shall be fixed by an Arbitrator to be appointed by the Committee of Lloyd's. The Arbitration shall (subject to the next succeeding Clause) be held in accordance with English law and shall be held in London.

Conduct of the Arbitration

11. The Arbitrator shall have power to obtain call for receive and act upon any such oral or documentary evidence or information (whether the same be strictly admissible as evidence or not) as he may think fit, and to conduct the Arbitration in such manner in all respects as he may think fit and shall if in his opinion the amount of the security demanded is excessive have power in his absolute discretion to condemn the Contractor in the whole or part of the expense of providing such security and to deduct the amount in which the Contractor is so condemned from the salvage remuneration. Unless the Arbitrator shall otherwise direct the parties shall be at liberty to adduce expert evidence at the

Arbitration. Any Award of the Arbitrator shall (subject to appeal as provided in this Agreement) be final and binding on all the parties concerned. The Arbitrator and the Committee of Lloyd's may charge reasonable fees for their services in connection with the Arbitration whether it proceeds to a hearing or not and all such fees shall be treated as part of the costs of the Arbitration. Interest at a rate per annum to be fixed by the Arbitrator from the expiration of 21 days (exclusive of Saturdays and Sundays or other days observed as general holidays at Lloyd's) from the date of the publication of the Award by the Committee of Lloyd's until the date of payment to the Committee of Lloyd's shall (subject to appeal as provided in this Agreement) be payable to the Contractor upon the amount of any sum awarded after deduction of any sums paid on account. Save as aforesaid the statutory provisions as to Arbitration for the time being in force in England shall apply.

Provisions as to Appeal

12. Any of the persons named under Clause 8 may appeal from the Award by giving written or telegraphic or telex Notice of Appeal to the Committee of Lloyd's within 14 days (exclusive of Saturdays and Sundays or other days observed as general holidays at Lloyd's) from the publication by the Committee of Lloyd's of the Award and may (without prejudice to their right of appeal under the first part of this Clause) within 7 days (exclusive of Saturdays and Sundays or other days observed as general holidays at Lloyd's) after receipt by them from the Committee of Lloyd's of notice of such appeal (such notice if sent by post to be deemed to be received on the day following that on which the said notice was posted) give written or telegraphic or telex Notice of Cross-Appeal to the Committee of Lloyd's. As soon as practicable after receipt of such notice or notices the Committee of Lloyd's shall refer the Appeal to the hearing and determination of a person or persons selected by it. Any Award of Appeal shall be final and binding on all the parties concerned.

Conduct of Appeal

13. No evidence other than the documents put in on the Arbitration and the Arbitrator's notes of the proceedings and oral evidence, if any, at the Arbitration and the Arbitrator's Reasons for his Award and the transcript, if any, of any evidence given at the Arbitration shall be used on the Appeal unless the Arbitrator or Arbitrators on the Appeal shall in his or their discretion call for or allow other evidence. The Arbitrator or Arbitrators on the Appeal may conduct the Arbitration on Appeal in such manner in all respects as he or they may think fit and may act upon any such evidence or information (whether the same be strictly admissible as evidence or not) as he or they may

think fit and may maintain increase or reduce the sum awarded by the Arbitrator with the like power as is conferred by Clause 11 on the Arbitrator to condemn the Contractor in the whole or part of the expense of providing security and to deduct the amount disallowed from the salvage remuneration. And he or they shall also make such order as he or they may think fit as to the payment of interest on the sum awarded to the Contractor. The Arbitrator or Arbitrators on the Appeal may direct in what manner the costs of the Arbitration and of the Arbitration on Appeal shall be borne and paid and he or they and the Committee of Lloyd's may charge reasonable fees for their services in connection with the Arbitration on Appeal whether it proceeds to a hearing or not and all such fees shall be treated as part of the costs of the Arbitration on Appeal. Save as aforesaid the statutory provisions as to Arbitration for the time being in force in England shall apply.

Provisions as to Payment

14. (a) In case of arbitration if no Notice of Appeal be received by the Committee of Lloyd's within 14 days (exclusive of Saturdays and Sundays or other days observed as general holidays at Lloyd's) after the publication by the Committee of the Award the Committee shall call upon the party or parties concerned to pay the amount awarded and in the event of non-payment shall realize or enforce the security and pay therefrom to the Contractor (whose receipt shall be a good discharge to it) the amount awarded to him together with interest as hereinbefore provided.

(b) If Notice of Appeal be received by the Committee of Lloyd's in accordance with the provisions of Clause 12 thereof it shall as soon as but not until the Award on Appeal has been published by it, call upon the party or parties concerned to pay the amount awarded and in the event of non-payment shall realize or enforce the security and pay therefrom to the Contractor (whose receipt shall be a good discharge to it) the amount awarded to him together with interest if any in such manner as shall comply with the provisions of the Award on Appeal.

(c) If the Award or Award on Appeal provides that the costs of the Arbitration or of the Arbitration on Appeal or any part of such costs shall be borne by the Contractor, such costs may be deducted from the amount awarded before payment is made to the Contractor by the Committee of Lloyd's, unless satisfactory security is provided by the Contractor for the payment of such costs.

(d) If any sum shall become payable to the Contractor as remuneration for his services and/or interest and/or costs as the result of an agreement made between the Contractor and the parties interested in the property salved or any of them the Committee of Lloyd's in the event of non-payment shall realize or endorce the security and pay therefrom to the Contractor (whose receipt shall be a good discharge to it) the amount agreed upon between the parties.

(e) Without prejudice to the provisions of Clause 4 hereof, the liability of the Committee of Llloyd's shall be limited in any event to the amount of security held by it.

General Provisions

15. Notwithstanding anything hereinbefore contained should the operations be only partially successful without any negligence or want of ordinary skill and care on the part of the Contractor or of any person by him employed in the operations, and any portion of the vessel or her appurtenances or her stores or the cargo be salved by the Contractor, he shall be entitled to reasonable remuneration and such reasonable remuneration shall be fixed in case of difference by arbitration in manner hereinbefore prescribed.

16. The Master or other person signing this Agreement on behalf of the property to be salved enters into this Agreement as Agent for the vessel her cargo and freight and the respective owners thereof and binds each (but not the one for the other or himself personally) to the due performance thereof.

17. In considering what sume of money have been expended by the Contractor in rendering the services and/or in fixing the amount of the Award or Award on Appeal the Arbitrator or Arbitrator or Arbitrators on Appeal shall to such an extent and in so far as it mey ba fair and just in all the circumstances give effect to any change or changes in the value of money or rates of exchange which may have occurred between the completion of the services and the date on which the Award or the Award on Appeal is made.

18. Any Award, notice, authority, order, or other document signed by the Chairman of Lloyd's or any person authorised by the Committee of Lloyd's for the purpose shall be deemed to have been duly made or given by the Committee of Lloyd's and shall have the same force and effect in all respects as it it has been signed by every member of the Committee of Lloyd's.

For and on behalf of the Contractor

....

(To be signed either by the Contractor personally or by The Master of the salving vessel or other person whose name is inserted in line 3 of this Agreement).

For and on behalf of the Owners of property to be salved

....

(To be signed by the Master or other person whose name is inserted in line 1 of this Agreement).

Appendix XX

A SUMMARY OF THE LOCAL RULES ON NAVIGATION APPLIED IN SOME PORTS IN THE UNITED KINGDOM

As mentioned earlier Rule 1 (b) states that the local rules on navigation shall "conform as closely as possible" to the International Regulations. S. 421 of the Merchant Shipping Act, 1894 states:

"(1) Any rules made before or after the passing of this Act under the authority of any local Act, concerning lights and signals to be carried, or the steps for avoiding collision to be taken, by vessels navigating the waters of any harbour, river, or other inland navigation, shall, notwithstanding anything in this Act, have full effect.

(2) Where any such rules are not and cannot be made, Her Majesty in Council on the application of any person having authority over such waters, or, if there is no such person, any person interested in the navigation thereof, may make such rules and those rules shall, as regards vessels navigating the said waters, be of the same force as if they were part of the collision regulations."

The local rules on navigation applied in the various ports in the United Kingdom are numerous and are constantly changing. They are made under local Acts, Order in Council or even by Notices to Mariners. The distinction between rules made under a local Act, which by sub. (1) are to "have full effect", and those made by Order in Council, which under sub. (2) are to be "of the same force as if they were part of the Collision Regulations" are of no legal or practical importance.

The following is a summary of the rules on navigation applied in some ports in the United Kingdom.

Bristol

The International Collision Regulations apply to navigation in this port. The only regulation which is promulgated by Notice to Mariners is that pertaining to signals to be displayed by dredgers. M. Notice No. 16 of 1972 states:

DREDGERS WORKING AT ENTRANCE TO CUMBERLAND BASIN, RIVER AVON

1. NOTICE IS HEREBY GIVEN THAT from the 10th July, 1972 and until further notice, a GRAB DREDGER or SUCTION DREDGER will be working from time to time in the approach to Cumberland Basin, Bristol City Docks.

2. The GRAB DREDGER will, when conditions are suitable, lie to two anchors, one forward and one aft, and may also have lines ashore. The anchors may lead well ahead and astern of the ship.

3. The Dredgers will be working from about two hours before High Water until one hour after High Water.

4. When working, the Dredgers will exhibit the following signals:

BY NIGHT

Signal	Meaning
1 Red Light on each side	Vessels must not pass on either side
2 Red Lights in a vertical line on one side and 1 Red Light on the other side	Vessels must pass on that side only on which the 2 Red Lights are exhibited
2 Red Lights in a vertical line on each side	Vessels may pass on either side

BY DAY

Black Balls in the same positions and having similar meanings will be substituted in lieu of the above-mentioned Red Lights.

NOTE: These instructions are not intended in any way to relieve any person in charge of a vessel from responsibility for proper and careful navigation.

5. When vessels are about to pass the GRAB DREDGER she will, if necessary, slack down one or more of her chains, but should an emergency prevent her from doing so she will sound 3 blasts in succession, viz. 2 short blasts followed by 1 prolonged blast on her siren as a warning signal.

6. ALL VESSELS ARE WARNED TO KEEP CLEAR OF THE DREDGER AND MOORINGS AND TO PASS AT SLOW SPEED.

Cromarty Firth

The Cromarty Firth Port Authority Order, 1973 deals, among other things, with the movement of vessels in the port, mainly the declaration of the draught of the vessels; directions to vessels at the docks and failure to comply with the directions.

Dover

The Traffic Control Signals within the harbour have been promulgated by Notices to Mariners. As to the outer harbour, the Traffic Control Signals are provided for in Bye-Laws 5 and 12.

Firth of Forth

The Forth Port Authority published in 1975 directions to vessels navigating in the Firth of Forth relating to: the use of VHF radio; clearance of outward or shifting vessels; clearance of inward vessels; reporting points; anchorages and movements of VLCCs.

Harwich

The Bye-Laws for the Regulation of the Harbour of Harwich, 1954 and their supplementary Bye-Laws of 1961, deal, among other things, with the authority of the harbour master; the movement of the vessels within the harbour; and places where anchorage are prohibited. Rule 14 of the Bye-Laws provides that the International Collision Regulations apply to the movements of vessels except as otherwise provided by the Bye-Laws.

In addition, there are Bye-Laws for regulating the discharging, loading, etc. of Petroleum Spirit and Carbide of Calcium, 1950; and the Explosives Bye-Laws, 1965. The movements of yachts, cruisers and the areas where water ski-ing are permitted are regulated by Bye-Laws, 1966.

London

The Port of London River (Amendment) Bye-Laws, 1970 was made in pursuant of s. 162 of the Port of London Act, 1968. The Bye-Laws deal with the duties of masters of the vessels; mooring and berthing; steering and sailing; lights and daymarks; sound signals; towing and pushing; signals of vessels approaching Tower Bridge, Richmond Lock; River duties of tonnage; and noise and smoke.

Manchester

Bye-Laws, 1963 deal, among other things, with: rules for preventing obstructions to navigation, nuisance and fires, etc.; use of quays, sheds, etc.; ferries; vehicular traffic; trespass and damage. Also in force are the Manchester Ship Canal Bye-Laws, 1973 and the Manchester Ship Canal Petroleum Bye-Laws, 1973.

Medway

The Medway Ports River Bye-Laws, 1973 is divided into the following six parts:

I Interpretation;
II Lights, Daymarks and Signals;
III Navigation;
IV Mooring and Anchorage;
V Allington Lock; and
VI Miscellaneous[1].

Mersey Channel Collision Rules

Pursuant to s. 421 (2) of the Merchant Shipping Act, 1894 and the Mersey Channels Act, 1897 Concerning the Lights or Signals to be carried and the Steps for Avoiding Collision, Order in Council was made on June 7, 1960[2] and amended on February 4, 1970 on the Mersey Channel Collision Rules[3]. These Rules deal with marks and lights by day and night for vessels which have on board explosives and petroleum spirit (Rules 3 and 4); the lights for tug and tow (Rules 5 and 6); a power floating crane (Rule 6); a power-driven vessel at anchor (Rules 8 and 9); a vessel aground or beached (Rule 10); and dredgers (Rule 12). Rules 14 and 15 explain the meaning of the fairways in the River Mersey and prohibit the movement of any vessel which may impede the traffic passing up and down the Rock Channel. The rest of the rules concern the launching of vessels[4].

Milford Haven

The Milford Haven Conservancy (Harbour) Bye-Laws, 1973 are divided into the following parts:

I Preliminary;
II Lights, Day Marks and Signals;
III Harbourmaster;
IV Navigation;
V Mooring and Anchoring; and
VI Miscellaneous.

Southampton

The Southampton Harbour Board Bye-Laws[5] are divided into the following parts:

---

1. See also The Shipmasters Guide for the River Medway and the Swale, 1973 and the River Medway Emergency & Oil Pollution Plans, 1970.
2. S.I. 1960, No. 977.
3. S.I. 1970, No. 160.
4. See also Notice to Mariners No. 14 of 1974.
5. See also The Southampton Railway Company Bye-Laws, 1924 (relating to Southampton Docks); The Petroleum Spirit Bye-Laws, 1975; and the Sea Fisheries Bye-Laws, 1974.

I Preliminary;
II Navigation and Moorings;
III Discharging and Taking in of Cargo, Ballast, etc., and Traffic Generally; and
IV Licensed Boatmen and Barrowmen.

A number of Notice to Mariners[1] are issued to regulate the signals and the speed of the vessels in the port.

Tees and Hartlepool

The Tees Bye-Laws are, at present, under revision. However, in 1976, the Tees and Hartlepool Port Authority published general directions relating to:

(i) navigation and control of vessels in the Tees; and
(ii) navigation and control of vessels carrying dangerous goods in the Tees[2].

Notice to Mariners No. 1 of 1975 concerns the port information services and Notice to Mariners No. 3 of 1976 deals with Traffic Control Signals in the River Tees.

Tyne

The Bye-Laws of the Tyne Authority consist of 147 clauses and are divided into nine parts. These Bye-Laws are under revision.

---

1. The following are the Notices to Mariners relating to Southampton port:
   Notice to Mariners No. 52 of 1972;
   Notice to Mariners No. 5 of 1973;
   Notice to Mariners - Speed of Vessels in the Port Area No. 70 of 1973;
   Notice to Mariners No. 33 of 1974;
   Notice to Mariners No. 47 of 1975;
   Notice to Mariners No. 46(T) of 1975;
   Notice to Mariners No. 42 of 1975; and
   Notice to Mariners No. 10 of 1976.
   For the port of Portsmouth see:
   Portsmouth Local Notice to Mariners No. 13 of 1976; and
   Portsmouth Local Notice to Mariners No. 18 of 1976.
2. See also the Draft Code of Practice for the Handling and Movement of Dangerous Bulk Liquid Cargoes, June 1976.

Index

ABANDONMENT
  of wreck, 18
ACTION
  consolidation, 68
  in personam. See JURISDICTION
  in rem. See JURISDICTION
  limitation of actions. See LIMITATION OF LIABILITY
  staying actions, 68, 69
ACTION TO AVOID COLLISION
  action leading to a close quarters situation, 138, 139, 140
  decisive actions, 131
  good seamanship, 131
AGONY OF THE MOMENT
  alternative dangers, 17
  dilemma, 17
AGROUND
  lights, 226
  meaning of, 225
ALTERATION OF COURSE
  avoiding alteration of course to port, 206
  close quarters situation, 138, 139, 140
  departure from the course,178
  effective, 138
  failure to alter course, 153
  keeping the course, 178
  to avoid collision, 131, 137
ANCHOR
  at anchor, 225
  dragging, 225
  failure to exhibit lights,226
ARREST
  arrest of ship, 72
  beneficially owned, 73
  convention 1952, text, 299
  lien, 71, 72
  sister ship, 73
ASSESSORS. See JURISDICTION
BREACH OF STATUTORY DUTY
  breach, 11
BRUSSELS CONVENTIONS. See INTERNATIONAL CONVENTIONS
BUOYAGE
  Maritime Buoyage Systems, 2, 283, 284
BURDEN OF PROOF
  departure from the Rules, 96
  inevitable accident, 14
CARE, DUTY OF. See FAULT
CERTIFICATES
  cancellation of, 55
CIVIL LIABILITY. See FAULT
CLOSE-HAULED. See SAILING VESSELS
CLOSE QUARTERS SITUATION
  bad look-out for not appreciating a close quarters situation, 141
  meaning of, 138
COLLISION
  civil liability, 9
  criminal liability, 51
  crown ships, 81
COMMAND, NOT UNDER
  definition, 99
  difficulties which do not justify not under command lights, 101
  lights and shapes, 222, 223
  overtaking, 168
COMPASS
  bearings, 119
  gyro, as evidence, 76
  reliance on, 168
CONTRIBUTORY NEGLIGENCE. See FAULT
CONVENTIONS. See INTERNATIONAL CONVENTIONS
COSTS
  costs to follow the event, 70
  discretion of the court, 69
  offer to settle, 70
COURSE AND SPEED
  course maintained until it is safe, 197
  crossing, 172
  duty to keep course and speed, 114
  safe speed, 113

stand-on vessel, 188, 193, 194, 195
CRIMINAL LIABILITY
Brussels Convention, 1952, text, 297
distress signals, 55
drunkenness, 55, 56
endangering life on board the ship, 53
formal investigation, 58
high seas, 51, 52
inquiries, 56, 57
pollution, 56
territorial waters, 51
CROSSING
approaching pilot station,183
duties of, 171, 172
failure to observe, 178
meaning of, 174,176
narrow channel, 184, 185
overtaking vessels distinguished, 186, 187
when to apply, 174
when to cease, 177
DAMAGES
apportionment, 25, 27
both to blame collision clause, 31
cargo, 31
common law rule, 24
consequential damage, 35
contribution between wrongdoers, 34
foreign currency, 32, 33
recovery against two negligent vessels, 34
remoteness of damages, 34
revision of apportionment by Court of Appeal, 30
DEFINITIONS
all-round light, 216
fishing vessel, 98
flashing light, 216
in sight of one another, 104
length and breadth, 104
masthead, 216
power-driven vessel, 98
restricted visibility, 104
sailing vessel, 98
seaplane, 99
sidelights, 216
sternlight, 216
towing light, 216
under way, 103
vessel, 96
vessel constrained by her draught, 103, 204
vessel not under command, 99
vessel restricted in her ability to manoeuvre, 102, 103
DISTRESS SIGNAL
Maritime Distress System, 3
regulations, 55
EVIDENCE
burden of proof, 75
documentary evidence, 75
gyro-compasses, 76
notices to mariners, 77
photographs, 76
statements inaccurate, 76
FAULT
agony of the moment, 17
breach of a statutory duty, 11
care and skill, 9
cause unknown, 16, 17
causing damage without collision, 14
error amounts to fault, 10
failure of machinery, 15
force of wind, 15
inevitable accident. See INEVITABLE ACCIDENT
interlocked faults, 13
mixed faults, 12
pilot, 21
practice. See JURISDICTION
presumption of fault abolished, 11
remoteness, 34
removal of wreck, 18, 19
salvor, 23
skill, care, 9
standard of care, 10
successive faults, 12
tug and tow. See TOWAGE
FISHING VESSELS
keep out of the way, 201, 202
lights and shapes, 221, 222
meaning of engaged in fishing, 98
responsibility towards power-driven vessels, 202

FOG AND RESTRICTED VISIBILITY
conduct of vessels, 205
excessive speed, 213, 214
fog thickened, 126
in a canal, 116, 124, 126, 127, 135
in or near an area, 206
GIVE WAY VESSEL
actions to be taken, 190
failure to observe her duty, 179
failure to sound the signal,191
timely actions, 190
INEVITABLE ACCIDENT
cause could not be determined, 16
failure of machinery, 15
force of wind, 15
inevitable mistake distinguished, 14
meaning, 14
what must be proved, 14
INTERACTION
meaning, 170
INTERNATIONAL CONVENTIONS
Arrest of Seagoing Ships, 1952, 62, text, 299
Civil Jurisdiction, 1952, 62, text, 294
Collisions, 1910, 25, text,290
Inland Navigation, 1960, text, 305
Limitation of Liability, 39, text of 1976 Convention, 311
Penal Jurisdiction, 1952, 52, text, 297
INTERPRETATION
international character, 78
rules of, 78, 79
JURISDICTION
assessors, 66, 67
consolidation, 68
costs, 69, 70, 71
exercise of, 61
high seas, 82
in rem, 61
in personam, 61
practice, 66
service out of the jurisdiction, 65
staying actions, 69
territorial waters, 83
KEEP HER COURSE AND SPEED
action by stand-on vessel,192
crossing, 172
duty of the stand-on vessel, 194
failure to, 194, 195
meaning of course and speed, 193
KEEP OUT OF THE WAY
action by give-way vessel, 190
action by stand-on vessel, 192
duty of the overtaking vessel, 163, 164, 166
fishing vessels, 204
sailing vessels, 162
LIEN
maritime liens, 71
LIGHTS, SHAPES
air-cushion vehicle, 218
anchored and aground, 225
exhibiting wrong lights, 215
fishing vessels, 221
not under command, 222
other lights, 215
pilot vessels, 224
power-driven vessels underway, 218
ranges, 217
sailing vessels, 220
seaplane, 226
towing and pushing, 219, 220
vessels constrained by their draught, 224
LIMITATION OF LIABILITY
amount of limitation, 43
construction of 1958 Act, 39
fault or privity, 40
fund, 44
period within which action must be taken, 48
pilotage authority, 47
procedures, 45
tug and tow, 45
LOCAL RULES OF NAVIGATION
breach of the, 134, 153

in certain ports in the United Kingdom, 333
in the United Kingdom, 84
in foreign waters, 86
LOOK-OUT
bad look-out which contributed to collision, 108, 109, 110, 111, 112
conversation diverting the attention, 109
duties of the person on, 106
leaving the post, 106
maintaining a proper look-out, 107
meaning of, 105
M Notice on look-out, 107
place of, 106
MEASURES OF DAMAGES - See DAMAGES
MISDEMEANOUR
failure to assist after collision, 54, 55
NARROW CHANNEL
aground, 148
breach of the local rules,153
crossing ahead, 143
keep as near as possible to outer limit, 143, 152
meaning of, 144
mid-channel, 145
speed, 151, 153
NAUTICAL ASSESSORS. See JURISDICTION
NEGLIGENCE. See FAULT
NUCLEAR SHIPS
recommendations applicable to, text, 285
ONUS OF PROOF. See BURDEN OF PROOF
OVERTAKING VESSEL
crossing ships distinguished, 186, 187
duty of overtaking vessel, 164
test adopted, 163
PENAL LIABILITY. See CRIMINAL LIABILITY
PILOTAGE
fog, 127
liability for negligence, 22
lights, 224
meaning, 21
relationship between master and pilot, 22
PRACTICE. See JURISDICTION
RADAR
British vessels over 1,600 tons must carry radar, 120
failure to keep a radar look-out, 109
failure to use, 122
look-out does not replace radar watch, 121
plotting, 122
use of, 121
REMOTENESS OF DAMAGES. See DAMAGES
REMOVAL OF WRECK. See WRECK
RESTRICTED VISIBILITY. See FOG
RISK OF COLLISION
case of doubt, 118
cases where risk of collision exist, 190
crossing, 171, 172
head-on situation, 170
mandatory requirement, 119
SAILING VESSELS
definition, 98
International Yacht Racing Rules, 1977, 162
lights and shapes, 220, 221
rules to be followed by, 162
SEAMANSHIP
action to avoid collision,131
course and speed, 193
look-out, 105
ordinary practice of seamen, 89, 91, 93
SEAPLANES
definitions, 99
lights and shapes, 226
SEPARATION SCHEMES
aims, 156
avoid anchoring in, 155
avoid crossing in, 155
factors to be considered, 157
fishing vessels, 155
in the territorial waters,160
mandatory, 157
on the high seas, 160
sailing vessels, 155

SPEED
consequences, 118
excessive speed, 127, 129
factors to be taken into account, 115, 116
fog, 127
meaning of safe speed, 113,114
STAND-ON VESSEL
action by, 192
course and speed, 193
crossing situation, 200
duties, 172
TRAFFIC SEPARATION SCHEMES. See SEPARATION SCHEMES
TOWAGE
duties of the tow, 20
duties of the tug, 19
liability for collision, 21
lights and shapes, 219
UNDER WAY
definition of, 103
lights and shapes, 218, 220
responsibility, 201
WRECK
marking, 2, 18
powers of Trinity House, 19
removal, 19